RACE

The
Woodrow
Wilson
Center
Press

Washington, D.C.

» «

The
Johns
Hopkins
University
Press

Baltimore

London

RACE

The History of an Idea in the West

» «

Ivan Hannaford

Editorial offices:
The Woodrow Wilson Center Press
370 L'Enfant Promenade, S.W., Suite 704
Washington, D.C. 20024-2518
Telephone 202-287-3000, ext. 218

Order from:
The Johns Hopkins University Press
Hampden Station
Baltimore, Maryland 21211
Telephone 1-800-537-5487

2 4 6 8 9 7 5 3 1

Library of Congress Cataloging-in-Publication Data

Hannaford, Ivan.
    Race : the history of an idea in the West / Ivan Hannaford.
      p.   cm.
    Includes bibliographical references and index.
    ISBN 0-8018-5222-6 (cloth : alk. paper). — ISBN 0-8018-5223-4
(paper : alk. paper)
      1. Race awareness—History.   2. Racism—History.   I. Title.
HT1507.H36   1996
    305.8—dc20

96-4162
CIP

Design: Adrianne Onderdonk Dudden

Woodrow Wilson International Center for Scholars

Contents

Foreword

Bernard Crick

The transmission of scholarly knowledge to the public is a fortuitous process at best and always involves long time lags. Critical history usually only makes small, slow gains, despite its weight of learned armor, against popular resistance fueled by widespread nationalist myths. Sometimes the "revisionist" historians (now more often a term of abuse than one of praise) are reviled by political intellectuals and the press as unpatriotic troublemakers. When it is grudgingly conceded that what they say may, in part, be true, it is labeled as most unhelpful to current social purposes. And, anyway, it is all a matter of subjective opinion, isn't it? That is the populist basis of highbrow academic, postmodernist, deconstructionist ideology.

Intellectuals might be supposed to be a bridge between the scholarly and the public mind, especially when matters of understanding are of great political and social importance. But I read and encounter so many intellectuals who assume that nationalism is a perennial human phenomenon and seem quite unable to imagine any other ties of obligation by which societies were bound together under government (such as religious belief, dynastic loyalty, tradition, fear, self-interest, civic patriotism, desire for law and order) before the invention and diffusion of nationalist ideology in late-eighteenth-century Europe with—arguably—some few premonitions or preconditions in the previous century. Certainly there is no turning the clock back, whether one considers nationalism a curse of modernity or a unique blessing.

The case of race is even more muddled and confused. Many people, who denounce racism nobly and boldly, sniffing it out in the most unexpected contexts, attack ideas of racial superiority by asserting the equality of races, rather than the equality of men and women. Even those who concede that no biological definition of race can possibly serve as a general theory of history and an explanation of individual human characteristics, capabilities, and worth—and even those who accept that such pseudoexplanations are invented ideologies—still cannot imagine a world in which such a comprehensive ideology or myth did not exist; or if the idea existed at all, then highly marginal and speculative and no guide or clue to understanding social organization. So people conclude that racial identification, while it must always be mediated, can never be rejected fully. Even if the Greeks and the Romans, the Celts and the Saxons, were not, strictly speaking, races, did they not believe that they were? Ivan Hannaford's long-labored research gives the unusually clear answer, "No."

Most modern scholarly writing on race by social scientists and historians combats the idea of racial prejudice and reveals the sad extent of discrimination. But Hannaford reminds us that there is a double prejudice. The belief that there has always been such a real and socially important thing as race precedes modern race prejudice. I add the caveat "socially important," for Hannaford is simply not concerned with assessing the amount of heat and light generated by claims that there are small differences of intelligence (however defined) between groups perceived as races. *Even if* that were true and the assumptions of such research sound, those small alleged differences (I tread every step carefully in this fought-over minefield) could not possibly carry the explanatory weight that racial theorists and even some eugenicists would attach to them in explaining different formations of culture—compared to many, many other factors: class, law, tradition, education, and so on; still less could they validate moral judgments. Hannaford, however, shows that the existence of racial thought in the ancient and medieval worlds is almost entirely an invention of nineteenth-century historians and psuedohistorians (such as Enlightenment biologists and zoologists constructing huge *a priori* schemes for the universal classification of species). He demonstrates how this invention gave itself the authority of ancestry by mistranslating ancient texts, either from ignorance or deliberate tendentiousness, or more subtly and respectably by an unhistorical and anachronistic use of new concepts of the translators' times to translate somewhat similar ancient terms. If one is completely seized with a new big idea one usually can find what one sets out to find in old texts. For example, Heinrich von Treitschke's now little read histories of Germany were once the great texts of "respectable" racial theory.

The "Anglo-Saxon destiny" historians such as John Fiske in the United States or Sir John Seeley in the United Kingdom looked up to him, but none of these gentlemen went on to advocate ethnic cleansing, even though they created an intellectual precondition for people to believe that that would be helpful. But Treitschke's use of medieval and classical sources, while it appeared scholarly, would fail modern standards of translation badly, let alone criteria of scientific method. Scholarly intellectual history has made real advances in our time. Texts and the concepts within them are now examined in the context of their times to gain the contemporary meaning of the concepts, which is often very different from ours.

Hannaford employs these methods meticulously in what is, astonishingly, the first scholarly history of the idea of race. There have been some highly unscholarly ones, in both a racist vein and an antiracist vein. The difficulty of a history of race, it soon emerges, is that no premodern author believed that culture was a product of biologically determined factors. Eric Voegelin in his monumental *Order and History* sees the symbol of blood and the blood relationship as universal, but it is only important as a mass ideology, rather than as an ancient esoteric mystery, in the modern world. There were and are so many other different explanations of how cultures are constituted, continue, and change or evolve, not all of them mutually exclusive. Aristotle, for instance, attributed physical differences between peoples to climate, but some modern translators say that he was using that as an explanation of race—a concept he would not have understood. But so deeply rooted is the belief either in the objective existence of racial determination or the idea that people held this fallacious belief that Ivan Hannaford felt the need to perform the great service in Part I of this book of reexamining, not merely the classical texts used by the modern progenitors of racial theory, but also esoteric, cabalistic, astrological, and occult texts that have influenced popular thought (what Hannah Arendt once loftily called "the metaphysics of the gutter"). He approaches an astonishing range of literature with great empathy, and from the beginning of his work, he quite expected to find what he did not find: racial theory. Perhaps never has so much ground been covered to reach such a negative conclusion, but it is an extremely important negation. One does not have to be a Popperian (though I think we are both a little Popperian) to see that knowledge advances both by refutation and by assertion. But to turn the negative assertion of Part I on its head, the positive assertion is that racial conditioning is not part of the human condition.

Among groups subject to racial prejudice the defense can be developed that they are a race as good as any other, or even in some respects better. This is a defense that is as dangerous as it is unneeded. To use the rhetoric of the enemy to fight the enemy is often to become the enemy. For it is at most a culture that needs defending and asserting, not a race; and, of course, the same is true of human rights. Reading Hannaford makes me (though I now go beyond his argument) even more worried about attempts to invent and assert legal doctrines of group rights. Individual civil rights are good enough to do the job. The difficulty with asserting group rights (whether based on racial, ethnic, or religious identifications) is that if those identifications are held to be legally and morally superior to individual rights, then it follows that these groups have rights, or will feel that they have rights, not merely against detractors but over all the individuals who are members of their group—not to act differently, not to leave the group, not to marry or to have sexual relationships outside it. This is an entirely different matter from making deliberate political concessions when necessary, when desired, when generally acceptable, to groups who suffer discrimination. Hannaford does not make a case for an atomic individualism. We are all both individual and social beings, but we are social in relation to a plurality of groups, none of which alone determines our identity or claims our exclusive allegiance. And even among those groups formed by racial stereotyping, race can be but one attribute and identity among many.

The second part of this profound and challenging book seeks to redress a general, almost complete ignorance (which I shared before reading this) about who were the progenitors of racial thought. The confusion of the biological with the social, which is crucial to racial thinking, leads the author into largely forgotten byways of the history of science, as well as of social and political philosophy. Few now can claim to grasp even the outlines of both, as thinkers of the eighteenth and early nineteenth centuries still claimed—often rashly. We can now be more clear in distinguishing fact from value and empirical generalizations from moral judgments. Because members of every human species, however labeled, can in fact copulate and procreate with others, the racial theorist has to ascend or descend to the dubious psychology of intelligence testing in order to attempt to validate a naked moral judgment. But even that does not work perfectly. Had I been both very, very intelligent and very market oriented, I should have mated with a dim but strong, healthy, lithe, and muscular (perfectly stereotypical) nonwhite partner in order to breed the most sought after football or tennis superhero of our times. Of course, like the story of George Bernard Shaw and Mrs. Patrick Campbell, it could equally well have had the opposite effect to that intended. But racial theorists invariably employ an outmoded concept of causality that has difficulty with statistical probability.

Most of those who believed in racial theory, or still do, are not racist in the sense of Houston Stewart Chamberlain who first advocated in the 1890s the compulsive cleansing of the good bloodstock and the elimination or segregation of the bad. But racial theory, if not a sufficient condition for active racism, is a necessary condition. Mere dislike and fear of strangers, literally the "outlandish," is common to most cultures at most times (and is what some historians have sometimes innocently confused with racial reaction); never before this century did it reach the extent of deliberate state policies of genocide, compulsory sterilization of the feeble-minded, or legal apartheid. Examples of large-scale elimination of heretics and infidels can be found before the modern era, but these were religious matters. Also ethnic prejudice only shades into racial prejudice when the belief that a culture is an extended family with blood ties also seeks to prohibit and punish marriage in or out of the *ethne*. Some ultraorthodox religious beliefs can at times seem to me remarkably like racial beliefs, both in dogma and in behavior; Hannaford would argue that precisely by the nature of those beliefs they are not for universal application or emulation. We cannot all be among the chosen, whether Jewish or Calvinist.

Arendt has said that our times have seen only two comprehensive ideologies—economic determinism (whether of the Marxist or the market kind) and racialism. Eric Voegelin pointed to the unique dangers of political religions taking on a racial dress. Hannaford has traced for the first time the etiology of this damnable but pervasive term "race," and in showing that it is uniquely modern, not universal, he has not so much landed us with another possible guilt and "burden of our times," but given us clear ground for hope that what is culturally created can be culturally deconstructed. And the alternative? Hannaford reminds us that before the determinism of either race or the market there was a long established Western tradition, honored and remembered even when it could not be practiced, that human societies were self-made creations of citizens. Loyalty was given, not to myths of race, but to civic institutions that were worthy of loyalty.

» «

I am honored to write this since Hannaford invoked my *In Defence of Politics* as one among many advocacies or remembrances of this great civic tradition that needs no racial barriers or ethnic crutches. But we both merely echo, above all, Aristotle, Machiavelli, the political thought of *The Federalist Papers*, and, in our times, Arendt. Hannaford sadly noted that after the time of Darwin:

> [I]t was generally agreed that classical political theory had little or nothing to offer Western industrial society. . . . The tests of true belonging [to a state] were no longer decided on action as a citizen but upon the purity of language, color and shape. And since none of these tests could ever be fully satisfied, all that was left in place of political settlement were ideas of assimilation, naturalization, evacuation, exclusion, expulsion, and finally liquidation.

May I add a word about the author? He read the proofs but died before seeing the book. I have not called him Dr. Hannaford nor Professor because he was neither when he wrote this, although he received an Honorary D. Litt. He came to the London School of Economics as a part-time mature student, taking a master's degree in political thought under Michael Oakeshott while teaching a great many hours and students at one of the former British Polytechnics, now Kingston University. But his talents, common sense, and ability to grasp large issues calmly (all of which show in this work) soon saw him dragged from teaching into high administration, although, he told me, "to retain my sanity I taught clandestinely." More to the present point, he became deeply intrigued by a suggestion that Oakeshott had made to him that the story of Ham's delinquency was similar to that of the Tower of Babel. For over twenty years Hannaford worked in his spare time on this history, originally uncertain what he would find and as surprised as the reader at what he did not find as well as what he did. Only in the last few years did a few of us become aware, through a paper he gave at the annual Political Thought Conference at Oxford, of how important this work was. Rumor could make it sound obsessive and eccentric, but reading it showed it to be outstanding scholarship, bold in extent but cautious and trustworthy in method and tone. Some who heard the paper were able to steer him toward two fruitful, if belated, periods of working leisure at Wolfson College, Cambridge, and then at the Woodrow Wilson Center. Although my bread has come from the university all my life, I take a sardonic pleasure in seeing this book as outstanding proof that private scholarship is still possible when the will and skill are there and the importance of the subject possesses the author.

Publisher's Note

Late into the stage of supervising the correction of proofs for this book, Ivan Hannaford died of motor neuron disease on February 14, 1996. He did not leave instructions regarding acknowledgments, but at the risk of making some important omission, we wish to name a number of people who supported the writing and publication of this book.

First and most important, without the loving care and support of his wife, Marjatta Hannaford, Mr. Hannaford could not have brought this project to completion.

Gregory Weller of the University of Northern British Columbia contributed to the development of Mr. Hannaford's ideas through many conversations during Mr. Hannaford's time at Lakehead University in Canada. Donald Horowitz of Duke University, Quentin Skinner of Christ College, Cambridge, David Harris Sacks of Reed College, and Frank M. Snowden, Jr., of Howard University all read the manuscript in its early stages and provided critiques of it. Bernard Crick, who wrote the foreword, also read and commented on the manuscript and supported Mr. Hannaford's project early, middle, and late. Because Dr. Crick is in residence at the Woodrow Wilson Center as a fellow in 1995–1996, he has been readily available to advise the Woodrow Wilson Center Press during editing and typesetting.

Professor Joe Bailey, head of the School of Social Sciences at Kingston University, provided vital logistical support during the editing of the manuscript and correction of the proofs. Anne Poole and Terry Sullivan of Kingston

University helped with fact checking and completing bibliographic references during editing and proofreading.

To all of these, my colleagues and I extend our heartfelt thanks.

Joseph F. Brinley, Jr., Director
Woodrow Wilson Center Press

Western History and Thought before Race

»«

I

Many people—many nations—can find themselves
holding, more or less unwittingly, that 'every stranger is
an enemy.' For the most part this conviction lies deep
down like some latent infection: it betrays itself on in
random, disconnected acts, and does not lie at the base
of a system of reason. But when this does come about,
when the unspoken dogma becomes the major premiss
in a syllogism, then at the end of the chain there is
the Lager. Here is the conception of the world carried
to its logical conclusion; so long as the conception subsists, the conclusion remains to threaten us. The story
of the death camps should be understood by everyone as
a sinister alarm signal.

Primo Levi, If This Is a Man

There is perhaps no question about which such absolute
ignorance prevails among highly cultured, indeed
learned men, as the question of the essence and
significance of the idea of "race."

Houston Stewart Chamberlain,
Grundlagen des Neunzehnten Jahrhunderts

There are many words which have been made to suffer
constant misuse; but there is none which suffers more
abundantly, or with sadder consequences, than the word
Race.

Ernest Barker, National Character

Among the words that can be all things to all men,
the word "Race" has a fair claim to being the most
common, the most ambiguous, and the most explosive.

Jacques Barzun, Race: A Study in Superstition

In the Beginning 1

There is an idea abroad, accepted as much by cloistered intellectuals as by ordinary people going about their daily business, that everybody knows what race is. The idea of race is a self-evident "fact," requiring no protracted thought. That a person is of a different color, appearance, disposition, or culture, or speaks a different language, immediately implies a specific race. We assume that the racial and ethnic diversity we see all around us has always existed as a historical, social, and biological fact that needs no further interrogation.

This idea, that human beings are obviously members of races, begs the whole question by saying that all meanings of race are finally reducible to "the biological transmission of innate qualities,"[1] or that race is an all-pervading natural phenomenon, an awesome and mysterious primordial force operating mechanically or organically, materially or spiritually, through all historical and prehistorical time. It is an idea which perpetuates and reinforces the notion that human beings belong to, or have always thought that they belonged to, enormous physico-natural families of primates divisible into "races" and sub-divisible into "ethnic groups." It takes as a matter of common sense that individuals are linked in some eventless way by common blood, climate, soil, *Kultur*, language, mental disposition, or some commonplace feature such as shape and color of eyes, skin pigmentation, size and shape of nose, slope of forehead, cranial capacity, depth of voice, smell of body, weight of breasts, and length of penes. These "facts" are more often than not taken for granted and enshrined as "givens" in value-free studies of race and the course of daily life. They are used in support of the notion that human beings are descended from

3

common material origins and are possessed of recognizable physical, mental, and cultural traits that are transmitted biologically and are used more often than not to group and classify people into four, five, twelve, or thirty-eight divisions, usually in some arbitrary hierarchical order.

It is the uncritical acceptance of the concept of race that I seek to interrogate in this book. In the modern world we have become so accustomed to thinking within a framework of race and ethnicity that we are quite unable to conceive of a past that may not have had this framework. As a consequence, the ethnic prism through which we have interpreted the past blocks out a wide range of thought on human experience and conduct, producing not an understanding or even an explanation, but an optical illusion—a human phantasmagoria. By this means the past has been transformed as much in the quiet of the study as in the hurly-burly of the street into colorful labels exemplifying how the conflict by the Greeks, Etruscans, and Latins, and the destruction of Carthage by Rome, bear an accurate resemblance to the racial and ethnic conflicts we see with nauseating frequency on our television screens.

My study is focused in the following ways. First, it traces the raciation and racialization of Western history and science since antiquity without the encumbrance of the intriguing controversy raging at the moment in the physical, historical, social, and political sciences as to whether there are races or not. For the most part the vast array of "theories" of race that we handle with such largesse today are little more than catch-all explanations, convenient for present utilitarian purposes but lacking substance in the philosophic, scientific, historical, and philological sources that gave rise to their definitions and presuppositions. My book is an invitation *not* to accept that the history of Western thought has always been, and always will be, a history of racial thought. It is an invitation to begin exploring from a different and more difficult starting point, to resist the easy high road of finding meanings of race in "residual, atrophied and mummified forms," as José Ortega y Gasset puts it,[2] wherever we look in the past. It asks the reader not to accept the postulates of race as "givens" but to examine the past without the intellectual baggage acquired since the end of the seventeenth century. It is an invitation that may be declined.

Second, my study proceeds on the assumption that there is already sufficient evidence in scores of dictionaries and etymologies for us to see that the word "race," as used in Western languages, is of extremely recent origin. It entered the Spanish, Italian, French, English, and Scottish languages during

ORIGINS OF THE WORD "RACE"

The word "race" entered Western language late, coming into general use in Northern Europe about the middle of the sixteenth century. There is no word bearing a resemblance to it in Hebrew, Greek, or Roman literature. In 1910, W. W. Skeat proposed as its main meaning: "lineage, family, and breed."
Its etymology includes:

ARABIC	*râs:* chief, head, origin, beginning; entering European languages through southern Spain
CZECH	*raz:* artery, blood; in colloquial Czech, a butcher, a slaughterer of pigeons
DUTCH	*razen:* to rage
ENGLISH	*rice* (Anglo-Saxon): power, authority, kingship, kingdom, used as of a district or office, as ***bishop-rice***; *ras* (Middle English): a trial of speed, swift course, current
FRENCH	*race:* from *rassa:* a group of individuals who conspire
GERMAN	*reiza* (Old High German): a line, stroke, or mark; *rasen:* to rage
ICELANDIC	*ras:* a race, running; *rasa:* to rush headlong
ITALIAN	*ratio:* sort, species; *razza:* sort, species; race, kind, brood, stock, descent, lineage, pedigree; *razzina:* a little root
LATIN	*radix:* root; *ratio:* species; *raptia:* radix and ratio (not considered to be good roots for the word)
PORTUGUESE	*raça:* race, generation, origin, descent, lineage, tribe, family, stock, breed, strain, mankind; a crack in the hoof (horses and cattle), a sunbeam i.e. the idea of something singular in a straight line (as with Spanish raza)
SLAVONIC	*raz:* something to do with marching in order, pulling hand over hand
SPANISH	*raza:* in horse breeding, the strain of thoroughbred horses branded in order to be distinguished; in cloth, the uneven thread that is different from others in the weft; in families, slightly derogatory

SOURCES

Bloch, Oscar, and Walther von Wartburg. *Dictionnaire étymologique de la Langue Française.* 4th ed. Paris: Presses Universitaires de France, 1964.
Cotgrave, Randle. *Dictonarie of French and English.* London: Adam Islip, 1611.
Dover, Cedric. "Race: The Uses of the Word," *Man* 95 (April 1951): 55.
Florio, John. *Queen Anna's New World of Words.* 1611; reprint, Menston (Yorks): Scolar Press, 1968.
Littré, Paul-Emile. *Dictionnaire de la Langue Francaise.* Monte Carlo: 1972.
Michaelis, Novo. *Dicsonario Ilustrado.* Wiesbaden: Brookhaus, 1961.
Robert, Paul. *Dictionnaire Alphabétique et Analogique de la Langué Française.* Vols. 5 and 7. Paris: Societé du Nouveau Littre, 1965.
Sebastian de Covarrubias Horozco. *Tesoro de la lengua castellana o española.* Madrid: Luis Sanchez, 1811.
Skeat, W. W. *Etymological Dictionary,* 4th ed. Oxford: Clarendon, 1910.
Voegelin, Eric. "The Growth of the Race Idea." *Review of Politics* 2, no. 3 (July 1940): 283–317.

the period 1200–1500 and did not have the meaning that we attach to it now. In most Western languages its earliest meaning related to the swift course or current of a river or a trial of speed. In the later Middle Ages it sometimes was used to refer to the lineage or continuity of generations in families, especially royal or noble families. But it was not until the late seventeenth century that the pre-idea began to have a specific connotation different from that of *gens* (Latin, clan) and to be used in conjunction with a new term—"ethnic group." And it was not until after the French and American Revolutions and the social upheavals which followed that the idea of race was fully conceptualized and became deeply embedded in our understandings and explanations of the world. In other words, the dispositions and presuppositions of race and ethnicity were introduced—some would say "invented" or "fabricated"—in modern times and were the outcomes of a vast excrescence of recent thought on descent, generation, and inheritance.

Third, I shall explore why popular and intellectual discourse came to be in thrall to this attractive and powerful modern idea and why so much has been written in recent times on its sociology and psychology. How did it come to pass that people came to believe with such certainty that they were connected to, or separated from, other human beings racially and ethnically by reference to an assortment of surface descriptions derived from the uncertainties of dimension, proportion, pigmentation, hair texture, shape, and mental states? To answer that complex question, I shall look at texts as well as contexts—those economic, social, geographic, physiological, and psychological perspectives that have, for all their important discoveries, diminished the old emphasis on political rule as the basis for Western civilization. The emergence of the idea of race had something to do with the insouciant and often deliberate manipulation of texts by scientists and historians abandoning earlier paradigms of descent, generation, and right order (and especially the political order) for an even later one (the racial order). I shall contend that with Jean Bodin, Thomas Hobbes, John Locke, Baron de la Brède et de Montesquieu, Comte Henri de Boulanvilliers, and Abbé Jean-Baptiste Dubos the modern concept of race was made to stand in opposition to earlier accounts of generation and inheritance and that, given the postulates and suppositions of the ancients, race could not have been their creation, as is commonly supposed.

Fourth, I will show that the idea of race is inimical to Western *civilization* in the strict political sense of that word as it was understood before the Reformation. It is fundamentally an Enlightenment notion used within the structure of legitimate intellectual inquiry to explain complex human arrangements, such as caste and tribe, that are based on historical presuppositions and dispositions totally antipathetic to both politics *qua* politics and to race.

For these reasons I will not follow the orthodox route taken by modern social scientists, who tend to take race as a historyless given, nor will I devote much time to those works that seek to prove our natural affinity with Heidelberg Man, from the one hundred thousand genes and the billions of letters of each inherited genetic message, which may or may not make up our individual "racial" composition as human beings. That said, I acknowledge that the discoveries of Francis Crick, J. D. Watson, Maurice Wilkins, and Rosalind Franklin in the biological sciences[3] are challenging all past historical, philosophical, and theological explanations of existence to an extent that few people are yet able to comprehend. Above all else, these scientific works seriously call into question the definitions and presuppositions of race propounded with such certainty in the eighteenth and nineteenth centuries and upon which the tottering superstructure of modern intellectual investigation rests.

What we see in the analysis of the codes of deoxyribonucleic acid (DNA) is the portrayal, description, and quantification of complex nonlinear genetic relationships—the "new systematics," as they are called. The examination of species and subspecies from a genetic standpoint has introduced dynamic new ideas that have generated a fierce debate inside and outside scientific inquiry. Are there fixed, immutable physiological and mental differences among races, or not? Those who cling to the old view argue that there is still some evidence of genetic, sociobiological, or clinical differentiation that may be termed "racial." Those who contest that premise argue that advances in high-speed data processing permit the quantification of such vast numbers of biological characteristics of individuals and groupings that no generalized evidence of raciation can be discerned. All that can be said is that each individual is a complex organism of phenetic relationships, and the term "race" now obscures more than it illuminates. New discoveries have so fundamentally challenged the superstructure, substructure, and terminology of biological science that any scientific analysis which includes raciation must be flawed because it arises— like Georg Stahl's phlogiston theory, Johann Blumenbach's formative force, and August Weismann's germ-plasm theory—from *a priori* propositions. Such analysis is much more concerned with maintaining the postulates of past classifications and nomenclatures than with pursuing scientific explanation of the awful chaos of human variability.

It is too early to say whether these fascinating scientific debates will provide evidence of raciation in human material.[4] What we can be assured of is that there is now considerable confusion where once there appeared to be certainty. The more important question is how human beings came to accept the premises of raciation and racialization in the first place. How, in antiquity, did human beings come to exchange their membership in family, tribe, clan, and caste, for something that we call "the civic" and "the political," and then in a very short period of human existence come to consider abandoning it? The various multiple theories of race used to explain the phenomenon are inventions of modern times and stem from the combined contributions of physical anthropology, the biological and chemical sciences, and various sub-branches of history. Notwithstanding the general confusion about these "theories,"[5] it is obvious that the idea of race continues to be used freely and loosely within the framework of social, political, and historical inquiry, often without any desire to examine its premises. It is that area of confusion and complexity, of shifting interpretations and elisions among science, history, philosophy, and practice, that I wish to concentrate upon in this book.

My fifth contention is that the idea of race does not lie dormant in every society on all occasions and at all times, simply waiting to be discovered. The idea of race has a historical pedigree and authenticity *sui generis* that may be traced by careful exegesis of what people were thinking about when they acquired the postulates, suppositions, and dispositions to divide the world in a racial way. These writers must be distinguished in history from those who cannot be assumed to have had these dispositions simply because they used resembling words like "barbarian," "monster," *ethnos*, "brute," "wildman," and "slave." To resist carrying the categories of the present into the past, I shall reject outright any suggestion that illuminates the past by reference to *post hoc* racial differentiation and raciation. I shall begin with the argument, not by any means new, that there was a remarkable *absence* of race as an organizing idea during the Greco-Roman period, and that the idea was cobbled together as a pre-idea from a wide variety of vestigial sources during the thirteenth to the sixteenth centuries. I shall then show that the idea was imperfectly conceptualized with little or no "political" illumination in the seventeenth to the twentieth centuries, eventually to emerge as one of the dominant ideas of modern industrial and managerial civilization.

To meet the immediate criticism that there is abundant historical evidence of something that certainly looks like race in Greece and Rome, I shall argue that a paradigm of thinking politically, entering Western history from 1000 B.C., created an archetype of politics *qua* politics. Seen in terms of its postulates, political thinking was inherently and logically resistant to the idea of race as we understand it; it was more concerned with something called "the civic." In the modern civilization following the agricultural and industrial revolutions of the late eighteenth century there appeared a multiplicity of racial hypotheses that fundamentally challenged that complex political archetype and sought to derogate the emphasis it had placed upon "the civic" in explaining antiquity. Indeed, in the fully developed racial archetype that emerged at the end of the nineteenth century, the civic and political explanations of past were unwanted; the main objective of its proponents was a complete displacement of politics. None of these later philosophical, historical, and scientific hypotheses of race offered a fit, or useful, conception upon which to base an understanding of either past or present civil association, except in terms of perpetual war.

That is not to say that when, at a later stage in the book, I come to address contemporary problems of racial discrimination, integration, and equity I shall idealize or romanticize the political theory of antiquity. Indeed, I shall contend that the European writers from 1760 to 1914 already accomplished that extraordinary feat and were so successful in their derogation of the antique political archetype that any attempt to revivify real politics is now seen as romantic and idealist by so-called social realists. Modern historians, scientists, and social scientists are so steeped in an Enlightenment racial perception that they are deflected from seeing the significance of the antique political and civic interventions in Western experience. I am well aware that the problems of the post-Nietzschean age are not the problems of the ancient world, and I do not intend to be blind to the fact that ancient and Christian civilizations—and indeed the greatest neoclassical republic in history, the United States—were dependent on slaveholding, often iniquitously maintained in the name of faith. Antiquity was, in fact, riven by slavery and barbarism—but not by race, and for that reason the classical idea of politics still has something to say in our time.

In short, I will insist that race is *not* everywhere. My aim will be to mark the important transitions in thought from a historical situation in which people lacked the disposition to divide the world into racial or ethnic groupings to one in which there is a disposition to divide everything in that way, even to the extent of inferring it when it is obviously missing as an organizing idea. That means not only keeping a tight rein on the word "race" but distinguishing it from another important idea generally considered to be related, "politics."

» *The Political Idea*

The introduction of novel political and philosophical ways of looking at the world wrought radical change at a time when the familiar forms of governance—particularly the Phoenician, Sumerian, Egyptian, Sabaean, Chaldean, and Hebrew—relied heavily on tablets of stone handed down to kith and kin, tribe and clan. First in Greece, and then by example in Rome, the idea was advanced that politics was an autonomous human activity distinguishable from other kinds of human activity that may be chosen to govern complex communities. That activity arose at a particular time in Western history, and it occurred in a structural arrangement termed a "polity." In common with Aristotle, Cicero, Machiavelli, and in more recent times with Walter Bagehot, Lord Acton, Alfred E. Zimmern, Walter Lippmann, Michael Oakeshott, Theophile Simar, Sheldon Wolin, Hannah Arendt, Eric Voegelin, Bernard Crick, J. G. A. Pocock, Donald Kelley, and Quentin Skinner, I distinguish this political activity as peculiar, and only an occasional obtrusion into human affairs. Bernard Crick sees politics as only one possible response to the problem of order, and by no means the most usual. According to his definition, politics is a process of discussion that demands dialectic, public criticism of public proposals; it is a way of ruling divided societies without undue violence.[6] This structural arrangement has been labeled the antique model of state by Martin Bernal in *Black Athena*.[7] Like Bernal, I am interested in polity but especially in what it was that made politics distinctive, in what enabled politics to emerge at all in a world where previously order had depended on the observation of hierarchical rules pertaining to household, family, clan, and tribe. In Greece and Rome the transition from kith and kin to polity, from blood relationship to political relationship, cannot be explained using natural, evolutionary, or genetic criteria, as has been argued since the time of Thomas Hobbes and particularly by Sir Henry Maine in his magisterial *Ancient Law*.[8] The Greeks themselves believed that the transition depended on human action and that it sprang from *logos*, or reason. Thus, the emergence of political life and law (*polis* and *nomos*) was the outcome of a heated and controversial debate about words and letters (*logomachy*) in a public place (*agora*), which might lead to interesting solutions to the puzzles (*logogriph*) of human existence. One important suggestion arising from this discourse was that secular human beings might be persuaded to try a novel form of governance that provided options and alternatives to the prevailing forms of rule then surrounding them. It was not a matter of Nature, but a difficult and original choice.

What the Greeks chose, and the Romans copied, was an extremely novel form of governance, never complete in its application, that wrested them from a capricious Nature (*physis*) governed by the mechanical rules of subsistence and the inevitability of Death. It enabled them to exercise some choice about the direction that might be taken by a category of people called citizens engaged in disputes about their temporary existence. The actual structure within which that activity was conducted was imperfectly organized, its membership was inequitable and unequal, and the conduct of its business was bifurcated into two distinct spheres of influence—the private (subject to the rules of Nature and *physis*) and public (subject to the rules of Man and *polis-nomos*)—between which there was much friction. Since the Enlightenment we have become so accustomed to making judgments about this ancient polity in terms of its obvious failure to meet the highest ideals it set for itself philosophically and metaphysically—and so bewitched by the obvious presence of slaveholding, limitations on participation and speech, the lowly status of women, the accepted subservience and monotone of household, entrenched attitudes toward the barbarians, and the excesses of tyranny, oligarchy, and democracy—that we have failed to appreciate what an enormous leap it must have been to have achieved any consciousness of the civic idea and the political way at all.

The Greeks recognized that the theocratic and bureaucratic models of the Egyptians, Phoenicians, and Hebrews could not handle the social and economic complexities they faced. Human settlements now involved larger numbers of diverse peoples in affairs no longer possible of regulation by kings, priests, tribal leaders, and heads of households. Competing forces of intellect, money, population, and changing conditions of life required new sets of assumptions. The political idea contained at least eight novel features:

» a belief that *all* human beings have a common beginning and share in the uncertainties of this transitory life

» a greater concern for immediacy in the face of human mortality, and a consequent emphasis on human excellence (*arete*) achieved through knowledge

» the identification of a general public arrangement based on published rules (*nomos*) made by a category of people called citizens acting publicly, and not by heads of households acting privately

» the resolution of difference, the settlement and reconciliation of interests and beliefs, by "speech-gifted men" through sound, critical argument about ends

» the accommodation of difference by compromise, with a commitment to balance and moderation and allowance for the expression of dissatisfaction, doubt, and eccentricity

» the original theoretical distinction between private and public (household and polis), and the definition of how mortal denizens of the capricious realm of nature may become good citizens

» the institutionalization of risk and the clear delineation in the mechanisms of governance of the limits of public and private action

» an emphasis upon articulate public speech, argument, and discussion in a public place

The political idea involved a disposition to see people not in terms of where they came from and what they looked like but in terms of membership of a public arena. The Greeks invented the ideal of citizenship and its accompanying demand for the discharge of a civic duty that was clearly differentiated from duty to family, clan, or tribe. Citizenship held out the prospect of purpose in life. Those locked in the private world were, in contrast, *idiotes*, trapped in an endless, purposeless existence. The Greek political idea thus inhibited the holding of racial or ethnic categories as we have come to understand them in the modern world. That is not to say that there were no divisions. The invention of politics did not banish persecution, cruelty, oppression, and slavery from the Greek states or the Roman Republic and Empire, but divisions were not in any way based on the premises of race.

From the publication of Hobbes's *Leviathan*, in 1651, the reading of Greco-Roman texts has been deflected from political descriptions toward "naturalized" interpretations fed by the presuppositions of mass democracy, self-determination, and raciation and racialization. Whereas the principles of political life were first grounded in human action in *opposition* to Nature, they have now been shifted to a quite opposite view. The rights, duties, and obligations which once flowed from a politics that *released* man from Nature are now seen to be *in* Nature and directly derived from it regardless of the postulates of politics.

What intrudes upon the modern perception of politics is what modern writers like Ludwig Fleck, Jacques Barzun, Erik Erikson, and Primo Levi have described as the tendency of human beings to be mesmerized by a "carnal scourge," in Fleck's words, of race introduced into Western civilization in modern times. Our perception of race, claims Fleck, is little more than an unhistorical "ritual mechanical action," or as Barzun puts it, "an easy, vulgar method for dealing abstractly with a threat to comfort or pocketbook."[9] No matter how strong the wish of antiracists to wind up the past, to extirpate the infection, to find its essential cause, and of racists to mobilize its obvious power, it has to be recognized that the idea of race exercises a strong hold over both. Erik Erikson writes:

> After all the new insights that totalitarianism, nuclear warfare, and mass communications have forced us to face, it can no longer escape us that in all his past man has based his ideologies on mutually exclusive group identities in the form of "pseudo species": tribe, nation, caste, region, class, and so on. The question is: Will mankind realize that it is one species—or is it destined to remain divided into "pseudo-species" for ever playing out one (necessarily incomplete) version of mankind against all others until, in the dubious glory of the nuclear age, one version will have the power and the luck to destroy all the others just moments before it perishes itself.[10]

Primo Levi fears that when "every stranger is an enemy," the end will be the complete obliteration by war of all politics and all remembrance.[11]

It is for this reason that I have chosen to examine the relationship among politics, religion, and race historically and not sociologically. My history will not be the ideal historian's history or a scientist's history, although it will go to both occasionally for refreshment and provocation. Nor will it be a philosophical history that seeks to construct a new theory of race upon *ad hoc* hypotheses. My task is more modest, and one that was much influenced by Michael Oakeshott, who once casually suggested to me that race was worth looking at as an antonym to politics. My task is simply to be puzzled by an identity called "race" and to wonder what that really is, and why it had a certain character, and how it ever became possible. As I stated at the beginning, all that I claim is that this work focuses on the principles of civil association that have been in opposition to race in Western civilization. This book is not so much a history of social, political, and economic events that caused race to appear as a narrow examination of the intellectual contributions that have guided and shaped human ignorance.

» The Idea of Race

In Part I, covering a vast period from the ancient world to the Reformation, I shall demonstrate that until Augustine's reconciliation of faith and politics in the fifth century, the major divisions between people were more clearly understood as being between the civic and the barbarous. In Greece and Rome the organizing idea of race was absent so long as the political idea flourished to reconcile the volatile blood relationship (kinship) found in family, tribe, and clan, with the wider demands of the community. After the Reformation, Augustine's controlled biblical allegory on faith and politics was superseded by multiple accounts of existence derived from early Chaldean, Hermetic, and Cabalist writings. From these arcane threads a racial account of existence based upon blood, physiognomy, climate, land, soil, and language began to be woven into a richly embroidered blanket that challenged both faith and reason.

In Part II, covering the end of the seventeenth century to the present, I shall examine how the newly published criteria of natural history became the basis for inquiry into legitimate government. Writers like Montesquieu, David Hume, Johann Blumenbach, Immanuel Kant, Gotthold Lessing, Johann Gottlieb Fichte, Johann von Herder, and Edmund Burke contributed to the emergence of a self-conscious idea of race. When in the early nineteenth century the great German historian Barthold Georg Niebuhr fundamentally reexamined the past in light of the temper and character of the races, as demonstrated in their close affections, common names, and kindred blood and color, the stage was set for the discovery of the true origins of the ordinary people (the *Völker*) in the generalizations of philological and scientific inquiry rather than in the political histories, practical mechanisms, and virtues and vices of actual states and peoples (*populus*). Henceforth history was not the history of historical political communities of the Greco-Roman kind, but, as John Dunn puts it, transmogrifications of people into "races" on a universal scale.[12] In reconstructing the natural histories of types of peoples, anthropologists, philologists, and historians gave shape to an autonomous idea of race. After Charles Darwin, it was generally agreed that classical political theory had little or nothing to offer Western industrial society. Notions of state drew support from the new literatures of nation and race. The tests of true belonging were no longer decided on action as a citizen but upon the purity of language, color, and shape. And since none of these tests could ever be fully satisfied, all that was left in place of political settlement were ideas of assimilation, naturalization, evacuation, exclusion, expulsion, and finally liquidation.

In 1936, when Julian S. Huxley and A. C. Haddon tried to reinstate politics, their appeal was not to the values of the political state or to a historical reexamination of the realities of classical political theory but to a more scientific explanation of how the scientific racists had got it all wrong and how a more truly scientific politics might get it all right. The belief that a better education, a better scientific understanding of race and racism, a better social theory, will cure the disease of race thinking without politics is naive. Nor has what Oliver Cromwell Cox calls "the new orthodoxy of race relations" prevented the balkanization of the world.[13] This orthodoxy has in fact accelerated the process, creating a vocabulary by which the natural resentments of individuals and narrow tribal units are perceived to be due to ethnicity and to no other factor. In the 1990s we can now see a "politically correct" orthodoxy imposing itself insidiously upon the literature and language of politics, an orthodoxy that seeks to end racial discrimination not by political reasoning but by identifying pernicious race language wherever it appears and excising it forcefully from the literature.

I shall deliberately obtrude upon this orthodoxy by placing as much emphasis on texts in which the order of things was not always illuminated by the concept of race as on those that trace descent and generation. I shall examine the conduct of human affairs by explicit reference to the postulates, axioms, and assumptions of ethnology and sociology. I begin with the ancient world because it is a past sufficiently detached from the present Tower of Babel to mark out and identify unusual and eccentric elements in continuity and change, and also because it is a vantage point from which to observe the removal and reconstruction of important features of the human landscape. I make no excuse for the significance I attach to textual exegesis (particularly in the case of Plato and Aristotle, who have been grossly misinterpreted and overplayed), because one of the great problems of modern-day race relations is that few people have the slightest idea of the origin of the ideas and concepts they employ with such profligacy. This is as true for antiracists as for racists; indeed, it is true for all of us.

Above all, I hope to show in this book that the span of years allocated to each one of us, whoever we are, wherever we live, whatever the size of our nose, whatever the color of our skin, whatever the current state of our health, is short and very fragile. Hesiod's didactic poems, *Theogony* and *Works and Days*, with which I shall begin, teach us that the real choices in life are between chaos and order, the idiocy of private existence and the purpose of public life, the rule of blood and the state of being well-lawed. The fictitious unity of race whipped up by the philologists, anthropologists, historians, and social scientists of the nineteenth century as an alternative to the idea of citizenship in a political state has led us to forget a very important past. The *nemesis* that followed from the undermining of law by power we see in Dachau and Ausch-witz, and could see repeated if we are not attentive to politics from the Urals to Shannon, from Gibraltar to Murmansk, and from Brecon to the Balkans, as kinships shatter into thousands of self-determining ethnic fragments and ultimately into the utterly private world of self.

The Ancient World 2

During the nineteenth and twentieth centuries, many writers came to use the word "race" to claim that there were immutable major divisions of humankind, each with biologically transmitted characteristics. Sometimes the word was used to describe cultural characteristics such as language or religion, or sometimes hypothetically "pure" physical types. It was often used as a synonym for "species" and in this sense was associated with characteristics derived from Nature. This way of thinking about human beings assumed that each race was a homogeneous group of individuals biologically or linguistically similar to one another and systematically distinguishable from other groups by peculiar characteristics. *Homo sapiens* was treated as part of an animal kingdom and considered to be a suitable subject for zoology and zootomy, biology and biometry. Western Europeans did not come to this complicated new way of describing people without a great deal of difficulty, however, and without destroying or bypassing older views of humankind and society that are still relevant.

This new way of looking at human beings was clearly recognized by Friedrich Nietzsche, who at the end of the nineteenth century reflected that Greek life had come to be interpreted not in terms of its own mythologies, metaphysics, and politics, but in terms of modern mass democracy and constitutional representation and modern concepts of nobility. For Nietzsche, what held the Greeks together was not a crude set of natural utilitarian and scientific connections like race, nor politics as an intimation of constitutional representation in the modern liberal democratic state, nor their capacity to think and practice politics *qua* politics and to create an original civic disposition out of custom, but the knowledge of "terror and horror of existence" as they sat alone in a boat on a tempestuous sea. The important key to the true understanding of this perilous natural state, therefore, was in the imaginative argument that philosophy, politics, and modern science were all redundant as interpretative devices. The future human predicament could only be fully grasped by a greater insight into the meaning of art, music, drama, and tragedy, first glimpsed by the Greeks.

Nietzsche's is a future world without race and without classical politics and philosophy, a world uncluttered by past principles. For the ancients, however, the idea of a state based exclusively on a community bonded together against the internal and external stranger solely on the basis of kinship, blood relationship, and common likeness was the very idea that politics replaced. Politics was the highest end of human activity, and philosophy was the key to its understanding. In politics and philosophy rested the alternative to rule by demigods, intellectuals, priests, soldiers, entrepreneurs, sojourners, aliens, and capricious self-seekers, provided the political arrangement was based on good thought, good laws, good education, good arms, and good people bonded together by the practices of law and citizenship. It was this political notion of state that was abhorrent to Nietzsche, as well as to the eighteenth- and nineteenth-century romantics, historians, and natural philosophers.

It has become commonplace to assume that anthropological observations were afoot in fifth-century B.C. Greece, that Hesiod had a "standard scheme of archaeology" in his Ages of Man, that Anaximander was "almost Darwinian,"[1] that Plato's discussion of breeding in the *Republic* was the origin of the eugenic state, that the doctrine of the inferiority of the races was merely an extension of Aristotle's analysis of slavery in the *Politics*, or in watered down versions—and it is the watered down version that should worry us most— that the Greeks had an ethnocentric view of their world. All these opinions need to be exposed to a historical perspective of the Greco-Roman world that gives some credit to the confrontation of texts with texts and allows some small challenge to be made to those interpretations that place the greater emphasis upon social, economic, political, and cultural contexts conjured up only after the great revolutions of the eighteenth century.

It is true that Martin Bernal has recently moved the discussion forward with his elegant lament of the penetration of racism and continental chauvinism into modern historiography and philosophy of history. He has advanced the important argument that there are two models of Greek history: the essentially European Aryan model fabricated between 1785 and 1985, in which there was no place for the Egyptian, Phoenician, and African, and the inclusive ancient model conventionally held by the Greeks in the classical and hellenistic ages. Yet even he, who argues that the ancient model had no major internal deficiencies or weaknesses in explanatory power, and that it was overthrown for external reasons because eighteenth- and nineteenth-century romantics and racists could not tolerate the mixture of peoples, lamely capitulates to the commonplace nineteenth-century idea that Thucydides and Aristotle had racial intent.

Bernal also neglects the painstaking work of classical scholar Frank M. Snowden Jr., whose approach in *Blacks in Antiquity* was to examine the epigraphical, papyrological, numismatic, and archaeological evidence of the early encounters of white Europeans with dark and black Africans—called by the Greeks and Romans "Ethiopians," from the Greek "to burn" and "face." Homer called a people dwelling in the East and Far West "Ethiopian," and later the term applied generally to the inhabitants of Africa south of Egypt and to others of swarthy complexion. Snowden concludes that the Greeks who depicted dark peoples did so without antipathy to color and that generations of scholars have misinterpreted the Greeks and Romans by attributing to them racial attitudes they never possessed. These attitudes were born out of the self-same anthropological, biological, and sociological theories of the eighteenth and nineteenth centuries that Bernal examines in his massive work. Snowden chooses the word "Ethiopian" because it was "the yardstick by which antiquity measured colored peoples" and also because he considers that the pioneering work of Grace Hadley Beardsley in the 1930s, and studies that followed, had given scant treatment to the Ethiopian in the literature. In a later work, *Before Color Prejudice,* Snowden examines black-white contacts from the middle of the third millennium B.C. until the sixth century A.D. and concludes that despite "the association of blackness with ill omens, demons, the devil, and sin, there is in the extant records no stereotyped image of Ethiopians as the personification of demons or the devil." A sensitive study along the same line is Lloyd A. Thompson's *Romans and Blacks,* which demonstrates that Roman attitudes toward Ethiopians had nothing to do with the modern phenomenon of race and were of a kind very different from those commonly described by social scientists and historians as racist.[2]

Both Snowden and Thompson offer reinterpretations based on a scholarly assessment of the evidence. Well-documented histories that make no *a priori* assumptions about blackness or whiteness, they suggest an ambiguity as to what a black was and how he appeared in Greco-Roman antiquity and in the ordering of that world. They are, as Michael Oakeshott puts it, invitations "to share in a transaction between the generations,"[3] suggesting that we look again at the texts of classical political theory and interrogate them as carefully as Snowden inspects his pots and their iconography. And, if Snowden is correct that race and ethnocentricism were of little importance to the ancients, we must attempt to understand what it was in the literature that acted as a block on these ideas.

» *The Moral Science of* Eunomics

From the sixteenth century on, three important early Greek texts were plundered by writers for alleged insights into the racial and ethnic composition of the antique world. Hesiod's *Theogony* and *Works and Days* were used to illustrate the inherent superiority of the Greek over the barbarian and the division of the world into four parts or races. Herodotus' *Histories* were regarded by the physical anthropologists of the late eighteenth and nineteenth centuries, and especially by the great historian Barthold Georg Niebuhr, as the precursor of modern ethnography. Hippocrates' *Airs, Waters, and Places* was for Johann Gottfried von Herder and Alexander von Humboldt, as they looked out upon a new world of ethnic groupings arising from the differentiations of environment, climate, soil, and culture, historical proof of their newly invented cultural and climatic theories of existence.

Close examination of these early Greek works, however, uncovers no assumptions about the major divisions of mankind based upon the idea of biologically transmitted characteristics, and hence no theoretical notion of biological similarity or dissimilarity except in a crude humoral sense. There were no physically differentiated types, no word that approximates or resembles "race." *Homo sapiens* was not treated as an anatomical, anthropological, or zoological specimen; neither was there a clearly defined concept of species as we understand it. Only in the work of Hippocrates is there a suggestion that the nature of man may be analyzed on the basis of observed differences in air, water, and place, but his crude scheme owes more to the humors and to the analysis of soul than it does to a consistent biological theory or to environmental hypotheses of a later era.

That is not to say that there are no genealogies, no means of succession, no foundation for the understanding of human existence, no acknowledgment of differences between peoples. My argument is that the Greek account of the differences between the peoples of Greece, Asia Minor, and Ethiopia was based upon criteria entirely different from those introduced into Greece by interpreters of the late eighteenth and early nineteenth centuries. Greek concepts of time and nature were such that they saw the limits of existence determined not by any ideas of progress but by a cycle of successions and transitions from one corrupt or uncorrupt state to another in which the present was more important than the future. Man's place in the present nature of things was always subject to the cyclical movement of the times. His fragile existence on earth was determined by the vagaries of the moment, and the short space of time allotted by the throw of the dice. The intellectual and physical capacities given to him were all temporary and fleeting, and in the natural order of things he was but an ephemeral presence. In a short time his life, and the name he bore, would be forgotten. Challenged by Diomedes to give his name in the battle for Troy, Glaucus, son of Hippolochus, responded: "What does my lineage mean to you? Men in their generations are like the leaves of the trees. The wind blows and one year's leaves are scattered on the ground; but the trees burst into bud and put on fresh ones when the spring comes round. In the same way one generation flourishes and another nears its end."[4]

Yet the Greeks were not content with the idea that the whole of existence was subject to the will of the gods or to aleatory factors. There was something that man could do to ensure that his words and deeds lived on and cut across the monotonous and corrupting cycle of time. It is here that the important differentiation takes place between peoples. All men are subject to the races of time, but not all wish to break the cycle. The *barbaros* and *ethnos* are those who are content to watch time passing and turning; the *politikos* are those who, without aspiring to omniscience over the nature of things, by measured word and deed challenge *physis* with *nomos*. The barbarous state and the political state are distinguished on the basis of their capacity to exercise reason in the pursuit of human excellence beyond the limitations set by the declared judgments of the forebears (*themis*) or the customs and laws of primitive society. Those who perform political deeds will be remembered, and great deeds will thus be immortal. The flourishing of this political ideal in the ancient world blocked the advent of a category of race as a substantial antithesis to it.

HESIOD

There is no better starting point for the understanding of the emergence of politics than Hesiod's *Theogony,* a genealogical poem of the relationship between the gods and man written about 700 B.C.[5] Hesiod described the coming into being of the world, the conflict between malignant and beneficent powers, the mastery of the powers of Zeus, and the final establishment of his kingship. This mythological account seeks to illuminate the life of the immortal and mortal universe. Its metaphors are drawn from what we identified earlier as the political idea, and they seek to illustrate the kind of relationship that ought to exist between the gods and man.

There are three myths in the *Theogony* and *Works and Days.* The first, concerned with the general ordering of the lives of the gods and mortals, promotes the primary virtue of being well-lawed. Although about the family, clan, or age (*genea*), it has little to do with the naturalistic and materialistic conceptions of the universe so familiar to us today in "skin and bones" anthropology.

The noun *genos* is frequently translated as "race," but its prime meaning is to do with those seen to be bound together by descent in families, clans, and tribes in a historical sequence from generation to generation. *Agenealogetos* is to be without genealogy. A group held together only by custom and habit is said to live in *ethos,* inhabiting the capricious realm of natural necessity (*physis*). Those, like the Greeks, who have invented *poleis* occupy two spheres— the one they cannot escape, the private monotony of the endless, purposeless cycle of household, and the other they have chosen, the public world of the *agora* governed by *nomos.* Those who live outside *poleis,* and govern their affairs hierarchically (like households, solely according to custom and habit, observing the judgments of the forebears—*dike* and *themis*), are said to be *ethnos.* One who governs such an arrangement is an *ethnarch.*

The differentiation between Greek and non-Greek, between *ethnos* and *politikos,* is not race, but the ability to rise above the mortal life of custom and habit, demonstrating by human excellence (*arete*) a capacity to engage in speech, argument, discourse in a reasoned and gifted way in a public arena. Those who cannot speak the language of politics, do not choose to practice it, and are unable to recognize its essential requirements are said to be *barbaros.* Those who are *barbaros* share with the Greeks the terror and horror of natural existence, but are distinguished from them by their persistence in living brutishly and viciously (without letters) according to nature (*physis*), rather than according to man-made laws (*nomos*).

The distinctive characteristic of Hesiod's genealogy in this first myth is that Zeus, unlike the non-Greek gods, is *not* a tyrant or despot or a head of household (*ethnarch*). Zeus rules as a wise counselor, who exercises judgment over mortals and immortals alike, and his title to rule is acquired and secured by the display of excellent qualities (*arete*) that enable him not only to overcome the uncertainties of time, circumstance, and event but to master the Titans. Before the rule of Zeus, the universe was all chaos and disorder. With Zeus a place for politics and the political life is created through speech and reason in a public assembly of gods and men, good and bad, without preselection, gathered together at Olympus, to choose between Zeus and Kronos, the Titan, the progenitor of all disorderly government.

The *Theogony* posits a dominant antithesis between political rule and barbarity, civility and incivility, law and custom, *physis* and *nomos*. The poles are not Greek and "other races" unless we mistakenly interpret barbarity and incivility for race and collapse the distinction between *physis* and *nomos*. Barbarity, incivility, and viciousness are the qualities of all men in *ethos;* they derive from inarticulate speech, lack of choice, vengeance, amnesia, subterfuge, and arrogance, all of which lead inevitably and dramatically to *hubris* and ultimately, to *nemesis*. The rule of Zeus, by contrast, is the rule of *nomos*—unerring speech, interpretation of law, balanced and moderate verdicts, mature judgment, and the bringing of great disputes to a skillful conclusion by persuasion and political judgment. Zeus gains the support of the monstrous powers as well as the beneficent powers not by the counting of heads but by the exercise of good political judgment. His appeal is in language all are able to understand. In the terror and horror of *hubris* and *nemesis,* they see that none would lose and all would gain by giving him their support.

The myth is a moral tale teaching that the political way is the right way, that politics—positing public relationship with a thinking ruler—is to be preferred over all other ideas and forms of governance. But it is only a hope, later elaborated in *Works and Days,* and must be defended against other egregious forms of rule lest it die. The lesson of the *Theogony* is that with time and education, politics as a way of governing may serve to make the most barbarous and unpolitical into the civic. The work is an introductory tale about the state of being well-lawed, a prelude to what I call the science of *eunomics* (philosophical and political interpretation), not to *eugenics* (biometry).

In *Works and Days* Hesiod's introductory hymn to the Muses and his identification of the opposing spirits of good and bad are followed by two complementary myths on the human condition. The story of Prometheus and

Pandora illustrates that human institutions become diseased when the gods, man, and the denizens of the underworld fail to exercise proper choice—choice being the prime requirement of political life. Prometheus twice tries to outwit Zeus by the theft of the firesticks, thus doing what no astute political actor should do—placing himself in double jeopardy in a contest with someone already possessed of *arete*. Zeus punishes Prometheus and mankind by creating in Pandora's virgin breast wheedling words and treacherous ways. Out of oxymoron comes confusion and the endless chatter of dissonant voices. Only Hope, securely imprisoned under the lip of the jar, keeps alive the promise of *eunomia* in a well-ordered *polis*.

Hesiod's third myth is the Ages of Man. The Golden Age, an idea that would become entrenched in Western thought, was an age brought into being by the immortals. Before this age, Kronos, the clever deviser, had castrated Ouranus and ruled over the heavens bringing into being the malignant powers. Zeus overcame him and established his kingship by "the force of his hands." Thereafter men lived "like gods knowing no care, no terror of old age and death, apart from evil, free in an abundant nature." This *genos* became divinities, as Zeus decreed, and represented the powers of good guarding mortal men by watching over cases at law.

At this stage the Silver Age was introduced "unlike the Golden Age in thought and appearance," but second to them. This age refused to worship the gods and *hubris* set in. Zeus put them out of sight under the earth where they lie anonymously bearing some honor.

The Third Age, the Bronze, was completely unlike the Silver, and was devoted to *hubris* and the ignoble business of war. Zeus banished them to Hades leaving behind no glory and no name for them. He then created a Fourth Age—a divine age of heroes called demigods—a reintroduction of those who had lived earlier on the boundless earth. Some died in war, some fought in the Trojan Wars, some had the blessing bestowed upon them of life in the Isles of the Blessed where they feast forever with the gods.

The Fifth Age is the present age, an age of ceaseless labor, and one which will be destroyed by idle chatter, dissonance, dishonor of parents; an age when oaths will not be kept, when might will prevail over right, when *hubris* will triumph over honor.

This myth of the Ages of Man presents a five-part arrangement taken up by later writers as a scheme with a racial or ethnic intent.[6] As in the *Theogony,* the noun *genos* is freely translated as "race" by writers and translators from the end of the eighteenth century on, thus giving credence to the idea that somehow Hesiod's fivefold division is a major contribution to the science of ethnology. In fact, the divisions are degenerative phases in time, and the main point of the myth is that the gods and mortals were born of the same source and will forever be subject to the revolving cycle of time, sharing its horrific uncertainty.

The *Theogony* and *Works and Days* are introductory moral tales about the state of being well-lawed, and it is a short cut and a gross error to consider them as preludes to race thinking. There is no assumption that the Greeks are a people possessed of distinctive characteristics and qualities—physical, intellectual, and cultural—that mark them as superior; *all* men in nature are *ethnos.* There is no progressive historical sequence, no classification system, no developmental physiology or psychology.

What we do find in Hesiod is a deep human understanding of the problem that arises for all mankind when man is cut off from the identity and intimacy he finds in the *ethos* of family, tribe, and clan. Entering a world in which he is faced with the past as well as the present, man experiences a daily mental and physical conflict between beneficent and malignant powers. All change is cyclical, and its transitions are subject to the uncertainty of circumstance and event. Left to his own devices and to the mercy of time, man vacillates between good and bad, order and disorder. If he is to find a new genealogy, it must be through the exercise of choice, which is the true measure of human excellence and to be found in human institutions capable of moderating the influences of *hubris.*

HERODOTUS

The emphasis that Hesiod placed upon moral virtue and civility as the opposites of barbarity and viciousness are examined in a different way some three hundred years later in the works of Herodotus and Hippocrates. The *Histories* of Herodotus (ca. 484–420 B.C.), the alien of Halicarnassus, a Dorian town in Carnia, West Asia Minor, contain vivid descriptions of differences between peoples and animals in the ancient world and provide a mass of detail on sizes of skull, color of hair and skin, methods of subjugation, rank, manners, wealth, religion, agriculture, transport, trade, and dress of the peoples who lived in Egypt, Mesopotamia, southern Russia, and North Africa in the sixth and fifth centuries B.C.[7] These texts on cannibalism, lustfulness, and bestiality became a source book for early Roman and Christian writers on monstrosity and barbarity, and later for the physical and social anthropologists, craniologists, and historians of the eighteenth and nineteenth centuries. Often overlooked in these later interpretations is that there is an important political dimension which, if neglected or abridged, distorts the text and our real understanding of the complexity of Greek life.

Language and ways of living fascinate Herodotus. But the contrast he makes, for instance, between the Ethiopian, who is the tallest, best-looking, and longest lived (3.23), and the blue-eyed Scythian, the wandering grazier, who is grotesque, and uses the appallingly cruel social practices of skinning and strangulation in the conduct of his domestic affairs, arises not from racial or ethnic criteria but from his incapacity to create some kind of moral public life capable of regulating such awful practices. What matters most for the Greek is not whether people are Ethiopian or Scythian, Greek or barbarian, but whether the moral standards set in the Hesiodic myth about the political idea—the right conduct of human affairs and the proper ordering of the universe—are met or not. The real test then is whether man is willing to forsake the realm of the private where he is *ethnos* and lives monotonously in *ethos,* for the public realm of the *politikos.*

If, therefore, we follow the thread of the argument about being well-lawed and speech-gifted that Hesiod presented and resist the temptation to rush headlong into ethnological explanations, we find in fact that Herodotus subscribed to the notion that the greatest authorities on Greek history were not the Greeks but the Egyptians: "Nowhere are there so many marvellous things, nor in the whole world besides are there to be seen so many things of unspeakable greatness" (2.35). Indeed, Herodotus went so far as to say that Greece inherited the mechanisms of its learned assemblies, processions, services, customs, and practices from the considerable interchange between Greece and Egypt in ancient times: "Indeed, well nigh all the names of the gods came to Hellas from Egypt" (2.50). Second, in his discussions of the fundamental social differences among the Egyptians, Persians, Colchians, Scythians, and Ethiopians, he exercised extreme caution in ascribing appearance as a reason (2.104), and consistently held that these people had a common beginning and a common past, perhaps proven by the common practice of circumcision.

Herodotus' translator A. D. Godley warns in his introduction to Books 3 and 4: "Herodotus is seldom proof against the attractions of a moral tale" (p. xvi). What must distinguish the *Histories* is the attempt to establish a true cause, or causes, for difference in moral ends. In Herodotus' work what separates the cultivated man, the man of political ideas, from the brute and the barbarian is not an ethnological but a moral cause. To treat his text as a scientific or historical account of race and ethnicity is to create a spurious past and to focus, as Nietzsche does, upon *I want it thus* rather than *it was.*

There is no better illustration of Godley's point than in Herodotus' treatment of the confrontation in Book 1 between Solon, the lawgiver, the archon in whose constitution citizenship is mentioned for the first time, and Croesus, the barbarian of Sardis, who had amassed great riches and once ruled efficiently and despotically before he lost it all to Cyrus. Solon and Croesus share the same human experiences and are subject to the same whimsical twists and turns of Nature. The story does not have a happy or predictable ending— a victory and a reward for showing a disposition toward civic virtue—as one might expect. Its denouement is the accidental killing of the favorite son of Croesus following his one act of reluctant compliance with the argument of Solon that reconciliation, human kindness, and hospitality were to be preferred to cruelty. Such is the chance nature of life, and such is Solon's awful warning of the uncertain and contingent nature of politics.

Herodotus' distinction between the Greek and the Lydian expatriate is not the differentiation of skull, color of skin, and climatic variations, but, if we are prepared to look for it, a disposition on the part of Solon to promote the Greek ideal of the political man (*politikos*) in which politics, citizenship, and civic virtue are seen as the end (*telos*), in the face of Croesus' vehement refusal to entertain such a ludicrous, terrifying, and threatening idea. The argument that Croesus advances is that he *must* be the most blest of all men by virtue of his great wealth generated by necessity and fortune. Solon responds with three tales of simple men who have all the virtues of the Hesiodic myth: truthful utterance, excellence in life, private moderation, public honor, duty to parents and to the gods, and a glorious remembered death. Croesus is bitterly disappointed that Solon has placed civic virtue above wealth and has chosen common men rather than himself, the greatest of *ethnarchs.*

The mutual antipathy between Greek and barbarian shown in the work of Herodotus is not about the innate superiority of one over the other. It is about the fundamental nature of political life and the moral axioms that ought to guide it. Herodotus understood that the days of all mortals are finite and that however life may be ordered in terms of its intellectual, physiological, and material advantages, blessings flow from a wide range of opportunities that temporarily present themselves—wealth, strength, intellectual prowess. The Fates—Clotho, Atropos, Lachesis—the givers and takers of life, health, and old age, sometimes help and sometimes hinder. Life is a cycle of contingent events, and human beings, and especially politicians, must not think that they can outwit the gods. If they fail to exercise good judgment, *nemesis* will follow and retribution will be harsh.

The successful characters in Herodotus' narrative are not those endowed with special physiological, biological, cultural, or intellectual attributes; they are those who, *whatever their origin,* have risen above the vagaries and vicissitudes of the natural world and have demonstrated a judgment able to turn events to human advantage, to create options out of seemingly hopeless situations. Exercising good judgment through choice is a distinctive practice illuminated more by teachings about abstract notions of justice and civic virtue than by the precepts of efficient administration, economic enterprise, or religion and cosmology. Herodotus' barbarians are those who, for one reason or another, within and without the *polis,* have been unfortunate enough to be excluded from participation in a peculiar and novel way of life.

HIPPOCRATES

So far I have labored the point that the *ethnos* are those perceived by the Greeks to share everything in common with them in the realm of natural necessity (*ethos*) but differentiated by the absence of *polis, logos,* and citizenship. This relationship between the *politikos* and the *barbaros* was a distinctively different relationship from that described, for example, by Jean Bodin when he drew up his new scheme for a natural history of man in the sixteenth century, by Johann Blumenbach, the physical anthropologist, when he constructed his important category of "Caucasian" in the eighteenth century, and by Johann Gottfried von Herder and Alexander von Humboldt when they and their followers searched for historical proofs for their cultural and climatic theories about existence. For these writers Hippocrates' *Airs, Waters, and Places,*[8] rather than the histories of Herodotus, became a key text as well as a blueprint, albeit inaccurate, for the origins of what came to be termed as "the Caucasian races" of Europe.

Hippocrates (ca. 469–399 B.C.), like Herodotus, made interesting comparisons between the people of Europe and the people of the southeast coast of the Black Sea. His reflections on the lives of the Scythians, who had occupied the country between the Carpathians and the River Don from the first millennium and had become by 650 B.C. the masters of northwest Iran and eastern Turkey, were generally unfavorable, but they were founded upon physiological and biological hypotheses entirely different from those that we find in the eighteenth century writers. Hippocrates painted a picture of an inhospitable, stagnant, and foggy region inhabited by gross, fleshy, yellowish, corpulent people who speak with deep voices. The physical condition of the Scythians, who lived around Lake Maeotis (the Sea of Azov), had been shaped not by some developmental biological process but simply by the quantity of water present in their lower bowels. Indeed, the Scythians had so much moisture that it had to be cauterized by amputation to dry out the body, to check impotence, and to encourage lively physical activity. Sexuality and reproduction, claimed Hippocrates, depend on the presence or absence of moisture. Leanness improves coagulation of the seed; excessive moisture prevents its absorption. Effeminacy in rich Scythian males was perceived as a divine disease not arising out of natural causes: "I too think these diseases are divine, and so are all others, no one being more divine or more human than any other; all are alike, and all divine. Each of them has a nature of its own, and none arises out of its natural cause" (*Airs, Waters, and Places,* Book 22). Hippocrates concluded that the cause of this effeminacy was dress (wearing trousers), too much time in the saddle, and the practice of cutting a vein behind the ear. Hippocrates observed that the affliction, which put people in mortal fear, affected only the rich, and caustically remarked that if the cause were divine then one would expect it to be distributed more equally.

While Hippocrates put much greater emphasis upon the climatic factors than Herodotus, it is important to note that he did not see nature acting alone. His main assumption was that the weak and feeble dispositions of the peoples of Asia, their gentle and lazy temperament, were due not so much to underlying natural or climatic factors as to the important fact that they were ruled by monarchs and despots—that is, they were not in possession of the essential marks of politics: "All the inhabitants of Asia, whether Greek or non-Greek, who are not ruled by despots, but are independent, toiling for their own advantage, are the most warlike of men" (Book 16). But Hippocrates also believed that physique followed the shape and aspect of land and climate, both of which can modify the physical frame, and he acknowledged that on some occasions nature might be shaped by force. For instance, in communities where a long head is taken to be a sign of nobility a baby's head was sometimes bandaged from birth to shape it:

But as time went on the process became natural, so that custom no longer exercised compulsion. For the seed comes from all parts of the body, healthy seeds from healthy parts, diseased seeds from diseased parts. If, therefore, bald parents have for the most part bald children, grey-eyed parents grey-eyed children, squinting parents squinting children, and so on with other physical peculiarities, what prevents a long-headed parent having a long-headed child? (Book 16)

Having introduced the proposition that the health-giving properties of water and wind, the distinctive differences in beauty and size, the climate and relief of the inhabitants of Asia Minor and Europe, and particularly of the Scythians, Caucasians, Asians, and Europeans, may have some bearing upon life as well as the political qualities, Hippocrates tried to construct a crude scheme for making standard judgments about these different peoples. This attempt to establish a relationship between land, water, and man, which is a collection of interesting humoral observations rather than a systematic philosophical or scientific analysis, commanded the attention of future authors. The scheme, purged of its political connotations, and presented in diagrammatic form, featured in Bodin's new method for understanding history in the sixteenth century. Herodotus is also the principal author on climate, from whom Herder recommended a patient deduction of inference.

» *Plato:* Eunomia *versus* Eugenia

In 1879 J. R. Green wrote in his *History of the English People* that William Shakespeare's Caliban, Montaigne's *Essais,* and Richard Hakluyt's "races of mankind" had introduced the inductive philosophy that made possible a new and radical reinterpretation of prescientific histories of the "virtues and vices" of states, thus allowing the past to be expressed in terms of material, racial blood-bonds as the real factors that held "the people" together. For Green prescientific history went back to Edmund Spenser's *Faerie Queene* and "to the one critical event in the annals of English poetry"—the rule of King Arthur.[9] These Celtic origins, portraying the wonder and mystery of Plato's moral sense of beauty, were brilliantly transliterated in the works of the romantics and the great English historians John Mitchell Kemble, William Stubbs, and Edward Augustus Freeman, whom we will encounter when we come to consider the racialization and raciation of the nineteenth century.

A decade later the biometrist Francis Galton coined the word "eugenics" as a substitute for "eunomics" to describe the study of agencies under social control that may improve the racial qualities of future generations either physically or mentally. From that time the *Republic* of Plato (ca. 427–347 B.C.) was popularized, principally by Galton's colleague, Karl Pearson, as a text putting forward the original racial and eugenic argument in Western history. In more recent times Karl Popper has argued that Plato established the aim of breeding the master race with an account of rulers who were vastly superior in race, education, and scale of values—anticipating Oswald Spengler's *Decline of the West* and Aldous Huxley's *Brave New World*. Popper also saw racial ideas playing a role in Sparta and Plato's idealist historicism ultimately resting upon a biological base.[10] For Richard Crossman, Plato's *Republic* is written from a eugenic standpoint and based, like Bertrand Russell's interpretation of it, on the manipulation of eugenic principles.[11] The passages of Plato's text upon which his dubious reputation as the precursor of racial theory rests are to be found in the digression in Book 5 of the *Republic*, where discussion turns to the general treatment of wives and children and the status of the family, and particularly to consideration of selective breeding. The suppositions of Plato's biology appear in the cosmology of the *Timaeus*.[12]

THE *REPUBLIC*

In Book 5, Socrates is pressed by participants in the discourse into elaborating on a subject he had briefly introduced in Book 3: the Guardians' holding wives and children in common and the status of women. Socrates embarks upon this particular discussion with trepidation and with some suggestion that he is being forced into abandoning the philosophical principles he had set for himself. He proceeds only on the understanding that those assembled accept the assumptions made earlier about philosophical inquiry and its ends.

Having already established that men would be the Guardians of the *polis*, Socrates proposes that women should have the same upbringing and education as men, including bearing arms, horseback riding, and appearing naked in public exercise. Agreeing that "the notion of women exercising naked along with men in the wrestling schools . . . would be thought laughable, according to our present notions," Socrates cautions, "Now we have started on this subject, we must not be frightened of the many witticisms that might be aimed at such a revolution" (5.452).

Challenged on the basis of the group's earlier agreement "that different natures should have different occupations, and that the natures of man and woman are different," Socrates exclaims:

> It is extraordinary, Glaucon, what an effect the practice of debating has upon people. . . . They often seem to fall unconsciously into mere disputes which they mistake for reasonable argument, through being unable to draw the distinctions proper to their subject; and so, instead of a philosophical exchange of ideas, they go off in chase of contradictions which are purely verbal. . . . I am afraid we are slipping unconsciously into a dispute about words. (5.454)

But Socrates continues the line of debate thus initiated, leading those assembled to agree that

> If the only difference appears to be that the male begets and the female brings forth, we shall conclude that no difference between man and woman has yet been produced that is relevant to our purpose. . . . To conclude, then, there is no occupation concerned with the management of social affairs which belongs either to woman or to man, as such. Natural gifts are to be found here and there in both creatures alike; and every occupation is open to both, so far as their natures are concerned, though woman is for all purposes the weaker. . . . We come round, then, to our former position, that there is nothing contrary to nature in giving our Guardians' wives the same training for mind and body. (5.455)

Having "breasted the first wave without being swallowed up" (5.457), Socrates proposes "a law which follows from that principle and all that has gone before, namely that, of these Guardians, no one man and one woman are to set up house together privately: wives are to be held in common by all; so too are the children, and no parent is to know his own child, nor any child his parent" (5.457). "Unregulated unions would be a profanation in a state whose citizens lead the good life," Socrates continues. "The Rulers will not allow such a thing" (5.458). Then he states:

> It follows from what we have just said that, if we are to keep our flock at the highest pitch of excellence, there should be as many unions of the best of both sexes, and as few of the inferior, as possible, and that only the offspring of the better unions should be kept. And again, no one but the Rulers must know how all this is being effected; otherwise our herd of Guardians may become rebellious. (5.459)

It is easy enough to abstract from Plato's text the assumption that a case is being established for something resembling a modern eugenically based society. It is much more difficult to see the *Republic* as a painstaking attempt in its own time to set an entirely new standard by breaking with the old hierarchies and values of family and tradition and creating a world of abstract ideas, a new way of discussing the old question of Hesiod of what it is to be well-lawed in a rapidly diversifying society. It is important to begin, therefore, not with Socrates' reluctant digression on the community of wives and children, but with Plato's definition of the Philosopher in Book 5. This discussion is devoted to examining a new and different way of moving from the plausible philodoxical or mythological definitions of his predecessors on life in a household (*oikos*) toward the formulation of an idea of a community (*polis*) based wholly on reason, which has its end (*telos*) in wisdom and understanding and not, as is frequently argued, in practical application.

In Book 5 the Philosopher is defined as the lover of wisdom and truth rather than the purveyor of practice, as the reflector rather than the imitator, as the searcher for absolute beauty rather than the believer, the imaginer, or the conjector. The name "Philosopher" is reserved for a very small group of people: "those whose affections are set, in every case, on the reality" (5.480). The Philosopher is the Master of Truth, which should be the true end (*telos*) of logical inquiry.

In the *Republic* Socrates debates face to face with retired businessmen, speech writers, and teachers of rhetoric, whose ideas of justice based on honesty, conduct, reward and benefit, cooperation and compulsion, contract and power are tested by a searching question-and-answer method against a greater Idea of Justice arising from qualities recognizable in the individual soul (1.353). The analytical process stretches the concept of individual human soul to its logical limit so that from dialogue comes an Idea of a Polis not tied to existing ideas of *polis* but exemplifying the Idea of Justice. "Insofar as the quality of justice is concerned, there will be no difference between a just man and a just society," Socrates concludes (4.434). The emphasis is always upon the concept of an entire community based upon an assumption of individual Virtue, which must by definition be independent of race and sexuality, however much we may want it to be otherwise in our transliteration.

For Plato, and indeed for Aristotle, the practice of philosophy is an activity unique to the Greeks. Its principles, practices, and methods are new and quite radically different from those of the Phoenicians, Egyptians, Thracians, and

Scythians. "We must admit," says Socrates, "that the same elements and characters that appear in the state must exist in every one of us; where else could
they have come from? . . . The love of knowledge . . . would be ascribed to
our own part of the world, . . . the love of money . . . with Phoenicia and
Egypt" (4.435). The distinction Plato insists upon is not race but what the
people love.

Plato's discussion of breeding of flock at the highest pitch of excellence,
therefore, is only a contribution to the history of the idea of race if we subordinate and trivialize the importance of love of knowledge in the *Republic*. If
we are willing to concede that the fundamental division between Greek and
barbarian turns on distinctions between degrees of excellence (*arete*) in the
grasp of the new learning, particularly logical argument and discourse, and
then insist upon seeing in it a subliminal contribution to the germ of the idea
of race, we should understand that we invest in it a meaning derived from
postrevolutionary writings of the eighteenth century in which the past becomes a genetic history of cultural, spiritual, and statistical instances. The
British philosopher F. C. S. Schiller, who claimed reading Plato's *Republic* made
him a convinced eugenist, exemplifies this tendency. Socrates' discussion of
women, the family, breeding, and infanticide is hesitant because his companions force him to depart from the ends of philosophical discourse to explore
its means. The discussion of breeding is not a recommendation for eugenic
action but a model against which states may be compared to see whether they
come close to the abstract Idea of the most just and most rational. It is an
exercise not in eugenics but in *eunomics*.

Thus far I have argued the very opposite of Popper's argument that Plato's
philosophical construct of the ideal *polis* promotes the values of racial and
ethnic identities. On the contrary, in the ideal *eunomic polis*, guided wholly by
truth, by justice, there is no stranger; all will be regarded by the Guardians
as brother, sister, father, mother, son, daughter, grandchild, or grandparent,
and the natural relationship between each will be unknown. This ridding of
care, as Plato calls it, will give the Guardian "a life better and more honourable
than that of any Olympic victor; and we can hardly rank it on a level with the
life of a shoemaker or other artisan or of a farmer." In the unlikely event that
the Guardian should thirst for power and money and become childishly dis-
tracted, "then he will learn the wisdom of Hesiod's saying that the half is
more than the whole" (5.465–66).

For the moment it has to be recognized that in the philosophical process of reasoning away the mechanical aspects of family and kin and creating a bonding that depends on sharing organically and rationally in a community where all are doing what they are best suited to do in the timelessness of knowledge (all assumptions that put race and ethnicity out of court), Plato has moved away from the activity of politics as described in my introductory chapter and elevated it into the highest expression of life in a human community. Politics has become the dominant note, intellectually and spiritually, encompassing every aspect of life in a vision of a metaphysical citizenry shaped on the most virtuous aspects of family and kin. In contrast, Aristotle's philosophy is concerned more with exploring the nature and limits of "existing politics" as a practical activity in which the household and family are not dissolved away and the private interests of the realm of natural necessity (subsistence, reproduction, exchange, and division of labor) are identified as different from those of the general public arrangement of the *polis*. Aristotle's way to civic virtue is not through an elevated metaphysical notion of citizenry but through the active participation in public affairs of actual citizens who live in households and retain their familial relationships. In Aristotle's case the most virtuous person is not identified by color, or place, or wealth, or intellect, or culture, but by the opportunity he is given, and takes, to be a citizen of a virtuous *polis*. We shall see later how these distinctions become of critical importance in the battle for ascendancy between those who postulate "political" origins, and those who postulate racial origins.

THE *TIMAEUS*

In the *Timaeus* we observe at firsthand the historical foundation of what Popper calls Plato's "biological theory of social dynamics."[13] If there is any validity in the claim that there is some contribution here to racial theory, then again the text must stand up to close scrutiny in terms of its cosmology, origins, and causes. I do not think it does. The *Timaeus* is about civics and politics, and not about race.

As we shall see in some detail later, it was not until after the twelfth century that parts of the *Timaeus,* especially the Allegory of the Basin, were taken by the Hermeticists to postulate a relationship between kind and form and to show that the resemblances between parents and children, and the different qualities of human beings, were determined by external influences and emanations. This analysis put forward new natural origins for the universe, and new divisions by which the republics of the world may be analyzed and understood. Likewise, the Jewish Cabalists likened God to a craftsman fashioning the eyes, nostrils, and skin of peoples (not races) to a common pattern. Using a speculative theosophy and cosmogony that vicariously borrowed from the *Timaeus* and depended on a new doctrine—the Doctrine of the Countenance—it was argued that type was revealed from prototype, replica from archetype, microprosopus from macroprosopus, as shown in the evidence of the features and intelligence. Cornelius Agrippa transmitted a Christian interpretation of this literature into natural philosophy, and Jean Bodin established a new historical method for its treatment, introducing a cosmology explictly rejecting the *Timaeus* and substituting a reconstituted natural republic of the world crudely divided into races rather than into political divisions. Upon this foundation the romantic writers of the late eighteenth century, principally Immanuel Kant in his treatment of racial character and characterization, and Johann Gottlieb Fichte in his conception of an apolitical metaphysical idea of a pure Greece, derived from aesthetics and art rather than politics, put forward a tentative hypothesis of race as a fundamental variable in human affairs. From Immanuel Kant through Johann Gottfried Herder, Jules Michelet, Thomas Carlyle, Ernest Renan, and Matthew Arnold, the idea of a soulful evocative dream world of race was constructed upon what I shall now argue was a misinterpretation of the ends of both the *Republic* and the *Timaeus*.

The cosmology of the *Timaeus* begins with Solon's travels to the Delta, and, as we have seen in Herodotus' account of the journey, with the discovery that the Greeks have no history of their own: "O Solon, Solon, you Greeks are always children: there is no such thing as an old Greek" (22b.33). From records preserved in the Egyptian temples Solon discovers that the Athenian state was once the best governed in the known world and that the progenitors of Socrates' citizens were the survivors of a deluge that had engulfed the world in earlier times.

The beginning of Cosmos and the ultimate generation of mankind is set out by Timaeus, an astronomer. Timaeus accepts that Cosmos came into existence, is tangible, possessed of body, sensible and generated, corporeal and perceptible to the senses (28c.51). Existence is apprehensible by thought with the aid of reasoning because it is uniformly existent, unlike things always becoming, which are never existent.

Working to a unique, perfect, and eternal model, of which Cosmos was a copy, the Architect made a whole, complete form of intelligible things, binding together the four elements of fire, earth, air, and water. Cosmos was given a spherical shape with seven basic motions belonging to Reason and Intelligence, only one of which—revolving motion—was retained after the Architect had removed six "aberrations" of motion: "For since God desired to make it resemble most closely that intelligible Creature which is fairest of all in all ways most perfect, He constructed it as a Living Creature, one and visible, containing within itself all the living creatures which are by nature akin to itself" (30d.57). The Architect made only one such Cosmos, and it will continue to be unique of its kind.

At the center of this single spherical universe, circular in motion, and corporeal, the Architect placed a Soul, which was diffused throughout the whole of Cosmos. "And the Soul, being woven through the Heaven every way from the centre to the extremity, and enveloping it in a circle from without, and herself revolving within herself, began a divine beginning of unceasing and intelligent life throughout all time" (36e.73). Thence followed, according to a pattern—a design—time, sun, moon, planets, night, day, the divisions of time, wandering and wayward stars, and the popular deities; only then were living creatures—the inhabitants of air, water, and earth—introduced. But, the Architect did not bring these mortal creatures into existence directly; he drew up the eternal, one, perfect model—the idea of the thing—and the work of fashioning and copying was left to the gods and the popular deities, who imitate "the power showed by me in my generating you" (41c.89).

Here Timaeus introduces the notion that variety and mixture among the inhabitants of this world are brought about by intermediaries. For the time being it is sufficient to note that this process of flux and efflux results in innate sensation, common to all, proceeding from violent affection, desire mingled with pleasure and pain, and the different and opposite emotions of fear and anger revealed by character. The description of this mixture and division is contained in the Metaphor of the Mixing Bowl, which was purloined in the nineteenth century to illustrate the dangers of racial mixing, particularly in reference to immigration into the United States. But in the *Timaeus* the references are to political metaphors that exhort all living creatures to master emotion and to live justly so that they will return to an abode in a native star to live a blessed and just life. There are also warnings that if a man lives an unjust and cowardly life, and fails to master sensation, he will be turned into a woman's nature at the second birth (42b.93, 90e.249), and repeatedly changed into some bestial, barbarian form until he yields to the force of reason.

The metaphor of the political way is reinforced with a description of its antithesis—the terror and horror of "becoming and always never existing," which is the clash and chaos of the six irrational revolutions of sensation as they wrestle with Soul: "And whenever external sensations in their movement collide with these revolutions and sweep along with them also the whole vessel of the soul, then the revolutions, though actually mastered appear to have the mastery" (44a.97).

To escape the bonds of ignorance Plato reiterates the ominous message of the Hesiodic myth: if man fails to avail himself of Reason in the conduct of his affairs—and that means education in the ways of philosophy and politics—he will fail to achieve the highest end, which is the strengthening of Soul through civic virtue, and *nemesis* will overtake him.

Those who argue that Plato was a racial thinker point to three aspects in the *Timaeus* that suggest a racial orientation: the treatment of the senses; the anatomical examination of the body; and sex.

The Senses   In Plato's analysis the senses are innate and common to all. Only when the clash and chaos of sensation are quelled by Reason and Intelligence does the individual soul become consonant with Cosmos. The operating principle is the Model Form and Copy Form (the Mother and the Receptacle). The head, a spherical body containing the brain and imitating the form of All (44d.99, 73d.193), is the most divine part of the body. It is given transport and movement by the limbs, and the face and eyes are set in the front as leading parts of the soul. Through the eyes a pure fire streams from within and collides with the object of vision to bring about a sensation called seeing, which is the cause of the greatest benefit to mankind. Without vision there would be no account of the universe, of the circling of the planets, of number, of time, or of Philosophy (46b.107). By the same token sound and hearing are bestowed by the absolute unvarying revolution of Form in the varying revolution of Receptacle and are stabilized and harmonized by Reason.

Timaeus divides sensation into three parts: the first is invisible and imperceptible to the senses; the second is perceptible by sense; and the third, an ever-existing place. In this digression there is a fourth: the Nurse of Becoming, who sways unevenly in every part, exhibiting every variety of appearance. She is the symbol of uncertainty and chaos in all things and is to be carefully watched by the men of vision—the Philosophers.

Earlier I drew attention to Snowden and Thompson's conclusion, based upon a close examination of artifacts, that when dark peoples were depicted in antiquity there was little antipathy toward color in the racial sense that we understand it today. This lack of antipathy may have to do with a greater familiarity, as Bernal points out, among European, African, and Asiatic in the Mediterranean than has hitherto been supposed, but it may also arise from an entirely different understanding of the senses, and particularly of the relationship between sight and color. In the *Timaeus,* a major source book until the end of the sixteenth century, the affectation of taste, smell, sound, and color depend on the presumption that fire, earth, air, and water are solid bodies possessing depth. The examination of them is conducted geometrically and arithmetically in terms of their kinds and their forms and the causes that underlie their special qualities. Colors consist of a flame issuing from a body, and they possess particles so proportioned to a contracting and dilating visual stream as to produce a sensation (45c) in much the same way that astringent particles are felt on the tongue:

> These, therefore, are the names we must assign to them: that which dilates the visual stream is "white"; and the opposite thereof "black"; and the more rapid motion, being that of a different species of fire, which strikes upon the visual stream and dilates it as far as to the eyes, and penetrating and dissolving the very passages of the eyes causes a volume of fire and water which we call "tears." (68a.175)

There is, of course, a moral lesson paramount in this antique analysis of sensation; that necessary cause should be sought for the sake of divine cause, which brings us back irrevocably to the life of blessedness and the Good, the life of *eudaemonia,* or fulfillment, through *eunomia* found only in the new way of philosophizing about the political life. For Plato the naked sense perception of man in the Receptacle (the Mixing Bowl) is not sufficient cause, a conclusion entirely ruling out the kind of associationist and sensationalist thinking that so inspired the nineteenth-century race thinkers.

The Body   Nor does the analysis of the body in *Timaeus* lend much support for racialist thought. The mortal kind of soul is constructed by the sons of the Architect—the gods and the popular deities—and located within the chest. That part which contains courage and spirit is placed between the midriff and the neck, where it can listen to reason; the appetitive part, containing the liver, is tied up, like a savage, between the midriff and the navel. The fearful and unavoidable passions of pleasure (a lure to evil), pain (which extinguishes good), rashness and fear (foolish counselors), anger (hard to dissuade), and hope (ready to seduce) are in a separate chamber between head and chest, below the neck, so as to keep passion from polluting divine reason. The citadel of reason, the brain, a perfect globe containing the marrow—"the universal seed-stuff for every mortal kind" (72c.191)—is situated in the head, and the marrow, from which all bone and flesh are generated, is distributed throughout the body by the vertebral column, which, like the head, is encased in bone for protection.

Disease of the body then is the overstepping of the conditions of "proper order." Anything done out of the proper order, or out of sequence, interrupts the delicate balance of passion and reason, and brings disease. When the salt, serum, or phlegm in the blood is corrupted, the nutriment to the body is greatly affected. Wandering humors give rise to a variety of tempers and spirits, to excessive pleasure or pain, that may infiltrate the three regions of the soul—reason, courage, and appetite—thus disturbing the proportion of things. And as it is with the human body, so it is with the body politic: "When the soul engages, in public or in private, in teachings and battles of words carried on with controversy and contention, it makes the body inflamed and shakes it to pieces, and induces catarrhs; and thereby it deceives the majority of so-called physicians and makes them ascribe the malady to the wrong cause" (88a,b.239). Bad temper, bad spirit, rashness, cowardice, forgetfulness, and stupidity in man are reflected in the *polis,* which is thus debilitated by evil administration, private and public slander, and the triumph of irrationality over the rational.

Sex   Does the contrivance of sexual intercourse, as described in the *Timaeus,* allow for a racial hypothesis? In the construction of Cosmos the gods placed sexual love in both man and woman by boring a hole through the lung, kidneys, and bladder channel and into the column of the marrow, extending from the head down through the neck along the spine to an outlet that caused a vital appetite for emission and implanting. The male genitals are excitable and will not listen to the voice of reason; the female womb, if left without implantation and fruit, becomes vexatious, restless, and wandering. So male and female remain until desire and love unite them as visible creatures embracing the Cosmos and God. Again, the exhortation is Hesiodic: civic virtue tempers the ills of irrational sensation. The political way is set against the barbarian way. Those who spend cowardly or immoral lives and fail to master the sensations of sex and appetite will be reborn, not in the Heroic Age of exceptional mortals but in abandoned barbarian regimes where mortals live with anguish, pain, and no respite from evil.

PLATO AND RACE

Michel Foucault, in *The History of Sexuality,* argues it is unhistorical to consider that the antipathy between Greek and barbarian presupposes a certain racial resentment. To the ancients, blood is a mystical object with a symbolic function. Foucault sees racism not as a political ideology but as a scientific ideology emerging in a much later era and having very little to do with the Greeks.[14] All I am adding to his argument here is that careful attention to Plato's analysis of the senses, anatomy, and sex demonstrates the significance of politics, the civil state, and the love of knowledge in the formation of attitudes toward human beings, who share these elements in common. I have treated Plato's texts at length to show that, before a disposition could emerge to divide people in some other way than in terms of membership of a political state or its antithesis, the barbarian realm of natural necessity, a number of very important building blocks would have to be painfully removed and others deftly added. Plato argued philosophically for a movement away from domestic life toward a *polis* based in wisdom and understanding. To understand Plato in terms of race is to misunderstand him in all that he says about the state of well-being.

The *Timaeus* is not a historical foundation for what Popper and others call a biological theory of social dynamics but simply an account of the creation of a single, unique universe by an Architect, in which humans are encouraged to master sensation and to live justly. The Cosmos is a unique copy of a whole complete form of intelligible being, and all life in whatever form is infused with the highest attainment of Soul. Descent is not about the transmission of somatological characteristics. There is no biology to support a notion of racial "type"; that comes at a much later stage in the history of humankind. Indeed, the human body, in all its anatomical parts, is construed as a meeting place for sensation and reason, a chamber separating the mortal soul from the corrupting disease of irrationality and the excessive influences of the humors. Plato's *Republic* assumes a *polis* in which reason has been stretched to its logical limit to construct a concept of the most rational and most good, against which man can measure the *quality* of existing men, existing *poleis,* and existing constitutions and laws. Just as in the *Timaeus* the brain—the citadel of reason—delivers to the vital organs of the body messages on behalf of the mortal soul, so in the *Republic* the Guardians, involuntarily possessed of title to rule by virtue of their reason alone, engage in soulcraft on behalf of the body politic. There are too many impediments and obstacles to the idea of race in such a complex discourse, and it is grossly anachronistic to interpret it in such a way.

In sum, the passages in Plato's *Republic* that have been taken as evidence of early racial thought are those relating to the community of wives and children and the breeding of dogs. I argue that there was little or no interest in these passages until modern times because there was an awareness, since lost, of what it meant to do philosophy and politics.

In the first place the novel methodology adopted by Plato in which a single abstract idea, limited in definition, is expanded from micro to macro is not to be confused with anything to do with practice. Moreover, the analysis of that idea must not deviate from the original principle upon which the study has been based, namely that the most rational quality is that of the soul, and courage and appetite are lesser qualities. All inquiries that go outside those logical parameters are digressions and threaten the method. It is clear from Plato's analysis that eating, drinking, and sex are to do with the household, the private realm of subsistence, and that his interest is not in replicating the hierarchy that exists there. On the contrary, the whole purpose of his philosophical analysis is to put forward an abstract concept of *polis* which never did exist, and never could exist, and which is dependent on the Rational Soul doing what it is best suited to do involuntarily, so that all souls live in a state of being "well-lawed" in a wholly nomocratic organic body, against which tawdry existing models may be compared and tested. When Plato is tempted to discuss the community of wives and children and the breeding example he shrinks from it, because it illustrates the awful danger— the threat of *hubris* and *nemesis*—of the retreat into philodoxy, a reversion to the principles of soul governing courage and appetite, which have as their ends the perpetuation of the rules governing the running of armies and households. His prime interest is in *eunomics, eunomia,* and *eudaemonia;* to ascribe even a passing interest in eugenics and eugenia in interpreting him is to undermine the rules of the philosophical edifice he has so painfully constructed, and thereby to miscon-strue his end.

Secondly, the philosophical exercise is geared to the search for a more rational kind of visionary politics beyond the parameters of existing practical politics. Plato does not agree with Aristotle's argument that the end of the *polis* is the achievement of a balance between things private and things public, between the rules governing the diversities of households and the rules governing the running of public business in the *agora*. Plato goes the whole hog and seeks Unity according to a single quality of Soul (Reason); it is a metaphysical escape into soulcraft in which matters connected with eugenics and race are, to say the least, an irrelevance.

That is not to say that I do not acknowledge that the two passages I have quoted are unimportant in putting forward a case for race thinking and eugenics in our time. It is true that Sir Francis Galton coined the term "eugenics" in the nineteenth century to describe what he thought Plato was saying. But it was certainly not what Plato was actually saying, and it was not what philosophers and politicians gleaned from him in earlier times. What I am arguing is that in the works of Plato and Aristotle the complicated discourse is about the specific requirements necessary for philosophy and politics, not race, to exist at all in human existence. These two activities spell out the principles, procedures, and institutional arrangements that formed the rock bed upon which Western civil and political society was built and were for a long time antipathetic to race. In Western history the object was to overcome the terror and horror of existence, which enveloped all humanity, and to found a civil society in which the modicum of peace and tranquility witnessed in the Greek city-state might be extended to a wider range of citizens. Plato's digressions into breeding remain so until the newly invented "bi-ology" of the early nineteenth century finds an alliance with "ide-ology" to question every rule governing the principles, as well as the conduct, of that past civil and political society. It is that unholy alliance and the derogation of the rules governing antique political society, not Plato's digression itself, that is important in understanding the formation of the apolitical, philodoxical, and pseudo-scientific ideas of race and racism.

» *Aristotle:* Eunomics *and the Practice of Politics*

Two important aspects of the work of Aristotle (384–322 B.C.) have led to his being considered as a major progenitor of racialist thought. The first is the originality of his method in the *Physics,* in which there is a systematic differentiation of the life of man in Nature (*physis*) from the life of man in a *polis*.[15] For almost two thousand years the dialectics and logic of the *Physics*—the mutual exclusiveness of opposites by a process of thesis and antithesis, and the theory of material, formal, efficient, and final causality—were methodologically sufficient and satisfactory for finding a way through the complexities of this differentiated antithetical relationship. First, man as a thing had a material cause, the material from which he was made; man's formal cause was his essence, or humanness; the efficient cause was the maker or architect, and finally, the end of man was the *telos*. Accordingly, this fourfold teleological approach to the discovery of the nature of man could not be considered apart from the important concepts of *genus* and *species*, which were set out in the *Metaphysics*. Physics was part of metaphysics; metaphysics was part of physics. All were part of philosophy as an original way of teaching and learning. It followed that man had to be considered in relation to his material dimension, his essence, what made him, and what were his true ends. The genus and species of man, therefore, were parts of the essence of Universal Man, and the true forms of existence were apprehensible as a whole by the higher sections of intelligence (philosophy) in a carefully constructed and integrated rational universal schema.

From the end of the seventeenth century, principally in the works of Thomas Hobbes and John Locke, whom we will consider later, Aristotle's method was stripped of its essences, or formal causes, leaving room for a more intensive and systematic investigation and analysis of natural phenomena according to material causes apprehensible through sensation and association and ordered according to accuracy and consistency of rational observation. From then until the end of the eighteenth century Aristotle's classification system, and particularly his concepts of *genus* and *species*, were ingeniously adapted and materialized to work out an arrangement by which the natural realm could be radically separated from the metaphysical and reordered into divisions or classes—termed "races"—within a natural order of things. The greatest of these analysts were Carolus Linnaeus and Johann Friedrich Blumenbach, who, acknowledging their enormous debt to Aristotle's method, rigorously applied it to the analysis of plants, animals, and human beings, which they arranged naturally according to *genus* and *species*. Although Aristotle's *Physics* had contributed so much to the method, the differentiation he had insisted upon in his comparison of political life with natural life was neglected, then derogated, as we shall see. As a consequence, it became possible, through a "naturalized" history, for the *Politics* to be seen as anticipating the natural divisions and varieties of the modern political world. Its analysis of slavery was seized on as a moral and natural justification for differentiation and discrimination of the newly discovered races.

Second, Aristotle's *Politics,* in conjunction with the *Physics* and the *Metaphysics* and in the light of the *Nicomachean Ethics,* contains two important passages that have been vigorously massaged since the sixteenth century by writers to infer a racialist disposition. The first is: "The State has in all cases a natural existence . . . and hence man is naturally a political animal" (1.2). Therefore, man may be considered appropriate natural material for investigation by the new methods of the physical sciences, extrapolated from the *Physics.* The second is a series concerning slavery: "A slave then is an animate instrument or an assistant in an animate property . . . and thus a natural slave is a human being who is naturally not his own master but belongs to someone else" (1.4); "The principle of rule and subjection pervades all Nature . . . and we infer that the same principle is true of human beings generally" (1.5); "We conclude that slavery is in itself an institution natural and right" (1.6). Ergo, Aristotle recommends slavery, which resembles race, and hence he is a racist.

SPECIES AND GENUS

In the *Metaphysics,* Aristotle reviewed the arguments and methodologies of thinkers interested in the idea of genesis. Thales (624–548 B.C.) was the first to see the principle of genesis as water, because all things have a moist nature and water is the origin of moisture. Homer (ca. 800 B.C.) named Oceanus and Tethys as the parents of creation; the sacred river Styx was personified as their daughter. Anaximenes (588–524 B.C.) and Diogenes (440 B.C.–?) made air prior to water; Hippasus of Metapontum (588 B.C.) and Heraclitus of Ephesus (440 B.C.) cited fire; and Empedocles (495–435 B.C.) believed genesis came from fire, earth, air, and water—the four elements. Anaxagoras of Clazomenae (500–428 B.C.) saw an infinite generation and destruction by aggregation and segregation. From his review of these ancient arguments Aristotle suggested that one could expect to trace the only cause of things, as we see them, to a corporeal principle, or to several principles under a material beginning, or, as in the case of the Pythagoreans, to number. Aristotle noticed that Socrates and Plato had both for the first time concentrated thought upon definitions and had observed that the problem of origins and causes no longer applied simply to sensible things, which were always changing, but to entities of another kind—to Ideas. All sensible things were named after Ideas, for the many existed by participation in the Ideas that have the same name as they: "And anything can either be, or become, like another without being copied from it, so that whether Socrates exists or not a man like Socrates might come to be; and evidently this might be so even if Socrates were eternal" (991a.23–27).

Aristotle concluded that the weakness of the Physicists' argument was their assumption that the causes of the origins of Man could be found by a narrow and exclusive inquiry into material things. As we have seen, Aristotle argued that as a species Man was an Idea, an Essence, immutable and substantial, intelligible philosophically, and hence theoretically, by way of mathematics, physics, and theology. The classification and ordering of what life (*bios*) was like for particular men living closest to the essence of the *species* (Man) in political states, or, like the *genus*, animal, in opposed conditions of barbarity, brutishness, viciousness, and slavery, could best be understood in terms of a thorough investigation of quality, quantity, relation, time, space, and motion, and defined in terms of *genus*, property, and accident according to what man was "becoming," his first cause and his material differences.

Whatever the outcome of these complex inquiries, Aristotle remained convinced that Greek, Ethiopian, and barbarian were united in substance in the essence of man, and that the *genus* of man was more substantial than that of other *species* of animals. There is no impression in Aristotle that he regarded Athenian as a separate species, or that he was in the habit of treating Greek and barbarian as substantially different species in the practical works of the *Politics* or *Ethics*. [16]

But when John Locke came to consider the ideas of *species* and *genera* in his *Essay Concerning Human Understanding* (1690) he remarked upon the critical distinction made between these general and particular Ideas. For Locke, words meant nothing; they were but signs—inventions set up by the mind to represent things. The terms "Species," "Differentia," and "Genus" used by Aristotle and the Schoolmen were simply convenient definitions enabling things to be sorted out sensibly. Whereas these words had once made the world more intelligible, they were now little more than indicators of the fruitless, obscure, and unintelligible pursuit of abstractions. Therefore, debate about the essence of the species was a hopeless line of inquiry proving nothing.

In taking Aristotle's system for the classification of living things, and abandoning his essences, Locke and his successors, especially Linnaeus, unwittingly provided elbowroom for the dangerous idea that Aristotle's discussion on *species* and *genus* in the *Metaphysics* was no longer relevant, and that his practical works on politics, ethics, physiognomy, and color were little more than elegant Aristotelian arguments in favor of natural slavery and biological differentiation, both of which could be used to prove that he had a racial disposition.

The world of appearance—of color and of physiognomy—which Aristotle dealt with in *De coloribis, Physiognomonica, Eudemian Ethics,* and the *Magna moralia,* probably the work of Peripatetic writers, is intelligible (more accurately, apprehensible) by the lower sections of intelligence. For Aristotle this is a lesser and more uncertain form of knowledge than philosophy and should be handled with circumspection. In *De coloribis,* for instance, Aristotle did not take the Ethiopian to illustrate a racial antipathy but simply to show that darkness is not a color and does not have any magnitude or definite shape. Blackness is to do with the transmutation of the four elements when moisture is drawn from the inside by outside heat and dries up, settles, and becomes stale; whiteness is to do with heat remaining on the inside, and what then becomes visible to the senses is a moist, flabby exterior. Hair follows according to the percolating away of moisture toward the outer surface of skin and hair. White specimens are weaker than black, because they become too moist and rot like unhealthy fruit. White animals exhibiting qualities superior to their species result from nutriment turned inward. Differences in color depend, therefore, upon different degrees of moisture and leaking nutriment. Clyde K. M. Kluckhohn summarizes: "The Greeks did not have a well-defined concept of biological race. Only at the individual level was biology significant. . . . Men were not classified as white or black but as free or servile." Kluckhohn acknowledges that they were proud of being Greek, but references to barbarian were "in no sense a 'racial' category."

Some of the Greeks more than half formulated the principle of natural selection. On the other hand, they did not fall into the error of biological racism. They preferred the pertinence of geographical environment and culture. Human nature, both biological and psychological, was definitely plastic. Cultural diffusion played a significant role. For "culture" they did not have a focused single concept—we still do not have one that is truly sharp and clear—but they comprehended the general idea of culture better than anyone before Pufendorf in the sixteenth century.[17]

Physiognomonica, which is generally attributed to Aristotle, records three methods for examining physiognomy. First, the basis of physiognomic inference is the *genera* of animals, positing for each genus a peculiar animal form and consequently a mental character. It is then assumed that if a man resembles such and such a *genus* in form, he will also resemble it in soul. Second, the same procedure is applied, with inferences drawn not from animals but from human beings. For example, Egyptians, Thracians, and Scythians are distinguished by differences of appearance and character, and signs of character are drawn from these *genera* (the word used in the translation is "races"). Finally, characteristic facial expressions are taken as the basis for inferences about condition of mind.

Having considered these methods, the author concluded that the inferences which may be drawn are negligible. The first method—of selecting signs from beast to man—is made on wrong principles, for a complete likeness will never be found, only a resemblance: "You still have no right to assert that a man who resembles a given kind in body will resemble it in soul also" (1.805a.14). The third method is also defective because facial expression is an unreliable guide and the method used is also lacking in principle. There are very few signs that are peculiar to individual *genera;* most of them are common to more than one kind, and of what use is resemblance in a common attribute?

The final conclusion is that the whole subject of physiognomy is beset with methodological difficulty because it is very hard to get clear evidence from common signs and peculiar features. It is better to look at animals that have some mental outlook in common and then see what is natural to them and absent in others. That being the case, a choice has to be made from a large number of variables, and there must be one mental affection in common to see whether the signs apply. For this reason the special province of physiognomy is thought to have limited applicability and to have more to do with natural affection, mental content, and acquired affection, which on their occurrence modify the external signs the physiognomists interpret. Even in interpreting movement, gesture, color, facial expression, hair, growth, smoothness of skin, condition of flesh, and parts and build of the body there are methodological difficulties: "for the species more nearly resembles the individual and it is with *individuals* that physiognomy is concerned; for in physiognomy we try to infer from bodily signs the character of this or that particular person, and not the characters of the whole human race" (2.807a.25–30).

If it were possible to make the necessary connections between a sign, or signs, and mental or physical dispositions, then the method would be appropriate to the masters of the new philosophy: that is, when the premises are given, the necessary conclusion will be known. Physiognomy is unreliable because the characterization depends on so many different features, from which resemblances may be seen but not complete likenesses. The complexity of the problem is further demonstrated by listing some of the variables that might be considered in such an inquiry: size of feet and toes, ankles, lower leg, knock-knees, thighs, buttocks, belly, back, sides, chest, shoulders, neck, lips, nose, face, eyes, waist, forehead, size of head, ears, and hue (too black is a sign of cowardice, as in Ethiopians and Egyptians; but so, too, is white in women [6.812a.12]). The listing of the human qualities that go with these variables is uncertain as well.

What I have tried to introduce here is the idea that Aristotle's treatment of *genus, species,* and physiognomy are inextricably tied up with something now generally unintelligible to us called "the essences." It is clear that when we tentatively examine these complex abstractions, we discover a concept of *species* and *genus* as far removed from our modern rationalist understanding of it as Icarus is to supersonic aircraft. This ought to place enormous methodological restrictions upon how we interpret how the Greeks saw themselves and their relations to others in terms of material and mental criteria, such as race, color, physiognomy, and temperament, but unfortunately it does not. It was not until the seventeenth and eighteenth centuries that the concepts of *species* and *genus,* as understood by Plato and Aristotle in a remote past, were reprocessed by the rationalists and made intelligible to the modern world by stripping the essences, materializing them, and shifting the emphasis away from contemplation to action. It was only then *post hoc, ergo propter hoc* that it became possible to analyze and explain the ancient world according to the corporeal principle and to see it as an observable world more reliably explicable by the rational techniques of sense impression. It was only then that race was engaged as a principal organizing idea in the analysis and interpretation of the texts of the ancients.

Bearing this in mind, we come now to consider whether there is anything in the *Politics* that might lead us to conclude that Aristotle had a theory of race. The chapters in Book 1 that discuss man as a naturally political animal, slavery and the principle of rule and subjection, and the capacity of slaves, women, and children for virtue (2, 4–6, 8) were central to the long-running dispute about the justification for enslavement. At the Council at Valladolid in 1550, when the Spanish court was asked to pronounce on the status of the newly discovered peoples of America, the decision reached and promulgated throughout the Spanish colonies was that Aristotle's work as a whole was not to be taken as a justification for the natural superiority of one people over another. On the contrary, the pronouncement argued that the text clearly showed a contradistinction between nature and political life that had been neglected by all those calling upon Aristotle to justify slavery in the New World. In short, the theory of natural slavery and subordination had been considered apart from the more important part of the text—a coherent and consistent theory of political life.

ARENDT AND ARISTOTLE

In her study of race thinking, Hannah Arendt takes interpretation of the relationship between the brutish state and the political state to be critical for understanding the political thought of Aristotle and the ancient world.[18] In her view, failure to understand that fundamental relationship in Aristotle's work not only distorts the whole of his text but also reflects upon the way human beings resolve the dilemmas of the modern world. For Arendt, race thinking is either the outcome of reading history backward and finding it even where it does not exist, or, more reprehensible, not bothering to read the texts at all.

For Arendt politics does not appear as a commonplace activity in all societies at all times. It had a historical beginning in the literature and came long before there was any conception of an idea of race. As I have argued in the introduction, politics is distinctively different from other, earlier forms of governance, and Aristotle is the one writer who identifies philosophically its conceptual limits. Politics is but one way of organizing and ordering the affairs of mankind—a historical alternative to the priesthoods of the riverine civilizations, to the transcendent orders of the East, to the rational Philosopher Kings of Plato's *Republic,* to the hierarchies of tyranny, oligarchy, and democracy, and to the monotony of the household.

Arendt distinguishes the truly political man (*bios politikos*) as one who, unlike a slave or a barbarian, is able to devote time to an activity called politics, which takes place in a general arrangement of affairs called a *polis,* a unit small enough for people to know their neighbors and large enough for it to have an identifiable public dimension. In such an arrangement the end is not to make the *polis* like a household, which would be an imitation of known forms of governance. In Aristotle's analysis, political participation depends upon *release* from areas of life occupied by menial manual tasks usually associated with the household (*oikos*). The household is a primitive and natural association of people. Slaves and servants, those who perform the tasks of *oikia* by necessity, are not citizens. In turn citizenship depends upon the capability, the excellence of the truly free man to speak, to argue, to reason in a public place (*agora*) free from the trammels of the household, the family, the tribe, the clan. The excellence (*arete*) of the citizen depends on release and on leisure. Political man is a living being capable of speech, as distinguished from the barbarian, the slave, and the *ethnos* both inside and outside the general arrangement of *polis.* Slaves and barbarians are *aneu logou,* not because they are deprived of speech (all humans make peculiar sounds or speak different languages, and in nature are potentially political animals), but because they are not part of a way of life that the Greeks thought they had invented, in which speech, and only speech conducted in a particular fashion, made sense and in which the central concern of the citizen was not simply to uphold and conform to what had been the myths, rights, and judgments of the forebears but to talk about problems that may have been disposed of by quicker and more efficient means—by the imposition of solutions by physical force, by intellect (as in Plato's construct), or simply by the manipulation of economic resources by large-scale bureaucracies.

Arendt's view, which is in complete agreement with the interpretations of such writers as William L. Westermann, R. B. Onians, Moses Hadas, Clyde Kluckhohn, Herschel Baker, Alfred E. Zimmern, Moses Finley, Walter Bagehot, Benjamin Jowett, and Lord Acton, is that the Greeks considered themselves to be superior because they alone upheld the Homeric ideal of excellence (*arete*) through a new way of thinking and teaching, which had made itself manifest in the new science of politics. It was not a question of accentuating natural physique or natural character, which as we have seen was regarded as being everywhere more or less the same: it was simply that those who participated in this new activity were not strangers to one another (*xenos*); they were fellow citizens (*sympolitai*) bound together by friendship in a *polis* where action and speech (*praxis* and *lexis*) resulted in good law (*nomos*). Those who were not Greeks—foreigners or sojourners (*parepidemos*)—were described as *ethnos,* namely all those who lived in the provinces, and were held together by *ethos,* by the custom and habit of the household (*oikos*).

POLITICAL AND BARBARIAN STATES

It is clear from the above analysis that a great deal hinges on the interpretation of what Aristotle meant by governing politically. The chapters of Book 1 of the *Politics,* discussed above, are usually quoted without any reference to the criticisms of Plato's *Republic* made in Book 2, Chapters 2–5, in which Aristotle rejected the principle of Unity that Plato had adopted as the basis for his discourse regarding the community of Guardians, wives, and children. Aristotle regarded the principle of "mine" and "not mine" as a natural indication of the depth of love that people have for what is their own and concluded that Plato's emphasis on Unity would weaken rather than strengthen the bonds of mutual affection and increase rather than decrease interest and suspicion. In his consideration of the nature of the *polis* and citizenship in Book 3, Chapters 1–13, Aristotle made it very clear that the political "species" is not any kind of state, nor is citizenship merely to do with residence, place, environment, or legal right. The political state has intrinsically to do with participation, the holding of public office, and the exercise of judgment—the acquisition of the ability to make choices. Citizenship, as he conceived of it, was not citizenship for all, but had to do with descent from citizens on both sides and with having the qualification to be a citizen. Just as the good citizen was not identical with the good man, so the political state was different from the despotic. Human beings come from oblivion and go to oblivion, and the polity they inhabit changes from one perversion to another with the twists and turns of life and death.

The good state will be that which has as its *telos* Virtue, which will consist of material cause, formal cause, and efficient cause, and may be seen in each species according to quality, quantity, relation, time, place, and motion. Aristotle assumed there are natural differences between the people of the colder regions of Europe, the Greek people, and the peoples of Asia (4.71327b). Like Plato and Hippocrates, he regarded the peoples of the colder countries, and particularly the colder parts of Europe, as deficient in skill and intelligence but full of spirit (*thymos*). These peoples remain comparatively free but attain no political development and show no capacity for governing others. The peoples of Asia, on the other hand, who live in warmer climes, are endowed with

skill and intelligence but are deficient in spirit, which Aristotle believed accounted for their continuing to be subjects and slaves. In between are the
Greeks, who unite the qualities of both—spirit and intelligence—and thus
are both free (out of spirit) and politically developed (out of intelligence) and
show a capacity for governing other people.

The same array of differences can be seen in the Greeks themselves. Some
are one-sided in nature; others show a happy mixture of spirit and intelligence.
The people the legislator of a *polis* can most easily guide into ways of goodness
are those naturally endowed with intelligence and spirit—the faculty of soul
from which love (*philia*) and friendship (*koinon*) issue. But spirit (*thymos*) should
not be used as justification for being harsh to any Greek, or as Plato advocates
in the *Republic,* to strangers, to those who are not known—the barbarians
and the *ethnos.* Magnanimous men are not of stern disposition, except when
they deal with wrongdoers.

Aristotle's analysis of differences in peoples, and the treatment of those
who are not known, is based upon that faculty of soul from which friendship
issues, and it is common to all men living in variable conditions. The disposition to govern politically depends more or less upon the natural conditions
in which all people find themselves, but it is a mistake, Aristotle argued, to
assume, as Plato does in the *Republic* (2.375), that the affairs of a political
arrangement are analogous to guard dogs and households. If that were so,
then the rules for governing politically would be no different from those governing the conduct of life in a household, a family, or a tribe. The kind of
association in which politics is practiced and theorized about by the *politikos*—
he who is responsible for the affairs of a political arrangement—is distinctively
different from the familiar association of kin.

In Book 1, Chapter 2 of the *Politics,* Aristotle assumed that the *polis* is a
"species" of association, that all associations are instituted for some good,
and that to attain the good there has to be a union of those who cannot exist
without one another. In reproduction it is a union of male and female; in the
polis it is a relationship of ruler to ruled. Here Aristotle distinguished between
two elements: an element able "by virtue of its intelligence to exercise fore-
thought," and an element "able by virtue of its bodily power to do what the
other element plans." One is to do with thought, the other with the body.
The former is the ruling element, the latter the ruled. In a natural state of
slavery the ruled element is ruled over by the ruling element.

Aristotle perceived the barbarian states as ruled states, as paradigms of the master-slave relationship observed to be natural in the household. It is this absence of a free class practicing politics, and governing in turn, which is the cause of the uniform condition of slavery among the barbarians and the *ethnos,* and it is this feature that Sir Ernest Barker regards as the real cause of the Greek feeling of superiority over the barbarian.

Aristotle's distinction between a species of association that is political and dependent on human action and one that is barbarian requires further examination. He defined a slave as the property of a master, as belonging to the master, and as having no life or being other than belonging: "Anybody who by his nature is not his own man, but another's is by his nature a slave"; "anybody who, being a man, is an article of property is another man's"; "an article of property is an instrument intended for the purpose of action and separable from its possessor" (1.4).

Aristotle's hypothesis is that there is a principle of rule and subordination in nature at large, and it appears especially in the realm of animate creation. By virtue of this principle the soul rules the body and the master (who possesses the rational faculty of soul) rules the slave (who possesses bodily powers). But the actual world does not always conform to the rational explanation of it. Nature does not always clearly distinguish men born to be masters and men born to be slaves. The general consensus that the superior in goodness *ought* to rule over, and be master of, the inferior in goodness is not always clearly formulated, either philosophically or philodoxically:

> There are some who, clinging as they think to a sort of justice (for law is a sort of justice), assume that slavery in war is always and everywhere just [because it is warranted by law]. Simultaneously, however, they contradict that assumption; for in the first place it is possible that the original cause of war may not be just [in which case, in spite of the warrant of law, slaves so called will not be just], and in the second place no one would ever say that a person who does not deserve to be in a condition of slavery is really a slave (1.6.1255a). [Interpolations from Aristotle.]

Thus, Aristotle confessed, the Greeks do not like to call persons enslaved by war, slaves, and normally confine the term to the barbarians: "They are driven, in effect, to admit that there are some [i.e., the barbarians] who are everywhere and inherently slaves, and others [i.e., the Greeks] who are inherently free" (1.6.1255a).

Where the distinction between natural slave and natural freeman is clear, however, it is "beneficial and just that the former should be slave and the latter master" (1.6.1255b).[19] There is a community of interest and a relationship of friendship when both naturally merit the position in which they stand. The reverse is also true, and there is a conflict of interest amid enmity when slavery rests on legal sanction and superior power.

Aristotle did not pursue the antithesis further, but he held tenaciously that the Greek political and civil paradigm was a sign of distinctive difference between free political regimes and vicious, brutish regimes. He applied the same argument to nobility. The Greeks regard themselves as noble not only in their own country but absolutely, in all places, while the barbarians can be noble only in their own country: there is "one sort of nobility and freedom which is absolute and another which is relative" (1.6.1255a). The single criterion used by Aristotle for distinguishing between freeman and slave, noble and low born, Greek and barbarian, is the same in each case: the presence or absence of goodness.

Aristotle was appalled by the cannibalism, murder, and savagery of the barbarians of the Black Sea, the Achaens and Heniochi, and the inland peoples. He likened the nature of these fierce bandits to wolves and savage animals running wild in wanton pursuits, untrained in the disciplines, degraded in vulgarity (8.4.1338b). In the *Nicomachean Ethics* Aristotle asked why it is that some states are brutish (*theriodeis*) and some not. He identified three kinds of brutish state: some have an originally bad nature; some came to it by a severe injury to the system; and some acquire it by habit. Brutish states cannot be condemned because of their brutishness; they are outside the limits of civic virtue and civic vice. They are what they are because of the terror and horror of natural existence; the die was cast for them by nature. Vicious states, on the other hand, are those within the limits of civic virtue that have become perverted by folly, cowardice, and selfishness:

> And of foolish people those who by nature are thoughtless and live by their senses alone are brutish, like some races [note this translation of *gene*] of the distant barbarians, while those who are so as a result of disease (e.g., epilepsy) or of madness are morbid. . . . It is plain that some incontinence is brutish and some morbid, while only that which corresponds to human self-indulgence is continence simply.[20]

The lower animals "have no power of choice or calculation but, they are departures from the natural man, as, among men, madmen are" (1149b.33).

Not only is the distinction between brutish states, which live entirely by nature, and political states, which live by human act, an important one, as Arendt argues, but more so is the relationship between the brutish state and the vicious state. In Aristotle's analysis brutishness is less evil than vice because people live by their senses *by nature* or because of the affliction of a disease they could not help. Vice is more reprehensible because it occurs where there is a choice between living brutishly and living politically. There is lesser scope for friendship and justice in brutish states, in tyrannies, where the prime relationship is that of ruler and subject, than there is in a system in which citizens participate on a political basis.[21] Aristotle's brutish state is not a racial state but one naturally comprised of chance persons, isolated, cut off from the world, not bound together in a moral or legal compact. Its members shift aimlessly, subsisting only on grass and raw flesh.

> He who is without a polis, by reason of his own nature and not of some accident, is either a poor sort of being, or a being higher than man; he is like the man of whom Homer wrote in denunciation: "Clanless and lawless and heartless is he." The man who is such by nature [i.e., unable to join in the society of a *polis*] at once plunges into a passion for war. (*Politics* 1.2.1253a)

The brute, a prisoner of a private world, unable to calculate or choose, unable to participate through speech, is an *idiotes,* an "idiot."[22]

Arendt's broad argument is that the idea of race emerged in human history only when the idea of a society of free men of diverse origins practicing politics and governing themselves collapsed under the weight of institutions that came to have more in common with Aristotle's specification of "the vicious" and "the brutish" than with his major species of association, "the political." The dilemma for modern man was that he had forgotten the complex elements of "the political" and under the pressure of the liberal democratic state's alliance with scientism, had lapsed into forms based upon the new racial criteria.

In sum, the works of Aristotle offer a framework for the comparative analysis of political and barbarian states according to the principles and procedures of Greek philosophical method now quite unfamiliar to us and discredited. These principles and procedures break with the myths of the Homeric and Hesiodic periods, introducing a critical and comparative analysis of different kinds and conditions of states of nature and people. Within that framework Aristotle strove to distinguish appearance from essence, the *species* from the *genus*. As a principle for sorting classes of things, he looked to the way the soul, the spiritual essence, governed the body, and applied the principle of rule and subordination to all of nature. It is this principle of rule and subordination that later writers seized upon to demonstrate either that his philosophical method was deficient or that the relationship between the political state and the barbarian state was sufficient natural justification for the enslavement of "barbarians." In fact, although Aristotle recognized important points of difference between the Greeks and the barbarians and believed these differences should be discussed and analyzed, he did not ascribe these differences to race, physiognomy, climate, relief, air, or even environment in the sense that we understand those terms today. The profound difference is due to the peculiar way in which the Greek people chose to conduct their affairs. Above all else Aristotle's polity is not a chance happening; if it arises at all it is because people of different individual, social, and economic backgrounds make considered choices together as citizens to arrange themselves in a moral and legal compact that is guided and directed by the art and science of politics and by a sense of civic virtue, not by the command of the leader, or by abject submission to either nature or blind duty. As Herschel Baker has summarized: "Man could live brutishly, enslaved by animal passion and bound to matter; or he could live divinely, satisfying the natural demands of his sensitive soul under the guidance of reason. The chariot of his soul was drawn by all the forces of his intricate nature, but reason, proudly triumphant, was the driver who held in check the plunging beasts."[23] Aristotle's physics and biology may be unfamiliar, but that is no excuse for trying to rescue his scientific coherence in modern terms by imputing to him a nineteenth-century theory of race.

» *Conclusion: Meaning and Method*

The meaning of race that has signally impressed itself upon the thought and imagination of the modern world depends on the acceptance of the following premises:

1 that human beings are independent of ethical, moral, religious, and mythological laws or rules, and are subject to the laws of Nature; man is a primate, like a bat, a lemur, or an ape

2 that origins are only to be found in physical-mechanical motions or in simple ideas implanted on the mind by Nature, and that these provide a more rational explanation of beginnings than myth or legend

3 that descent is about the transmission of biological characteristics, once "blood," now "genes," sometimes linked via the concept of evolution to soul, spirit, or mind

4 that races may be distinguished and arranged hierarchically so as to allow recognition of peoples by "type"

5 that differences between human beings may be explained by reference to structural characteristics that are assumed to be held in common by people who may be grouped, classified, and ordered into divisions taken to be "real" because they are empirically observable

6 that all people, as part of nature, belong to an enormous physical or natural entity, divisible into "races," or subdivisible into "ethnic groups," which are regarded as actual things and that they are linked together in some way from these material origins

These premises are not to be found in the Greeks. What I have tried to show in this chapter is that, if we look to the Greeks themselves, we do not find Nature independent of ethics and morals. Among Aristotle's many accurate observations on fish, birds, crabs, lions, elephants, camels, and pigeons, there is no attempt to compare differences among European, Asiatic, and African human beings with the same systematic rigor. We scour in vain for some evidence of an analytical tool that permits of the division of mankind into racial groups. In *Parts of Animals* he says: "By 'common' I mean those which belong to all animals; by 'to a genus' those of animals whose differences from one another we see to be matters of degree. Bird is a genus. Man is a species, and so is everything not differentiated into subordinate groups. In the first place the common attributes may be called analogous, in the second generic, in the third specific" (1.645.21–27).

The characteristics and divisions of mankind that became so important after the Renaissance are not to be found in the Greeks. Their methods of philosophy, their classical political theory, could not conceive of man in terms of membership of a material species. Without the union of the physical-biological notion of self-preservation with the idea of a state based on the realization of Will, the Greeks were bereft of the means of constructing an idea of race. Instead they articulated a clear and unambiguous idea of the political way, especially in the regulation of small general associations of people of diverse backgrounds. They had much to teach on the subject of citizenship, civil association, and the devising of a civic disposition.

Until the end of the sixteenth century, the nature and origins of virtuous and vicious governance were mainly distinguished according to the principles and processes of the Greeks analyzed here. Even as late as the eighteenth century Aristotle was for Edmund Burke the great master of political ideas and of governance that had formed the ethical and practical base for Western civilization. For G. W. F. Hegel, Aristotle's political and ethical state would be realized and borne upward to a higher state in the processes of history and philosophy.

It is also true that some were not enthralled by Aristotle's political way, or by the old-fashioned methodologies of the Old Philosophers, and it is in their works that we see the emendation of Aristotle's method. Francis Bacon, Thomas Hobbes, John Locke, Jean Bodin, Montesquieu, and Georges Buffon echoed the poverty of politics in the face of the advancing natural way of looking at the world, stripped Aristotle's philosophy of the essences, and gave greater prominence to the method of his analysis, from which they laid claim to a more rational understanding of man's political as well as his biological, physiological, and psychological nature. Carolus Linnaeus elaborated Aristotle's ideas of *genus* and *species;* Johann Blumenbach used Aristotle's method to lay the foundation for modern physical anthropology. Johann Gottfried von Herder revived Aristotle's concept of the degeneration of the species and applied it toward understanding the differences between European and Negroid features, various forms of rule, and particularly to the cultures of the newly invented *Völker.* Barthold Georg Niebuhr asserted that the true historical perspective of Greco-Roman life should be race, not politics. Thereafter Aristotle's claim that the basis for good government was politics and political rule was put to one side in favor of the idea that diversity was a source of corruption and the regeneration of European life and literature would only come through the revival of the chivalrous Germanic racial elements of Christianity. John Mitchell Kemble condemned outright the conditions Aristotle attached to the origins and conduct of political life, reorienting notions of citizenship from politics toward a society based on arms, feuds, and the blood of the Teutonic founders. Alexander von Humboldt echoed arguments legitimizing slavery by pointing to Aristotle's *Politics* as the origin for the doctrine of the inferiority of the races. The Compte de Gobineau rejected Aristotle's ideas of civic virtue as arising from citizenship of a properly conducted political state, arguing that the health of a state does not depend on constitutions and the political way but on the natural state of society and its races. Matthew Arnold transformed the Hellenic notion of "politics" into a recently invented Indo-European force in contention with a Semitic force. Friedrich Wilhelm Nietzsche saw regeneration not in the politics of Aristotle but in the collective release of Will as expressed in music, art, literature, and poetry. Finally Francis Galton, Karl Pearson, and Houston Stewart Chamberlain fundamentally rejected the political state as having anything worthwhile to say at all about the conduct of lives while embracing the fundamental natural realities of racial inheritance they alleged Plato glimpsed in the *Republic*. Race is about this Hellenism consciously revived at the beginning of the nineteenth century by reading out the political idea from Greek texts.

Transitions from Greece to Rome 3

I have claimed in the opening chapters that the Hesiodic myths, the histories of Herodotus, the Hippocratian reflections on climate and relief, and the works of Plato and Aristotle do not offer much evidence of an organizing idea of race when seen according to their own lights. I have suggested that it was largely through the adaption of Plato and Aristotle's method that the history of Greece came to be "raciated" during a much later period in human history—a period closer to the scientific, historical, social, political, and economic concerns of our own time, which we shall examine in detail in the final chapters of this book. In this chapter I want simply to introduce, and then set to one side for the time being, the idea that from the time of the Reformation historiography was penetrated by a similar racialized interpretation of the long period of Roman history. This interpretation was characterized not so much by neglect of the political and civic dimensions of the relevant texts but by an explicit attack on a number of key Roman sources which were claimed to reveal, and then to confirm without a doubt, that the politics of Rome was nothing more than a surface superficiality. According to these interpretations, the true inspiration and greatness of Rome, as revealed in the texts, emanated from a society bonded not by politics and law, but by art and race. At this early stage I shall not discuss how these texts came to be used as a basis for an account of that "other Rome," but I shall focus instead on how the Romans symbolized an original attempt to deal constructively, and differently, with the problem of change from a strict relationship of family, kin, generation, and nobility to life in a *res-publica*. However complicated or irrelevant it may appear to the modern reader steeped in ideas originating in the early part of the nineteenth century, there is a nonracial story here that needs to be retold.

The texts I shall consider are those frequently quoted as authorities for race from the end of the eighteenth century. They include:

1 Polybius' *Histories* and Cicero's *De republica* and *De legibus*, which were taken by the Comte de Gobineau, Friedrich Nietzsche, and the racist Houston Stewart Chamberlain as offering overwhelming evidence of the fundamental weakness of classical concepts of citizenship and political civilization and as confirmation of Montesquieu's alternative, natural account, and Barthold Georg Niebuhr's novel hypothesis that Rome drew its lifeblood from consanguinity and from a fundamental racial antipathy between Etruscan and Latin, Carthaginian and Roman, Roman and German

2 Vergil's *Aeneid,* which was romanticized from the sixteenth century to confirm the hypothesis that the defeat of Carthage by Rome, and its ultimate destruction, were racial events of fundamental moral importance to the civilization of Europe and later in the nineteenth century as an event morally justified solely on grounds of the primacy of the state, the force of arms, and the Hobbesian right of conquest

3 Lucretius' *De rerum natura* and Sextus Empiricus' *Outlines of Pyrrhonism,* which explore the authority of sense impression in the context of *genus* and *species* and tentatively question the methods and limitations of Platonic and Aristotelian thought when examining the differences between peoples

4 Strabo's *Geographies* and Vitruvius' *On Architecture,* which discuss the influences of geography, climate, language, and music upon the divisions of the peoples

5 Tacitus' *Germania* and *Agricola,* in which the early beginnings of the Germans appear for the first time, and the work of Ammianus Marcellinus, who introduces the origins of the Saracens, Gauls, and Celts; both are considered to be writers plotting out a racial course

In the 1940s, Eric Voegelin's analysis of how the Greeks had distinguished between narrow groups of cognates arranged in close family relationships (*anchisteia*) and how the import of those relationships changed as they developed into *genos, phratria,* and *demes,* from which the idea of membership of a political body emerged, greatly influenced Hannah Arendt's work on race thinking.[1] Voegelin traces out the historical transitions from ideas based on the ancient idea of *polis,* to the later ideas associated with the mystical body of Christ, and finally to modern ideas of "skin and bones" anthropology. The key argument here is that, historically, the latter could not have appeared without the disposal of a number of ideas critical in ancient and Christian formulations of the body, generation, and right ordering, and that until these building blocks were finally removed by Carolus Linnaeus and Johann Friedrich Blumenbach, it was impossible to conceive of a world composed of races.

We have seen how Plato in the *Republic* and Aristotle in the *Politics* shaped and finished the two major foundation stones for citizenship in pressing the argument that citizens are made, not born. Plato's idea of citizenship arises from an assumed rational source—the human soul—and is concerned with harnessing reason, as opposed to crude opinion and naked interest, for the benefit of a whole community attuned to ethical ends. It is exclusive only because the processes and procedures of philosophy are exclusive and the Greek *polis* (the model) is the only appropriate test bed available; anything larger is not a *polis*. Aristotle's idea, unlike Plato's, is more concerned with giving proper weight to the expression of private opinion and interest, and balancing these expressions in a political assembly of individuals qualified by their speech and action to participate in the art of politics for the ethical ends of the *polis*.

As Voegelin shows, the principal idea that the Romans brought forward from Greece and put into practice in much larger units of human association is not to be confused with the modern liberal democratic notion of popular participation in the activity of state, as so many modern theorists infer. For Rome, the principal idea was that politics was a way in which human beings in a mortal existence could reconcile the different beliefs, traditions, motives, and interests according to the best procedures and practices of the Aristotelian nomocratic model. The emphasis was not democratic, but *eunomic*.

What appears, then, in this more complicated story of antiquity is neither a crude account of racial antipathy, as expressed by race thinkers from the sixteenth century on, nor the more insidious euphemism which says that if the ancients did not express it they must have intended it, but an invitation to examine the ways in which the Greeks and the Romans symbolized an original attempt to deal with the problems of change by means of politics *qua* politics. What they observed was a potential threat to the strict traditional relationship of family, kin, generation, and nobility; what they put in its place was an idea of political life as the antithesis of the conduct of life based upon anything as monotonous and degrading as the running of a household.

» Greek Notions of Political Citizenship and the Practicalities of Roman Life

The two writers who applied the Greek vision of the political are Polybius (ca. 200–118 B.C.), an Achaean internee who spent sixteen years of his life in Rome reflecting upon its people and institutions, and Cicero (106–43 B.C.), who developed a framework for political action based on a shrewd understanding of political and legal practice.

POLYBIUS

Polybius, a member of the Achaean League formed to protect the declining and disintegrating Greek *poleis,* was interned after the Romans had successfully defeated their Macedonian allies. The *Histories,* written for Greek and Roman, joined Heraclitus in rebuking poets and fablers who offer "tainted witnesses to disputed facts" and told fanciful stories about the sea and land opening itself up to travelers.[2] Polybius considered why it is that people who once had a reputation for virtue because of their hospitable nature and their piety to the gods have now become infamous for their cruelty and wickedness (4.20). The origin of these qualities lies not in some biological, histological, geographical, racial, or ethnic fault, for all men are subject to atmospheric conditions, the common cause of natural differences in feature and color: "Men by their very nature must perforce assimilate themselves [to atmospheric conditions], there being no other cause than this why separate nations and peoples dwelling widely apart differ so much from each other in character, feature, and colour as well as in most of their pursuits" (4.21). Rather, argued Polybius, the failure lies in wrong training from childhood, habitual violence, and the unscrupulousness of those in authority. It was only when the Cynaethians, the Arcadian *ethnos,* neglected the practice of public arts—music, drama, singing, and dancing—and devoted themselves exclusively to individual pursuits that they came to behave as savages, not like human beings but beasts.

For Polybius, therefore, difference in peoples arose from a failure to understand the peculiar nature and diversity of Greek political arrangements as practiced in the Republic of Rome. It had also to do with the inability to deal with the vagaries of fortune and chance (*tyche*). His model for the analysis of change was the Roman constitution and his source the Platonic theory of the natural transformation of government, which he thought was too subtle for ordinary people. Yet he provided a simplified summary of historical change beginning with the familiar story of inundation (6.4). As people instinctually herded together, leadership fell first to the bravest and strongest, and kingship followed only after notions of goodness and justice—and their opposites— began to be understood (6.5). These notions came into being because men are naturally inclined to sexual intercourse, the consequence of which is children. Unlike the animals, man possesses the faculty of *reason,* which allows him to reflect upon past, present, and future relations with kin and to notice those things that please and displease, to observe differences in conduct, to share gratitude for deeds done, and to feel resentment for injury to a close friend or neighbor, "imagining themselves in the same situation": "from all this there arises in everyone a notion of the meaning and theory of duty which is the beginning and end of justice" (6.6). Out of duty came the ability to distinguish between noble and base conduct, and people, claimed Polybius, will support the noble and avoid the base.

Every constitution that is simple and is based on one single principle is precarious because it is soon perverted into some corrupt form of that unity. Using the metaphor from nature of rust and iron, and woodworm to depict the corruption of a body politic laboriously built upon reason, Polybius saw changes taking place "necessarily and naturally" in a cycle from kingship to tyranny to aristocracy to oligarchy to democracy to the rule of force and violence and degeneration to the perfect savagery of the starting point. This is the course appointed by nature. Even as the great Roman Republic has come into being, so it will pass away.

For Polybius, it is this cycle of change, of perversion and corruption of good and just public forms by bad and unjust private forms by men who do not have "the power of bearing high-mindedly and bravely the complete reverses of fortune" that is the root cause of the different states of mankind, not race. It matters little whether a man is a Greek, Roman, Carthaginian, or Libyan; he is judged by a theory of moral duty and responsibility to a legitimate civil authority derived from a common historical past. Polybius held to the classical Greek idea that a civic disposition depends on a structural arrangement of public institutions in which the art of politics, properly conducted according to legitimate procedures, is of paramount importance in achieving and maintaining the good life.

We shall see later how Polybius' treatment of the destruction of Carthage (1.65) became during the nineteenth century a cliché for the justification of a race war. For the time being we must note that the differences in character that Polybius observed are not racial but those generally found between "a confused herd of barbarians" and men who have been brought up in an educated, law-abiding, and civilized community. When the Carthaginians were unable to meet the demands of mercenaries for arrears of pay, all sides failed to understand the subtle art of politics. Commanders lost the ability to address men in groups in languages they were able to understand, and private action was allowed free rein. Indulgence, piracy, mutiny, and savagery followed, as they always will in such unrestrained private arrangements. Polybius concluded that just as men's bodies become savage, brutalized, and quite incurable from ulcers and tumors, so "such malignant lividities and putrid ulcers often grow in the human soul, that no beast becomes at the end more wretched and cruel than man" (1.81).[3] In such circumstances, it is too late to whistle up political remedies. "Thus at the end," Polybius concluded, "they are utterly brutalised and no longer can be called human beings" (1.81).

CICERO

Writing a century later than Polybius, Cicero was much more concerned with the political theories of Plato and Aristotle as applied to the problem of Roman citizenship in the actual circumstances of his time. Cicero's is not an abstract philosophical analysis but an examination of the relationship of actual citizens to the legal institutions of Rome and its past and a proposal of what may be required to maintain the integrity of the Roman Republic in the future.[4] He concentrated on what can actually be achieved through the workings of constitutions and laws, written and unwritten, as they are applied to the diverse peoples who live within general public arrangements of larger and wider provincial, urban, and cosmopolitan dimensions than the Greek *polis*. In Book 2 of *De republica,* Cicero described not an ideal *res-publica* in the manner of Plato's *Republic* but an example of an actual city founded by a person at a place called Rome. In *De republica, De legibus,* and *De officiis,* Cicero posited the Roman citizen as one who has roots in the past, and more particularly in the legendary foundation (*origino*) created in 754 B.C., from which all legitimate and recognizable authority (*auctoritas*) flowed.

In *De republica* Cicero used the dialogue between Scipio and Laelius to clarify what he meant by a legitimate form of political rule (1.25–26). He explained that a *res-publica* is the property of a *res-populi,* a people not randomly brought together but associated in an original agreement with respect to justice for the general community at large and so in possession of a complex social and economic organization. The first cause of such an association is not so much the weakness of the individual as the tendency toward sociability that nature has implanted in man. Citizenship arises by mutual agreement to establish roots, to build, to worship together, and to assemble the diverse elements within a community for common purposes and ends under the jurisdiction of a deliberative body. This deliberative body must always owe its beginning to the same cause as that which produced the *res-publica,* and its functions, however well they may be performed by one man, selected citizens, or the whole body of the people, must conform to the agreement that first bound the people together. This relationship is a legal one, and it is fundamental to the ideal of *populus.* In modern democratic theory it is frequently confused with the barbarian idea of *Volk* (the folk).

Cicero believed that any one of the three forms of government—monarchy, aristocracy, and popular government—might hold the *res-publica* to the bond and bring about order and peace. Each has its advantages and disadvantages—"for before every one of them lies a slippery and precipitous path leading to a certain depraved form that is a close neighbour to it" (1.28). He argued that even in a *res-publica* where the power of the people is greatest, where there are elections and all the trappings of popular rule, where there is the expectation that decisions will always be taken, and judgments made, in the best interest of the people, there will always remain the conflict of interest of birth, wealth, privilege, and leadership.

For Cicero, men could become part of *societas hominem* in four ways:

1 through citizenship: sharing in the infinite and universal bond of common humanity (*gentis, nationis, linguae*) and through a clear relationship with fellow citizens of the same *civibus,* in which much was held in common (*res-publica, res-populi*); the bonds that held people together were religion (*re-ligare*), the law, and the past. The colonnades, streets, sculptures, courts, and suffrage were reminders of the public presence, and augmented the republic's past

2 through association with a smaller circle of kindred in the nursery of the *res-publica*—the family, worship, sacred places, house, hearth, and home

3 through friendship and service

4 through links with country (*patria*) "which embraces all our loves"; the Roman owed loyalty to *parentis, pater familias, patria,* and *res-publica* while foreigners were *peregrinae*

These ideas of membership of *societas hominem* are clarified in *De legibus*

(1.10.30). Cicero's society does not come about of its own accord; nor does it contain the somatological and psychological ingredients necessary for a racial society. It is in the first part composed of *consanguinei*—those related by blood—but family and kin are not a racial relationship. It also has its origins in what Cicero called a *patria, sacra, genus et maiorum*—the land people occupy, the sacred places, and the customs, habits, and judgments of forebears (2.4). For Cicero, as for Aristotle, any member of a *gens* could pass from the private world of the isolated, rootless, sundered man, which all in their natural state belong to, to the *civitatis* of speech-gifted men. The first *patria* is one brought about by birth; the second by law. Cicero was emphatic that "there is no human being of any race [*gens*] who, if he finds a guide, cannot attain to virtue." He cited Cato as an example: Cato, a Tuscan by birth, unknown and obscure, lowly in origin, but marked by virtue of the authority of the republic, its heroic deeds, its past legends, and by the virtue he acquired for himself as a good citizen of that republic.

Later writers, as the final chapters of this book will show, interpreted this concept of citizenship, this notion of a humanizing civilization brought about by politics, this idea of proper conduct creating a virtuous disposition toward civility, as the central weakness of the Greco-Roman conception of state because it impeded the "true civilization" of the ordinary natural people (*Volk*). Even the destruction of Carthage, seen by classical writers as an uncivilized act, became justification for a society based on kith and kin, and not on a *populus* bound together by law.

VERGIL

For the moment, however, I shall not pursue the idea that there was racial significance in the destruction of Carthage. Instead I shall follow the story that began with Polybius' and Cicero's application of Plato's and Aristotle's notions of political citizenship to the practicalities of Roman life. Even as Polybius and Cicero were writing, the republican form of governance that provided the foundation for the propagation of their ideas was disintegrating and Rome was entering a period of empire. It was then that Vergil (70– 19 B.C.) gathered together in *Aeneid*, the great epic of the first beginnings of Rome, the major themes of the state of being well-lawed from Hesiodic myth and the works of his predecessors.[5] Vergil's work, which was later purloined, romanticized, and racialized by countless writers, illustrates the moral virtue of the *via politica* and reinforces the Roman belief in the efficacy of a humanizing civilization that had released Rome's subjects from the whims of nature. The escape of Aeneas from destruction and the arduous voyage to a refuge in Carthage with Dido, the beautiful Phoenician queen, gives him what is expected from the good and just *societas hominem*—friendship, protection, and aid (*hospitium*), with the hope of permanent settlement: "The city I build is yours; draw up your ships; Trojan and Tyrian I shall treat with no distinction" (1.571.2).

But, the story is also one of torn loyalty and lost nobility as Aeneas and Dido struggle under the competitive influences of the gods, Venus and Juno, and are "caught in the snare of shameful passion" (4.186–216). Together they are transported by the inexorable march of happenings in the realm of natural necessity to the tragic death of Dido and to the commitment to destiny, chance, and fortune by Aeneas.

The central theme of Vergil's text is not about the Trojan, Carthaginian, or Latin races and the superiority of one over the other, but whether Aeneas will be diverted by passion and private interest from the glory of establishing a unique political community that has its *origino* at a place, Rome. The metaphors, analogies, and allusions used throughout are those of Greek and Roman politics, and the lessons drawn are political lessons by an enthusiastic "outsider" for the benefit of a Roman audience. When Aeneas decides to leave the comfort of Carthage, and the love of Dido, his choice is a political choice symbolizing all that is expected of a political actor in the *res-publica*. The choice is difficult, the interests finely balanced, and, like all true political happenings, the events are dramatic. Aeneas is spurred on by the intervention of the immortal in the affairs of mere mortals. Mercury cries, "What can you gain by living at wasteful leisure in African lands?" (4.250–83). Not daring to offend the gods, yet torn by civic duty, when he is finally denounced as traitorous by Dido the Carthaginian, he says, "It is not my own choice that I voyage onward to Italy" (4.348–77), and from her reply, "And when death's chill has parted my body from its breath wherever you go my spectre will be" (4.378–409), he knows that his decision, like all important decisions involving real political choice, will weigh him down for the rest of his days.

Dido's response to the right decision of Aeneas the True (Vergil refers to him as "the True" when he is doing right) is to turn away from politics, the art of persuasion, to magical spells to prevent his departure. But she is thwarted by Mercury, who warns Aeneas that he must take full advantage of "the times" and obey the advice of the gods (an unbeatable political mixture for fending off fortune and chance). The dawn departure is observed by Dido, who kills herself: "Life passed into the moving air" (4.673–705). The on-lookers assembled together in a public place, like citizens of *res-publica,* are left shattered and exhausted, yet relieved, by the enormity and tragedy of a de-cision selflessly and rightly taken by a man of *virtu.*

The intended lessons of the *Aeneid,* like the *Theogony,* are that nothing of value can be accomplished without resolve and that all is lost by inattention to public duty. The metaphors used throughout the epic have to do with the conduct of political life, political institutions, and political actors; they have no connection with theories of racial mixture or conflict. When Aeneas at the end is tested on the descent to the underworld, Charon, the warden of the crossing of the pools of Cocytus and the marsh of Styx, exercises the ultimate choice of those who have been buried and ritually honored in death. The remainder who roam unaccepted—remote and split assunder—are those who have had no public recognition in death by a *res-publica* bonded together by law and a glorious past. These are the resourceless ones, the apolitical beings who have fallen prey to the blandishments of the barbarian world of incivility and brutishness. In the moving imagery of the gathering of the silent Vergil reminds his readers of the consequences of abandoning the *via politica.* The hearing of the account of lives lived and changes made, the shaking of the urns of chance by Minos, the confrontation with the past, the judgments of fallen comrades, the censure and punishment for misdeeds ac-cording to the seriousness of the offense—all replicate and symbolize the processes of a citizenry living in a state of *eunomia.* As in the Hesiodic myth, those who set themselves up against the gods or imitated them by acting extrapolitically are dealt with severely: "Mad fool, to mimic by a clatter of bronze and the beat of horn-hooved horses the storm clouds and the bolt which may be copied by none" (6.583–618). Punishment will be exacted for those who dishonor parents, betray liege lords, commit adultery and incest, sell their homeland for gold, legislate in their own private interest, and the outcome of departing from "the good" and "the right" will be disastrous: "Be warned, learn righteousness; and learn to scorn no god" (6.619).

Yet Vergil does not promote the security of his ideal civil association simply by dwelling upon the fear of punishment for wrongdoing. In the *Aeneid* there are promises of reward for those who acted rightly. In the Fortunate Woods, the Homes of the Blest—where heroes of happier years roam dwelling in meadows forever fresh—Aeneas meets his father "like airy winds or the melting of a dream" (6.688–720). These passages present a moving description of a universe having its origins in Heaven, with all the inhabitants, men and beasts, bound together by spirit and mind, and the strength of the seed is fire.

The destiny of Aeneas is set in an understanding of classical political life that is set aside by later writers who see in Greek and Roman society manifestations of racial thinking. The task Aeneas faces is not the construction of a race upon natural origins, but the building of a Rome with *auctoritas,* founding it upon law, arms, and artifacts that augment (*augere*) the past and graft tradition to the present. The binding force is religion (*re-ligare*), and Aeneas has to grant mercy to the conquered, to constrain the haughty, to give vision for the future and, as a stranger, to bind himself to the kingdom of the Latins. Latinus says: "If these strangers shall exalt our name to the stars by mingling their blood with ours, descendants of their breed shall see all the world at their feet, guided and swayed by their will, wherever the sun passes on his returning way" (7.98–101).

It is interesting that H. Rushton Fairclough translates this passage, "whose blood shall exalt . . . and the children of whose *race* shall behold," when the operative words in the text are *generi, progenies,* and *sanguine.* And, while Vergil talks of *populi* and *gentes* in the context of the first encounter between Latinus and Aeneas, the translation talks of *nations* and *races* (7.235–38), thereby imposing misleading categories. Aeneas in his search for an alliance is offered friendship, protection, and the hand of Latinus' daughter, who is not permitted to be offered to any of Latinus' kind (7.265–71). Again we are reminded of the immense difficulty associated with the conduct of human affairs nomocratically and politically even when there appears to be plenty of room for agreement and maneuver. Alecto, the goddess of grief, intervenes to impede the marriage, to set brother against brother through hate and mischief, and to play on the resentment of the disappointed Latin suitor, Turnus, so that he burns the Trojan ships and tricks Aeneas into a final war to secure by force what could not be achieved by alliance. At the final signing of the treaty with the Arcadians, the Trojans are asked, "Qui genus?" They confer and conclude that everyone is related to the gods. The compact between Latium and Troy at the end of the *Aeneid* is not the imposition of one rule over another, but a political accommodation in which the Latins are permitted to retain their traditional language and dress. The settlement encourages respect for the customs of others and realizes the fine balance between unity and diversity that is always necessary in a well run state.

» *The Authority of Sense Impression*

In putting forward this nonracial interpretation of the Greeks and Romans, I am aware that conceptions of nature held by the Ionians, Pythagoreans, Physicists, and Peripatetics from the seventh century B.C. through to the coming of Galen might be interpreted as suggesting a racial inclination. But without exception they were dependent on anatomical and physiological doctrines that saw natural science in political, philosophical, and metaphysical terms. The early naturalistic schools, while positing the origins of life on the basis of natural analogy (water, slime, motion, sun, fossils, abiogenesis, atomistic degeneration, Intelligent Design, monstrosity) were enmeshed in mythology and quite unable to tear themselves away from the presence of the endless immortality of soul in all mortal things. Alcmaeon of Croton (500 B.C.), the Pythagorean anatomist and physiologist, wrote about bodily conditions and human affairs in terms of the opposites of health (an isonomy of hot, cold, wet, and dry) and disease (a monarchy, with the brain being the seat of thought and feeling). Empedocles of Acragas (492–432 B.C.) saw blood as the container of innate heat and the heart the carrier of *pneuma* (air and breath). Polybus, son-in-law of Hippocrates, provided the humoral doctrine that conceived of the human body as made up of elements of living matter—earth, air, fire, and water and influenced by blood, phlegm (*pituita*), black bile (*melancholia*), and yellow bile (*chole*). Even when Erasistratus of Chios (300 B.C.) challenged the humoral doctrine and substituted a physiological explanation that saw the heart as the center of an atomistic and naturalistic arterial system, he still described blood as a substance transmitting the vital spirit (*pneuma*) and believed that all men were subject, to varying degrees, to its stifling influences.

With these views in mind, however, I would like to consider briefly a diverse group of writers who express dissatisfaction with the political accounts of descent and generation we have so far considered. These texts have been revived from time to time, and, as we shall see later, are continuously referred to from the sixteenth century until modern times as major authorities for race thinking in the ancient world, as well as for the formulation of a new racial understanding of the modern.

EPICURUS AND LUCRETIUS

In Epicurus (341–270 B.C.), who had established the garden at Athens, we can already see a turning away from the tenets of classical political theory in a questioning of Plato's system of Ideas and Aristotle's essences and his reaction against the poetry and mythology of the Homeric and Hesiodic political myths. His follower, Lucretius (ca. 99–ca. 55 B.C.), in *De rerum natura,* using Epicurus' method of observation and testing on the basis of sense impression, paid greater attention to the material and natural origins of man as insurance against the loss of the political way.[6] But in both authors the unifying concept of *genus humanorum* was of paramount importance. It continued to be a shared compact of body and spirit, which for all men, Greek and barbarian alike, were inevitably separated by death.

SEXTUS EMPIRICUS

The great summarizer of these schools was Sextus Empiricus (A.D. 200), the greatest of the later Greek skeptics, who in his *Outlines of Pyrrhonism* (or *Hypotyposes*) and *Against the Dogmatists* formulated the antithesis of reason and sense and in the face of political collapse and the barbarian advance advocated an attitude of reserve and mental imperturbability to all the questions of knowledge and life so far considered.[7] In the *Outlines of Pyrrhonism* he reflected upon the distinguishing features of those who were not speech-gifted men enjoying the political life and experiencing the humanizing influence of choice (i.e., those living in brutish lands outside the realm of the political):

> The body of an Indian differs in shape from that of a Scythian; and it is said that what causes the variation is a difference in the predominant humours. Owing to this difference in the predominant humours the sense impressions also come to differ, as we indicated in our First Argument. So too in respect of choice and avoidance of external objects men exhibit great differences: thus Indians enjoy some things, our people other things, and the enjoyment of different things is an indication that we receive varying impressions from the underlying object. (1.80)

Sextus Empiricus compared the barbarians (rational animals who converse in utterances we do not understand) with animals who cannot speak and suggested that the division between Greek and barbarian was not as clear as it had appeared in the texts of the classical political theorists (1.74). For him, everything depends on sense impression; with varying time, circumstance and event, position, distance, and location, each object appears differently. Admixtures also affect the senses: "Thus our own complexion is of one hue in warm weather, of another in cold, and we should not be able to say what our complexion is, but only what it looks like in conjunction with each of these conditions" (1.125).

For Sextus Empiricus, differences in the origin and variety of body structure, differences in the relation of rational and irrational, differences in soul and body, differences in mental and physical states and dispositions, and especially differences in civic dispositions, depended on position, distance, and location and on the admixture, quantity, and constitution of the underlying objects. No object can be apprehended in its purity; it is always conditioned by the physical and mental state of the observer, and things linked to the object as it emerges into a world of time and space become relative to other things. We must, therefore, suspend judgment (epoche) on the nature of the objects, and observe the constancy and rarity of occurrences, making no positive assertion concerning absolute truth. It is sufficient to observe that there is a wide variety of conduct, law, habit, and ethics throughout the known world and antitheses abound.

From his comprehensive review of classical literature Sextus Empiricus concluded that the emphasis placed upon the excellence of the Greek (arete) in politics, philosophy, and law, and upon the absolutes of Justice and Injustice, Vice and Virtue, as contained in the "essences" of Greek philosophy, were overstated. He contradicted Heraclitus' view that all things are resolved into world conflagration and primeval fire (1.29). Reviewing Democritian and Cyrenaic thought, Protagorean doctrine, and academic philosophy, he concluded that all were unreliable, including skeptic philosophy, because everything has to be related to some sign or truth dependent upon sense impression. Sextus disputed Aristotle's relation of genus to species as that of potentiality to actuality—the actuality of the oak implicit in the potency of the acorn—arguing that it is impossible to conceive of opposite qualities, such as possessed by the multitude of species and particulars included in the genus, co-existing in the unity of the genus. If they do not all co-exist, the genus ceases to be inclusive of all its proper species and particulars; and if the genus includes none of the opposites, it is wholly unrelated to its particulars and has no claim to be termed a *genus*.

Looking at principles and origins, Sextus concluded that the existence of God is not self-evident (Book 3). He wondered whether anything causes anything. What is cause? We assume a cause because, if we do not, everything produced would be random. Cause has a certain plausibility about it, but we must know its effect from evidence we have examined closely and carefully. By a process of doubt we may be moved by a force (*arche*) that enables us to present antitheses in a form of argument (*tropoi*), which leads us to suspend judgment on some of these important questions and thereby to attain that peace of mind (*ataraxia*) which brings calm. If anything has to be agreed, it has to be with true proof, true criterion, and an approved proof: therefore, suspend judgment.

At this point Sextus examined the observed differences between peoples. In Athens sodomy is regarded as shameful and illegal, he reflected, and yet the Germani (not the Germans but a Persian tribe) have it as custom. Zeno and the cynics are indifferent to it. Intercourse with women in public is not thought to be shameful by the Indians. Prostitution and tattooing are in Egypt highly esteemed, and yet in Athens they are considered to be disgraceful: "Also, it is a shameful thing with us for men to wear earrings, but amongst some of the barbarians, like the Syrians, it is a token of nobility" (3.24.203). The Persian magi marry their own mothers and sisters, as do the Egyptians. Plato argues for wives in common, Zeno approves of masturbation, and Chrysippus in the *State* approves of incest. The eating of human flesh is regarded as reprehensible by the Greeks but is treated indifferently by whole tribes of barbarians: "Yet why should one speak of 'barbarians' when even Tydeus is said to have devoured the brains of his enemy, and the Stoic school declare that it is not wrong for a man to eat either other men's flesh or his own?" (3.24.207). In Greek literature abundant examples of bestiality, sodomy, incest, illegality, polygamy, piracy, and criminality show that "in regard to justice and injustice and the excellence of manliness, there is a great variety of opinion" (3.24.218).

Similar controversy existed about the existence of the gods, religious observance, and diet. The Jewish and Egyptian priests will not eat pig, Sextus observed, while the Libyans will not taste sheep, or the Syrians dove. In some cults it is lawful to eat fish, in others not. In Egypt it is unlawful to eat an animal's head, and onions and garlic are similarly proscribed, as are mint and parsley and beans. The Greeks do not touch dog, the Thracians do. If these rules existed "by nature," then we would all observe the same rules. Comparing the treatment of the dead by the Egyptians, Ethiopians, Indians, and Persians, Sextus concluded that some think death dreadful, while others suppose death to be preferred to living. All are matters of convention, and all are relative.

Seeing a diversity of usages and suspending judgment as to the natural existence of anything good or bad or (in general) fit or unfit to be done, Sextus completely rejected the art of living politically, as I have described it in Chapters 1 and 2, as logically unsound and undiscoverable. Effort and learning bring art, not nature, and Sextus was skeptical about the teaching of it.

We are left with an appeal to sense impression and an invitation to suspend judgment on all matters not supported by empirical evidence. However, there is no attempt in Sextus, or in Epicurus or Lucretius, to go beyond the criteria of Greek and barbarian, political and brutish, virtuous and vicious, rational and irrational—to convert observed differences into divisions that approximate in any way the "races of men." What Sextus Empiricus does is to recognize difference in the natural constitution of *genus humanorum*. We have to wait fourteen hundred years before a fundamental reclassification takes place that enables the diversities of *genus humanorum*, observed in such amazing detail in these works, to be explained by the new category of "race."

» *The Authority of Geography and Language*

In arousing an interest in the methodology of sense impression and its relationship to soulcraft and humoral biology, the opposites of *physis* and *nomos* impeded the emergence of a full-fledged "natural" basis for the division of mankind. The notion that Nature could stand alone, so to speak, could not proceed without abandoning the old Greco-Roman division of the political and the barbarian and some of the entanglements of the ideas of *polis* and *respublica*. In the fields of geography and architecture two writers tentatively explored the limits of these antitheses, keeping well within the boundaries of antique ideas yet providing a more detailed analysis than Hippocrates and Herodotus of what precisely the natural divisions of mankind might be and how they had come about. A close examination of the *Geographies* of Strabo, and to a lesser extent Vitruvius' *De architectura,* shows that while they were still preoccupied with the old notion of barbarity and brutishness, and what it was in politics that had rescued human beings from the clutches of a capricious Nature, a much stronger emphasis was now being placed upon the authority of an autonomous geography, climate, and language.

STRABO

In the *Geographies* Strabo (44/63 B.C.–A.D. 18/19), a descendant of Greek and Asiatic families, a native of Amasia, a visitor to Rome, a stoic, a talented summarizer of ancient thought on chorography and geography, reflected upon the works of Eratosthenes and Homer and their descriptions of the inhabited world, the differences of peoples, and the things men hold in common.[8] He disposed of fanciful tales of Hesiod, Alcmaeon, and Aeschylus on long-headed men, web-footed and dog-headed men, men with eyes in their breast, and one-eyed men, as nothing more than a taste for the marvelous. He had a similar distaste for the works of Herodotus.

Insisting on the familiar distinction between Greek and barbarian, which had to do with qualities pertaining to law, politics, education, and speech, Strabo began with an analysis of the inhabited world and its limits and differences, from Iberia in the West to India in the East (the antipodes), to Scythia in the North and Ethiopia in the remoteness of the South. The inhabited world, according to Strabo, was an island that could be known from the evidence of the senses. Those who set out to circumnavigate this island come back, claimed Strabo, not because of impediment but because of "destitutions and loneliness" (1.1.8). The Ethiopian, "the furthermost of men," is "sundered in twain" by his remoteness; in the North the men of the island of Britain are complete savages, and it is of no benefit whatsover to know them because of their isolation (2.5). Both dwell in the realm of natural necessity, of subsistence, and because of their barbarity and brutishness do not conduct themselves according to the rules of political life.

Here, then, is an island world divided into Greek and barbarian with a crude attempt at subdivision into Scythians, Celts, and Ethiopians. Repeating Eratosthenes' condemnation of the division of peoples according to natural criteria, Strabo argued it would be better to divide them according to the good and bad qualities, the virtues and vices, they all share in common: "Just as if those who have made such a division, placing some people in the category of censure, others in that of praise, did so for any other reason than that in some people there prevail the law abiding and the political instinct, and the qualities associated with education and powers of speech, whereas in other people the opposite characteristics prevail" (1.4.9). Strabo claimed that the distribution of animals, plants, and climates was not the result of design but "of accident and chance," "just as the differences of race, or of language" (2.3.6–7). Strabo believed that the arts, faculties, and institutions, once they made a beginning (and this is the important qualification), "flourish in any latitude whatsoever and in certain instances even in spite of the latitude; so that some local characteristics of a people come by nature, others by training and habit" (2.3.7–8).

In Book 14, Strabo speculated that the word "barbarian" was first used onomatopoetically to describe people who had difficulty enunciating Greek words and talked harshly and raucously. When the Greeks applied the word "barbarian" to all those who pronounced words thickly and harshly, they misused it as a general term, thus making a logical distinction between the Greeks and all other unusual and quaint peoples (*idiotetas*). Thus, said Strabo, after long acquaintance and intercourse this effect was seen to be the result not of thick pronunciation or any natural defect of the vocal organs, "but of the peculiarities of their several languages" (14.2.28–29).

The distinction Strabo makes between peoples is based, therefore, upon the fundamental Greco-Roman assumptions we have already explored about the antitheses of the life of the barbarian, and life governed by the rules of politics, as informed and illuminated by the essential distinctions made between the two realms of *physis* and *nomos*. My point is that the linguistic and geographical divisions are understandable only within the terms of reference set by those assumptions. I accept that the divisions bear a remarkable resemblance to the ones that we now use in physical and social anthropology to specify and describe what are now thought to be racial and ethnic divisions of human beings. But, without some extraordinary intellectual leap performed for us by historians and scientists of a later era, we cannot conjure up from the evidence of Strabo's own linguistic and geographical divisions a republic of the world that is in any way dependent on the idea of race. Strabo's divisions are still to do with politics and nature in opposition to one another, with politics as the significant idea.

VITRUVIUS

In *De architectura* Vitruvius (late 1st cent. B.C.–early 1st cent. A.D.), the military engineer and architect of the Augustan Age who sought to design his buildings to suit the climate and latitude, put forward a more precise division of mankind.[9] But, like Strabo, he expressed the reasons for the division in the language of political philosophy. Vitruvius accepted that variations in mind, shape, quality of body, language were due to climatic variations (6.1.3), but his theory of climate rested upon a Hippocratian foundation of heat and moisture. Those who live in the South are smaller in stature, dark in complexion, and possessed of curly hair, black eyes, strong legs, and thin blood. The thinness of their blood is caused by the sun's intensity drawing out moisture. Southerners are resistant to heat and fever because they are nourished by heat; Northerners are weak in the face of fever but fearless in war because of the fullness of their blood.

Like Strabo, Vitruvius was uneasy with explanations of difference derived from the uncertainties of the world of natural necessity—of boring monotone—and more comfortable with explanations drawn from a human world separated from the rules governing the natural world—that is, with the political realm. He analyzed the quality of sound of the human voice, upon which the conduct of political life, citizenship, law, and education so much depend (6.1.5). From this analysis of speech-gifted men flowed an assessment of the intellectual capabilities of different peoples (in generibus gentium dispares) occupying a world of limits, levels, and horizons sloping away from North to South like the strings of a musical instrument. The lowest point on the horizon, away from the level of East and West, is in the South. Here voices are shrill and thin, because in the South the pitch of the instrument is high, and as one proceeds toward the level (Greece), the pitch relaxes and then becomes deeper in tone.

Vitruvius' explanatory system is adjusted to musical harmony by temperature. As people moved away from the middle region toward the isolation of the outer limits of the universe—to the perimeter of polis, away from the central facts of political life toward savagery and brutality—the accent is driven by greater or lesser moisture toward higher or lower notes. Southerly people, because the atmosphere is rare and hot, have sharp and bright minds and "are more readily and swiftly moved to the imagination of expedients" (6.1.9). Northerners are chilled by damp, stagnant air, and have sluggish minds like snakes in cold places:

> But those who are born in colder regions, by their fearless courage are better equipped for the clash of arms, yet by their slowness of mind they rush on without reflection, and through lack of tactics are balked of their purpose. Since,

therefore, the disposition of the world is such by Nature, and all other nations differ by their unbalanced temperament, it is in the true mean within the space of all the world and the regions of the earth, that the Roman people holds its territory. (6.1.10)

Unlike Strabo, Vitruvius seemed to believe that the observable differences may not be entirely due to accident or chance or to language. He was much more disposed to recognize that the divine mind has allotted to Rome a propitious region from which to rule the world and into which the planets of Jupiter, Mars, and Saturn intervene from time to time to influence events.

Apart from Strabo's excursions into etymology to explain the relationship of Greek and barbarian and Vitruvius' suggestion that the pitch of voice and the quality of mind and body have something to do with the humane conduct of affairs, there is nothing in this vast literature, which describes the then known world country-by-country, that suggests an idea of race or ethnocentricity. There *is* a fundamental division, but it is of little historical profit to see it as being racial or ethnic.[10] What we see in the texts, as we saw in Aristotle, Plato, Hippocrates, and Herodotus, is an attempt to encourage by improved sense observation a move toward a moral civic life geared to the political way. The human beings we are asked to observe are different human beings of one species (using the term in its Aristotelian sense) inhabiting a world of infinite variety, which may be brought from barbarity to civility through attention to excellence (*arete*) and good government dependent on politics, citizenship, education, and law—a humanizing civilization seeking to escape the clutches of barbarity and viciousness.

» *The Authority of the Historical Record*

When later writers began to reexamine the justification for title to rule in authorities other than those transmitted to them by antiquity, they became interested in elaborating on the brief account given by Vitruvius of the barbarian peoples who inhabited the North, and Strabo's divisions. Two sources were used to establish the pedigree of these peoples. The first account is by Cornelius Tacitus (ca. A.D. 55–ca. 117) in *Germania* and *Agricola,* in which for the first time there appear references to the early beginnings of the Germans, and the second is in Ammianus Marcellinus (A.D. 330–393), who deals with the origins of the Saracens, Gauls, and Celts. Both texts are mere fragments, but both assume vast importance in later times as textual justification for establishing title to rule and for deciding upon the characteristics of physical appearance, mental traits, organizational divisions, and geographical and ethnic origins of whole populations of human beings.

TACITUS

In *Germania* and *Agricola* Cornelius Tacitus confessed that although he was skeptical about their origins because of the lack of reliable records and their isolation from other men, he supposed that the Germans were an indigenous people and only very slightly blended with new arrivals (*gentium adventibus et hospitii mixtos*).[11] The country is inhospitable, inaccessible, harsh of climate and "pleasant neither to live in nor look upon" (2). Tacitus believed that the beginning of this *genus* was a god, Tuisto, and his son Mannus and his three sons, whose tribes expelled the Gauls, until the whole people were called by the artificial name "Germans." He acknowledged with little enthusiasm the accounts of the presence of Hercules and Ulysses in Germany at some time:

> Personally I associate myself with the opinions of those who hold that in the people of Germany there has been given to the world a *gentem* [trans., "race"] unmixed by marriage with other races, a peculiar people and pure, like no one but themselves, whence it comes that their physique, so far as can be said with their vast numbers, is identical; fierce blue eyes, red hair, tall frames, powerful only spasmodically, not correspondingly tolerant of labour and hard work and by no means habituated to bearing thirst and heat; to cold and hunger, thanks to the climate and the soil they are accustomed. (4)

Tacitus devoted much time to his descriptions of German divination, lawmaking, and governance, concluding that "the most complimentary expression of assent is military approbation" (11). He also considered the tribal divisions within Germany and Gaul and the customs, habits, institutions, religions, and climate of these northerly peoples.

In *Agricola,* the biography of his father-in-law, Gnaeus Julius Agricola, Tacitus considered for the first time who were the first inhabitants of Britain, and he compared immigrant and indigenous among them. The conclusion he reached was that climatic conditions stamped a certain physique on the human body. The red hair and large limbs of the Caledonians suggested a German origin; the swarthy faces of the Silures (of Glamorgan, Brecon, and Monmouth) and the curly quality of their hair suggested a passage at some time of these peoples from Iberia.

As we shall see later, these brief references to the Germans (mere fragments of the past) came to be of immense importance to modern scholars searching for new ways of accounting for descent and generation and the right ordering of mankind. E. H. Warmington in his introduction to *Germania* says, "Tacitus' Germania is by far the fullest and most valuable treatise of its kind which has come down to us from ancient to modern times; and was with reason called by scholars of the Renaissance 'libellus aureus' 'a booklet of gold.'"

AMMIANUS MARCELLINUS

Imitating Tacitus, Ammianus Marcellinus, who was born in Antioch of Greek parents, educated in the Latin of the Eastern Empire, and then served in the Roman army, looked into the past for truthful accounts of the history of Rome and lamented the passing of the political way.[12] An acute observer of human experience, he owed much to Cicero. He wrote of the Saracens, "whom we never found desirable either as friends or as enemies, ranging up and down the country, in a brief space of time laid waste whatever they could find, like rapacious kites." They are a people constantly moving, of no settled abode, and sexually active: "so much for this dangerous tribe" (*Hactenu de natione periciosa*) (14.4.1–7).

Ammianus' account of fourth-century Rome emphasized lawlessness and savagery, in which people had been stripped of life and rank in burnings and beatings by men of noble rank. The political practices of law, accusation, cross-examination, and evidence had perished, replaced by torture and forced confession, by treachery and flattery.

> Furthermore there is no doubt that when once upon a time Rome was the abode of all the virtues, many of the nobles detained here foreigners of free birth by various kindly attentions, as the Lotus-eaters of Homer [*Odyssey* 9.84ff.] did by the sweetness of their fruits. But now the vain arrogance of some men regards everything born outside the pomerium of our city as worthless, except the childless and unwedded; and it is beyond belief with what various kinds of obsequiousness men without children are counted at Rome. (14.6.21–22)

For the origin of the Gauls and the Celts Ammianus looked to Timagines, a Greek of Alexandria who was accurate in the language. Some asserted that the first Gauls were aborigenes, called "Celts" from the king's name and "Galatae" from the Greek word for Gauls. Others said they were of Dorian origin. The Druids said that they were part indigenous, but also driven by war from their homes across the Rhine. Others stressed the Trojan origin after the destruction by Greece. But Ammianus considered the most important account to be of the settlement by Hercules, son of Amphytrion, who overcame the tyrants Geryon and Tauriscus, who respectively oppressed Spain and Gaul and, having won, took high-born women to wife and begat large numbers who settled districts. The region was also settled by a people from Asia (the Phocaeans) who, in order to avoid Harpagus, prefect of Cyprus, set sail for Italy and founded Velia (Castellamare della Bruca), and Massilia (Marseilles), and under the influence of the Bards and Euhages and the Druids investigated questions of the sublime and attempted to explain the secret laws of nature. The Druids, who were loftier than the rest in intellect, were elevated by their investigation of obscure and profound subjects and "scorning all things human, pronounced the soul immortal" (15.9.8).

» *The Authority of Magic: Apuleius*

But, if sense impression and milieu are not sufficient to break the hold that the moral political life had over the Greeks and Romans, then what is left? The African Lucius Apuleius (ca. 124–ca. 170), writing at the end of the second century A.D., eliminated entirely classical philosophy, politics, sense impression, geography, and Roman *auctoritas,* and put in its place the powerful force of magic. A 1566 introduction to *The Golden Ass* states that this book is "a figure of man's life" touching upon the nature and manners of mortal men "egging them forward from their asinal form to their human and perfect shape."[13]

Apuleius regenerated the mind from brutish and beastly custom not by the traditional symbols of classical political theory but by allowing his hero, transformed by magic into a libidinous ass, to roam freely, bereft of all reason and virtue, through the experiences of life. It is not applying his mind to the art of living through the activity of politics that interests Apuleius; it is only by the excellent arts of magic and the study of sciences that Lucius, the ass, will be brought to "the right and very shape of a man" (p. xvii); only by

devouring "the sweet rose of reason and virtue" (p. xvii) without the interces-
sion of God or the gods will he be released from the affliction he faces.

Unlike the *Theogony, Works and Days,* and the *Aeneid*, this work is no longer
an affirmation of the symbols and values of the good life lived by speech-gifted
men in a civil political community. It is the celebration of the methods and
the values of magic as opposed to philosophy. Apuleius' narrative begins with
a Greek, Lucius, telling his story of a journey to Thessaly, the birthplace of
enchantment and sorcery, where Socrates, his companion, is enslaved, like the
Indians, Ethiopians, and Antipodeans, to the magic of Meroe. Socrates dies
in mysterious circumstances after Lucius dreams of his murder at the hands
of Meroe. In Book 2.2, Lucius, "of comely stature, his graceful slenderness,
his delicate colour, his hair yellow and not too foppishly dressed, his grey and
quick eyes shining like unto the eagle's, his blooming countenance in all points,
and his grave and comely gait," is enticed into liaisons with the black art, and
encounters Fotis the ravishing servant girl, who introduces him to clandestine
love, fortune-telling, and Egyptian prophecy. Fotis arranges for him to spy on
Pamphile, the magician, who is about to turn herself into an owl to meet her
secret lover. Lucius persuades Fotis, who claims she knows the ingredients of
the magic ointment, to turn him into an owl. Instead he is transformed into
an ass, a brute beast, and, while Fotis searches for the roses of reason to
change him back to man, he roams the world, reviled, beaten, used, sometimes
playing the part of the good ass, sometimes the bad, observing the mystery
and deception of life.

There are two important allegories in Apuleius—the allegory of Cupid
and Psyche, and the seduction of Arete, the wife of Barbarus,[14] by Philesith-
erus. Both have outcomes which depend upon trickery, ritual, visions, obla-
tions, sacrifice, stars, snakes, and jewels; both reject the political symbols of
Hesiod and Vergil and propose that more is to be gained by insincerity and
wickedness, and less to be learned from the teachings of the ancient philosophers, than from the informed inquisitiveness of a randy ass. In the allegory
of Cupid and Psyche, the virgin who by her very appearance challenged the
immortal beauty of Venus, Pleasure is born of an illegitimate and dishonest
relationship. In the allegory of Arete honor was satisfied with the flimsiest of
untested alibis. Throughout the text Lucius is introduced into the private
mysteries of Isis and Osiris (Book 11), the natural mother of all things, the
initial progeny of the worlds of the Phrygians, Athenians, Cyprians, Sicilians,
Ethiopians, Eleusians, and Egyptians, so as to avoid the inconveniences and

difficulties of the political sources of Greece and Rome. It is not human action conducted in accordance with established legal procedures and practices that restored Lucius to his human shape but the intervention of the great Egyptian priest, who by the power of the sovereign goddess transformed him in a wink from beast to man by the administration of the magic roses.

» *Conclusion: Challenges to the Political Way*

In summary, during this important period in Western history Polybius, Cicero, and Vergil used their considerable ingenuity and practical skill to give authority to an institutional and legal framework (a *nomocracy*) capable of accommodating the differences of quaint and strange peoples within a well-ordered citizenry. The major categories within their discourses are *res-publica* and *res-populi*—differentiated private peoples bound together in a nexus of law and in a common citizenship and engaging together in the language of politics.

It is of considerable importance to my thesis that these peoples are not biological natural entities as we perceive of them today. They are not, as the nineteenth-century historians supposed, *Volk* living in a self-determining *Volk-staat;* they are aggregations of people bound together by a compact of law in an authoritative historical association. But in this transition from Greece to Rome there appear four important challenges to the Greek idea that the political realm was distinctively different from other human arrangements. The first was based on the evidence of sense impression—the careful analysis and comparison of the actual differences in practices and conventions of the quaint and strange peoples inhabiting the barbarian natural world. The second reexamined the work of Hippocrates and Herodotus on climate, land, relief, and soil, in an attempt to establish new divisions for mankind other than those of the political. The third introduced the idea that the barbarians themselves may have a history as it searched for origins in sources other than those of Homer, Hesiod, and Romulus and Remus. Finally, an interest in the stories of first beginnings turned away from the utterances of speech-gifted men in political places (nomocratic rule) to the prognostications of magicians and sorcerers roaming the world.

Jews, Christians, Moors, and Barbarians

My arguments so far have been based on the understanding that Greek and Roman ideas of political life were original and distinctively different from those that had hitherto prevailed. The political way was to allow people, who were naturally tied to the household by virtue of the need to subsist and to reproduce, to "pass" by the mechanism of citizenship from the private realm into a public arena. Here they would judge, and be judged, not by the criteria of birth and chance, but by their word and deed and their overall contribution to the well-being of the general community.

I have also posited a complementary idea that philosophy *qua* philosophy had given human beings the opportunity to think about the problems of being and becoming and that politics had given them an opportunity to debate the ends and aims of the general community to which they belonged. The tailoring of the law to allow full expression of public opinion (however limited the notion of "public" may have been) concerning the constitutional basis of the law, and its operation, was considered by the Greeks and Romans to be the very essence of this distinctively different way of conducting life. I have added to these two important arguments the thought that this *eunomic* approach was pliable and flexible and fundamentally opposed to the rigidity of existing theocratic and bureaucratic systems of thought and governance, and that it had arrested the development of a consistently worked out theory of race.

The Greeks and Romans were also concerned, however, with the origins of *polis* and *res-publica. Genesis,* from the noun *genos,* frequently and wrongly translated as "race," had to do with families, clans, and the ages of man as well as with birth, noble descent, and those bound together by common origin. The word was also closely connected with *ethos, ethnos,* and *barbaros*—those without civilization, citizenship, and *logos.* In the Hebrew literature a similar distinction existed between those who are *'am* or *laom* (of Israel as the chosen people) and *goyim* (those grouped by clan and natural descent). In the Vulgate, the word *gentiles,* from the Latin *gens,* was used to distinguish those who were members of nations other than the Jewish. Israel is the people, *'am* or *laom,* God's own possession (Exod. 19.5), and the rest of mankind are the Gentiles (Deut. 4.27, 18.9), the Israelites' neighbors, who lured them into the worship of false gods. In the Septuagint and in the Vulgate the words *ethne* and *ethnos* are used to describe those who are *goyim*—those who were dispersed after the confusion of tongues following the Tower of Babel and who have their first beginnings in sin (Gen. 11). To the Jews, Gentiles were unclean, and the Gentile world, essentially the political world of the Greeks, had no permanent existence. Politics and the political state of Greco-Roman civilization were transient and unwanted. God had vouched that *'am* will not be destroyed by the *goyim;* it is Rome that will be destroyed.

Whereas for the Greeks the distinction between Greek and barbarian was a matter of teaching and learning and governing—philosophically and politically—for the Hebrews the distinction between the *'am* and the *goyim* was a matter of faith and Yahweh's grace. The distinction was based not on *race* but on a fundamental difference in the relationship between God and man. The stranger (*ger*) may be accommodated; he may be brought into the house by conversion, thereby becoming *ger tzedek,* an honored one.

At the end of the Roman Republic the people who appear in the Gospel of John as having set themselves against *faith* are described as "ethnics" whether they are from Greece, Rome, or Israel. For Christians, faith is now a synchronization of God's grace in the Hebrew sense and of faith in Christ. God becomes the God of Jew and Gentile alike, and the distinction between them through a difference in faith has been removed: now *all* have the potential of belonging to God by virtue of their faith in Christ. In the Pauline letters the ethnics are no longer the non-Greek barbarians (those who do not have politics and philosophy), the Gentiles, or the *goyim* (those who are unclean and do not have the Hebrew faith); the ethnics are now the heathen—those who do not share in the body of the faithful in Christ. Moreover, *gens, gentiles,* and *ethnos* are no longer strangers, shifting sojourners in ethnic apolitical lands in the Greek sense; they have entered the household of God, into fellowship and citizenship through the medium of faith.

» *The Rise of Faith*

The collapse of the city-state and the Roman Republic ushered in a period from the first century A.D. to the sack of Rome by Aleric and his Goths in 410 when the peculiar activity the Greeks and Romans called politics was called into question by the rise of faith and religion.

JOSEPHUS AND THE COVENANT

The first full-fledged assault on the political idea came from Flavius Josephus (A.D. 37–ca. 95), a Jewish general and historian who was keenly aware of the distinctions between faith and politics. In *Contra Apion* (A.D. 75) he rebuked those Greeks who doubted the truth of his massive *Antiquities of the Jews*.[1] Addressed to Apion, the son of Posidonius, a Greco-Egyptian, the polemic denounced Greek philosophy and politics as dishonest, unoriginal, and un-historical while praising the superior skills of Chaldean, Egyptian, and Phoe-nician historiographers and genealogists. Josephus resolved the conflict be-tween faith and politics by the outright rejection of Greek *nomocracy* in favor of a theocratic form of rule based upon the Mosaic Code and the Covenant. He defended his position through five biblical stories that have since become pivotal to the understanding of race thinking in Western Europe: the Creation, Cain and Abel, the Tower of Babel, the division of the world into three parts and the curse on Ham's posterity, and Moses' exhortation to his people in the wilderness.

The Creation   In Book 1.1 Josephus described Moses' account of the Cre-ation. Suggesting that after the seventh day Moses "begins to talk philosophi-cally," Josephus implies that we should interpret the story as enigmatic, wise, and decently allegorical. During the Middle Ages, the story of Creation be-came critical in discussions about race.

In the Hebrew tongue, Adam means "one that is red" and Eve, "the mother of all living" (1.1.2). Adam was told that he should abstain from eating the fruit of the tree of knowledge in the Garden of Eden, but Eve was per-suaded by the Serpent to taste, Both Adam and Eve became aware of their nakedness and covered themselves with fig leaves. Conscious of sin, Adam accused Eve, and Eve accused the Serpent. God punished Adam. "He also made Eve liable to the inconvenience of breeding, and the sharp pains of bringing forth children" (1.1.4). The Serpent was deprived of speech, and Adam and Eve were moved to another place.

Cain and Abel   In Book I.2 Josephus recounted the transgression of Cain, who slew his brother and gave himself up to the pursuit of bodily pleasure and violence, thus introducing craftiness and cunning into the world. Seth, righteous for seven years, also transgressed, bringing unease and worry to Noah. God loved Noah: "yet he not only condemned those other men for their wickedness, but determined to destroy the whole race [note trans.] of mankind, and to make another race that should be pure from wickedness" (1.3.2).

God sent the Flood to destroy the transgressors. In Book I.3 Josephus described the Ark, its dimensions, and the many sorts of creatures that entered it. His confirming source is Berossus, the Chaldean, who became the authority for the propagation of the Hamitic heresy, one of the main supports for race thinking in sixteenth-century England.

The Tower of Babel   After the Ark came to rest in Armenia, the place of descent, Noah's sons Shem, Ham, and Japhet were encouraged to colonize the world, but, Josephus warned, "they, imagining the prosperity they enjoyed was not derived from the favor of God, but supposing that their own power was the proper cause of the plentiful condition they were in, did not obey him" (1.4.1).

Nimrod, the strong and bold grandson of Ham, persuaded the people to ascribe their happiness not to God but to themselves. To be revenged on God if he punished them again by flood, Nimrod said that he would build a tower too high for the waters to reach. And so the tower was built, and God decided not to punish the people by destroying this ludicrous structure but to cause a tumult among them "by producing in them divers languages; and causing that, through the multitude of those languages, they should not be able to understand one another. The place wherein they built the tower is now called Babylon; because of the confusion of that language which they readily understood before; for the Hebrews mean by the word Babel, Confusion" (1.4.3).

And so the people were spread over all the earth, losing their names in the dispersal. In Josephus' account, some new names were those the people gave themselves to make their names more intelligible to the local inhabitants and others were names the Greeks gave them, names that sounded good in

Greek and were easily understood by the Greeks. Josephus suggested that the Greeks gave the people Greek names so as to set agreeable forms of government over them as if they were derived from the Greeks themselves. In the nineteenth century, the Tower of Babel and the confusion of tongues became the obsession of historical and scientific philologists.

The Division of the World and the Curse on Ham's Posterity   In his account of the habitation of the world after the Flood, Josephus divided the world into three parts: Japhet inhabits Europe; Shem has the region of the Indian Ocean, Persia, Chaldea, and Armenia; and Ham dwells in the land of Africa, Egypt, and Libya. Noah cultivated vines and made wine, after which

> he offered sacrifice, and feasted, and, being drunk, he fell asleep and lay naked in an unseemly manner. When his youngest son saw this, he came laughing, and showed to him his brethren; but they covered their father's nakedness. And when Noah was made sensible of what had been done, he prayed for prosperity to his other sons; but for Ham, he did not curse him, by reason of his nearness in blood, but cursed his posterity. And when the rest of them escaped that curse, he inflicted it on the children of Canaan. (1.6.3)

From Josephus through Jean Bodin in the sixteenth century, this account remained the orthodox interpretation of the division of mankind, despite the continuous remonstrances of the Roman Catholic Church.

Moses' Exhortation   According to Josephus, after forty years in the wilderness Moses exhorted his people:

> O children of Israel! there is but one source of happiness for all mankind, the favour of God; for he alone is able to give good things to those that deserve them, and to deprive those of them that sin against him; towards whom, if you behave yourselves according to his will, and according to what I, who well understand his mind, do exhort you to, you will both be esteemed blessed, and you will be admired by all men; and will never come into misfortunes, nor cease to be happy: you will then preserve the possession of good things you already have, and will quickly obtain those that you are at present in want of,—only do you be obedient to those whom God would have you to follow. (4.8.2)

Following the exhortation in 4.8.2 are six governmental precepts:

i) They must not prefer any other constitutional form "before the laws now given you"

ii) They must not disregard that way of divine worship nor change it in any other form. God's presence will enable them "to despise the opposition of all mankind"

iii) Virtue will be the principal reward for following these precepts and will bring undisputed reputation with posterity

iv) They must accept that the laws come by divine revelation

v) They must observe the Commandments and heed the advice of leaders, control passion; otherwise they "will forfeit the favor of God" and all will be reversed

vi) They must destroy their enemies because they will corrupt proper institutions. "for by this means alone the safety of your own happy constitution can be firmly secured to you." Extirpation of the Canaanites is also discussed in 4.8.42 and 44

This is followed in 4.8.4–16 with a description of the laws and constitution and what must be done to deal with temples, blasphemy, tithes, prostitution, dress, sacrifice, conduct, commemoration, judgments, murder, boundaries, plantations, agriculture, punishment, marriage, family relationships, poison, wells, and interest.

The description of the Ten Commandments in 4.8.44 appears to be presented in a political form, when Moses gathers together in an assembly the whole community, including wives, children, and slaves, and warns them not to dissolve the constitution or to change the law. If they do, God's vengeance will follow.

The Covenant and the Political Way   Josephus unequivocally embraced aristocratic rule based on strict religious piety exercised in accordance with unchanging precepts laid down in a Covenant between man and a supreme divine Governor and following historical texts known to be true. He emphasized the limitation of opposition, the control of passion, the avoidance of the uncertain political way, and a complete severance from the "talking-shop" of Greek philosophy.

The faith that Josephus expressed in his polemic was not intended to bridge the gap between Jew and Gentile, Christian and Christian, pagan Greek and barbarian; it was an affirmation of faith in an eternal God. Josephus fixed his gaze upon a single God who had created the world and all the peoples in it, but much later his work was taken to be a confirmation of the vulgar notion that the origins of race may be traced to these Hebrew teachings about a chosen people of pure blood. This notion was erroneous, as Hebrew piety contains the possibility of conversion of the stranger into the faith. The idea of a nucleus of true believers must also be understood in light of the history of the Israelites.

It is important to recognize that the Bible conceives mankind as derived from a common ancestor and records the drama of human obedience to and defection from the will of God. It also includes divine instructions that furnish the measure for human conduct. Its genealogical registers are not a simple genealogy for the Hebrew people, tracing descent from Adam, but, as Eric Voegelin has argued, fix on Shem as the nodal point. They served a practical purpose. Following the Flood and the division of the world by Noah's sons, "clans of pure descent, uncontaminated by marriage with foreigners, were to be the ruling class of the new settlements in Jerusalem and the surrounding towns." To establish descent clan heads traced their ancestry to Shem, the "Named One," the abstraction by which Israel is distinguished from a symbolically anonymous mankind (Adam, or "Man"). Moreover the Covenant at Mount Sinai, the dominant experience in the creation of the Hebrews as a unified group, required a new genealogical construction. It was a divine revelation of true order valid for all mankind but made to a particular group at a particular time. "Hence," explains Voegelin, "there could be, and historically there was, differentiated from it both the idea of mankind under one God and the idea of a nucleus of true believers."[2] The Covenant implied a governmental arrangement dependent on the will of God as expressed in the Commandments. Law was not, as in the Greco-Roman view, to be brokered by different kinds of citizens sharing ideas in the public life of the *agora;* it was a given.

THE AUGUSTINIAN COMPACT

The task of reinstating politics amid a bewildering variety of new faiths fell to a North African Christian from Souk-Ahras in western Algeria, Augustine of Hippo (A.D. 354–430). Augustine wrote *De civitate Dei* (ca. A.D. 413–26) only a few years after the Goths sacked Rome.[3] The barbarians who had dwelled beyond the fringes of classical civilization now occupied the epicenter of politics, and Augustine was compelled to search history for an explanation as well as for an understanding of what could bridge the gaps between the old civility, the new faiths, and barbarian invasion, between politics and faith, between the political and the natural.

In his comprehensive examination of the confused, contradictory, and complicated Hebrew, Phoenician, Egyptian, Chaldean, Roman, and Greek genealogical accounts, Augustine considered very carefully the positions taken by the Pythagoreans and the Ionics and concluded that Plato's account of the creation in the *Timaeus* (8.11) was probably closest to the Mosaic account of the deliverance of the Hebrews out of Egypt beginning in Exodus 3.14 with God's name and his imutability. [I am who I am, or in some versions I am that I am.] On the other hand he set to one side with contempt the works of Hermes Trismegistus and Lucius Apuleius, who interposed between God and man demons and spirits dwelling in visible objects, and he rejected Origen's arguments that earthly bodies were inhabited by sinful souls according to the degree of sin. The imagery of the Roman and Greek gods and Greek notions of natural theogony were similarly disposed of as outrageous. Augustine argued that "the deserts of sons are not to be estimated by the qualities of bodies" (1.11.23). For that reason the works of Pliny and Aulus Gellius, with their horrific accounts of Pygmies, Skiopodes, Cynocephali, Androgyni, and Hermaphrodites, were not to be regarded as reliable sources for determining whether these monstrous peoples were really of the stock of Adam or the sons of Noah. All such accounts of monstrosity had to be treated with circumspection, since all men born of Adam were rational and mortal and, whatever the state of their bodies, were human. Boethius (A.D. 475–525), speaking from Rome in a later generation, agreed that all humankind on earth arose from the same origin. But he emphasized life's transitory nature. However much the body's good qualities may be overesteemed, and its beauty praised, it is all superficial and may be turned to worms in the burning of a three-day fever.[4]

Augustine preferred to see his own work not as a historically correct account of the beginning of mankind but as a prophetic insight: "So in this prophetic history some things are narrated which have no significance, but are, as it were, the framework to which the significant things are attached" (16.2). In that framework the five stories of Josephus remain central to the story, but Augustine reinterpreted the tripartite division of the world (15.27). The Chaldean, Berossus, whose work survives in fragments quoted by Josephus, had stressed the transgression of Ham, the middle son of Noah who had sinned against him by divulging his sleeping nakedness and been banished to the dark regions of Africa, forever carrying the taint of corruption. Augustine took the text in Genesis 9.25—"a servant shall he be unto his brethren" (from the Latin *servus,* to preserve a captive in war for the purposes of service)—to show that Noah's curse upon Canaan, the son of Ham, had a quite different allegorical meaning. In Augustine's interpretation the Ark, which rescued Noah from the Deluge, was the image of the City of God sojourning in the world, a symbol of the Church rescued by the wood, upon which hung the Mediator, Christ. Its dimensions represented the human body (15.26), and its entryway, the sword wound of Christ. Those who entered were those who came to Christ. Augustine recalled that when Shem and Japhet came upon the sleeping Noah they entered backwards, not looking upon his nakedness, and they covered Noah's body (the symbol for Christ's passion) with a garment (the sacrament), for which they were both blessed (Gen. 9.26–27).

In this important Christian allegory, Shem was the flesh of whom Christ was born, the circumcised Jew; Japhet represented the uncircumcised Greek, the house of Christ, the Church; and Ham, the hot, restless one separated from both, represented heresy: "The tribe of heretics, not with spirit, not of patience, but of impatience, with which the breasts of heretics are wont to blaze, and with which they disturb the peace of the saints" (16.2). Ham's children were symbolically those shifting sojourners in ethnic lands who were outside the household of God, and not of the faith.[5]

Augustine's version of the division of the world, which he was at pains to make clear would always suffer from excessive allegorical interpretation, was both Christian and Roman: by faith in Christ *all* men could be members of the City of God. Christ replaced Romulus as the founder of the City (21.22.6). Ham was merely the symbol of the man in isolation, the clanless, lawless, heartless man who, like heathen ethnics, did not know God: "However, not only those who are openly separated from the Church, but all those who glory in the Christian name, and at the same time lead abandoned lives, may without absurdity be seen to be figured by Noah's middle son" (16.2). For Augustine the division between Shem, Ham, and Japhet, between Hebrew, African, and European, is not racial but a matter of those who live according to God and those who live according to man.

Defining all men as rational and mortal, Augustine was left with the problem of reconciling philosophically those matters having to do with faith and the pressing realities of the earthly city, the secular vale of tears. Augustine resolved the difficulty in two ways. First, in proclaiming the alternative histories as profane and heretical, he declared it blasphemous to say or believe that any other than God was the creator of Nature (1.12.25). The nature of the fetus and its corresponding lineaments and color were produced of none but the most high God (1.12.25). The city of God on earth was the institution of the Church, now rising in Rome as the administrative and economic structure of the Roman Empire declined, and men entered it through *conversion*. It did not matter which son of Noah they were descended from, whether they were speech-gifted or mute, barbarian, brutish, or vicious, black or white: "But whoever is anywhere born a man, that is, a rational mortal animal, no matter what unusual appearance he presents in color, movement, sound, nor how particular he is in some power, part or quality of his nature, no Christian can doubt that he springs from one protoplast" (16.8). All were eligible for membership by faith in *communitas, christianitas,* and *humanitas.*

Second, Augustine recognized that membership in a Christian community and faith alone would not resolve the complexities of secular existence. Unlike his predecessors, he did not believe that existence could proceed solely on the basis of following the fixed precepts of sacred texts. On the contrary, his acceptance of the complete and unchanging whole concept of the Creator—expressed as a Trinity of Father, Son, and Holy Ghost—allowed him to introduce the interventionist institutions and practices of *ecclesia* and *regna* (Church and State) to hold authority until the Second Coming. His syncretic solution temporarily legitimized an agency—the Church—established to provide moral guidance and pragmatic advice to rulers who had to rule and subjects who had to obey. At the same time it permitted co-existence with rulers who had priorities other than those of faith. Augustine achieved this remarkable feat by retaining the important political elements of Greco-Roman experience in the practices of dialogue and conciliation between the Church and State and among the people of Western Europe, North Africa, and Northern Europe, who were not of the faith. The dichotomy between matters of faith and politics, which Josephus had solved by disposing of politics and *nomocracy* altogether in favor of theocracy, was resolved in *De civitate Dei* by giving some small encouragement to the antique idea of *citizenship,* of being well-lawed, of cultivating a civic disposition within a *res-publica* serving a *populus* bound together in a nexus of law. In this way, Augustine hoped, the worst excesses of blind faith within the Church would be tempered, as well as the inevitable tendencies to corruption in tyranny, oligarchy, and democracy in the State.

THE RISE OF ISLAM

This Augustinian compact between Church and State was to last in Western Europe for a millennium. It laid the foundations for a stimulating, but contentious, intellectual and religious dispute among Christians, barbarians, and Jews within a temporizing "political" discourse. But, this continuous intellectual discourse was made more difficult when, in the eighth century, another novel and dynamic force was introduced from across the Straits of Gibraltar.

In the fragmentary evidence of Roman writers, the stories of the fablers, and the written evidence of the Holy Koran (the gradual revelation and recitation of the Creator), there is a record of the aboriginal peoples of Arabia called the Sabaeans and Himyarites, who were divided tribally into the Adites of the Yemen, the Thamudites of Northern Arabia, and the Canaanites and Philistines. These proud peoples were pagans, who, during the period of antiquity so far described, had stubbornly resisted the power of the Persians, Greeks, and Romans and had refused to accept the words of the Hebrew prophets and Syrian and Abyssinian Christians. They preferred instead to worship idols and to express themselves orally in odes, camel drivers' songs, profane poetry, and myths. They were bound together not by Greek politics and philosophy, nor by religion, but by the honor of the household and the tribe, and their god was called Allah, a heathen reference point for fixing disputes between subordinate multiple gods and demons, called kobolds and jinns. For these fierce tribal peoples descent was claimed from Ishmael, son of Abraham, and Mecca was the place that Adam had constructed where the idols were gathered together declaring the splendor of magic and idolatry. This period is referred to by Muhammad the Prophet as a period of wildness and savagery, not unlike the condition of barbarism, brutishness, and viciousness that we have seen described in the classical Greek and Roman texts. For the Greek and Roman the *polis* and *res-publica* were ways of putting an end to barbarity, brutishness, and viciousness; for the Prophet Muhammad it was *hilm*—the moral responsibility of life in a new religious community.

Muhammad was born in the Year of the Elephant (570–71) when the Yemeni made an expedition against the Quraish trading center of Mecca, where they saw for the first time the elephants from Abyssinia. The fragmentary story of Muhammad's childhood appears in the Holy Koran (93.7-8-9). He was an ascetic, versed in Christian and Hebrew religion, who, turning away from the idolatry and profanity of his kin, sought a new way of teaching them to prepare for the coming day of judgment. Muhammad withdrew, and in his fortieth year was called to be a prophet by the angel Gabriel at Mount Hira (Sura 96.1–20, the Sura of the Drop of Blood). When Gabriel left him, Muhammad doubted the revelation of prophecy and knowledge he had been given, and Gabriel came to him a second time. (Sura 74.2:1 "O thou that has wrapped *thyself with thy mantle.*") Thereafter he was said to be possessed of prophecy, knowledge, and certainty. He formed a community of the faithful at Mecca but made a compromise with his own tribe, the Quraish, by acknowledging the existence of their gods, whereupon they prostrated themselves before him. (Sura 53.20,21:1 "Now tell *me* about Lat and Uzza, and Mannat, the third one, another *goddess.* . . . Nay, to Allah belong the Hereafter and this *world.*") Muhammad admitted his guilt, and was visited again by Gabriel, who, repeating the sura said that Muhammad had mouthed words that had not been revealed to him. Allah was not divisible; His Word was greater than the authority of all temporizing compromises and settlements. Muhammad's retraction of the compromise he had made with the Quraish did not find favor, and his threats of coming judgment now fell on deaf ears. (Sura 16.105:1 "As for those who do not believe in the Signs of Allah, surely, Allah will not guide them, and they shall have a grievous punishment.")

For a time Muhammad continued to preach surrender to the will of Allah (*islam*) and to denounce idolatry, but with little success among his own people. In 619–20 he encountered inhabitants of Medina who did not ridicule him and treat him as a forger, as his own people had done. He asked to seek refuge with them and in the following year went with some followers to Medina to preach and to instruct the strangers (the First Homage and the Second Homage) and was hailed as a prophet. In April 622 the Migration (*Hegira*) from Mecca to Medina took place, symbolizing the rejection of kin and the foundation of a community based on unswerving faith:

> The Migration was undoubtedly essential to the establishment of Islam. It was necessary that Muhammad should cut himself off from his own people in order that he might found a community in which not blood but religion formed the sole bond that was recognized.[6]

From this time forth, the faith flourished throughout all Arabia. How relevant was it to the story of race as we have told it so far? Unlike the Augustinian account considered earlier, the Holy Koran was a revealed text set down gradually in a series (*sura*) from an original text in Heaven to the Prophet, Muhammad, the last of a line that extended back through Jesus to Moses. It was a text that unashamedly eschewed compromise and affirmed the indivisibility of Allah. In interpreting meaning, the emphasis was placed first upon faith in the word, and then upon consideration of the opposites of truth and falsehood. Those who did not believe were outside the community of the faithful (*ummah*). Therefore the Holy Koran contained a foundation for legislation and belief, traditions (*sunnah*), community (*ijmah*), and individual thought (*ijtihad*) that regulated all aspects of life, including duty to God, neighbor, and self. Surrender of the individual to the will of God (*islam*) was a necessary condition of both religious and social life. The five pillars of the faith—prayer, welfare tax, fast, pilgrimage, and profession of faith—outlined the correct procedures and practices, both private and public, for attainment of brotherhood in faith. Unlike the Augustinian compact between Church and State, Islam united the spiritual and the temporal in a social system that was wholly religious. It would be spread throughout the world through *jihad*, or holy war, for unbelievers could have no merit however moral their actions might be. Western philosophy was an error, a turning away from the judgment of the Creator (82.10–13), and Christianity a wrong doctrine (9.30–31).

A CONVERGENT CIVILIZATION

The Hebrew, Christian, and Muslim accounts of descent and generation considered here have much in common in their genealogies but differ considerably in several important respects. The Hebrew and Muslim accounts attached great significance to the divine nature of the law as revealed by God through a prophet or teacher. The practices of everyday life were governed in their entirety and in very precise detail by religious texts, rules, and precepts. Existence on earth was centered in the worship of God. In a direct relationship between God and man, there was no place for political thinking. These accounts were faithfully synchronic. The relationship between man and God was synchronized by faith, leaving no room for politics.

On the other hand, the Christian account, as narrated by Augustine, was dualist, syncretic, and technically hypocritical in the best Greek sense of the word: that is, it had a high potential for dissimulation, pretense, and the acting out of politics. In its emphasis on the role of the Church as an agency legitimately established to provide moral guidance and pragmatic advice for rulers, the ecclesiastical triumphed over the political. But the metaphors Augustine cleverly selected to describe the three cities—the City of God (or righteousness), the city of God on earth as part of that city, and the earthly city—were drawn from Greek and Roman political life. Although politics as an autonomous activity and political rule as a form of governance were not accorded the prominence they had in the thought of Aristotle or Cicero, they informed Augustine's notions of citizenship and of the relationship between *ecclesia* and *regna*. In short, Augustine's *De civitate Dei* did not entirely renounce Greek and Roman political symbols, and as a result the Christian community was not depoliticized to the extent advocated in the Hebrew and Muslim texts. These distinctions were to have immense importance in determining the relationship among the three communities during the millennium that followed the sack of Rome by the barbarians. With some difficulty, the three faiths managed to reconcile their divergent political and religious approaches in a rich, convergent civilization in Western Europe. But after 1200 a resurgence of interest in profane history and a fascination with monstrosity, unnatural shape, and hidden causes in blood unleashed tendencies that culminated in the expulsion of the Jews and Moors from Spain and thereafter in the foundation of an apolitical world full of races.

» *Purity of Blood and Expulsion*

Moses Maimonides, the greatest teacher of the Hebrew world, was pivotal to the shift in Western thought after 1200. This Jewish scholar, physician, and philosopher opened the way for scientific inquiry by reintroducing Aristotelian thought without violating the biblical declaration that Nature had one Creator. His argument that "God is a free cause, but a rational one, and his rationality lies in the homogeneity of his creation" created a new interest in logic and metaphysics within his own faith and presented a challenge to the Augustinian formulation of the Christian doctrine as well as to Islam. Leon Roth has argued that Maimonides' emphasis upon the rationality and practicality of the Mosaic Code for the conduct of civilized life for all men helped define the notion of contract that would have great influence in the foundation of international law in the sixteenth and seventeenth centuries.[7]

But while Maimonides laid the foundations for rationality, scientific thinking, international law, and comparative cultural anthropology and gave value to ethics as a specific human science dependent not on the intervention of a beneficent anthropomorphic god but upon the acts of man, his thought had a dark side as well. In Maimonides there is an inherent distrust of philosophy *qua* philosophy—just as there is in Josephus—and an increasing emphasis on a revealed truth emanating from an incorporeal God. Sidestepping Aristotle's analysis of difference and variety in human affairs, Maimonides retreated into the fixed rules of the Hebraic law and excluded without mercy those who are unclean and would defile faith. In a bitter irony, Maimonides' arguments were first turned against his own people in 1492, the year Europeans and Americans celebrate for its "discovery of new worlds." That year, the Jews were expelled from Spain. A decade later, Muslims were also banished.

THE MOORISH INVASION OF EUROPE

In my view the Jewish and Moorish presence in Spain occupies an important place in history because it provides an example of significant human migration and settlement over a long period of time without the necessity of using the convenient catchall explanation of race. Racial and ethnic explanation has become so familiar to us today in Whig descriptions of the recent "occupation" of the Americas and the formation of the modern European states that we quickly forget that the Jews had achieved a significant, honorable, and recognized place in Spain for almost fifteen hundred years and the Moors for eight hundred years that was not determined "racially," but in accordance with acknowledged political ideas, practices, and procedures. It was the suspension of that *via politica* that brought to an abrupt and catastrophic end a long period of the *modus vivendi,* and heralded a future era of coterminous (racial) self-determination.

To understand the political significance of Maimonides' thought, it is necessary to turn to the Iberian Peninsula, where Christian, Jew, and Muslim coexisted for many centuries. When the Moors invaded Spain in A.D. 711, they not only initiated a fundamental Islamic presence in that part of Europe that lasted almost eight hundred years but encountered a Jewish presence that had been a major intellectual, social, religious, and economic force since the beginning of the Roman Empire.

After the consolidation of the teachings of Muhammad by his close friends who formed the Orthodox Khalifate (632–61), the Word was spread from Medina to Persia and Syria. With the assassination of the last of his true descendants, Ali, the title was taken by Mu'Awiya, the governor of Syria, and during the next century Damascus rivaled Persia as the center of power and learning under the Umayyad dynasty (661–750). It was the Umayyad dynasty that broke the restraints placed upon the Arab world by Roman and Greek history and finally took the faith into Morocco, West Africa, and Europe. In 711 the military governor in North Africa, Tarik, took four ships to reconnoiter the paradise he had heard about across the commanding straits and landed at Jabal Tarik (the Mountain of Tarik, corrupted to Gibral-tar). Within two years two large forces had defeated the West Goths, and had reached the Pyrenees. By 732 the Arabs under Abdar-Rahman, the deposed leader of the Umayyad dynasty in Damascus, had established a Moorish dynasty in Spain and had occupied territories as far north as Tours.

In his literary analysis of this period, Nicholson makes the important point that this early Umayyad period was more about conquest and less about spreading the faith, simply because there were those within the faith who argued that conversion would not bring equality with the vanquished natives.[8] Nicholson believed that this controversy about equality and conversion was deeply rooted in pre-Islamic literature, which Nicholson mistakenly believed to be "racial" in content (6.280). It was not until the Abbasids, claiming closer descent from the Prophet, seized power from the Umayyads that this pre-Islamic literary dispute began to be resolved. From 750 the Abbasid dynasty at Baghdad created a center of Persian learning and literature which lasted until it, too, was engulfed by the Mongol hordes of Ghenghis Khan in 1258.

It was during this period of Abbasid high learning that the Moors were defeated at Tours (732), driven out of Narbonne by the Frankish barbarian Pippin, and forced to take up fortified positions south of the Pyrenees. In 801, when the Frankish kings embraced Christianity, the Moors retreated further to Cordova (929) where, with the support of the Berbers of North Africa, they established an Islamic center to rival Baghdad. A new injection of faith regenerated the whole of Moorish Spain within the region of Andalus and the Maghrib when Yusuf ibn Tashfin, a warrior mystic, crossed from North Africa in about 1090 to establish the Almoravid dynasty. This advance was further consolidated with the new movement of Al-Muwwahhidin in Morocco, whose founder Ibn Tumart and his lieutenant Abd Al Mumin crossed into Andalusia and had by 1157 brought nearly half of the Iberian Peninsula under their rule. It was not until after their defeat by the Moors at Alarcos in 1195 that the Christians became sufficiently united to deal with this invasion, which they finally accomplished with a decisive victory at Las Navas de Tolosa in 1212, bringing to an end five hundred years of conquest and military occupation.

In the middle years of the Abbasid dynasty, in Bukhara, Central Asia, Avicenna (Ibn-Sina) was born of Persian parents (980). He showed intellectual promise at a very early age, and at sixteen he was able to recite the Koran and to carry out simple medical procedures. In 1013 he began his *Canon of Medicine,* which from the twelfth to the seventeenth centuries became the standard guide to medical practice in European universities, although it was not in translation until the fourteenth century. The canon did not offer the standard Gallenic and Hippocratian medical hypotheses. Instead, it concentrated on describing in five books a method of classifying the parts of the body and the types of diseases. In order to justify theologically his interest in the modification of Galen and Hippocrates, Avicenna also sought to reconcile the logic of Aristotle's *Metaphysics* and Platonism with his own understanding of the revealed Word of the Holy Koran. He was extremely interested in Aristotle's essences and forms and tried to show how they may be examined by the intellect in three different ways—metaphysically, physically, and logically. Oliver Leaman in his *Introduction to Mediaeval Islamic Philosophy* argues that al Ghazali (1058–1111), a mystic Persian thinker, contested this attempt to incorporate Greek philosophy into Arabic thought in his *The Refutations of the Philosophers,* and that this contestation was taken up and moderated in Muslim Spain by Averroes.

Averroes, Ibn Rushd, was born at Cordova in 1126. During the early part of his life he experienced the ebb and flow of conflict between Muslim and Christian, but the crossing of the Al-Muwwahhadin from the Magreb in 1157 stopped for a time the worst excesses of the incursions of the Christian princes into Adalusia from the North. During this period great mosques were built and learning flourished under a tight legal system that more strictly observed the literal interpretation of the Holy Koran. Like Avicenna, Averroes held Aristotle in high esteem but did not believe that a mystic interpretation of the essences and forms was necessary to understand the word of Allah, who was one and indivisible. The eternal truths lay in the words and teachings revealed by the Prophet, and could not be reduced to metaphysical propositions. For a time he found favor with the legalistic Islamic authorities in his opposition to al Ghazali's mysticism, and he served as an esteemed judge in Seville, Cordova, and Morocco. But, for Averroes that which Aristotle distinguished as "science," that is, mathematics, physics, and theology, as opposed to practical politics and ethics, should continue to look at and classify things methodically as they are in reality. It was this flexible "Greeking in" of the Islamic texts along the lines suggested earlier by Avicenna that eventually led him into difficulties, and before his death in 1198, he fell out of favor amongst his own people. However, the seed sown in the fertile intellectual soil of Muslim Spain bore fruit in the new universities of Europe at Paris, Oxford, and Padua. Averroes had a profound influence on the interpretation there of Aristotle's poetry, metaphysics, and physics among the Schoolmen and their opponents, and particularly on the encouragement of critical analysis in law and medicine.

Although the rich Muslim scholarship we have briefly described was in the Aristotelian tradition and contemplated almost every aspect of life—mind, the heavens, generation, plants, senses, ethics, aesthetics, physics, logic, and law—it has to be said that it halted when it came to the most compromising document of all, Aristotle's *Politics*. Until the death of Averroes the continuing military threat between the faiths was agitated by the idea of a Moorish *jihad,* a holy war to unite all under Islam, and eventually by the idea of a Christian crusade to expel the Moors from the body of the faithful. The conflict was essentially religious, but it was prosecuted intellectually on the Christian side under the banner of Church and State in an uneasy alliance between the teachings of Augustine's *De civitate Dei* and the reintroduction of Aristotle's *Politics*. It is worth noting that during the Middle Ages the great Christian thinkers, that is to say those seeking accommodation between Church and State, states and states, by the *via politica* were Saint Thomas Aquinas, Dante, Marsilius, and Machiavelli. Their discourse on politics *qua* politics was of little or no interest to the Islamic thinkers, who were much more interested in an enduring law interpreted according to the Word.

It would be wrong, however, to portray the struggle as fanatical. In the long intervals between the wars life went on, and over eight hundred years there was significant accommodation between the two faiths. The Moors had economic and technological advances to offer, and in the early days Castilian monarchs sought to attract them with privileges, exemptions, and rights within Christian communities. By the thirteenth century, and particularly during the reign of Alfonso X (1252–84), the Moors, or Mudejares—Muslims who remained after the Christian reconquest—had laws describing their rights and were sometimes given exclusive possession of small towns, where Christians were forbidden to enter. In these separate communities the Moors conducted their own affairs under the authority of local magistrates and officials while remaining part of a wider community through the contribution they made to its nonreligious life. In larger towns the Moorish communities were segregated into special communities (*aljamas*) surrounded by walls (*barrios*). These divisions were not racial; they were religious.

JEWISH SEPARATENESS

Similar accommodations were made for Jewish communities. The great historian of the Jews, Heinrich Graetz, sets the zenith of their medieval history at the time of the death of Moses Maimonides (1205), when, after more than a thousand years of settlement in Spain, they, too, had come to possess their own town life, jurisdiction, councils, and revenue administration and were linked throughout Iberia by a highly intellectual religious system of rabbinical authority and law. It is important to note that their law was not the formulation of law of the Greco-Roman political state so eloquently described and proscribed for them by Josephus, but a law based on the ancient Hebrew texts and genealogical registers and steeped in a deep suspicion of the politics and philosophy of Greece and Rome.

The rabbis derived their authority from the kings, who obtained revenue from them through taxation, import duties, and the billeting of soldiers and from a special levy of thirty denarii to compensate for the thirty pieces of silver Judas received for his betrayal of Christ. These payments were made a moral obligation by the rabbis, and the communities (*burghettos*) soon became a reliable source of finance, credit, and management for the kings as well as a haven of safety where Jews could exercise their religious rites. Again the division is not racial; like the *aljamas,* the *burghetto* began as place of protection for those who wished to practice their religion outside the sphere of *ecclesia* and *regna* and for whom there was no expectation of compromise or conciliation in matters of faith.

That is not to say there were no disputes between faiths or that there was a cozy relationship without persecution and cruelty. As Lukyn Williams has shown, even in the years before Moses Maimonides, the Jews were seen as the violators of the canon law of the Church, attacking the authority of its teachings and institutions and threatening its very spirit and soul. This was not a racial threat; it was religious. Williams carefully analyzes a thousand years of unsuccessful attempts by irritated Christian scholars to bring the Jews to Christ through intellectual persuasion and dialogue in public places.[9] As Valeriu Marcu has observed, the Jews within their walled *burghettos* were bound to a rigid law and textual exegesis that would yield neither to Arabian and Greek philosophy based on imagination and sense perception, nor to teachings and practices based on Roman republican forms of authority, tradition, and politics.[10] For the Jew religion was all. There was no place for the tradition of compromise that informed the Greco-Roman political state.

CASTE

If this state of being religiously separate and politically mute, as were the Moors in their *aljamas* and the Jews in their *burghettos,* cannot be described as a racial division, then what can we call it? The Christians considered themselves superior because of their Christian religion, which derived from the authoritative Roman account of Augustine. Islam, which recognized no division between the spiritual and the temporal, created a unified religious social system of believers that through *jihad* posed a constant threat to Christians. The Jews were seen as living in captivity forever, a constant reminder of those who had crucified Christ. Americo Castro explains this urge to share in a common life yet not lose a distinct identity not as an expression of racial difference but as a passionate desire to preserve a noble spiritual lineage. This concern for "good lineage" and the retention of its purity is called *casta* (the word a recent arrival), and the *castizos* are those of good family and descent. While the three communities were separated from one another religiously, they were bound together through the idea of being *castizos,* members of an important group with a legitimate lineage. While the Moors and Jews were depoliticized by their own teachings, the Christians were split into religious and political spheres of influence with increasing signs of the appearance of strong professional bureaucracies. Castro does not apply the term "race" to these divisions: "Let the matter of biological antecedents—that which is called race—be left to zoology."[11]

Like Snowden and Thompson in their assessments of Greece and Rome, Castro's view suggests that historians should not be tempted into anticipating the appearance of a race state before the essential intellectual components are in place. If anything, this period of European history invites attention because of the *absence* of the idea of race in the face of substantial migration of peoples of different faiths who had to be painfully accommodated over long periods of time by and through the principles and practices and processes of classical political theory. But from 1100 onward the nature of the relationships among these peoples of different faiths began to change.

MOSES MAIMONIDES AND THE
REINTRODUCTION OF REASON

The changes that began after 1100 had an important bearing upon the emergence of an idea of race. First, Moses Maimonides, born in Cordova on March 30, 1135, then at the very center of the Muslim world, sought to speak for Jewish *castizos* in the face of Christian and Islamic intolerance brought about by an upsurge of Islamic invasion. He also turned to examine the introversion and introspection of his own people, living forever in a depoliticized state in which the rabbis were the undisputed literal interpreters of the ancient Hebrew texts and no other constitution was allowed. In *The Guide for the Perplexed,* written after he had fled to Cairo to avoid persecution, Maimonides set out, in the language of Greek teaching and thinking, his opposition to the system and method of Islamic theology (*kalam*), thereby reinstating that which Josephus had termed dishonest, unoriginal, and unhistorical.[12] In considering each term applied to God in the Hebrew texts, Maimonides carefully defined, either by identifying with some transcendental term or metaphysical term, or by skillfully using simile or allegory, a relationship that came closer to what he considered the true meaning of Hebrew, Muslim, and Christian scripture. His main difficulty was with the Mutakallemim (orthodox Islamic) writings, which saw God as a corporeal being and man as having divine attributes. Maimonides contested these conclusions because they placed too much reliance upon the literal interpretation of texts. In his view the whole question of God's relationship to man was open to wider Greek metaphysical speculation.

The Creation   Maimonides' account of Creation followed the familiar pattern from God to Adam to Moses to the spread over the earth of different families and different languages, and it differed little from earlier discourses by Josephus and Augustine on the subject or from the revelations of Muhammad. Affirming that God is incorporeal, Maimonides argued that there is no similarity between God and his creatures: "Anything predicated of God is totally different from our attributes; no definition can comprehend both: therefore His existence and that of any other being totally differ from each other, and the term existence is applied to both homonymously" (1.35.49). The literal assumption that God is a corporeal being was nothing more than a concession to idolatry, the worship of graven images, and should be resisted: "God has no organs, or, what is the same, He is not corporeal; His actions are accomplished by His Essence, not by any organ" (1.46.62).

In this extremely difficult "Greeking in" of the Mutakallemim and Hebrew texts, Maimonides revived that part of Aristotelian philosophy that applied to existence, essences, and origins to validate the Pentateuch and the Prophets as a fit study and text for his own people and for those Greco-Roman Christians and Muslims who were perplexed. Although he seemed to imply that reliance upon anything other than the Torah was heretical, he employed the philosophical system of Aristotle to show that God is the "cause" of every event and the Creator of the universe. In using Aristotle's explanations of existence and creation, Maimonides was able to establish a compatibility between the scriptural account of Creation and the philosophical account of the causes of production and destruction of matter, light and dark, heat and cold. Hence, the biblical stories were more likely to yield, in his view, to allegorical than literal interpretation. He urged that they be carefully studied, chapter by chapter, to find what is consistent with the philosopher's view and what is not.

Second, as well as accepting Aristotle's explanation of existence and creation, Maimonides also accepted that part of the *Politics* which argued that man was naturally a social animal and by nature forms communities. Man is the highest form of creation, differentiated from other living beings and composed of the largest number of constituent elements: "This is the reason why the human race contains such a great variety of individuals, that we cannot discover two persons exactly alike in any moral quality, or in external appearance" (2.40.232). These two propositions had the further effect of loosening the emphasis placed upon literal exegesis, particularly within the Hebrew community, and they opened a way for a deeper inquiry into natural human difference, variety, and appearance, which had been brushed to one side by Augustine in his much earlier analysis, and more recently resuscitated by the Islamic writers.

In this more comprehensive analysis of Creation Maimonides focused on deformity and unnatural shape, or monstrosity, as it appeared in the mystical passages of the Torah: "It is well known that there are men whose face is like that of other animals; thus the face of some person is like that of a lion, that of another person like that of an ox, and so on; and man's face is described according as the form of his face resembles the form of the face of other animals" (3.1.252).

Maimonides warned that these interpretations of difference and variety in individuals may be contrary to Law and Reason and that one should proceed with caution. Deformity was seen as a disorder of action (innate or not) having its origin in transient substance, not form. Man's shortcomings (passion, lust, gluttony, vice) were all due to the substance of the body, while merits were due exclusively to form. In this tension between substance and form, body and soul, the best and most perfect being that can be formed of blood and semen is the species of man, who is differentiated from other living matter because he is living, reasonable, and mortal. Where deformity occurs it is strange and exceptional, out of step with the perpetuation by a repeated succession of genesis and destruction of the most perfect being formed of matter. On this earth, man is superior to all other living beings, but when it comes to the spheres and intelligences, he is exceedingly inferior.

It is important to note, however, that Maimonides did not support the theory held by Aristotle, A Shariyah, and Mu'tazilites that everything in human affairs may be attributed to chance, Divine Will, or Divine Wisdom, respectively. Rather, Maimonides held to the view that everything in human affairs is due to the merits of man, with each individual having a share of Divine Providence in proportion to his perfection. He shared with Augustine the view that the astrological works of the Sabeans, Hermetists, Kasdims, Egyptians, and Chaldeans were utterly lacking in true science, second-class precepts claiming to perform wonderful things. Maimonides scornfully rejected the influence of the stars, natural remedies, witchcraft, and demons and regarded the wide availability of Arabic texts on these subjects as a dangerous encouragement to idolatry. He regarded Abraham as meritorious in rejecting Sabean worship of the sun and stars. Remnants of the Sabeans, explained Maimonides, are found "in the remote corners of the earth, like the savage Turks in the extreme North, and the Indians in the extreme South" (3.29.315).

The Law and Genealogy   For Maimonides, there is only one true set of rational precepts concerning the relationship between man and man, and man and God, and these are contained in the Jewish law and confirmed by Aristotelian method.

He proceeded to establish the more important principle that the sole object of the law was for the benefit of man. He sought to demonstrate the wider applicability of the Commandments. It was his view that every one of the 613 precepts of the Mosaic Code inculcated some universal truth and had as its purpose the removal of erroneous opinion, the establishment of proper relations within society, the diminution of evil, and training in good behavior—all of which would be acceptable to reasonable men in all the nations of the world. The Mosaic Code was justifiable not simply in terms of faith but by its efficacy in the political terms of Aristotle and Augustine. The Law was a matter of opinion, morals, and social conduct as well as of faith. Its chief object was to teach the truth that aimed at removing injustice from mankind, particularly debarring those actions that disturb the social order and economy of the family, such as intemperate eating, drinking, and sexual intercourse. In this light, burnt offerings and sacrifice were of only secondary importance. The direction of Maimonides' argument was to urge greater religious tolerance and flexibility within the Jewish community.

Having established that the law is for man's benefit, Maimonides affirmed that statutes must be definite, unconditional, and general. The law cannot be made, like medicine, to vary according to different persons, times, and circumstances. It has to be certain and known (3.34).

Maimonides then divided the precepts of Jewish law into fourteen classes covering such things as business transactions, loans, rites, ceremonies, sacrifices, cleanliness, food consumption, and sex, and subdivided each into two classes, those pertaining to relations between men and those pertaining to man's relationship to God. He showed each class to be correct and useful. He again rejected the idolatry of the Sabeans, Kasdims, and Chaldeans, and especially that of the Egyptians and the Canaanites, warning against witchcraft relating to plants, animals, and minerals and practices such as painting trees and putting blood on the land. In medicine, he claimed the law permits "everything that has been verified by experiment, although it cannot be explained away by analogy" (3.38.335).

Yet Maimonides' account of the law, however well justified by reference to Aristotelian philosophical method, still remained rooted in theocracy. His perception of law and its purposes derived from a most excellent relationship between God and his creatures. Maimonides shared with Josephus the distrust of secular *nomocracy* and of hypocritical Aristotelian politics.

While Maimonides recognized a duty to the slave and the freeborn (3.38.34), his concern did not extend to sinners. Augustine had broadly invited all—Greek, Gentile, Ethiopian, barbarian, monster, slave, and sinner—by faith to enter into the body of the faithful in Christ, but Maimonides took a more rigorous stand. Mercy for sinners, he claimed, was cruel to *all* creatures, and pleas from them for help must be refused. He strictly followed the tenets of the Jewish law, condemning all defilement and uncleanliness arising from wrongful practices relating to eating, menstruation, leprosy, semen, food, and animals. Maimonides did not accept Sextus Empiricus' sensationalist view that the existence of bewildering diversity in religious observance, diet, usage, and attitudes to death were matters of convention. On the contrary, he refused either to suspend judgment on these matters altogether or to seek a political accommodation in the spirit of compromise and reconciliation. Instead he used Aristotle to support his retreat into the private institutional arrangements of family and household. With his cornerstone the Jewish law, he condemned prostitution, incest, and intercourse "between root and branch," and degrading carnal pleasure and gastronomy. There was no suggestion in his work, however, that his disapproval of copulation between different species had anything to do with the mixture of "races." He opposed "unnatural sex" that violated established codes of religious practice and intermarriage with other nations lest it "make thy sons go awhoring after their Gods" (3.29.379, see also Exod. 34.16). Endogamy, as in days of old, was "a fence against idolatry."

Maimonides' concern about intermarriage left him with the complex problem of genealogy—of being of good lineage—which required some explanation in light of what was happening around him. He applied jurisprudence to the manner in which nations branched from a common root and were caused to mix and disperse. For him, genealogies were not useless repetitions of superfluous historical matter but a practical necessity, as they establish identities and recount incidents witnessed by people in the past from which people in the present must learn if they are to make their way in the world. Although Maimonides was seeking to confirm the legitimacy of the Hebrew genealogy, he opened up the wider possibility for other peoples to become interested in alternative genealogies and to seek greater accuracy in the pursuit of their own particular records. We shall see later how this avenue comes to be used as an awful tool against the Jews.

The Allegory of the King's Palace   To exemplify the relationship of faith and reason, Maimonides presented the metaphor of the king's palace. It begins by proposing that some of the king's subjects live in his country and some live abroad. Of those who live in the country, some have turned their backs to the palace and face in another direction. Some are desirous to go to the palace to minister before the king but have not yet seen the palace walls. Some reach the outer walls of the palace and go in search of the entrance gate. Others pass through to the antechamber and to the innermost court, and some actually gain an audience with the king.

Maimonides likened those who are around the palace walls in search of the gate to those who know mathematical science and logic. Those who enter the gate have physics, and those who enter the innermost court and gain an audience with the king have reached the beginning of understanding, with a grasp of natural philosophy and metaphysics. In contrast, those who are in the country but have their backs to the palace are believers who hold false doctrines, which they have adopted in consequence of great mistakes of speculation or received in error from others who misled them. Those who are abroad are without religion altogether, whether it be based on tradition or speculation. These are, explained Maimonides, "the extreme Turks that wander about in the north, the Kushites who live in the south, and those in our country who are like these. I consider these as irrational beings, and not as human beings; they are below mankind, but above monkeys, since they have the form and shape of man, a mental faculty above that of the monkey" (3.50.384). But those who hold false doctrines within the country (the followers of Muhammad and the supposed descendants of Ham) recede more as they appear to proceed: "They are worse than the first class [i.e., the Turks and the Kushites], and under certain circumstances it may be necessary to slay them, and to extirpate their doctrines, in order that others should not be misled" (3.51.384).

For the first time in Western thought people are described as beyond the bounds of rationality; they are not human. Others, rational but lacking in faith, are perceived as so dangerous to the position of the rational and the faithful that their extirpation from the face of the earth is justified. As Roth points out, Maimonides made an enormous contribution to Western civilization by regenerating a lost interest in logic, mathematics, physics, science, and metaphysics. And while he established a platform that might have eventually produced a political rapprochement among the three faiths, it led instead into a cul-de-sac of blind faith and a justification of extirpation.

THE DEGRADATION OF THE JEWS

Maimonides' argument came to be applied with great force against his own people just at the moment in Spanish history when the Jews were factionalized and open to attack. Graetz sees a dismal gloom descending on medieval history after the death of Maimonides: "Maimuni's death and the ascendancy of the Papacy were two misfortunes for Judaism which removed it from its lofty position to the deepest degradation."[13]

Graetz believes the reasons for the decline may be traced to Pope Innocent III (1198–1216), who at first was ready to continue the practice of acknowledging the political status of the Jews within the body of the faithful and protecting them from unjust treatment within the earthly city. During the Crusades, when under the Cross the Crusaders were absolved from sin and free to Jew-bait, Innocent promulgated a *Constitutio Judaeorum* in the Roman and Greek tradition of *nomocratic* rule. It required monarchs to respect the cemeteries of Jews and to protect them from molestation, confiscation of property, and arbitrary punishment for offenses. In Spain, where tolerance had been shown to the Jewish community for a millennium, Don Pedro II, king of Aragon (crowned by Pope Innocent III in 1204), and Alfonso the Noble, king of Castile (1158–1214), were both reprimanded by Innocent for taking protection too far and positively favoring Jewish heresy within their midst. Innocent threatened excommunication to any Christian who carried on intercourse, financial and otherwise, with Jews. In 1208 he wrote to Count Nevers: "The Jews, like the fratricide Cain, are doomed to wander about the earth as fugitives and vagabonds, and their faces must be covered with insult."[14]

In Graetz's account, two significant events changed Innocent's traditional practice of governance by acknowledged political rules into a crusade in the name of the faith. The first occurred on July 22, 1209, when Innocent moved against the Albigenses in southern France, whom he regarded as heretics because they had listened to the biblical exegesis of Jewish teachers and had declared the Jewish interpretation of portions of the Scripture to be a more accurate interpretation than that of the Papacy. They had thereby challenged the absolutism of papal authority. The city of Béziers was surrounded by papal forces wielding the spiritual and the secular sword. When Innocent was asked by the military commander how to distinguish between true Catholics and heretics, Innocent replied, "Strike down; God will recognize his own." The town was stormed and twenty thousand people were massacred. Thus began a reign of terror against blasphemy and heresy across Western Europe. In 1211 the Jews were forced into a migration to Jerusalem. The second event, perceived as a threat to Christian Europe, was the invasion of southern Spain by Almohade Prince of the Faithful of Africa and South Spain, Abu-Yussuff Almansur and the capture of Salvatierra in September 1211. Alfonso the Noble called upon Innocent for help in repelling this attack, and an Ultramontane force was sent under the command of the Cistercian monk, Arnold, who had been responsible for the massacre at Béziers in 1209. In the course of this crusade against the Crescent, Arnold was offended by the protection given to the Jews in Castile and openly attacked them. The first attack on the Jews in Spain thus came not from fanatical Spanish monarchs, but from the outside intervention of a soldier intent on ignoring the rules of papal politics.

These events initiated a reconsideration of the political status of the Jews. In France, at the Paris Synod, it was proposed to ban Jews from employing Christian servants and Christians from attending Jewish women in confinement. This proposal was considered at the Montpelier Synod in 1214 but dropped following strong Jewish representation and argument. However, Innocent summoned a general ecumenical council at Rome and was able to consolidate the power of the Church in the states as well as to impose new impositions upon the Jews. Four of the seventy decrees passed by this Fourth Lateran Council (1215), which also founded the Dominican and Franciscan orders, applied to Jews. Christian princes were formally forbidden to give offices to Jews on pain of excommunication. They were encouraged to watch over their Jewish subjects so as to curb usury and extract tithes and the Easter reminder. In these good works they were to be more closely monitored by the Church. That in itself presented little difficulty for the Christian princes, for they were used to temporizing and bending the pope's decrees to suit their own convenience and advantage, and they had little intention of allowing the pope to consolidate his power over them by that means. What was more important, and was to have a devastating effect upon the history of Western civilization, was a new requirement that Jews in all Christian countries should wear a dress distinguished from that of the Christians to prevent mischievous intermarriage. From their twelfth year, all Jewish men were to wear in their hats, and all Jewish women in their bonnets, a badge.

The idea of a badge of identification was copied from Almohade Prince of the Faithful of Africa and South Spain, Abu-Yussuff Almansur, who had insisted that Jews who converted to Islam should wear a hideous dress, with long sleeves, reaching to the feet, and, in place of the traditional turban, large bonnets of the ugliest shape. Abu-Yussuff was not sure whether converts to Islam were genuine, and he decided that if they were, he would not oppose intermarriage. However, if they were simply posing, he would kill them. Because he could not be sure either way, he chose a hideous uniform to mark out those converts who were strictly observing the practices of the faith and regularly attending to its daily rituals. Abu-Yussuff's successor, Abu-Abdullah Mahomet Alnasir, changed this hideous dress to yellow garments and turbans: "By this colour of raiment the class of people who were outwardly Moslems, yet in their heart of hearts still Jews, was characterized in the first decade of the thirteenth century in the Kingdom of Morocco."[15] Although in 1219 Pope Honorius III gave a dispensation freeing the Jews of Castile from wearing the badge, James I of Aragon enforced it in 1228 and was popular for so doing.

The identity badge marked an important turning point for the Jews. No longer were they to be recognized as part of a religious and political community by virtue of their contribution as human beings to the general public arrangements of states. The residual "citizenship" they had enjoyed for a thousand years, and the homes they had found after their dispersal, were further degraded by state assemblies, provincial councils, and royal cabinets expressly set up to consider their exclusion from all affairs of state. That the exclusion could be accomplished with the utmost efficiency, it was necessary to impose on the Jews a clear identity which implied a denial of their identity as human beings. Their complex genealogy, their dignity and their self-respect, and their historical reality was reduced to the form of a badge of prescribed shape, color, length, and breadth. Graetz points to November 30, 1215, as the day the Jews in Europe were forced to take the first step toward becoming things.

THE BLACK DEATH AND PERSECUTION IN THE NORTH

Notwithstanding these novel strictures and the execration heaped upon them, the Jews continued to enjoy varying degrees of protection and prosperity throughout Western Europe in the early fourteenth century. Pope Gregory IX protected the Jews of France from the Crusaders in 1236 and in 1240 ordered the princes of Spain to seize the books of the Jews and hand them over to the Dominicans and Franciscans for safekeeping. It was not until the Black Death carried away a large proportion of the world's population in the middle of the fourteenth century that the degradation of the Jews took a new direction. Because the Jews appeared to have suffered less from the plague than the general population, it was rumored that they were the originators of the disease. Suspicion fell on the Spanish Jews, who were said to have sent messengers with boxes of poison from Toledo through a settler in Savoy, with the aid of a rabbi and a rich Jew, who were claimed to be dealers. The poison was supposed to have been prepared by Jewish doctors of the black art in Spain, who were said to have used the skin of the basilisk, spiders, frogs, lizards, the hearts of Christians ritually sacrificed, and a fragment of the Host beaten into a soft mass. Graetz claims that these rumors were not discouraged by the Church and were seized upon and exaggerated by ignorant people. They gained ground in southern France, where in 1348 the Black Death claimed many lives. Jews were burned there, and the slaughter spread to Catalonia and Aragon, where traditionally Jews had been granted protection. Attempts to burn Jews in Barcelona in 1348 were foiled by distinguished citizens, but that same year, at Cervera, eighteen Jews were killed. Still, in Spain the Church, the grandees, and the princes supported Jews and were prepared to come to their aid.

Some small measure of the protection given to Jews can be seen from the bull issued by Pope Clement VI in 1348 prohibiting anyone from killing without judicial sentence, from forcibly baptizing Jews, and from despoiling Jewish goods. It also stated that the charges against the Jews were plainly absurd, as the affliction of the plague was being visited upon Jews and Christians alike. But though published to the whole of Catholic Christendom, the bull did little to stem the tide of rumor and obloquy outside Spain. As Graetz says, "The child had become more powerful than its parent, wild fancy stronger than the Papacy."[16]

The decision to banish Jews from political communities, to put them outside the protection of *nomos,* began to have frightening consequences. At Lake Geneva four Jews were tortured and alleged to have revealed the names of the persons from whom they had received poison and where they had hidden it. They denounced themselves and all Jews as guilty. Further pressure by the judges upon two of them—a woman and her son—brought further admissions of poisoning. The confessions were recorded and signed, and the accused were burned at the stake with all those Jews who lived in the region of Lake Geneva and Savoy. The poisoning rumor spread throughout Switzerland, and at the end of 1348 there were further trials and confessions. The consuls at Bern sent reports of the trials to Basel, Freiburg, Strasbourg, and Cologne implying that the Jews were guilty of widespread poisoning. A Jew was sent in chains to Cologne to demonstrate the diabolical plans of the Jews. In Zurich charges of well poisoning and ritual child murder were laid against Jews; those found guilty were burned at the stake, and the remainder of the Jewish community was expelled from the city. As the plague spread, the attacks upon the Jews increased and further charges were made against them in Constance, St. Gallen, Lindau, Überlingen, and Schaffhausen. Some municipalities like Strasbourg and Wintertur continued to give protection to their Jewish communities, but at the Council of Benfelden in 1348, which met to consider the Jewish question, these municipalities were outvoted, and at the end of the year Jews were banished from all cities of the Upper Rhine. The Jews of Alsace were declared outlaws, and they met the same fate in Basel, where on January 9, 1349, all Jews in the city were burned to death and Jews prohibited from settlement there for two hundred years. In January 1349 all Jews at Freiburg were burned at the stake with the exception of twelve rich men, who were allowed to live in order to disclose the names of creditors. Then on Saint Valentine's Day in Strasbourg, which had been one of the sympathetic municipalities, two thousand Jews were imprisoned and burned at the stake. Following the practice at Basel, Jews were banned from the city for one hundred years.

At Worms, the oldest community in Germany, where Charles IV (German king, 1347–78, and Holy Roman emperor, 1355–78) had shown liberality in giving the citizens, including the Jews, freedom to dispose of their own property as they wished, it was decreed that Jews should be burned. Twelve Jews pleaded for mercy, and when refused were said to have killed the councillors. There seems to be some doubt about this story, but the fact remains that four hundred Jews burned themselves to death there in March 1349. Similar large-scale outbreaks occurred at Oppenheim, Frankfurt, Mainz (where six thousand Jews perished), Erfurt, and Breslau as well as in Austria, where in Vienna the entire Jewish congregation killed themselves in the synagogue. There was also widespread persecution in Bavaria, Swabia, Augsburg, Würzburg, Munich, and Würtemberg, and in Magdeburg, Hanover, and Hungary.

The process of extirpation for those whose backs were turned to the palace wall in Maimonides' allegory had begun in earnest. What had started as an intellectual argument in favor of greater religious tolerance and flexibility within the Jewish community, and lent support to those outside Jewry who sought a more genuinely political accommodation among the three castes, was turned upon its head. The Jews became the idolators in the allegory, and the Christian community was no longer perplexed about what its course of action should be in dealing with them.

After the worst effects of the plague had abated, however, the bans on the Jews in Germany were lifted and they were encouraged to return to provide services for the Church, the princes, and the municipalities. In France they were attracted back by Manessier de Vesoul, a Jew, with a decree issued by the king in March 1360 giving unrestricted entry to any part of the country with an entry charge on the head of each household and an annual tax that provided much-needed revenue for the Crown. The terms of this decree are interesting because they demonstrate the extent to which France was prepared to go to establish a political status for these immigrants. The usual provisions are there concerning the protection of trade, interest rates, property, and freedom from forced conversion, and there are promises of protection against violence by the nobles and the clergy. But the most important political concession is the establishment of a separate judiciary with a prince of the royal blood acting as protector and a tribunal of no appeal consisting of two rabbis and four assessors to hear cases. Where there was a conviction, the property of the guilty party was to be forfeited to the king and also the rabbis within the community were to be fined. Attracted by these concessions, Jews entered France in large numbers.

Subsequently, however, the medical and legal professions complained of unfair competition, questioning the qualification of Jews to practice and objecting to the special extrajudicial concessions they had been given. The clergy also complained that Jews were no longer wearing the prescribed badge of identity. The king backed down on the original concession and permitted the entry of only those Jews who had passed the required examinations. Henceforth all Jews, with the exception of those with special privileges (like Manessier and so-called court Jews), were to wear a red and white wheel-shaped badge (*rouelle*) the size of the royal seal.

THE PROBLEM OF CONVERSION IN SPAIN

In Spain the plight of the Jews, although serious, was not as hopeless as in the North, where the well-poisoning and ritual-killing rumors seem to have received widespread credence. It is true that the Jews suffered from supporting the unsuccessful Don Pedro (1350–69) in the civil war against his brother

Henry (1369–79) and that the "Jewish influence" in the claim to succession did not do the Jews any good, but neither Pedro nor Henry yielded to petitions for their exclusion from state employment and from their rights to farm taxes. Jews were still regarded as part of political communities, and although they were being plundered vicariously whenever the opportunity arose, they were still wanted by the princes, the grandees, the Church, and the institutions of learning and industry for the expert services they provided.

Nevertheless, as Valeriu Marcu shows, the Jews were forced to wear a badge of identity for two main reasons. First, the rabbis resented what they regarded as the blasphemy of current Greek and Muslim interpretations of the Torah in light of the rediscovery of Aristotle's method. Lacking the wisdom of Maimonides they immured themselves in Cabalist orthodoxy and imposed on their own carefully organized communities the same kind of harsh moral strictures that Spanish law was imposing upon Christians associating with them. The law said that any Jew found consorting with a Christian woman would be burned alive. The rabbis responded with an ordinance approving the facial mutilation of Jewish women who mixed with Christian men "that these Jewesses might lose their attraction for lovers."[17]

Second, it was obvious to the bishops that the Jews, who comprised about 10 percent of the population, had a mastery of investment, financial advice, literature, science, and medicine. The response of the Christian community was to impose draconian ordinances withdrawing economic privileges, evacuating them from dispersed communities outside the ghettos, and forbidding Christian association with Jews. Jews were required to let their hair and beards grow and wear a long gown of the coarsest material to mark out their sin. Marcu argues that this was a symbol of putting out to savagery—a banishment to isolated communities of those who did not share in Grace. The *burghettos* which had started out as "safe havens" thus became institutions of containment.

To avoid the obvious inconveniences of these impositions, many Jews who had lived in Spain for generations were willing to be baptized, and from the end of the fourteenth century large number of Jews adopted Christianity. Moreover, the old principle that forcible conversion was a sacrilege, instituted at the Fourth Council of Toledo in 633, was largely abandoned in favor of the argument of John Duns Scotus (1308) that forcible conversion was legitimate in the case of children and that in the case of adults it was better to compel to do good than to do ill with impunity.

Many Jews and Arabs thus went over to Christianity following mob attacks on *burghettos* and *aljamas*. In addition, since the time of Raymond of Penyafort (ca. 1240), the Church had acquired the services of priests and bishops who were trained in Arabic and Hebrew and skilled in entering into formal disputes with Jews. Their arguments were supported by those of men like Jerome de Sante Fé, who, as Joshua of Lorca, had been brought up as a Jew and a physician but, following baptism, wrote *The Scourge of the Jews,* a scurrilous polemic against them. Solomon Halevi (1350–1435), rabbi of Burgos, who was baptized Paulus de Santa Maria after seeing a vision following the sacking of the ghetto by the mob, became archbishop of Burgos and, like Jerome, prosecuted his newfound faith with the intellectual rigor of a zealot. Alphonso d'Espina, a former rabbi, as rector of Salamanca University and judge of the Supreme Council of the Inquisition, drew public attention to the privileged positions of Jews at court, in the Church, in trade and finance, and in the professions, and he argued for their extermination on grounds that they believed in demons and were tainted with a poisonous infection. He pleaded with the pope to absolve anyone from sin who killed a Jew and advocated taking Jewish children from their parents and baptizing them to remove any taint of Jewishness.

The conversion of large numbers of Jews to Christianity, for whatever reason, initiated a process of assimilation between the old *castizos* that lasted some forty years. But while professing Christianity, many converted Jews (or *conversos*) remained faithful to the Law of Moses in the privacy of the family. After a time faithful Christians became concerned about these "pretense Christians" and were galled when they saw *conversos* in important positions in the state, Church, finance, and industry and acting as luminaries in all branches of science and intellectual inquiry. A fresh series of attacks targeted not the immured Jews within the ghettos but the *conversos,* who came to be seen as cheats in religion and faith, swindlers, diabolical wizards, and quacks. Eventually *conversos* came to be called *marranos*—swine who were damned to distinguish them from orthodox Jews and true Christians.

Until this time, three fixed castes had co-existed in a limited physical area through a political arrangement that permitted two faiths to continue their practices within the walls of *aljamas* and *burghettos* within the cities. In general a measure of protection was granted to them by the monarchs and the Christian church in return for the valuable services they rendered to the community at large. Each one of the faiths had a clear genealogy, and each believed that it belonged to a noble and divine order that could be proved by reference to sacred texts. The emergence of a class of people who had *no* legitimate genealogy—the *conversos* and the *marranos*—raised very real questions about their place in the order of things and their relationship one to another. Those who had associated with the *marranos* (and there were few who were not so sexually compromised), and had benefited from the relationship, rushed to protect them; those who wanted them out of the way pressed for their extirpation. The ancient genealogies based upon exegesis from religious texts were becoming factionalized, and the search began for new accounts of descent and generation and for more convenient recipes for the right ordering of human affairs. As Marcu points out:

> The Inquisition was being prepared in the minds of the people for thirty years before the appearance of Torquemada. It is true that by the time the eve of the Inquisition had arrived, almost half the Jews in Spain had been baptised. But these Catholics, writes one conversant with their history, were in a preponderant majority, more closely connected with Jewry than is generally assumed. They submitted to force and were Christians only in appearance, but they lived as Jews and observed the laws and prescriptions of Jewish ritual.[18]

As we have seen, the *conversos* and the *marranos,* and indeed the *moriscos,* as the Muslims in Spain were called, depended for protection on the continued intervention of the Church at Rome and on an uneasy balance of power between the Church and the states in Spain. But, as the power of the Roman Church weakened with the rise of autonomous states, there was an increasing tendency to seek alliances with national churches, and the position of the Jews became more exposed. In Spain during the reign of Ferdinand and Isabella (1474–1504), resentment of interference from Rome brought the Spanish Church into an alliance with the monarch to seek out and destroy heresy in whatever form it appeared. The king appointed Filipp Barberisse, a Sicilian priest, Cardinal Mendoza of Seville, and the queen's father confessor, Thomas Torquemada, to attack sin and assist him in exercising proper control over independent municipalities, factious provinces, *conversos, marranos, moriscos,* and recalcitrant grandees.

Cardinal Mendoza had been charged by Isabella, who was uncertain about proceeding against the *marranos,* to deal with them moderately in accordance with established rules of inquiry and to treat them with propriety. Mendoza ordered the priests to record the number of *marranos* resident in each diocese, ostensibly to determine the extent of the problem set for him by the monarchs.

In fact, this methodical census augmented the badge in marking people who had hitherto escaped identification by their outward profession and espousal of faith and by their willingness (or unwillingness) to live separate lives within the *burghetto* or *aljama*. Those who had left the walled enclosures and had become converts or apostates were now named on an official list, and the way was open for tests to be applied to determine whether they were judged to be heretics. Mendoza's census was accompanied by a breviary for converts in the dioceses. The *marranos*, steeped in a tradition of dispute and argument, attacked the breviary in a series of pamphlets, thereby confirming the suspicions of those most opposed to them that they were Christian in name only and that, secreted like poison within the body of the faithful, they constituted a serious threat not only to the faith but to the health of the body politic.

THE SPANISH INQUISITION

In 1480 the first tribunal of the Inquisition met at Andalusia under the authority of Ferdinand and Isabella with the grand inquisitor, Torquemada, appointed by the king and confirmed by the pope.[19] In earlier times the tribunals had conducted themselves as ecclesiastical courts and had operated more or less in accordance with the Augustinian principle that it was for the Church to decide and advise in matters of faith and for the State to wield the earthly sword of execution. And so the ecclesiastical courts had in the past concerned themselves with heresy and blasphemy and any matter of conduct that went against the true religion. The old Inquisition, despite its record of cruelty, was essentially a *nomocratic* political institution that permitted of a certain measure of dispute about principles and practice, was uncertain in the judgments it handed down, and allowed a final appeal to the highest judicial authority at Rome. The new tribunal was different in two very important respects. First, because of the declining influence of the Papacy, the tempering effects of the bulls of Sixtus VI and Alexander VI were not felt within Spain. The tribunal, although acting as if it were an ecclesiastical court with all the recognizable political practices and procedures and all the ecclesiastical trappings, was in fact a law unto itself, encouraged by the administrative needs of a newly emerging state. Second, a new test based upon the idea of purity of blood (*limpio de sangre*) was introduced into the deliberations of the tribunal, which had the effect of turning the search for heresy within the faith into a search for the defilement of blood wherever it might be found. To this point the king, the bishops, and the nobles in Europe had claimed legitimate descent from a variety of complicated genealogies, all of which were accommodated one way or the other within the Christian belief in a common descent from Adam. But the historical sources upon which these genealogies were based were uncertain, and the tests applied were not exact. The English had competing Trojan, Roman, Celtic, Germanic, and Hebrew myths of origin; the French looked to Troy, to Rome, to the myths of a Gallic or Frankish past. The Spanish myth that noble descent could be traced to those heroes who had resisted the Moorish invader in the eighth century and had managed to keep themselves free from the taint of the blood of the infidel intruders was taken by the tribunal to be the main test of whether a man was a true Castilian or not, and every man was required to prove what could not possibly be proved— the purity of his pedigree on the evidence of blood. The grandees who had taken *conversos* into their families, the Church that had permitted rabbis to join its ranks, the princes who had used the financial and intellectual skills of the Jews and the Moors, and particularly the *marranos* who were clearly identified by Mendoza's head count—all came under suspicion and were "on trial" whether they were summoned or not. The *marranos,* who were quite unable to prove purity of blood, and saw the test as a hurdle impossible to jump, fled to the protection of sympathetic grandees or to Rome. The Inquisition in Seville treated this flight as one more proof that they were in fact apostates, and the nobles who were sheltering them were forced to return them in chains by the thousands as obvious heretics. Their plight worsened when a revolt of *marranos* and Roman Catholics at Seville was betrayed and when appeals for justice on grounds that the Inquisition was unconstitutional fell on deaf ears.

The Inquisition proceeded to nurture the old rumor that the *marranos* were not only apostates but as Jews consumed the blood of Christian children after ritual murder. At the trial of Benito Garcia, a baptized Jew, Torquemada revealed confessions of apostasy and ritual murder that had been obtained by deception when a converted Jew was planted in Garcia's cell. Garcia was said to have been aided and abetted by rabbis and to have admitted to the murder of a Castilian boy. The revelations of guilt were made in serial installments fed by rumor and innuendo, an interesting apolitical technique used to great effect in the nineteenth-century trial of Alfred Dreyfus. During a long-drawn-out trial, Torquemada played upon the fear of ritual child murder to gain maximum impact upon the mob. Garcia was dragged to the court where, instead of meekly submitting to its judgment, he courageously condemned the Inquisition, branded Torquemada as the Antichrist, embraced the traditional Jewish laws, and renounced the Christian faith. In that final defiant act he provided Torquemada with a cast-iron proof that the Jews were universally blasphemous and devious, a murderous threat to Christian people.

THE EXPULSION OF THE JEWS AND MOORS

On January 2, 1492, Granada fell, and the Moors were beaten. Ferdinand and Isabella formally occupied the Alhambra, and almost eight hundred years of Arab occupation effectively came to an end. But even at this late date treaties were made under oath with the Moors giving them privileged status and generous terms, as subjects of the Crown. The oath of capitulation at Granada also referred to Jews as privileged subjects, but Torquemada took exception to these clauses on grounds that they were blasphemous. Ferdinand agreed to banish the Jews, and despite the pleas of his finance minister, himself a Jew, that the Jews had a noble pedigree and a place in the history of Spain, banishment was agreed in a proclamation signed at Alhambra on March 31, 1492. The Jews were given three months to leave. Their property was confiscated or sold for a pittance. They were cast adrift as *peregrinos,* as wandering stateless people, after a millennium of habitation in the Iberian Peninsula. Of the three hundred thousand remaining in Spain, very few submitted to baptism. Pope Alexander VI received some of them into the papal territories of Venice and Naples; some went to Bayonne, Nantes, and Bordeaux; and others went to England, Holland, Belgium, Sweden, and Denmark. About fifty thousand went to Constantinople, where they were permitted to wear a white fez to distinguish them as Jews.

Under the terms of the treaty of 1492, the Moors were given rights of property and conscience and were permitted to live in full enjoyment of religious and civil liberty under Ferdinand and Isabella. But their security was not to last long. In 1499 Francisco Jiménez de Cisneros, archbishop of Toledo, adopted once again the policy of forcible conversion, and the Maimonidean horror that had befallen the Jews came upon the Moors with greater ferocity. A period of terror and mass conversions followed, and the edict for their expulsion from Spain was finally issued on February 12, 1502. During the next eight years more than a million *moriscos,* the majority of whom knew no other place than Spain, were banished from Europe with no respect for their lives. Very few survived to make their way across the Straits of Gibraltar.

» *Conclusion: The Mark of Cain*

The decline and degradation of the Jews and their expulsion from a country they had inhabited for a millennium, together with the decimation of the Moors in Spain, suggest that the events following the Albigensian Massacre and the invasion from the South in 1211 are critical to understanding the idea of race in Western civilization, though sadly neglected in national and racial histories. Resonances of the expulsion and extirpation live on in our time, and not simply in the minds of those who are overtly racist. I have tried to show that Augustine's treatment of the non-Christian confined arguments about genealogy to a religious context and a spiritual lineage. In whatever form man appeared, it was clear that he issued from one protoplasm. Eight centuries later Maimonides, a Jewish scholar of immense intellectual authority, significantly altered the account of Creation by describing the Turks, Indians, and Kushites as remnants of the Sabean worshipers. What follows from this fundamental departure from Augustine and from Greco-Roman principle and practice was exposure of people outside the law of king and church to unprovoked attack. Because their idolatrous ways were seen as a threat to the true faith, their extirpation from the face of the earth could be justified.

Following the terror of the Black Death and the arguments of Duns Scotus for the forcible conversion of children, the logic of Maimonides was used against the Jews, then the Moors, then *all* peoples who did not conform to the artificial tests of identity devised by regimes that had abandoned all pretense of understanding Aristotelian and Ciceronian concepts of a political state. The twenty thousand who perished at Béziers were treated not as *nomoi,* or even as *barbaroi,* but as the faceless, anonymous victims of war. After the massacre the rules governing papal politics were ignored, and the ground was cleared for what Primo Levi calls "the unspoken dogma," which later becomes "the major premiss in a syllogism" that "every stranger is an enemy."[20]

The Fourth Lateran Council's turning away from the art of politics—from speaking, arguing, and reasoning about uncertain ends—and its failure to accommodate within the idea of political community the notion that peoples of different faiths and interests *may* co-exist within a civil association—signaled the end for a time to the disposition to think politically and act with civility. It may be argued that the council ended for all time the idea of citizenship of the kind cherished by the Greeks and Romans and introduced a new era of thinking in which the state or condition of war came to be treated as a normal and natural part of existence, not as the antithesis of the humane political order advocated in the politics of Aristotle, Polybius, Cicero, and Thomas Aquinas. But the council's relevance to the idea of race, which had not yet been clearly articulated, was that it introduced artificial badges and bonnets of identity designed to exclude those who hitherto had been included as *nomoi,* to identify those who were compromised publicly by what they were privately. In place of love of knowledge and human excellence in writing and speech, we find the simple test of purity of blood, devised by converted Jews. Impossible for anyone to meet, it produced the tragic downward cycle of rumor and the serial release of private information for public consumption by a greedy audience of voyeurs who had hitherto been satisfied by confused and inaccurate genealogies. Later I shall show that at the end of the nineteenth century, when race thinking had reached its apogee and the idea of semitism had appeared as a novel concept, these themes reappear in a new guise. They owe their origins more to these arcane and obscure arguments about faith than we have hitherto admitted.

Finally, what we can identify historically is the neglect of argument and counterargument in determining decrees relating to the levying of taxes and the regulation of the affairs of citizens within the three communities embraced by the public arrangement we call state. With the arrival of a quick-fix tribunal acting as judge and executor on these matters, the classical idea of the political state was modified to exclude people from a civil association on the basis of rumor rather than the evidence given before a properly constituted magistracy. The side-stepping of political discourse reduced humanness to a few distinguishing marks, with the application of a test of blood to determine who was of good lineage to satisfy the requirements of an absolutist state. The badge that distinguished people who could not be set apart by their physical appearance in later times became the mark of Cain and then absorbed by logic and association of ideas into the mark of race.

Monsters and the Occult

Augustine had looked with contempt upon the works of Hermes Trismegistus, Pliny, and Aulus Gellius, with their accounts of horrific monsters, arguing, "No matter what unusual appearance he presents in colour, movement, sound, nor how peculiar he is in power, part or quality of his nature, no Christian can doubt that he springs from one protoplast" (15.8). Nevertheless, the fascination with monstrosity continued unabated. John Block Friedman, in *The Monstrous Races in Medieval Art and Thought,* has provided abundant scholarly evidence of this interest from the literature, art, maps, manuscripts, illuminated letters, icons, and theological debate of a wide range of Western writers. Pliny's collection of wondrous stories from Homer, the depiction of Saracens with dog heads, and Jews as grotesque cynocephali, the genealogical narratives of Cain and Ham, and Hippocratian and Aristotelian arguments about heat, cold, and moisture were all ingeniously combined to delight the imagination or to play on fear of the unknown. Isidore of Seville (ca. 560–636), claims Friedman, "made a bold inductive transfer from individual monstrous births to the idea of monstrous races." In literature villains became monsters, like Beowulf's adversary Grendel. Cain's murder of Abel appears in *Piers Plowman* as hatred associated with ugliness, violence with deformity. Not until after the fifteenth century would interest in "the monster" be superseded by the notion of the "noble savage," but, Friedman concludes, "The myths of the monstrous races, though geographically obsolete, were too vital to discard. They provide a ready and familiar way of looking at the native people of the New World."[1]

» *The Secret Texts*

Friedman demonstrates that the fascination with monstrosity led directly to the transition from *gens* to race, but I think there is another way we might proceed without resort to racial or ethnological criteria. In the fourteenth-century debate about the human status of monsters by jurists like Bartolus of Saxoferrato (1314–57) and Baldus de Ubaldis (1319–1400), Guido da Baysio (d. 1313), and the Dominican Thomas of Cantimpré, the answers to the practical problems of monstrosity followed the authorities of canon law and Scholastic theology. In the final analysis the important decision as to whether two things agreeing in form agree in nature, which was central to the dispute, was made in the context of the discourse on religion and faith in Latin, and not in the context of race as the word appeared later in the vernacular European languages. For these reasons I suggest that a more profitable approach to understanding the transition from *gens* to race might be to turn to the secret texts of the Hermetists and Cabalists, which present a more direct challenge to the *via politica* and the disposition to civility that I have traced in earlier chapters. These texts deserve greater attention than they have hitherto enjoyed, the Hermitica because they have an impact upon the writers who influence the developing idea of race from the fourteenth to the seventeenth centuries, and the Cabala because it casts a long shadow over the "scientific" understanding of race from the end of the nineteenth century to our time.

THE HERMETICA

Some two hundred years before Josephus rebuked the Greeks for making false claims about the novelty of their philosophy and preferring the politics of speech-gifted men to the theocracy of Moses, there was much speculation about a set of texts said to have been written by the Egyptian god of wisdom, Thoth. These secret texts may have been written by Egyptian Platonists who were dissatisfied with dogmas and built up an oral philosophic religion based on seeking after God and then recorded their statements as they went along. The texts, the Hermetica, borrow from Platonic and stoic sources, and although they are supposed to reveal secret information from Egyptian sources, there is little Egyptian doctrine.[2] The style is the philosophic discourses; the teacher, called Hermes Trismegistus, is fictitious, and the pupil is, variously, Tat, or Asclepius, or Ammon.

The conversations between Hermes and his pupil are easily recognizable from Plato's *Timaeus* and from the works of Hesiod, Vergil, and Apuleius. They are about the attainment of gnosis, which is the knowledge of God and union with God without the need to conform to an infallible scripture or for any intermediary in the relationship between God and man. The text contains a complicated discussion of *genus,* which is conceptualized as type, and form, in which changing human forms vary as copies of *genus* according to time, place, climatic condition, and astrological influences. In the analysis there is also an attempt to move away from the division of the world into the three parts following the biblical story of Shem, Ham, and Japhet and to reorient the world geographically toward the South and East in the shape and form of man. None of these conversations is racial, but four aspects of the text surface in the literature of the natural and social sciences down to our time.

The Allegory of the Basin puts forward the proposition that man is subject indirectly to powerful Gnostic cosmic forces which pervade the universe through a process of emanation and are most easily observable in the evil manifestations of impure birth and distorted human shape. The affairs of man are watched over by troops of demons who are subject to the sun and the command of the planets and who use pestilence, earthquake, and tempest to punish impiety. At the time of one's birth these demons make their way into the body and enter those irrational parts of the soul that feel desire and repugnance. If God shines forth from the rational parts of the soul, then the demons are defeated; if not, then they hold sway in all that may be observed around us. Politics becomes nothing more than a demonic activity, its utterances a babel, and civic virtue has no value.

The second proposition is that every living being, whatever its kind, whether it be mortal or immortal, rational or irrational, with or without soul, bears the likeness of its kind according to the character of that kind. The human race is taken as an example of something which has a common form, so that individual man can be recognized by his appearance (*aspectus*) as being a man. But for all the sameness of form, men differ from one another according to origin, time, and the cycle of the Zodiac. A physically deformed man, therefore, possesses the group of qualities included under the general concept of "man" but not the qualities of the ideal man. "Thus the type [the generic form *species* is the Latin word] persists unchanged, but generates at successive instants copies of itself as numerous and different as are the movements in the revolution of the sphere of heaven; for the sphere of heaven changes as it revolves, but the type neither changes nor revolves" (Asclepius 3.35.329).

This view challenges the Augustinian view that God alone disposes of cause down to the last member of the nether world, that the production of the fetus is by God alone, without intermediaries, and that all humankind issues from one protoplast. It leaves the way open at a much later historical stage for the introduction of the idea that human beings may be identified according to type within the overall concept of *genus humanorum,* and to the eventual labeling of these types as "races."

Third, discussion of the Zodiac, demons, and comets as visible messengers announcing destined events postulates the notion of a universe populated by human beings who cannot be called rational animals in intellect or body without outside intervention. This notion contradicts everything that Augustine would say about man as a rational creature descended of Adam.

Finally, in Hermes' descriptions of Creation we have an astrological system influenced by sun and moon, Saturn, Zeus, and Mercury conferring spiritual qualities of nobility upon righteous kings, founders of cities, lawgivers, genuine philosophers, and trustworthy prophets according to the geographical position they inhabit to the North, South, East, or West of an earth shaped in the image of a human being lying on his back. The secret engine that drives the universe is the system of the stars "linked to unerring and inevitable fate, by which all things in men's lives, from their birth to their final destruction, shall of necessity be brought into subjection" (Kore Kosmu, Isis to Horus 23.48.485). These images and world divisions reappear in Moses Maimonides and Jean Bodin, but most significant is the role played by cosmic force in the formation of the parts of the body and mind, which becomes increasingly important in the formulation of the idea of race as it emerges from the sixteenth to the twentieth century.

With the Hermetists there is a weakening of the Aristotelian and Ciceronian idea that man is a political animal struggling against the odds to create some kind of civic disposition out of his peculiar and uncertain association as a citizen in a secular political community of diverse human beings. We have entered a world in which cosmic and astrological forces begin to make the running and to challenge Augustine's careful but precarious separation of faith and politics. It is a world in which the efficacy of both ecclesiastical and political agencies begins to be questioned. Dipping into the basin of emanating knowledge is claimed to give better insight into differences in birth, shape, geographical distribution, impurity, *genus,* type, and form than ever could be achieved by the public debate of speech-gifted secular political men.

THE CABALA

If the Hermetists were long on intuition, they were short on method, and it is to the Cabalists that we have to look for the ingenious combination of both. Like the Hermetists, the Cabalists set out to record the oral traditions of people at the end of the classical Greek and Roman period. The *Zohar,* a collection of texts, treatises, extracts, and fragments that purports to record the discourses between Rabbi Simeon ben Yohai and other Jewish exegetes,[3] was probably written during the second century A.D., although some would argue that it was written in its entirety in the thirteenth century, when it was first made generally known by Moses de Leon of Granada. The work is a turning away from ratiocination to intuition as a means of discovering a speculative theology, theosophy, and cosmogony and deserves to be included in any attempt to understand the historical significance of the superstitions behind alchemy, astrology, and magic. It held attractions for Christian scholars, who recognized Christian elements in it and has, Arthur Edward Waite has pointed out, a curious modern ring.[4] Here are clear signs of a new direction in the study of man's physiological and psychological make up that not only circumvent the experiential and essentially anthropomorphic accounts of descent and generation and the right ordering of human affairs of the Greco-Roman political processes but present a universe rooted in numerical symbols that reappear in the anthropological, geographical, topographical, chorographical, and biological descriptions of nineteenth-century race thinkers.

Waite's view is that we should be careful to separate the administrative tradition of the Talmud and the Mishna, the magical tradition of the Hebrews in the ancient texts (that is, the tradition of exegesis practiced by the traditional methods of Hebrew scholarship), from this theoretical Cabala. The term Cabala should be applied only to the subdivisions of the Doctrine of Creation and the Doctrine of the Chariot, which were novel descriptions of Genesis couched in the language of theogony, cosmogony, and physiognomy mainly derived from Plato's *Timaeus* and Aristotle's *On Physiognomy.* By this ingenious means the Cabalists created a mysterious transcendental explanation of the universe, which, because it was expressed in incomprehensible cryptograms, did not directly offend the Talmudic exegetical tradition, Arab science, or Western speculative philosophy. For these reasons I shall begin with the related doctrines central to this arcane text—the Doctrine of Creation and the Doctrine of the Chariot, and the Doctrine of the Countenances.

The Doctrine of Creation and the Doctrine of the Chariot   What distinguishes the Cabalist presentation of the five stories of the Creation from the versions of Josephus, Augustine, and Maimonides is the emphasis on a system of emanation, which introduced the idea that the world was born, and may be explained by those who know, from the greater certainty of numerology and etymology.

The raw materials of this system of emanation, which are the letters of the Hebrew alphabet in reverse order, are described in the prologue to the *Zohar.* When the Holy One was about to make the world, all the letters were embryonic, and they came forward to present themselves individually to Him in reverse order. Each letter was rejected in turn, and He decided eventually to create the world with Beth. (The letter Aleph did not present herself because Beth had already been chosen, and the Lord told Aleph that she would be the expression of unity on which all calculation and operation of the world would be based: A = 1 !)

According to the interpretation of the Cabalists, the first words of Genesis 1, "In the beginning," were revealed in the second letter of the alphabet, B, *Bereshith,* meaning "in the beginning, with wisdom." Apart from allusion, the description of Creation did not follow the authoritative, literal interpretations of Genesis 1–6 familiar to Talmudic scholars and Christian thinkers but proceeded in accordance with the working out of a set of obscurely coded letters to heighten mystery and illusion. For the Cabalist there was an ideal form and likeness of Man revealed in the likenesses of Man, Lion, Ox, and Eagle engraved on a supernal prototype, a Chariot. Man as he appears in the world below possesses some elements of these ideal forms and likenesses, but they are not permanent; supernal beings, in contrast, are formed without any outer covering to be modified.

Creation proceeded from void to form by the arrangement of letters. The story included the seduction of Eve by the Serpent and the birth of the two sons, Cain and Abel, out of the slime of the Serpent. From Cain's side came the evil species—demons, evil spirits, and necromancers. From Abel came a more merciful class, yet not wholly beneficial. "The right kind was not produced until Seth came, who is the first ancestor of all the generations of the righteous, and from whom the world was propagated" (1.36b.137). Cain carried the burden of being a defective, unfinished creature carrying an aspect (*aspectus*) unlike that of any other human being (1.47b–48a). All the invisible ones—the demons, the monsters of the Hermetists—who hover around doing mischief to man, possess the mark of Cain.

The account of the Deluge in the *Zohar* is also much more dramatic and mysterious (Gen. 6–11) than the account in the works of Josephus, Augustine, and Maimonides. Grounded in numerology and etymology, it contains tantalizing allusions to Greco-Roman political concepts, which are not fully developed as they are in Aquinas, Marsilius of Padua, and Machiavelli. The Ark and Noah are taken to be symbols of a supernal pattern. Having seen that life on earth was corrupt, God sent the destroyer (1.60b.196). Noah was warned by God, and he entered the ark as the righteous one with his three sons and their womenfolk. All the animals of the field and the birds went with him, and God blotted out the rest, leaving absolutely nothing. It was from this time forward that the facial impress was changed from the supernal prototype (1.71a) to the imprint of Man, Lion, Ox, and Eagle, and the rainbow was the mystic symbol of the setting of these marks. In the *Zohar*'s account of the resettlement of the earth, the three sons of Noah are named: Shem is symbolic of the right side, Ham of the left side, and Japhet a purple mixture. Ham is the father of Canaan and represents refuse, the dross of gold, and the rousing of unclean spirits by the ancient Serpent. Ham is also the notorious "world darkener" who observed Noah when he was drunk from the wine of his hastily planted vineyard and in his drunkenness was uncovered and lost his mental balance, revealing a breach in the world. Canaan seized the opportunity to steal the mystical symbol of the covenant: "Therefore Noah said, CURSED BE CANAAN, since through him the curse returned to the world. A SLAVE OF SLAVES HE SHALL BE" (1.73b.249) in words that correspond to the curse addressed to the Serpent (Gen. 3.14). The account concludes with a description of the Tower of Babel, the confusion of tongues, and Sodom and Gomorrah.

In my view, these stories detract from accounts of human order that arise from the efforts of men acting politically, teaching independently, and thinking abstractly about a variety of human experiences and relationships. They lead directly into a world in which everything is established by God's will and by the manifestations of His presence, hidden or otherwise, in all phenomena. We shall see how the emergence of an idea of race is inextricably linked to an increasing preference for these profane stories—the legend of Noah, the curse of Ham, the mark of Cain—as literal explanations for the origins and divisions of man. Above all, it is a system rooted in a theory of emanation complemented by physiognomical thinking.

The second book of the *Zohar* concerns the working out of the permanent forms of man as they exist in the letters and numbers with the likenesses of man as they exist in this world—from prototype to type. The assumption is that there is no part of the human body which does not have a counterpart in the world as a whole: "For as man's body consists of members and parts of various ranks all acting and reacting upon each other so as to form one organism, so does the world at large consist of a hierarchy of created things, which when they properly act and react upon each other together form literally one organic body" (2.134a, 134b.36). The seduction of Eve by the Serpent is taken to be the beginning of defilement, accursedness, and death for men in general, and the curse upon Ham and Canaan for particular men. Many evil and magical powers came to interfere, to administer, and eventually to dominate the world: the left end, the outer, "the end of all flesh," symbolizing the defiled; the right end, the inner, the spirit, symbolizing the holy (2.152b.89).

The holding out against the forces of the night who attempt to deflect the righteous from their true course is the subject of Book 3. The story begins with a commentary on the text, "That the Lord (YHWH) had brought Israel out of Egypt," and reflects upon the transition from the name Elohim in previous verses to the name YHWH. Elohim indicates the Shekinah who protected Israel in exile and was always present with them and with Moses; YHWH signifies the supreme emanation that brought the Israelites out of Egypt and is known by the symbol JUBILEE. When it was known that Jethro, one of the Egyptian Pharaoh's three wise men, converted to the worship of the true God of Israel, the whole world gave up idols (3.68a ff.; cf. Exod. 18).

This story prompts a discussion by three rabbis on paganism—what it is and how it can be interpreted in light of the Word. Jethro's coming to Moses in the desert is symbolized as the coming to "the mountain of the Lord" of the sojourners and the proselytes who desire to participate in the mystery of joining a holy supernal sphere: "Yet is he called 'Ger' [proselyte, lit. sojourner], a person living out of his own country, because he has left his own people and kin and taken up his abode in a new place" (3.70a.218). Strangers may join the Jews, but they must give up their strangeness. Josephus' advice holds: that the Jews should not prefer any governmental form other than the one already given to them and that they must not neglect their existing way of divine worship. The key governmental arrangement is not the Greco-Roman state—an arrangement capable of accommodating a variety of citizens whose private lives are distinguishable from the public life of *agora;* it is a governmental arrangement dependent on the will of God, as expressed in a covenant, which will hold fast until the coming of the Lord. The law does not arise from the actions of speech-gifted men acting expediently and politically in contingent circumstances to create a civic disposition; it is a given.

In this analysis of type and prototype, we see the Cabala occupying ground left void between the Greco-Roman political view of the world and Hebrew genealogy that depended on tracing inheritance back to a named one, whose identity was lost in antiquity, and beyond him to a true God of all humankind. The Cabalist system embellishes the five stories of Creation far beyond their biblical origins to explain the defilement of man through the intervention of demons.

The Doctrine of the Countenances   The rabbis create from the book of the generations of man the most ingenious revelation so far encountered of the inner meaning of the features of man—the hair, forehead, eyes, lips, face, lines of the hands, and the ears. By these seven features the different types of man can be recognized and related back to the Creation, the Fall, and the curse upon Canaan and Ham, the "world darkener," who in later versions of the story becomes the African. The shape, size, color, and movement of each visible part of the human body is connected to a series of letters that reveal the hidden secrets of these images. A fine round forehead, for instance, is a sign of great penetration, and the man who possesses it will be cheerful, kind to all, and have a high intellectual interest. He will become very proficient in the Torah, and when he speaks three large wrinkles appear on the forehead, and three smaller ones above each eye. He is straightforward in word and deed, and he cares nothing for anyone. His allies will benefit from association with him and profit in secular matters. The signs show that symbolically he belongs not to the region of justice but to love and mercy, and he should avoid the law because he will be unlucky in it. The rabbis then produce a comparative analysis of large unrounded foreheads, large rounded foreheads, large and uneven foreheads, sharply rising foreheads, together with a bewildering array of mysterious signs by which they may truly be known. A similar analysis is made of color of hair, eyes, size of lips, ears, and the lines of the hand to reveal disposition, nature, temperament, and intelligence.

These aids to recognition put forward the idea that from these mysteries, and from the comprehension of the Torah, the hidden propensities of men may be found. This Doctrine of the Countenances, in other words, holds that there are visible natural signs which may give a clue to what men are really like behind the mask. The features of the face "are moulded by the impress of the inner face which is concealed in the spirit residing within" (3.73b.224). This spirit produces outward traits, which are recognizable to the wise, and the true features are discernible from the spirit. It is important to notice here that the interpretation is not of actual facial characteristics but of outward appearances of the spirit emanating from the soul within; not until the work of Immanuel Kant and Franz Xaver Messerschmidt in the eighteenth century will these individual characteristics reappear in the sciences of craniology, cephalometry, and biometry.

The spirit and soul are discernible through the design of the letters of the alphabet imprinted on the face. There are four designs as they appear in the Doctrine of the Chariot:

Man: He who walks in the way of truth, recognizable by those who know the mysteries of inner wisdom. The design issues forth and becomes the *outer form* of a man (3.74b.226).

Lion: He who turns to the Lord and is able to counter evil. The good spirit may be detected in the veins, nose, movement, and color of the face.

Ox: He who deserts the Torah and follows iniquity. Another spirit takes up the abode of the good spirit and impresses itself upon the outer lineaments.

Eagle: He who perpetually repairs the defects of his past. All signs in the countenance have been lost by this weakness of spirit (3.75a.227–28).

Archetype and Replica   In this system, everything that is below corresponds with what is above. Microcosmic man is the reflection of the spirit expressed in various forms and layers. Archetypal Adam—the idea of man emanating from a source of primeval light—was first portrayed and engraved without the cooperation of the female; a second man, a replica, was taken from the archetypal seed and energy of the first and placed within the female. The text suggests that Cain was produced of the energy of Adam. From the vast countenance, termed the macroprosopus, emanates the lesser countenance, the microprosopus, which possesses bodily shape and form. Defilement is ingeniously shifted to the female side by pointing out that the text does not say "*he* begat" but "*she* bare a son."

The world is likewise ordered by hierarchy. The earth is divided into seven parts, one higher than the other, with the Land of Israel being at the peak and Jerusalem occupying the highest point. The creatures in these seven worlds are all different, some having strange and monstrous appearances. But how do the Cabalists account for the difference if all are descended of the one Adam? They conclude that the highest earth, called Tebel (inhabited world), which is attached to the upper firmament and to the supreme name, is reserved for man; as a consequence man is superior to all other creatures. The lower creatures come from the moisture of the earth, which brings forth various kinds of short-lived crustacea and cortices. In that lower world there also dwell strange races who live as long as other men and whose appearance is due to the nature of the air (4.10a.344).

The Cabala's analysis of type and prototype, of the relationship between microprosopus and macroprosopus, introduces "type thinking" into the study of man. The Doctrine of the Countenances has had a much greater influence upon rational thought than we dare to admit, and it continues to shape modern race thinking. The idea that the prototype is replicated through the intervention of demons in all living things and the notion that the features of an individual man have something fundamental to say about his likely behavior and disposition undermine the value of the political way and the virtue of citizenship. With bodily features as mysterious signs related to the curse on Ham and Canaan, Aristotle's warning that physiognomical criteria should not be given precedence over philosophical and political criteria is dismissed. We enter a world in which the natural relationship between microcosmic and macrocosmic man becomes of prime importance.

» *The Spread of the Occult*

In *The Christian Interpretation of the Cabala in the Renaissance*, Joseph Leon Blau distinguishes between ordinary matters of religion, which are determined daily by people of simple faith without fuss and bother, and those serious religious issues arising from time to time that bring whole systems of authority into doubt and spark interest in new dogmas and new forms of inquiry.[5]

Sometimes orthodoxy is reaffirmed, but sometimes a few people generate idiosyncratic constructs by virtue of their claim to be able to penetrate through to truths not revealed to ordinary folk. In debate surrounding the Cabala, three doctrines received occult emphasis and mystical significance: the transcendence of God, the literal interpretation of the Scriptures, and redemption of mankind through the Messiah. Blau argues that these doctrines emerged in three ways. The first is in a *theory of emanation,* which, as we have seen, is central to Cabalist thought and is shared with the Hermetic writers. The Creation and governance of the world are carried on by intermediaries who are part of creation but whose powers emanate from God. This theory is fundamentally opposed to classical political theory, which is concerned with what is happening to citizens of this world today and with providing legal and constitutional remedies for the conflicts of interest that arise from mortal life in a secular community. The second doctrine relates to the inflexibility of the rules laid down in the Torah, which led to the development of an *exegetical system* of some complexity and permitted the development of techniques that place undue emphasis on an occult theory of Creation in which letters, numbers, signs, and words play a more significant role than the practice of politics in the regulation of human affairs. Finally, the *doctrine of redemption* led to a system of theosophy based on intuitive knowledge of the divine—pantheistic and naturally mystic—that employed scriptural exegesis to reveal doctrines and truths hidden from ordinary political actors.

The two principal exponents of these doctrines were Johann Reuchlin (1455–1522), who was initiated into the Cabala by Giovanni Pico della Mirandola (1463–94), who drew upon Benjamin Recanati's (1290–1350) commentary on the *Zohar,* and Paracelsus (1493–1541), the Swiss physician and alchemist. In Reuchlin's *De verbo mirificio* (1494), a discussion by a Jew, a Christian, and an Epicurean results in the middle, Christian viewpoint being accepted by the disputants. Again in *De arte cabalistica* a Pythagorean, a Muslim, and a Jewish Cabalist engage in a dialogue, with the result that the Jew, Simon of Franfort, who has a reputation among Jews exiled from Spain, expresses his relief at the consolation he finds in the study of incomprehensible numerically based schemes of the Cabala.[6] The text, a collection of treatises from classical, Christian, Arab, and Hebrew sources, is extremely difficult to follow. Although it reached England in 1532, it had been exposed as early as 1509 by one of the most distinguished of the writers on magic in the sixteenth century, Henry Cornelius Agrippa of Nettesheim (1486–1535).

AGRIPPA

In the *De occulta philosophia,* first published in 1533 and translated into English in 1651, Agrippa provided the first methodical description of the Cabalist system.[7] In three books—on natural philosophy, mathematical philosophy, and theology—this work was the starting point in understanding the occult for Latin-reading scholars and of immense authority and repute. Drawing on the *Zohar* as well as the literature of Greece and Rome, and quoting Plato, Pythagoras, Lucius Apuleius, and Hermes Trismegistus, Agrippa attempted to specify the philosophical principles upon which all forms of magic were supposed to proceed. The most important book is the third, which provides a doctrine of angels, demons, souls of men, and correspondences with classical mythology. All created things, high to low, follow a defined order. Before the end of his life Agrippa recorded his opinion that the Cabalistic art was merely "a rhapsody of superstition," its mysteries "wrested from Holy Scriptures," a play with allegory proving nothing.[8] Perhaps we may one day come to think the same about the idea of race?

Natural Philosophy   According to Agrippa, natural philosophy concerns the nature of things that are in the world. Inquiring into causes, effects, times, places, fashions, events, their whole and their parts, natural philosophy is about beasts, man, fire, earth, air, and water. Mathematical philosophy concerns the quantity of natural bodies as extended into three dimensions, so as to conceive of the motion and course of celestial bodies. Theology is what God is—mind and intelligence—and has to do with the virtues of words and figures and the mysteries of the seals. Agrippa advocated a deep study of natural philosophy, in which is found the quality of things and the occult properties of every being, but he warned that without the support of mathematics and theology it is impossible to understand the rationality of magic, which comprehends, unites, and actuates the three faculties.

For Agrippa, the four elements of fire, earth, air, and water are wondrous and have celestial sources. They exist in stones, metals, plants, and animals, and their characteristics are composed together and diffused through everything, including the stars. Some virtues depend immediately upon the elements, such as heating, cooling, moistening, and drying (first qualities); others are compounded of elements, including evaporating, mitigating, burning, and opening (secondary qualities). Together these qualities act upon the limbs and the members to provoke a happening, such as a healing, which is treated as a third quality: "Whosover shall know how to reduce those of one order into those of another, impure into pure, compounded into simple, and shall know how to understand distinctly the nature, virtue and power of them in number, degrees and order, without dividing the substance, he shall easily attain to the knowledge and perfect operation of all Natural things and Celestial secrets" (4.41).

Nevertheless, there are qualities and happenings not explicable in terms of the elements. Their causes lie hidden. Man's intellect cannot reach out to find them. Agrippa went beyond the boundaries of Cabalist thought to select oddities—land-living fish, the digestive system of the ostrich, crickets in the hearth, Noah's ark joined together with bitumen so that it was preserved for a thousand years upon the mountains of Armenia (10.61)—to illustrate his point.

Generally, the elements move to one another: fire to fire, water to water, like to like. But since the soul of the world is diffused through all things and acts as a medium infusing all things, clearly some happenings do not come from the likenesses of elemental relationships but from above. These causes are hidden; they are not open to sense and reason. For instance, when God acts alone, miraculous happenings take place: Joshua and the sun standing still, Daniel in the fire, Christ crucified and resurrected. There are also qualities in the animal world that can be seen in man, and remedies and cures may be passed from one to the other through common, friendly vibrations (magic). Dissimilarities are also passed between bodies, and remedies may be found by seeking out antidotes or opposites. There are also evil influences and enmities between things, and Agrippa invited an investigation of their properties and distribution, how these similarities, differences, and oppositions may be employed.

The Ordering of Things   Two Platonic ideas are important in Agrippa's analysis. First, he explained that all inferior bodies are exemplified by superior ideas; the idea of the thing consists of wholeness or oneness, simple, immutable, pure, indivisible, incorporeal. The nature of all ideas, therefore, is Very Goodness itself (God) by way of cause. Second, ideas in God are but one form, but in the soul of the world they are many. Ideas are placed in the minds of things, joined or separated from the body, and by degrees are distinguished more and more.

Under this Platonic system there is stamped upon each corporeal form an ideal form; nature is infused by small seeds of form, and ideas are the essential cause of every species and every one of its virtues. In Agrippa's account, however, there are between the One and the Many intermediary stars, which give to each species the celestial shape or figure suitable to it and from which proceeds a wonderful "power of operating." Individuals come under a horoscope or celestial constellation and "contract" the essence to receive something that adds to the species. This contracting together of horoscope, celestial constellation, and essence produces something more than that received directly from the species. This contraction accounts for prodigy, which is determined partly by God, partly from the conjunction of the planets, and partly from the "obedientialness" of matter and disposition. Agrippa ingeniously combined the works of Plato, Avicenna, Hermes, and Albertus Magnus to produce his own account of unexplained happenings, such as magnetism, static electricity, the effects of plants on the digestive system, and phosphorescent light. He concluded that the form and virtue of things come from Plato's Ideas; ruling and governing from the Intelligences (Avicenna); disposing from the aspect of the Heavens (Hermes); and answering from the influences of the Heavens and the temper of the elements contained in the specific form of things (Albertus). For a thing to have a specific form, all these combinations have to agree and be consonant with one another.

Agrippa demonstrated how inferior things are subject to superior, and how bodies, actions, and dispositions of men are ascribed to stars and signs according to Hermetic explanations. He accepted that it is difficult to know exactly the relationship between the stars and the signs by color, odor, and effect, but argued that systematic investigation of relationships, conjunctions, similarities, and dissimilarities in plants and animals might help reveal what is presently hidden to the senses and reason: "But he who knows how to compare these divisions of provinces according to the Division of the Stars, with the Ministry of the Ruling Intelligences, and Blessings of the Tribes of Israel, the Lots of the Apostles, and Typical Seals of the Sacred Scripture, shall be able to obtain great and prophetic oracles, concerning every region of things to come" (31.106).

All natural things have seals and characters that distinguish them: bay trees, bones, shoulder blades, wood, sulphur, pitch, oil, mixtures, bees, honey, giants, trees, oysters, stones, horses' tails:

> Forth is the band and continuity of Nature, that all superior virtue doth flow through inferior with a long and continued series, dispersing its rays even to the very last things; and inferiors, through their superiors, come to the very Supreme of all. For so inferiors are successively joined to their superiors, that there proceeds an influence from their head, the First Cause, as a certain string, if one end can be touched the whole doth presently shake, and such a touch doth sound to the other end; and at the motion of an inferior the superior also is moved, the which the other doth answer, as strings in a lute well tuned. (37.120)

Agrippa produced a scheme for good and bad geographical locations relating to the courses of the earth, planets, and stars (47.145). He extended his interest in locations of influence to include the nature of color, which he described as a descent of a store of light into celestial bodies from God, the true light. The Son is overflowing brightness, and the Holy Ghost brings brightness exceeding all Intelligences: "an abundant joy beyond all bounds of reason" (49.146). In dark bodies, light has a certain beneficial and generative virtue, penetrating to the center and beaming forth.

According to Agrippa, man's gestures and countenance are subject to the influences of the heavens. Saturn produces melancholy, Jupiter open honesty, Mars cruelty and anger, the Sun honor and courage. Venus dances and laughs, and Mercury is inconstant, quick, and variable. The Moon is changeable and poisonous.

The heavens also influence color and shape. Saturn is black and yellow, rough skinned with great veins, hairy, has little eyes, frowning forehead, thin beard, great lips, eyes intent on the ground, heavy gait, and is crafty, a witty seducer, and murderous. Jupiter is pale, darkish red, handsome of body, of goodly stature, with large pupils, short nostrils, great teeth, curled hair, and good disposition and manners. Mars has red hair, round face, yellowish eyes, a sharp look, and is jocund, bold, proud, and crafty. The Sun is tawny, yellow-black dashed with red, short of stature, without much hair, has a handsome body, yellow eyes, is wise, faithful, and desires praise. Venus tends toward blackness but also white with a mixture of red, a handsome body, fair and round face, fair hair, fair eyes, good manners, honest love, and is kind, patient, and jocund. Mercury has not much white or black, a long face, high forehead, fair eyes, straight nose, thin beard, long fingers, and is ingenious, a turncoat, subject to many fortunes. The Moon is white mixed with a little red, has fair stature, round face, eyes not fully black, a flowing forehead, and is kind, gentle, and sociable.

Such signs and signatures do not show how one is to act, however. For actions, Agrippa turned to the texts of the astrologers, upon whom the figures of physiognomy, metoposcopy, and the arts of divination depend.

The Theory of Emanation   Agrippa's theory of emanation enabled him to turn away from a theory of citizenship based on complex arguments about the nature of political experience toward an occult theory of Creation containing within it a theosophy like the Hermetists and the Cabalists. This theosophy, which placed great emphasis upon technical interpretation and explained human diversity in terms of numbers, letters, signs, and symbols ordered according to time, place, and appearance, was a tremendously powerful tool in the hands of those who were attempting to unlock the secrets of the universe, and remains so to this day.

Agrippa's exegetical system urged the close examination of phenomena according to the rules of natural philosophy, mathematics, and theology. At the same time, unexplained phenomena and hidden causes were accorded a place in the existing hierarchy of things by reference to the assumed rationality of magic. It is very interesting that the publication of this occult philosophy (at the heart of which is the central Cabalist Doctrine of the Countenance) coincided with the European discovery of Africa and America and with the first common usages of the word "race" in European languages as well as with a description of life as a course, a rush, an onward movement of the heavenly bodies, a fast-running dangerous stream. It is no accident that the legend of Noah, the curse of Ham, the mark of Cain, and the division of the world were used to account for these unfamiliar worlds. Agrippa's work provided a theoretical framework in which northern Europeans could understand the "monstrous," "uncivil" peoples they encountered on their hazardous travels to unknown lands.

In summary, the works of Agrippa provide a Christian setting for the practice of natural magic. Introducing Hermetic and Cabalist thought into natural philosophy, Agrippa challenged the hierarchical ordering of things as expressed by Scholastic writers. He opened the way to understanding man in terms of geographical location, an approach later developed by Jean Bodin, Montesquieu, and the nineteenth-century environmentalists.

PARACELSUS

Blau's suggestion that Agrippa was pivotal to the development of new dogma and forms of inquiry during this period is enhanced by Allen G. Debus's study of Paracelsian science, which examines the search for a new key to nature through the discipline of chemistry.[9] Debus argues that the followers of Paracelsus bridge the gap between ancient and medieval sources in the search for an acceptable Christian interpretation of nature in chemistry. They believed that personal, commonsense observation of the microcosmic and the macrocosmic, with the aid of the divine grace of God, was a better guide to understanding than textual exegesis, thus setting in motion a rejection of past authorities that would make possible the great discoveries of planetary motion by Johannes Kepler, circulation by William Harvey, Robert Boyle's vacuum, and Isaac Newton's laws of motion. But this is no neat progression. Debus focuses on the numerous lesser discoveries by chemical analogy that were introduced to replace the logical truths and maxims of Aristotle and Galen. Alchemy was one way around Scholastic logic and argument, and it led to a refreshing revival of interest in Babylonian and Alexandrine texts, including the Hermetica and the Cabala. It also led to a reexamination of Aristotle's *Metaphysics* and *Politics,* hitherto the foundations of ethics and politics, to an interest in color change and transmutation as guides to understanding the world, and to new methods of practical experiment. In sum, inquiry was directed away from the subtleties of Scholastic science, philosophy, and theology toward an emphasis upon humanity, history, and a new moral philosophy that had something to say about the problems of daily life, education, and navigation, the working out of which are seen in the works of Erasmus, Rabelais, Pico della Mirandola, and others.

Theophrastus Phillipus Aureleous Bombastus von Hohenheim (1493–1541), who gave himself the name Para (above) Celsus (the first-century physician), approached the systematic understanding of nature through the study of medicine and chemistry rather than through a preoccupation with the stars. His *Volumen medicinea paramirum* (1520) encouraged the natural philosopher to learn all there is to know about the firmament and the earth, the relationships between the two, and the astral emanations from the Creator that impress themselves as signatures upon all things. Paracelsus saw the universe as a living natural unit charged through and through with occult forces, and man was a natural part of that life. He actively and provocatively discouraged the reading of the works of Galen and Avicenna, both of whom exercised great influence on the Schoolmen, preferring instead to lecture on the basis of experience, to recommend the study of nature, and to put his faith in the wisdom of magic. His wanderings in England, Ireland, Scotland, Egypt, Jerusalem, and Constantinople developed his interest in alchemy and chemistry, and at Ferrara in 1516 he rejected the view that the stars and planets controlled parts of the body or that the ancient philosophers had much useful to say about medicine. On June 24, 1527, the *monarcha medicorum,* as he called himself, defiantly and symbolically burned the texts of Avicenna and Galen in front of the university at Basel, claiming that they knew nothing of chemistry, which was the key to the understanding of nature.

This new moral philosophy does not stand apart from the way in which men came to see themselves as belonging to "races." Paracelsus shifted the emphasis from natural magic toward chemistry and medicine as the means for discovering new truths. Man was still subject to occult astral forces, but they could be better understood by reference to the analogies drawn from the signs of chemistry and medicine than from biblical sources or the texts of the Greco-Roman world. This new approach raised the significance of color change and anatomical dissection in the analysis of visible instances of monstrosity and incivility and, as we shall later see, led to a fundamental reexamination of the signatures and marks of Cain and Ham and the existing division of the world into three parts.

VESALIUS

Andreas Vesalius (1514–64) provided a similar transition through morphology. Vesalius was born in Brussels and educated in Paris and Louvain, where Arab medicine was popular, graduating in Padua as a doctor of medicine in 1537. His major work, *De humani corporis fabrica libri septem,* was published in 1543, when he was appointed to the household of the Holy Roman emperor. Later he was a physician to Philip II's court at Madrid. Pursuing the interest in human anatomy inspired by Leonardo da Vinci (1452–1518) and Albrecht Dürer (1471–1528), Vesalius concentrated upon the dissection and accurate drawing of the human body, cadavers, and bones. His work was produced by the new printing press, and the illustrations were said to have been prepared in the studio of Titian using wood blocks.

Julian Huxley and A. C. Haddon describe Vesalius as "the first to expound publicly and systematically the structure of man's body as based directly on his own observation and researches," but John Saunders and Charles O'Malley warn against seeing his work as a great leap forward in the development toward an "objective" science. Rather, they see him as still tangled up with the structure of Scholasticism and Gallenist and Hippocratian thought, concerned even at this late date with concepts of plethora, plenitude, and pleroma and the processes and procedures of bleeding as a remedy for illness. Like Paracelsus, Vesalius had been openly critical of Galen and had demonstrated his dissection methods publicly to show that Galen had not used human cadavers but those of dogs, pigs, and monkeys. But Vesalius lacked a clearly formulated scientific method. Yet, whereas Galen had used calendars of bloodletting determined by astronomy and meteorology with reference to Hippocrates and to later astrological works, Vesalius insisted upon repeated dissection and demonstration for the establishment of a hypothesis based on the observation of facts. Only in *Fabrica* (1543) did Vesalius approach modern science in addressing the question whether the method of anatomy could corroborate speculation. By shifting attention from authority to the empirical observation of outcomes, he established a new method of dissection in medicine, which would have great significance in the analysis of corrupt political and religious systems.[10]

» Conclusion: New Divisions

In the Middle Ages the old divisions between political man and barbarian man still pertained. But the Hermetists and Cabalists provided a new Christian focus for a transformed Hebrew genealogy. As the stories of Ham and Canaan—the clanless, hearthless ones—which Augustine had branded as symbols of heresy and profanity, moved to center stage, humankind became divided into "types." According to the Cabalist interpretations, these divisions could be divined in the eyes, nostrils, and skin, prototype to type, from macroprosopus to microprosopus, through the action of demons and intelligences. Agrippa provided the theoretical framework for a new treatment of man. Paracelsus turned attention to chemistry, anatomy, and color change, and Vesalius contributed a materialist's understanding of blood, bones, and the cadaver. Their complex arguments made it possible to contemplate, but not yet to realize, a world comprised of races.

New Methods, New Worlds, and the Search for Origins 6

Between the expulsion of the Jews and Moors from Spain and the landing of the first Negro in the North American colonies in 1619, the word "race" entered Western languages. It originally had a multiplicity of meanings that mostly related to running, mathematical or astrological lines, millstreams, ships' wakes, marks, and courses. The word also denoted being of good, noble, and pure lineage, and in Christian Europe directly related to membership in an ancient and exclusive noble order of kings and bishops and to a particular time sequence (*cursus*) that had its authority (*auctoritas*) and origin (*origino*) in a historical past stretching back to Rome. This order was at the outset resistant to any counterclaim from Trojan, Saxon, Arthurian, Celtic, Gallic, Frankish, Jewish, and Moorish sources, which were regarded as mere legends and fables. The works of Bartolomé de Las Casas, Niccolo Machiavelli, and John Foxe exemplify the old political order that contained and constrained this early idea of race; their influence had to be removed before "race" could assume a specific meaning and develop from pre-idea into idea.

It is unhistorical to perceive the concept of race before the appearance of physical anthropology proper, because the human body, as portrayed up to the time of the Renaissance and Reformation, could not be detached from the ideas of *polis* and *ecclesia*. Membership in both was inextricably bound to political theory and Christian theology, and both implied a specific form of citizenship and civil order that derived its practical and moral values from the thought of the ancient world, Augustine's *De civitate Dei*, and the Scholastics of the Middle Ages rather than from natural history and biological science. The identity of the person (insofar as he had any identity at all—and precious few had!) and his membership of the order of things, was in the first instance essentially "political" and led back to the *Timaeus*, the *Republic*, and particularly to Aristotle's *The Politics*. In the second instance membership was "ecclesiastical" and was determined by participation as willing partners in the Sacrament, which brought membership of the mystical body of the faithful in Christ. These ideas lead back to Augustine's *De civitate Dei*, and the Scholastics of the Middle Ages. In both instances a people (*populus*) was bound together and assumed its identity through law (*nomos*) and faith, and not through biology, secular history, and an autonomous physical or moral order. But after the expulsion of the Jews and the Moors from Spain, and from the time of the voyages of discovery, a wide variety of new reasons was adduced to account for the startling differences Europeans encountered in the fabulous new lands. Above all, what astonished the discoverers and reformers was the contrast between known public ways of governance and what appeared to be the barbarity, brutishness, and viciousness of private existence in realms bereft of all recognizable and legitimate public dimension and showing few familiar signs of civility and letters. The idea of the ancient race was reformulated in the 1560s first by the new historical methodology of Jean Bodin and second by François Hotman's rejection of the old authorities of Greece and Rome as the source of German and Frankish institutions.

Following the Reformation, and particularly after the accession of Elizabeth in England, lay people searching for alternative accounts of generation and the right ordering of mankind found answers not in the antique political theories of Aristotle or in Machiavelli's refurbishment of them but in a confused hodgepodge of hidden causes derived from Hermetic and Cabalist sources. In place of long-standing Catholic authorities, the Protestants substituted vicariously from the works of Luther and Calvin and, as the printing press made the literature of witchcraft, sorcery, and astrology more widely available, a new description of race was infiltrated into the old description from the fraudulent rehashing of the heretic, but extremely attractive, Chaldean version of the story of Noah, the transgression of Ham, and the division of the world.

Still, no fundamental amendment was made to the exclusive idea of a race and order of kings and bishops until Galileo, William Harvey, Francis Bacon, and René Descartes so fundamentally changed the understanding of nature that people questioned royal supremacy in ecclesiastical matters and promoted alternative laws of inheritance for the newly discovered peoples—as well as for the Germanic peoples of Europe. Not until the early years of the seventeenth century did the idea of race begin to take its familiar modern form. Ultimately Richard Verstegan's search for an elect German *gens*, an aboriginal people who had conquered the known world in a dimly remembered past, focused attention upon an "ancient nobility," a race, having its origin in a common German and Saxon source.

» *The Old Political Order*

Americo Castro argues that until the forcible repatriation of the *moriscos* and the expulsion of the Jews, there was no such thing as Spain as we understand it today. What existed was a conglomeration of peoples of different faiths, "none of which could survive without the other two." It was not until one caste—the Christian caste consisting of old Christians and *conversos*—took over the Hebrew notion of purity of blood (*limpio de sangre*)—that the idea of collective life began to yield to the idea that authority now came through blood.[1]

LAS CASAS

If purity of blood, mystical and magical and not yet biological, justified the purity of Christian lineage, then what was the position of the newly discovered peoples of unequal degrees of civilization in the infidel lands of Africa, America, and the East Indies? Both Bartolomé de Las Casas (1474–1566) and Francisco de Vitoria, orthodox Christian thinkers, had to meet the usual arguments that these peoples could be brought to Christ by force because of sin, idolatry, and offenses against the natural law. Numerous bulls issued by the Church from the eleventh century onward declared papal authority over infidel lands "on the authority of the omnipotent God delegated to us through St. Peter and the Vicariate of Jesus Christ which we exercise on earth." The conversion of the Indian was thus as much political as it was spiritual and ecclesiastical. The counterargument of Las Casas and Vitoria was that the Indian was a neighbor in the strict Greco-Roman, Christian political sense. Because he possessed reason, he should not be deprived of political liberty or title to property by force, and he should not be reduced to slavery because he had the potential to become not only a part of the body of the faithful in Christ (*christianitas*) but also a citizen of *res-publica*.

But, on his return from the Indies in 1547, Las Casas was confronted with a different argument—the argument used earlier by Maimonides—that wars against Indians were just because as *people* they were inferior by nature: they were as children to adults, women to men, cruel to mild, monkeys to men. They were without law, property, and civilization; they were Aristotle's *barbaros* by nature and might, on the same grounds as the Jews and the Moors, be forcibly converted or extirpated from the face of the earth.

Las Casas's response to this argument was made at Valladolid on July 8, 1550, when he confronted Gines de Sepulveda, and others who argued that the Indians were thick skulled, lazy, and shiftless before a special group of theologians charged with deciding how a just conquest was to be conducted in accordance with known rules. No record exists of the proceedings, and the judges did not give a verdict, but Las Casas's case, while acknowledging Aristotle's point that some men may be by nature slaves, rejected outright Sepulveda's case that Indians were by nature inferior on grounds it had misinterpreted Aristotelian theory of slavery and nature: "All the people of the world are men. . . . All have understanding and volition, all have the five external senses and the four interior senses, and are moved by the objects of these, take satisfaction in goodness and feel pleasure with happy and delicious things, all regret and abhor evil."[2] Las Casas's work was widely circulated in Spain and used as the main authority in the conquest in South America to check unfettered economic exploitation of the Spanish colonies, to permit the Crown and the Church to retain some minimum jurisdiction over the nature of government and politics, to question just title in law, and, most important, to temper the worst aspects of the doctrine of purity of blood that had so devastated the Jews and Moors.[3]

That is not to say that exploitation, persecution, and slavery did not exist in colonial South America or that they were any less cruel. It simply indicates that although the old authorities were weakening there was no new formulation of race in Spanish, Portuguese, and Italian contexts. The patriarchal feudal system transported across the Atlantic operated without the prejudice, discrimination, and race hatred that marked the colonization of North America.[4]

LORENZETTI AND MACHIAVELLI

Then what prevented the initial development of an idea of race based on blood and anatomy? Between 1337 and 1339 Ambrogio Lorenzetti (died ca. 1348) painted a cycle of frescoes in the Palazzo Pubblico at Siena, ascribing fright-ening consequences to neglect of the art of politics.[5] The fresco symbolizing good government depicts an aged monarch clad in the black and white of the Sienese coat of arms, holding a scepter and shield on which is painted the Madonna. On either side of the throne are seated the civic virtues of Justice, Temperance, Magnanimity, Prudence, the three divisions of time (Praeterium, Presens, and Futurum), Fortitude, and Peace (a magnificent creature holding an olive branch with her foot firmly placed on a helmet and shield, the em-blems of war). Around the head of the monarch flutter the theological virtues of Faith, Hope, and Charity, and around his feet are the legendary founders of Siena, sons of Remus, the link with *origino* and *auctoritas*. Justice sits looking to Wisdom above her, who holds a book and scales. In each plate of the scales is an angel: one crowning a citizen and beheading another, the other pointing a sword and spear at one citizen while pouring coins into the barrel of another. Both symbolize the place of force and law in the state, and both plates are held by Justice and linked by a slender cord to Concord, who sits below Justice, holding a carpenter's plane, the symbol of equality of all citizens before the law. Both cords are attached to the counselors of the republic as they move in procession with the monarch, under the protection of the knights, to pay homage to good government.

On the opposite wall is Lorenzetti's allegory of bad government—a dia-bolical lord with fangs, horns, mail armor, a sword in one hand and a goblet in the other. The lord is surrounded by Cruelty, Perfidy, Fraud, Anger, Discord, and War. Above the countryside fly Tyranny, Avarice, and Vainglory, and Justice lies in chains. The land is devastated, and armed bands plunder, pillage, rape, and murder beneath the gaze of winged Terror.

For this Renaissance master good government is grounded in citizenship, participation, and the state of being well-lawed. We can see the same preoc-cupation in the next century in Niccolo Machiavelli's Florentine triptych, *The Prince*, *The Discourses on the First Ten Books of Titus Livius*, and *The Art of War*.[6] Machiavelli (1469–1527) attempted to work out a new route by reaffirming Aristotelian and Polybian authorities for moral virtue. He did not take up the notion of purity of blood, nor did he seek guidance from the Christian faith or from the arcana of the Hermetists and Cabalists. His portrayal of the new political state was founded upon the revival of the art of politics among citi-zens possessing political *virtu*. Only occasionally did he use biblical sources, and then only to illustrate the good effects of government soundly and flexibly based on good law, good arms, and good education, and the evil effects that flow from unrestrained private acts. The ends judged to be good are those that secure the long-term security and peace of the autonomous political state unfettered by fanatical faith and corrupt religion.

In *The Prince*, the most read and the least understood of his works, especially in Northern Europe, and in *The Art of War*, which has much to say about the conduct of politics as the antithesis of war, Machiavelli diverted attention momentarily from the centerpiece of the Aristotelian form of *The Discourses* and considered those conditions that erode and undermine the state in which political liberty flourishes. Here we are dramatically confronted with the armed despot of Lorenzetti's allegory of bad government, who is required by necessity to operate where there is no *auctor*, no *re-ligio*, no remembrance of the past. In these dire circumstances of corruption and license, also described in detail in Aristotle's tyrannical, oligarchic, and democratic forms, men have forgotten the *auctoritas maiorum*, the trinity is broken, and all Greco-Roman notions of being a people (*populus*) bound by a compact of law have been suspended. In such a corrupted state of affairs, in such times, there is no civic disposition, no citizenship, no politics—only the negative options of abject submission to Fortuna, to natural necessity, or to war. According to Hannah Arendt it was this theoretical model of *The Discourses* that, until the willful demolition of the political elements of Aristotle's *Politics* during the eighteenth and nineteenth centuries, provided the main buttress in Western history against those vicious and barbarian forms of governance that gave rise to the idea of race.[7]

Castro's claim that the old authorities still had a stranglehold over the idea of a co-existent life, and that it hindered the emergence of the idea of purity of blood, is confirmed in the tenacity with which Machiavelli held to the proposition that man should not succumb to Fortune or take for granted the moral and religious virtues of faith, hope, and charity, which, in Lorenzetti's allegory, float over the monarch's head. To secure secular justice, temperance, magnanimity, and prudence, the prince will have to act. The insecure state in a condition of natural necessity will require the artifices that pertain to war; the secure political state will require the artifices of peace and a capacity to adjust flexibly to the times. In both instances—in peace and in war—the military are indispensable. In *The Prince*, the military leader uses all means at his disposal with impunity to combat Fortune. In *The Discourses*, the military leader gives the insignia of war to the citizens, for there can be no proper conduct of political affairs until the corrupt private forces of the mercenary and auxiliary are subordinated to the authority of a public body possessed of *virtu* (3.25). Hence Machiavelli's best polity is that which has authority vested in it publicly and in which power is exercised according to known legal procedures and practices, which provide for public accusation and legal remedy by speech-gifted men. The new art of politics lies in a return to the civic disposition of the ancient republic. In *The Art of War* the interlocutor, Fabrizio, is asked to say what things he would introduce in imitation of the art of the ancients, and he replies: "To honour and reward virtu; not to scorn poverty; to value good order and discipline in their armies; to oblige citizens to love one another, to decline faction, and to prefer the good of the public to any private interest, and other such principles which would be compatible enough with these times" (1.35).

Of course, in the achievement of such a state much will depend on the judicious exercise of Aristotelian choice, particularly in the selection of the militia, who will always pose a threat to the well-being of any state, however well contrived, because of the corruptibility of man. Therefore, the militia must be rooted in a noble citzenry and chosen (*delectus*), like the citizen, from those who have an interest and a stake in the stability and order of the secular state. Random choice from the *demos*—from gentlemen, quacks, mobs, and thieves—is no choice in the sense that Aristotle and Machiavelli use the term. For Machiavelli choice rests upon an understanding of what it means to be a citizen, and it has little to do with the utilitarian principle of counting heads that emerged in the nineteenth century. Choice is the ability of a man of political *virtu* to distinguish between untutored conjecture and intelligent debate about the realities that surround him. It is precisely because of the failure to choose wisely that Rome and its empire had degenerated. It had lost the public character of the political state in a misalliance with the Christian Church and had absorbed the worst aspects of a passive Christian religion, allowing the notion of active citizenship and political liberty to be debilitated by the classical vices of tyranny, avarice, and vainglory. Man forgetting the art of politics forgot the art of war (*Art of War*, 1.1–79).

Absorbed by the idea and ideals of political citizenship and what it means to be a man of *virtu* in a political state, Machiavelli had little time for the notions of purity of blood that were beginning to be taken up in Northern Europe. His observations on the differences in people derive not from ponderous analyses of color, climate, forms of body, and planetary influence but from everday experience: Germans are overorganized, Frenchmen renowned for principle and scholarship, the English not to be relied upon, the Italians poor fighters. Where the essential institutional forms of governance are missing, as in Africa and Asia, there can be no politics and no political *virtu* (2.76–80).

THE RACE AND ORDER OF KINGS

We now know that Machiavelli's overt attempt to return to the ancient structures and values of the Roman Republic and to revive interest in the best examples of genuine political action drawn from the histories of Rome and Greece was immediately under attack (or, more accurately, ripe for plunder) by those who contended that the origins of good government lay in faith, in nature, in economic freedom, and in an entirely different historical methodology. Machiavelli's theory of state bore no resemblance to those states that began to form in Europe during the late sixteenth and early seventeenth centuries. In time a different argument emerged, holding that men are not only independent of ethical, moral, religious, and political rules but that such rules may be formulated more rationally from the laws of nature than from the tenets of the Old Philosophers and the Christian Fathers. With this change came the idea that origins and differences may be explained not by reference to political reality or faith but by reference to structural characteristics— physical and anatomical—and mechanical motions or associations, assumed to be held equally by all, that permit of the division of mankind into empirically observable groupings, ultimately called "races."

But even in those parts of Europe away from the influence of Rome, the old authorities did not yield immediately to this new ordering of things according to nature. James Bryce, in his famous lecture on the Balkan crisis that immediately preceded World War I, warned against assuming that race consciousness had been omnipresent throughout European history. He contended, as we have, that religion had been so entangled with dynastic ambitions of the sovereigns of France, Spain, Austria, and the lesser German states that it curbed the growth of racial feeling. Nearly every "race" was itself divided, and while these inner divisions, too, retarded the growth of racial consciousness, "yet both in the consciousness and the antagonism the racial strain was weak. No nation, hardly even France which had most claim to lead the rest, vaunted its own art or letters to the disparagement of others: each was willing, and very wisely, to learn what it could from without."[8]

But Julian S. Huxley and A. C. Haddon put forward a contrary view, suggesting that John Foxe's *Acts and Monuments*, published in 1570, was the starting point for race as denoting the descendants of a single person or couple, and hence the beginnings of a conscious feeling of race in England and Western Europe. In this text Foxe (1516–87) aimed to set forth at large "the whole *Race* and Course of the Church from the primitive age to these latter times of ours."[9] To dissociate his work from the contemporaneous practice of writing fables about the past, he explained that his book would be methodical, certain in proof, well qualified in style and expression, and rich in variety. Above all, it would be based on records. Using tables to describe the seven kingdoms of the Saxons, Foxe stated that Ofricus Deirorum and Eaufridus Bernicia "are put out of the *race of Kings* because they revolted from the Christian faith" (1.122). His long description of the history of these often "unchristian and infidel" kingdoms concludes: "And thus standeth the *order and race* of the Saxon Kings reigning together with the Britains in this Realm" (1.124). Thus, although Foxe used the word "race," it denoted membership of kings and bishops in an order and course of things, a category not open to everyone and not evidence of a biological coupling. In Foxe's perception of the past, history is a chronology of events, a catalogue of instances in which those noted for Christian action appear. Kings and bishops may be put out of the race for unchristian action, either in their dealings with Realm (a political body) or Church (an ecclesiastical body). Foxe's notion of race is not the starting point for the modern idea.

» *A New Historical Methodology*

If Las Casas, Lorenzetti, Machiavelli, and Foxe did not provide new thought patterns to connect a conception of a noble and ecclesiastical society with notions of purity of blood and race, then where is the bridge from the one to the other? I do not think there is one single architect or designer for the idea of race that eventually emerged in the eighteenth century. Rather, the bridge seems to have been constructed from flimsy materials by a disconnected series of thinkers bent on developing a variety of whimsical and speculative projects.

BODIN

One of these thinkers was undoubtedly Jean Bodin, whose massive *Method for the Easy Comprehension of History* (1565) provided a rambling, inconsistent, and partial account of generation and right order that turned away from Machia-velli's emphasis upon citizenship and institutional forms of rule and radically altered the symbols of the political and the ecclesiastical, establishing an en-tirely new basis for the appraisal of divine, natural, and human legislation.[10]

Jean Bodin (1530–96) was Angevin by birth and received a legal education at the University of Toulouse. He wrote his treatise in 1565, and thirteen Latin editions followed from 1566 to 1650. In seeking a method that would disen-tangle the interpretation of divine history from the encumbrances of Roman law and authority, Bodin took the first step in secularizing divine history and heralded the beginnings of a "natural" history of the peoples who actually exist on this earth in a present time.

In the dedication to Jean Tessier, president of the Court of Inquests, Bodin set out his intention to trace the main types and divisions of the universal law, down to the lowest, and to lay down postulates, rules, and lists of interpre-tation. Bodin laid out the corpus of the law for forensic analysis according to the rules of the Paracelsian anatomists: law was no longer about the rote learning and pedantry of the grammarians, the philosophers, and theologians; it was to do with the collection and collation of legislation acquired from a variety of civil and military disciplines and geographical sources. The laws of the Greeks, Persians, Egyptians, Romans, and Hebrews were to be placed on the anatomist's slab, dissected into their essential parts, and divided according to type.

Method for the Easy Comprehension of History did not assume that history was only for the tutored or that the interpretations of the origins of man given by the biblical exegetes and classical writers were not open to question. Bodin gave divine history entirely to the theologians, and natural history to the philosophers; he would focus on the history of man. Like Machiavelli, Bodin was interested in "a new route" to the discovery of rules governing human action in the history of man and his laws. But, unlike Machiavelli, Bodin's route did not lead back to a reformation of politics, citizenship, and law based on the classical ecclesiastical and political sources. Instead it looked to a his-tory of mankind divided up into peoples and dispositions arranged according to astrological and astronomical influences, climate, language, geographical location, and ordered by means of the historical phases and sequences of legal formularies, later to be termed "races" in the works of Montesquieu.

Bodin argued that the interpretation of characteristics of human beings can best be drawn from the enduring character of nature rather than from the institutional forms of man, which vary from time to time and place to place and are, as a consequence, unreliable. He took the propositions made in the crude divisions of Hippocrates and Strabo that northerners were different from southerners and explored further those traits and innate natures visible in both. To do this, he had to place the whole of the universe in a modern setting, breaking with the familiar biblical and Hamitic account of origins (without forsaking entirely the tripartite division) and abandoning the traditional analysis of *polis* and *res-publica* into monarchy, aristocracy, and mixed polity and their private, vicious opposites. Bodin proposed a schematic grouping of the world into Scythian, German, African, and "Middler" divided according to the form of the body and distinguished by color. A further division into Mediterranean, Baltic, and Middler retained the tripartite structure and invested it with characteristics distinguishable by the senses: voice, eye color, and body form. Thus the blackness of the African and the whiteness of the Scythian, the old division between man and brute, was no longer wholly dependent on ancient classical sources but more upon the patient forensic analysis of habits of mind and body and upon the visible effects of reproduction and migration. While introducing geographical and astronomical dimensions to his study, Bodin still relied heavily upon the slender evidence of Tacitus for the qualities of the Germans, and upon empirical analysis of "types" of men subject to the influences of an inborn nature, the planets, and blood. These sources made it difficult for him in every instance to square the form of the body with existing forms of governance. The position of the Britains, Irish, Danes, Gotlanders, Upper and Lower Germans, and Scythians was clear enough: they now occupied the propitious epicenter of politics that had once been the preserve of the Greeks and the Romans. But that left the French, northern Spanish, some Italians, Swedes, Franks, and Norwegians living in latitudes that did not properly fit the new geographical pattern. Moreover, Bodin's hostility toward the classical writers served only to embellish the old stories with new traits neglected by the ancients without providing a consistent explanation to replace the humoral theory of the generation of heat. As laid down in the teachings of Cabalist sources, the peoples at the extremities of *res-publica* and their laws could now be known by the position they occupied geographically according to three stages in history presided over by Saturn, Jove, and Jupiter. Still, there is some ambivalence in Bodin's tests of the physical form and origins of the peoples. Much depends on language, the situation and character of the region, the reliability of the writer, and the degree of mixture that has taken place since the Deluge, and only the Jews can boast of having such an antiquity.

So, what relevance does this confused and inconsistent source have to the elusive pre-idea of race? As we have seen, Bodin used cosmography, rather than divine sources, biblical stories, classical texts, or Scholastic maxims, for understanding past and present. He emphasized sense impression—touch, taste, sense, smell, and association—in attempting to discover a new route to the rules governing human actions. He extended his historical interests beyond the Greco-Roman and Hebrew origins to include the Chaldeans, Africans, Germans, and Gauls. His analysis embraced a wide variety of types of men, who do not share in a common humanity by political means but who are what they are by virtue of an innate nature under the influences of the stars. He was much influenced by the secret texts of the Cabalists. All these shifts resulted in the first carefully worked out, diagrammatic division of mankind based upon natural divisions, driven not by ecclesiastical and political principles and practices but by the influences of geography, climate, language, the planets, and accompanied by an invocation to the mystical qualities of the blood.

Bodin's new divisions of mankind became powerful vehicles for the transmission of superstitious generalizations to the scientific classifiers of the eighteenth century. His division of historical time into stages permitted his important conclusion that in the history of the world the North was at the beginning of its ascendancy.

HOTMAN

However much Bodin's rambling discourse may have excited interest in fascinating stories of origins rooted in blood, language, and planetary influence, he, like Machiavelli, had failed to account for the beginnings, growth, and decline of states in an analysis of legislation. Instead François Hotman (1524–90) was the first to use legislation as a means for examining the "true" origins of existing peoples, thus opening a path for the more detailed study of his immediate successors Verstegan and Montesquieu.[11]

In the preface to *Franco Gallia*, which was dedicated to Lord Frederick, count Palatine of the Rhine, duke of Bavaria, and first elector of the Holy Roman Empire, Hotman reflected upon the "monstrous doctrine of indifference, attributed to the Epicureans and Cynics" that permitted the renunciation of inborn love of country (*innata patriae*) for the sake of present usefulness.[12] Hotman praised Homer's love of native soil (*natale solum*) and the sentiments that attach themselves to birthplace—to the soil, to friends and neighbors, and to contemporaries. But sometimes tyrants bring savagery to citizens. The question was then whether the good citizen was justified in giving up care and affection for country on account of his country's neglect of him. Hotman answered that the citizen must not desert the country in its hour of need but should stay and seek remedies. Hotman praised Lord Frederick for the peace he had brought to the Palatinate during the past sixteen years, and, turning to the old Frankish and Germanic historians, he contended that the country (*nostra Republica*) had flourished for a thousand years and would "return to health when it is restored by some act of divine beneficence into its ancient and, so to speak, its natural state" (preface, p. 143).

Hotman made several important points. His first task was to provide an adequate grounding for his country's constitution in Roman and Greek sources while at the same time acknowledging the significance of a Gallic past. He contended that when the Romans reduced Gaul to servitude under the burden of taxes, garrisons, and tributes, they had represented tyranny rather than political liberty.

The immediate question of the renaming of Gaul—to France, Franciam, or Franco-Gallia—was important to Hotman, and he devoted considerable effort to exploring all historical authorities that had attested to the name "Frank." Rejecting the fablers, Hotman suggested that the name derived from a particular event or occasion (*ex re et occasione*): "It was when those who declared themselves foremost in the recovery of liberty [*liberos*] called themselves Franks, by which they were understood among the Germans to mean free men, exempt from servitude" (5.201). He rejected claims that Charlemagne had enacted a hereditary kingship for the Franks, drawing on numerous examples from history to assert that before Charlemagne the kingdom of Franco-Gallia was not hereditary, "but was transferred by the choice of the people" (7.245).

Thus "Frank" came to be used in popular speech to mean *pro libero et immuni* (free and immune), and from it the noun "franchise," a sanctuary, and the verb "enfranchise," to set at liberty. Citing Johannes Aventinus, who found legal authority derived from the Teutonic words for liberty, *freyghait* and *freyghun*, Hotman emphasized the notion of being of free and noble birth, not submitting to any form of servitude (5.203), and also referred to "Frank" as derived from a play on the word "ferocity," the characteristic of those who refused to pay tribute to the emperor. Hotman used Tacitus as authority for the description of the Franks as *libertatis auctores*. Associating the name with the throwing off of tyrants and kings, Hotman argued that Frankish kings were elected by consent as guardians of liberty (6.221) and that it was the Franks who freed the Gauls from Roman tyranny. The Franks intermingled with the Gauls (*commixti*)—translated as the "assimilation of two races," but Hotman himself said, "Now that our community has been formed from the two nations of Gauls and Franks, they were altogether united in spirit" (*unaque iam e duabus Gallorum et Francorum gentibus civitate facta, universi coniunctis animis*) (5.217n).

Hotman linked the grounding of the constitution and the origin of the Frankish name with a novel formulation of the laws of inheritance, again based on antique political authorities but having relevance to his Franco-Gallian argument. He reaffirmed that inheritance was habitually transferred by votes and decisions of the estates and peoples assembled in a council of the kingdom—the council of gentis. The patrimonial estates of the king belonged to the king himself, whereas the ownership of the domain of the king remained with the people, and no part of it could be alienated by the king without resort to popular authority. In a complex argument based on the assumption that until the time of Charlemagne there were two branches of Franks—the Franks in Gaul and the Salic Franks beyond the Rhine near the river Sala— and that Salic law was distinct from public law based on custom and practice, Hotman concluded that the Franks acquired the form of their constitution not from the Gauls but from the German peoples and the form was free: the election and removal of a monarch did not involve compulsion, did not depend on escorts or mercenaries brought in from outside, and was not judged by the comfort and will of the one who occupied the throne but by the ease and desire of the republic. Upon four foundations, then—the constitution, the Frankish name, the laws of inheritance, and the two divisions of Salic and Frankish law—Hotman constructed a model with the symmetry of the Ciceronian republic. Its emphasis was upon constitutional custom and the discovery, not of new lands and new methods, but of an ancient constitution grounded in immemorial custom.

While it is difficult to discover any relevance to the idea of race in either Bodin or Hotman, and on the face of it the two seem to have little in common, Bodin's powerful suggestion that knowing the innate nature of man is important for the understanding of the current ascendancy of the North made it necessary to justify the origins of the peoples who inhabit these lands out-side of Roman law. This is what Hotman accomplished. The significance of Hotman's work is that it turned attention to the inhabitants of the North and fixed the origin of their ancient constitution, as well as the first beginnings of the German and French *gentis* (as opposed to "race"), not in 754 B.C. in the original conflict between the patricians and the plebeians, but in the fifth century A.D. For Hotman, the past could be known, understood, and proven through a search for origins in language and names and the diligent study of laws of inheritance. Bodin and Hotman represent the historical remnants of nonracial arguments concerning law and religion. Not for one moment could they have imagined how important their works would be in the development of something as alien and dynamic as the idea of race.

» *Renaissance England and the Voyages of Discovery*

In considering the works of the ancients, I have argued that the old sheet anchors of political and philosophical discourse held in the face of the Hermetic and Cabalist storm and that no coherent hypothesis of "race"—other than that of an exclusive race of kings and bishops—emerged until late in Western civilization. In the nineteenth century, however, the period of ecclesiastical and political reform that we shall now come to consider was seen as providing the main economic and spiritual determinants of modern race prejudice. Race was seen as the direct outcome of changes in the mode of production and distribution as applied to the market manipulation of people as things, or the onward march of the barbarian Franks and Gauls in Western civilization acting out in Nation and Race the reformed and purified spirituality of a new northern Christianity. It followed that modern race consciousness and ethnocentricity were accelerations of forces that had been there from time immemorial.

But Bryce's contention that race consciousness was neither an antique phenomenon, nor directly attributable to the sea changes that were taking place in the Renaissance and Reformation, should at least raise a modicum of doubt. Quentin Skinner has shown in his remarkable panoramic overview of the period the immense complexities and confusions of the conflict between faith and reason, religion and politics. Christopher Morris describes the Elizabethan phase as "a cluttered lumber room" and explains, "Where the Catholic philosopher looked for the laws by which God made things work, the Protestant looked for miracles and arbitrary acts cutting across all known and knowable laws." Felix Raab contends that in England "the game of power politics was on" with little or no understanding of the principles and precepts of political theory and that when theoretical justification was required, Englishmen turned to theological or astrological sources couched in terms of "Christian society." The realities of Machiavelli's political life were "glimpsed but not revealed." Louis B. Wright describes the Elizabethan era as a time when the homily, table talk, drama, handbooks, chronologies, sermons, entertaining genealogies, astrology, and alchemy were considered much more reliable guides to the ethical and moral laws of life than philosophical and political theory. Still, education was believed to be "an instrument of salvation (religious, economic and social) which would teach the way of life leading to business prosperity, social advancement, and an eventual seat at the right hand of God with Abraham and Isaac."[13]

STEREOTYPES AND SHAKESPEARE

Before we consider the literature of Elizabethan England, it is worth reminding ourselves that the noun "stereotype" is derived from mass production print processes and, significantly, depends for its efficiency upon an object called a "cliché"—a connection the inventor of modern race relations must have understood in abandoning history and philosophy for a journalistic approach to "the problem" of race. The essential characteristic of a stereotype is that it is a stock mental picture, and although some branches of history may justify its use, in intellectual history it is the stereotype itself that continues to hold us in thrall to the idea of race.

Our most prevalent stereotype of Elizabethan England is that which adduces a virulent "ethnocentricity" from the evidence of William Shakespeare's Othello, Shylock, and Caliban.[14] But in Shakespeare (1564–1616) there are far too many complex ironies, contradictions, disjunctive parallels, and antitheses to make crude racial type casting academically possible. At every twist and turn in his works we are confronted with the enduring good of the antique state, with its deep understanding of justice, virtue, civility, and Christian order—all ranged against the unrestrained forces of an alien and barbaric new world. Thus, when we appear to see in Shakespeare manifestations of racial prejudice, are we perceiving through a preconception, "a ritual mechanical action," as Ludwig Fleck calls it,[15] or an acting back into a past of ideas originating in later times? Our villain-guide Iago tells us that love is "merely a lust of the blood and a permission of the will" and that the marriage of Othello and Desdemona is "a frail vow betwixt an erring barbarian [*sic*] and a supersubtle Venetian" (*Othello* 1.3). Iago's "Put money in thy purse" speech to Roderigo is often cited as one of the best examples of human prejudice in the English language, as are Prospero's references to Caliban in *The Tempest* (1.2) and Shylock's "Hath not a Jew eyes?" speech in *The Merchant of Venice* (3.1). Yet these are quick-fix interpretations that ignore the complex human relationships of Shakespeare's characters and the tension in his works between civility and savagery, between political order and barbaric chaos. Is Iago to be believed, the man who tosses away virtue as "a fig!'tis in ourselves that we are thus, or thus" (1.3)? With this brief and provocative digression, we come appropriately to a third important description of hidden causes that infiltrated itself into Foxe's account of the ancient race and order of kings and bishops and eventually added flavor to Bodin's innovative methodology.

HOLINSHED

From 1570 until the end of the century, the fabulous and mythological accounts of generation and settlement that Foxe had painstakingly tried to avoid were given great impetus by the *Chronicles of England, Scotland, and Ireland, called Holinshed's.*[16] Raphael Holinshed (died ca. 1580), a Cambridge historian, continued Reginald Wolfe's project to prepare a Protestant universal geography and history based on accounts available in English. First published in 1578, it appeared in a more comprehensive edition in 1587, following Holinshed's death. Shakespeare used the second edition as a sourcebook for his works, as did many later popular historians.

Holinshed rejected Catholic records and sources, including Augustine, turning instead to an anthology of the missing volumes of Berossus of Babylon, Metasthenes the Persian, Archilochus, and Q. Fabius Pictor published in 1498 by Annius of Viterbo (1432–1502), which gave popular credence to an alternative "historical" genealogy and helped to undermine the traditional version of the settlement of the earth. Although Annius was soon revealed to be a forger,[17] his work remained an inspiration and a fertile source for an alternative inquiry into the origins of mankind. Here the diverse usages of the word "race" began to take on a specific meaning and become applicable not simply to kings and bishops but to other noble and professional men.

Holinshed's imaginative account of the first beginnings of Britain cited the Samothes and the giant Albion who "repaired hither with a companie of his owne *race* proceeding from Cham [Ham], and not onelie annexed the same to his owne dominion, but brought all such in like sort as he found here of the line of Japhet, into miserable seruitude and most extreame thraldome" (1.4.9). In his first edition the Britons appear as a confused ragbag of peoples of mixed blood coming out of Spain, Ireland, Gaul, and Belgium and subject to successive Samothean, Trojan, Roman, Saxon, Danish, and Norman conquests. The Scots, a mixed people of Scythian and Spanish blood, came out of Ireland, and, although long settled, they were reputed to be most "Scithian-like and barbarous" and "longest without letters" (1.4.13–14).

In the second edition the story of settlement and genealogy was greatly expanded with even more fabulous and unreliable material, again liberally drawn from Annius on Berossus and again recounting the story of the giant Albion who landed in Britain and subdued the Samotheans: "And so . . . this Iland was first called by the name of Albion hauing at one time both the name and inhabitants changed from the line of Iaphet unto the accursed *race of Cham*" (1.1.3). Cham was a sorcerer and a monstrous giant, Holinshed continued, and this "*race* of giants" was derived from Henoch, son of Cain, "of whom that pestilent *race* descended" (1.5.16). This is "a *race* of those men" who taught witchcraft, sorcery, and buggery "as branches from odius and abbominable root, or streames derived from a most filthie and horrible stinking puddle" (1.9.37), "although their posterities are now consumed, and their monstrous *races* utterlie worne out of knowledge" (1.5.15). The line of the accursed Ham was finally destroyed by Brutus, leader of the Trojan remnant who, after pagan sacrifice and a prophetic dream, left Greece for a vision of a land beyond Gaul where giants dwell, "for there thou shalt find out An everduring seat, and Troie shall rise anew, Unto thy *race*, of whom shall kings be borne no dout, That with their mightie power the world shall whole subdew" (1.2.440). This entertaining account of Brutus' annihilation of the line of Cham was accompanied by a recapitulation of the genealogies from Ethelwulfe (6.10.63) back to Shem and Adam and by a rehearsal of the Spanish, Italian, Saxon, French, and German genealogies out of Hesperus, Aeneas, Woden, Thrace, and Giveston.

HAKLUYT

In 1589, two years after the publication of the second edition of the *Chronicles*, Richard Hakluyt (ca. 1552–1616) in his *Principal Navigations, Voyages, Traffiques, and Discoveries of the English Nation* more carefully observed Foxe's principle that history should rely not on descriptions of marvelous and fabulous origins but on authenticated records, acts, and monuments.[18] Hakluyt's test of legitimacy and title to rule followed the familiar idea of a well-ordered civic arrangement acting publicly to combat the private excesses of barbarousness, brutishness, and incivility. For the most part Hakluyt's legitimate genealogy is maintained if the civil order and course of things are drawn from authoritative historical records prepared by those in the service of kings and bishops. What sets people apart—"without"—is that, "like the wild Irish," they do not belong to a realm (*regna*) and, like the Lapps and Finns, "they neither know God nor yet good order" and "all studies and letters of humanitie they refuse" (2.266).

Hakluyt's judgments of what constituted good government would not have been unfamiliar to Vitoria, Las Casas, or Machiavelli. He reprinted early instructions given to John Cabot, which set out a right order for the proper conduct of a public enterprise of discovery (2.197–200). They prohibited the imposition of religion, laws, and rites upon the newly discovered peoples, who must be treated carefully, "so as to induce their barbarous natures to a liking and mutuall societie with us" (8.99), and with a view of learning about their natures and dispositions. This common recognition of the principles and procedures of what was thought to be the mark of good government characterized the reports in Hakluyt of Richard Cheinie's voyages passing through Russia to Persia from 1563 to 1565; Laurence Chapman's venture in Persia in 1568; Angrimus Jonas's powerful correction of the scurrilous reports brought back from Iceland by the German cosmographers Gamma Frisius, Sebastian Munster, and Albert Krantz (1448–1517); Sir George Peckham's account of Sir Humphrey Gilbert's visit to Newfoundland in 1583; and Walter Raleigh's account of the discovery of Guiana in 1595, which pleaded with the queen not to leave these territories to the "spoile and sackage of common persons" (10.342). But as the enterprises encountered difficulties, including ambush, betrayal, and ransom, allusions to witchcraft, sorcery, and humoral disposition increased. And while in the early accounts captains conceded that drunkenness, idolatry, lust, and gambling were as commonplace among their own men as among the people they encountered, after Sir Martin Frobisher's voyages, their comments were less cautious: "What knowledge they have of God, or what Idoll they adore, we have no perfect intelligence, I thinke them rather Anthropophagi, or devourers of man's flesh than otherwize" (7.227).

This most striking departure from the early, ordered public framework is contained in George Best's *True Discourse of the Three Voyages of Discoverie, for the Finding of a Passage to Cathaya, by the Northwest*, which was originally published in 1578 and is included in Hakluyt's compilation. In this account Best, who accompanied Frobisher in 1576, 1577, and 1578, sought to prove by experience and reason that natural causes accounted for the fundamental differences in men (7.261–65). Following comparative study of the peoples occupying the regions of the world, Best concluded that the Hippocratian hypothesis that people are black because of the parching heat of the sun, or because of their geographical position, was wrong. He cited abundant examples of different peoples living in similar latitudes with entirely different physical characteristics:

> I my selfe have seene an Ethiopian as blacke as a cole brought unto England, who taking a faire English wife, begat a sonne in all respects as blacke as the father was, although England was his native country, and an English woman his mother; whereby it seemeth this blacknes proceedeth rather of some natural infection of that man, which was so strong, that neither the nature of the Clime, neither the good complexion of the mother concurring, could any thing alter, and therefore, we cannot impute it to the nature of the Clime.

Blackness, Best concluded, must be due to some other hidden cause, which he identified as a natural infection that proceeds by lineal descent: "and so all the progenie of them descended, are still polluted with the same blot of infection." This infection does not proceed from a biological cause but from Berossus' account:

> It manifestly and plainely appeareth by holy Scripture, that after the generall inundation and the overflowing of the earth, there remained no moe men alive but Noe and his three sonees, SEM, CHAM, and JAPHET, who onely were left to possesse and inhabite the whole face of the earth: therefore all the sundry discents that until this present day have inhabited the whole earth, must neede come of the off-spring either of Sem, Cham, or Japhet, as the onely sonnes of Noe, who *all three being white*, and their wives also, by course of nature should have begotten and brought forth white children.

Best explained that the Devil caused Ham to transgress the laws of inheritance and to indulge in carnal copulation. Thus his sons were marked with a black badge to symbolize loathsomeness and banished to the cursed and degenerate voids of Africa, where they lived as idolators, witches, drunkards, sodomites, and enchanters.

From the time of Best, the African appeared in literature as someone outside the reach of classical Aristotelian politics. He was marked, not with an artificial badge and hideous raiment like the Jew, but with a natural badge of pigmentation understood to be caused by a natural infection brought about by an unnatural act encouraged by an evil spirit.[19]

WITCHCRAFT, ASTROLOGY, AND THE HUMORS

Best's fable received strong support from a variety of different sources on witchcraft, astrology, and the humors. Perhaps the most entertaining of them was Reginald Scot, a writer well versed in the works of Bodin and Cornelius Agrippa, who in *The Discoverie of Witchcraft* (1584) set out, tongue in cheek, to put down Bodin, the champion of witches, as well as Jakob Sprenger and Heinrich Kramer, the compilers of *Malleus maleficarum* or *Hexenhammer*, the standard textbook on witchcraft in Germany.[20] Scot's inquiry was conducted with wit and compassion for the fate of the wrongly accused. It drew upon Hermes Trismegistus, the Platonists, John Calvin's confutation of Dionysius in the *Institutes*, the Cabalists, Talmudists, and the Schoolmen to show that the power and glory of God will prevail over witchcraft. Nevertheless, Scot accepted the existence of spirits and devils, and used Paracelsus as an authority on the Huns, who were, he said, begotten of a liaison between the Incubi and a group of witches banished into the desert by the king of the Goths. From this unhealthy union—for the Incubi suffered a "natural" disease of the blood—arose a savage and untamed nation, who spoke a language more like that of the devilish, brutish beasts than articulate, cultivated men. Yet Scot did not always seek explanations in mysteries and superstition; he also appealed to simple reason:

> We read also of a woman that brought foorth a young blacke Moore, by means of an old blacke Moore who was in hir house at the time of her conception, who she held in phantasie, as is supposed: Howbeit, a gelous husband will not be satisfied with such phantasticall imaginations. For in truth a blacke Moore never faileth to beget blacke children, ow what colour soever the other be: Et sic e contra. (*Discoverie of Witchcraft*, 13.16)

Timothy Bright in his *Treatise of Melancholy* (1586) examined the relationship between the humors and the blood more thoroughly.[21] He probed the influences of weather, region, and "mind disposing of mind" upon different peoples living in different places. He believed that "choler, fleume, bloud and melancholy"—the inward sources of hastiness, sadness, dullness, and cheerfulness—were affected by weather, location, and mind and themselves influenced the nutritive juices that produce healthy and unhealthy dispositions, causing people to act in particular ways. Butchers, for example, are intimately acquainted with slaughter and have a disposition to cruelty; ploughman have a low calling and are not renowned for their devastating wit; Asians are mild, gentle, and unfit for war because of the constant air in that region; Europeans are naturally tough, hard, and stern because of their greater exposure to the elements.

These obscure works chosen from an endless list of Elizabethan writers are for the time being sufficient to show the great importance being attached to the humors, the external influences upon the inward senses, and the simple and compound dispositions that come about when one works upon the other under the shadow of witchcraft and sorcery. The tensions among "hidden causes," natural philosophy, and ancient nobility were to play an important part in loosening the ties of an exclusive and ancient royal race.

» *Nobility and Race, Logic and Reason*

The sticking point for the conversion of an exclusive idea of race into an inclusive one was the old Roman Catholic interpretation of what was "natural." The traditional account of generation was founded on a first beginning at Rome and a stream of authority that flowed naturally through Church and State. Protestants no longer had such recognizable, legitimate, and acceptable symbols to guide them. The English adventurers explored a depoliticized world in which, both in theory and in practice, the public regulation of the pope and the king was becoming less effective. Increasingly the external world came to be treated as a wholly private realm detached from the Catholic precepts of natural law and from the new international law that was beginning to be developed in the sixteenth century.

ACOSTA

Some writers, like Joseph Acosta and Samuel Purchas, were not content to be carried along on a wave of "confused assimilation and eclectism," as Meyrick

Heath Carré calls it, without looking back to the old order of things. In putting forward his description of the new world in conflict with the old, Acosta in *The Natural and Morall Historie of the East and West Indies*, published in England in 1604, had plainly shied away from superstition, signs, or prognostication.[22] Acosta was much more concerned about the rich diversity of troupes, lineages, nations, realms, empires, cities, and commonwealths that he saw around him, and the reasons for the differences between them.

Acosta glimpsed the possibility that the South American Indian may have come to the New World by a land bridge by way of the Atlantic islands and that there may be some biblical evidence for the migration of the Jews in earlier times. He concluded that the reason he could find no first beginning of the Indians was because they had no writing and no certain remembrance of their founders (24.77). Although his natural history rested upon moral history founded on God's truth, the story of the Garden of Eden, and acceptance of Christian faith, he was still puzzled by the similarities between animal and animal, man and man, both in the Indies and in Europe, especially if all the remnants found refuge in the Ark of Noah. He avoided speculation on grounds that it would be idolatrous to give natural phenomena a status more important than God's governance and, like Las Casas, rejected the view "perswading ourselves that the Indianes affaires deserve no other respect, but as of venison that is taken in the forest, and brought for our use and delight" (6.432).

Acosta put forward the old argument of Aristotle's antique state that the laws, privileges, and customs of the Indies, where compatible with Christian teaching, should be maintained and kept as the fundamental law, and their social virtues should be stimulated and encouraged. He firmly believed that there was no nation, however barbarous, that had not something good to be said for it, and indeed no commonwealth, however well ordered, that had not something bad. He insisted that there was little benefit to be gained from the study of the Indian people if there was no attempt to understand their beginnings and to compare their way of life with the natural and moral history of a well-ordered commonwealth. He believed that the Indians possessed reason, and, although they were "without," had the capacity and the potential to participate in political life.

PURCHAS

In his *Pilgrimages* (1613) Samuel Purchas (ca. 1577–1626) also acknowledged the influence of Las Casas, but only in condemning the forcible conversion practiced by the Spaniards—"this Hell-monster of their bloudie Catholocisme."[23] Purchas successfully manipulated his natural history in an anti-Catholic direction, somewhat in accord with Holinshed's individual Protestant history, so that it would be of use to philosophers, students of politics, and geographers. Purchas's account of the Creation, the Fall, the nature of religion, the Flood, the repeopling of the world, and the division of the tongues followed the familiar line. But whereas Foxe found the *race and course* of Church and Kingdom in antique records, Purchas's account is investigative and reconstructive. God no longer appears over Nature but *in* Nature, and His presence is indicated in the contrast between chaos and order in the nature of things.

For Purchas, as for Bodin, there was a chaotic Platonist stage before the first beginning brought about by one who is the author from whom Nature emanates to infuse the divisions of mankind with the image of God in man: "This image of God appeared in the Soule properly, secondly in the bodie (not as the Anthropomorphite Heretikes, and Popish Image-Makers imagine, but as the instrument of the Soule), and lastly in the whole person" (3.11). Purchas was ambivalent about some involuntary infusion polluting the soul and body, as Best had described, and emphatically denied that the stain was passed through sexual intercourse. He reaffirmed Thomas Aquinas' teaching that the power of the seed prepares the body to receive the Soul. Here Purchas reintroduced Cain as the first divider of religion, marked "that he might be an example to the future generations, branded also by the Lord with some sensible marke, to exempt him, and terrifie others from that bloodie crueltie, and cursed as a runnagate and wanderer" (6.28) and reconsidered a variety of different accounts of the Flood and Noah. Of all of these he held Berossus the most suspect: "That Berossus, which we now have, is not so much as the ghost, or carkasse, and scarce a few bones of the carkasse of that famous Chaldean Author, mentioned in the Ancients, but the dreams of Annius, (no new thing in this last age) coined for the most part in his name" (7.33). Yet Purchas perversely returned to Berossus for the causes for difference, found in the Tower of Babel and the legend of Ham, who was cursed for his sins of self-abuse, public corruption, sodomy, dishonesty, and incest. Ham was banished, and his descendants were horrific: "Their nether lippe was thicke and redde, and so great that it hung downe to their brest, and it together with their gummes bloudie: their teeth great, and on each side one very large: their eyes standing out: terrible they were to looke upon" (12.538).

But Purchas did not agree with Best's hypothesis that natural infection resulting from Ham's secret indulgence in carnal copulation was the cause of the natural blackness of the African. He also rejected Hippocrates' hypothesis that blackness is caused by leaking nutriment and heat, and Herodotus' attribution of difference to the color of the parent's sperm. Like Acosta, he hesitated to delve too deeply into these mysteries. Like Best, he stopped with the stories of Cain, Babel, and Ham, not pressing his argument to the point of making men members of different natural "races." For the moment the religious stories were sufficient. For Purchas, the diversity of humankind has less to do with monstrosity than with lack of religion and civility. Indeed it is evidence of God's wondrous handiwork: "The tawney Morre, black Negro, duskie Libyan, ash-coloured Indian, olive-coloured American. should with the whiter European become one sheepe-fold, under one great shepheard, til this mortalitie being swallowed up of life, wee may all be one, as he and the father are one. . . . Without any more distinction of colour, Nation, language, sexe, condition al may bee One in him that is ONE, and only blessed forever" (6.14.545–46).

FLORIO

In 1578, the same year that Holinshed's *Chronicles* were published, there appeared a description of the manners and customs of the people by the son of an Italian immigrant to England. Giovanni Florio's *First Fruites* was followed in 1603 by his translation of Michel Montaigne's *Essais*, and then in 1611 by his great lexicon of useful words and phrases, *Queen Anne's New World of Words*.[24]

In attractive and free-flowing language "of familiar speech, merry proverbs, witty sentences, and golden sayings," Florio (1553–1625) described in his *First Fruites* the manners of the various nations without seeking to establish how a noble and renowned English nation appeared in antiquity and what were its origins. In these superficial reflections, with no reference to Berossus or to the Old Philosophers, Florio described what people could easily see for themselves:

> Tel me of curtesie if you know the customes of certaine nations, I know you know thé. I wyl tel you as briefly as I can. . . . The Ethiopians are a certaine people of Caria, they are simple, foule, and slaves: the Carthaginians are false, and deceivers: those of Babylon, are malitious, and corrupted the Persians are gluttonous, and drunkardes: the Cicilians are very niggards, & yet faithful.those

of Caspia are cruel: they of Lesbia, filthy the Scithians lawelesse: the Corinthians, fornicatours: the Boctians, very rude: the Simerians, very beastly: they of La-cedemonia, very hardye: the Athenians, delicate: the Romans proud and glorious: the Spaniards, trauelers, disdainful, and despisers: the Italians, proude and reuengers: the Frenchme, crafty and fierce: the Germanes, warriours: the Sax-ons, dissemblers: those of Sueuia, tatlers: the Britayne (an Englishman) a busy body: the Irisheman, wylde: the Cimbrian, seditious, and horrible: the Boemian, very discourteous, and desirous of newes: the Scottishman, periured: the Vandal, mutable: the Bauarian, a scoffer. Of other I do not well remember. Verily I yeelde you thankes for this, with a good hart." (30.70)

Like his compatriot Machiavelli, Florio was careful not to set great store by these descriptions. Beauty and ugliness were only skin deep, and horrible vices were often concealed behind beautiful faces. In time all will be devoured by the worms: "Lastly, we are al one like thing, and we walke all towarde the grave: and when we are out of this world, what difference will there be be-twwene the faire & the foule? verily none" (38.87).

In the *World of Words*, which remained a standard lexicon for students and doctors throughout the seventeenth century, Florio confined his description of race to those of high nobility, and in his translation of Montaigne he also used "race" to mean those of "royall blood." Yet in his treatment of the orders and degrees of the ordinary people, for whom he had a great deal of affection, there was an enticement for others to delve deeper into the entitlement for membership in race.

RACE AND THE ESTABLISHED ORDER

In Hakluyt and Holinshed, and much later in more sophisticated form in the works of Pierre Charron, there is this same curiosity to know what it means to be a member of an ancient nobility. In Hakluyt's *Principal Voyages*, René Laudonnière, writing in 1587 of events that took place in the 1560s, told how John Ribault attempted to persuade his men to settle in Florida, instead of returning home, where they were unknown to the king of the realm and the great estates of the land, they were descended of poor stock, and they did not know the profession of arms. As common men, they were not descended of "*a noble race*," though "if vertue were regarded, ther would more be found worthy to deserve the title, and by good right to be named noble and valiant" (8.469).

In the void of Florida, Ribault had held out some prospect that some men might be able to enter a noble race by their own efforts, but it went no further than that. Men saw themselves as Christians in an established political order, which was set out in Holinshed's *Chronicles* as (1) gentlemen (kings, princes, dukes, marques, earls, viscounts, barons, knights, esquires); (2) citizens or burgesses; (3) yeomen, who are artificers; (4) laborers and husbandmen (2.5). Holinshed included in his "race" all those who are described as "gentlemen" or "Esquire (commonly called squire) from the French word, and so much in Latine as Scutiger vel armiger, and such are all those which beare armes, or armoires, testimonies of their *race* from whence they be descended" (2.5). The term "esquire" distinguished a noble fighting man from a common soldier.

> Gentlemen be those whome *their race and bloud*, or at the least their vertues doo make noble and knowne. The Latines called them Nobiles & generosos, as the French do Nobles or Gentle hommes. The etymologie of the name expoundeth the efficacie of the word: for as Gens in Latine betokeneth the *race and surname*: so the Romans had Cornelios, Sergios, Appios, Curios, Papyrios, Scipiones, Fabios, Aemilios, Iulios, Brutos &C: of which, who were Agnati, and therefore kept the name, were also called Gentiles, gentlemen of that or that *house and race*. (2.5.273)

Although Holinshed's definition is wider than Florio's, he was opposed to including new gentlemen—the university men, physicians, and captains who "go in wider buskens than his legs will beare." He speculated that too much was being made of new virtues and outward appearances, and the "old smell of ancient race is being neglected" (2.5.273).

CHARRON

In 1612 Samson Lennard, a genealogist and heraldic visitor, or inspector, translated Pierre Charron's *De la sagesse*,[25] first published in Bordeaux in 1601. Charron (1541–1603) was a student and friend of Montaigne who came under attack in France for his skepticism and atheism. In this massive text, he devoted forty-three chapters to the four moral virtues of prudence, justice, fortitude, and temperance; sixty-two chapters to the knowledge of self and the human condition; and the whole of Book 2 to the enunciation of the principal rules of wisdom.

Charron's account of Genesis (41.151–53) owed much to Platonism, and his descriptions of diversity and inequality were taken from Pliny, Herodotus, and Plutarch. Like Hakluyt and Purchas, he was profoundly disturbed by observed differences in the shape and manners of newly discovered peoples, as illustrated in his long account of monstrosity and deformity. Charron conceded that man and beast may be one in nature and that in some circumstances the gap between the excellent beast and the base man may be narrower than that between the base man and the great man. But Nature is one, and since all differences are derived from the spirit appearing in so many diverse parts, jurisdictions, and degrees, "We must now at the last learn to know many by these distinctions, and differences that are in him, which are divers, according to the many parts in man, many reasons, and means to compare and consider him" (41.153).

It followed, therefore, that a system was necessary to categorize and classify these differences according to Reason. Charron's fivefold classification was similar to Bodin's but encompassed all that is Man—spiritual, physical, acquired, public, private, apparent, and secret—which was further subdivided into five formats elaborately worked out in carefully constructed tables according to *natural* distinctions, such as location, country, sun, air, climate, color, features, complexion, countenance, and manners. This table was then subdivided according to degrees and parts of the body according to the parts of the world—North, South, and Middle—following closely the pattern we examined in Bodin's work. Charron ascribed to each part a distinctive "nature," arising partly from natural phenomena and partly from the spirit, religion, and manners of the people. The causes of the differences of peoples, and the proofs, were to be found in bringing together body and spirit, in the inequality and difference in inward natural heat, and humors, and the influences of the planets, which Charron further analyzed into three specific sorts of people born into the world—Northerners, Middlers, and Southerners—who may be identified according to the force and sufficiency of spirit in each organized in a complex matrix of human qualities and proofs (42.164).

Only after this detailed exploration of the four capital distinctions of nature, spirit, accident of estate, and accident of condition and profession of life did Charron consider the fifth capital distinction, the favors and disfavors of Nature and Fortune, and here is his first reference to the theme of *race*. Like Holinshed, Hakluyt, Florio, and Ribault, Charron regarded nobility as a quality *not* found everywhere. Race is an honorable thing established by reason for public utility:

It is divers, diversley taken and understood, and according to divers nations and judgements, it hath divers kinds. According to the generall and common opinion and custome, it is *a qualitie of a race or stock*. Aristotle saith, that it is *the antiquitie of a race and of riches*. Plutarch calleth it *the virtue of a race*, meaning thereby a certain habite and qualitie contained in the linage. What this qualitie or virtue is, all are not wholly of one accord, saving in this, that it is profitable to the weal-publick. (59.197)

Charron's conception is that race is an exclusive quality: not all men are noble, and not all members of a civil society are members of races:

For to some, and the greater part of this qualitie is militarie, to others it is politick, litarie to those that are wise, palatine of the Prince. But *the militarie hath the advantage above the rest*: for beside the service that it yieldeth to the weal publick as the rest do, it is painfull, laborious, dangerous; whereby it is recounted more worthy and commendable. So hath it carried with us by excellencie, the honourable title of Valor. . . . That is to say a long continuance of this qualitie by many degrees and races, and time out of mind, whereby they are called in our language Gentlemen, that is to say of a race, house, familie, carrying of long time the same name, and the same profession. For he is truly and entirely noble, who maketh a single profession of publick virtue, serving his Prince and Countrey, and being descended of parents and ancestors that have done the same. (59.197–98)

At this stage in English history, to belong to a race was to belong to a noble family with a valorous ancestry and a profession of public service and virtue. Race was no longer the reserve of kings and bishops. It had come to include fighting men and lay men of the learned and legal professions. But, it is born of a nobility that arises from active "political" eye—of governance, not nature. A nobility that comes by blood is, unreliable:

This is a personal and acquired nobilite and considered with rigour it is rude, that one come from the house of a Butcher or Vintner should be held for noble, whatsoever service hc hath done for the Common-weal. Nevertheless, this opinion hath place in many nations, namely, with the Turks, contemners of ancient nobilite, and esteeming of no other but personall and actuall militarie valour; or only antiquitie of race without profesion of the qualitie; this is in bloud and purely naturall. (59.199)

That which is natural and of the blood is another man's quality, and it is vanity to think otherwise: "I scarce account those things ours which descend from our linage and ancestours, or anything which we our selves have not done; no man hath lived for our glory and renown. Neither are we to account ours which hath been before us. . . . What good is it to a blind man, that his parents have been well-sighted, or to him that stammereth that his Grandfather was eloquent?" (59.199).

In Charron's extremely important text, therefore, race does *not* have a quality, natural or spiritual, that is its own and is prior to public service, achievement, and profession. A nobility based on blood and nature is lesser, necessary but subordinate in character. Gentlemen now belong to races. And yet if dependence on the general claim of race and ancestry for entry to the nobility is to be ruled out, so by the same token is the granting of nobility solely on the strength of public service and profession:

> It is a foul thing to degenerate, and to belie a man's own race. The nobility that is given by the bounty and letters patent of the Prince, if it have no other reason, it is shameful, and rather dishonourable than honourable; it is a nobility on parchment, bought with silver or favour, and not by blood as it ought. If it be given for merit and notable services, it is personal and acquired, as hath been said. (52.200)

BLUNDEVILLE

Even in Charron's extension of the definition of race to include gentlemen and bearers of arms, there is marked absence of an argument that all men are members of races in nature. The idea was still tied to the old notion of races and orders of kings and bishops, and partial emendations of it. But in 1589 Thomas Blundeville began in his *Description of Mappes and Cardes* to try to understand *place* and *things* on the basis of a logical analysis of generation and its processes.[26] He drew upon Gerardus Mercator (1512–94) for charts, Ptolemy (121–151 A.D.) for map projections, and Gamma Frisius (1508–55) for longitude and triangulation and arrived at a division of the world into four parts (Africa, Asia, Europe, and America), thus casting doubt upon the Arthurian legend of settlement of the inhospitable North and correcting the inaccuracies of navigation so as to minimize the perils of journeys to inhospitable lands. *His Exercises Containing Six Treatises* followed in 1594, written for gentlemen not versed in cosmography, either terrestrial or celestial, who wished to know more about the principles of navigation as well as arithmetic, geometry, mathematics, and triangulation. This time he went to Petrus Plancius and John Blagrave, as well as translating Albrecht Dürer's treatise on the art of painting, which he hoped would be helpful to the joiner, carpenter, and mason.

Blundeville accepted that the world was created by God Almighty of the same blood. Issuing forth from Noah's Ark, its peoples may be distinguished in terms of quality and shape of body, color, and size, which he divided into Patagonians, who exceed all other people in greatness; Chinese, who have broad faces, little eyes, flat noses, little beards, and those with small feet who are counted as beautiful; Africans, who have "grosser and thicker lips" than other people, and the inhabitants of Agysimba and Guinea and the lands near Cape of Good Hope, who are black and do not differ much from Oriental Indians; and the Abyssinians or Moors of Egypt, who are duskish in color like the inhabitants of Barbary and are called white Moors, and those that dwell between them and the Nigrites, or black Moors, who are yellowish in color. Blundeville quickly passed over the stories told about pygmies and monsters, such as are described in Charron's work: "All these are meere lyes, invented by vaine men to bring fooles into admiration, for monsters are as well borne in Europe, as in other parts of the world" (263). With this marvelous dismissal of the Plinian monsters, Blundeville calmly proceeded to distinguish and divide according to geographical location, with accounts of faiths and ceremonies practiced in different places.

In *The Art of Logike* Blundeville advanced his most important definitions of what a place is and how argument and demonstration should be conducted, and confutation constructed. He set out a massive table designed to enable those in dispute to know the nature and power of each argument they use in divine and human affairs. When dealing with place, explained Blundeville, the Old Schoolmen rely upon a division into two kinds: one on maxim (a general rule approved and received of all logicians so that no man will deny it), and the other a difference of maxim, which is the proper name of every place whereby a maxim is known from another and to what place every maxim belongs. For Blundeville these maxims serve as sheet anchors, as places of refuge, when adversaries deny conclusions. Hence, when speaking of stock or birth he claimed, "Of this place you may reason thus: Hee had strong parents, Ergo he is strong. He came of an evill *race*, Ergo it is no marvaile though he bee evill disposed" (4.2.75).

Using these maxims as support in argument, Blundeville also based his logical view of generation and corruption upon divine authorities and Holy Scripture, and all else was judged *logically*, with the birth of Christ as good, just as its logical opposite, and particularly barbarism and incivility, were evil. His construct of true and false was built on logical opposites.

If Blundeville had stopped with divine authorities and maxims, there would have been nothing very remarkable about his work. But he next turned to human authorities, which he described as expressing themselves in three ways: first in written form in histories, laws, statutes, decrees, judgments, ruled cases, maxims, proverbs, general rules, patents, warrants, licenses, commissions, charters, deeds, releases, court rolls, extents, accounts, obligations, indentures, testimonies, and the like; second in things spoken, as in freely uttered confessions, testimonies, rumors, opinions, wise speeches, and forced confessions by oath or torture; and third in the custom and usage of the people. All three forms had to be looked at logically and tested against the truth of the world to see whether they supported the propositions of virtue against vice, and civility against barbarism.

BACON

What we find in Blundeville, therefore, is a new signpost: a guide to action that, while retaining the old appreciation of civility as a virtue and barbarism as a vice, governed the way in which the practices of the newly discovered peoples were perceived and the new authorities upon which judgments must be made. Blundeville's texts not only spread a wider understanding of the need for accuracy in navigation, but they gave an impetus to another kind of voyage of discovery into a rich variety of written and spoken human authorities based upon a logical analysis rather than upon the *ad hoc* sense impressions of brilliant and intuitive men like Shakespeare and Florio. This new analytical method, which is clearly visible in the works of Charron, came to be employed more fully after the publication in 1605 of Francis Bacon's *Twoo Bookes of the Proficience and Advancement of Learning*, which introduced a world in which climate, geography, and anthropology began to be seen as natural foundations for political life and allowed for the establishment of a new method by which working models could be built from the observation of diverse parts, so that all revealed and traditional ways could be measured and a new ordering of things established through the effective force of reason.[27]

Like Blundeville, Bacon (1561–1626) was still committed to the idea of

God as the First Cause, but he warned that straying into the field of knowledge would tempt the Serpent. He realized that for man to pick the first fruits of the Tree of Knowledge he must avoid the temptation to be a law unto himself: man must not be seduced by "vayne Philosophie." And so Bacon brought about a neat compromise between biblical exegesis and the advancement of learning about nature through a logical attack on those branches of learning that "[soften] mens minds and bringeth them to a love of leisure and privatnesse" (1.7), and he sought to achieve a compatibility between the pursuit of learning and the discipline and honor of arms, which he found in Roman experience and practice. For Bacon the arts of government as favored in the poetry and historiography of Vergil, Livy, Marcus Terentius Varro, and Cicero had in the past held back "Rudenes and Barbarisme" (1.12), and it was better that learning be in the hands of learned men than in those of the Church.

Bacon remarked that the opening up of the literature and language of the ancients to a wider audience following the Lutheran revolt had undoubtedly brought an exact study of language and a flourishing style of speech, but it also led to an excess of superficial trivia: "It seems to me that Pigmalions frenzie is a good embleeme or portraiture of this vanitie: for wordes are but the Images of matter, and except they have life of reason and invention: to fall in love with them, is all one, to fall in love with a Picture" (1.19). He suggested that the universal truths propounded by the Schoolmen, at times cloistered and introverted, required some stirring up, not only to exalt God but to benefit the state.

Finally, Bacon drew attention to the marked tendency to rely on unverified ecclesiastical reports of miracles or on superstition and unhistorical sources. He urged a move away from single obsessive studies such as theology, mathematics, logic, or the pursuit of alchemical chimeras, so as to put in perspective the overemphasis on the mind and understanding of man: "If a man meditates on the frame of nature, the earth with men upon it, it will not seem much other than an ant hill, some carry corn, some their young, some go empty, and all go to and fro 'a little heape of dust' " (1.42). Elsewhere he stated, "Howebeit, I doe not meane when I speake of use and action, that end before mentioned of the applying of knowledge to luker and profession; for I am not ignorant how much that diverteth and interrupteth the prosecution and advauncement of knowledge; like unto the goulden ball throwne before Atalanta, which while shee goeth aside, and stoopeth to take up, the *race* is hindred" (1.26).

Given these vanities and weaknesses, Bacon turned to natural history and asserted that Pliny, Geronimo Cardano, Albertus Magnus, and the Arabians had been too lightly accepted; as a consequence fabulous untrue matter had been faked. Aristotle's diligent and exquisite history of living creatures had been mixed with vain and feigned matter and not given the consideration it deserved. Too much attention had been paid to the Cabalistic arts and enigmatic writing. The error, as he saw it, was that the ancient world was not being treated as the ancient world; instead it was being presented by computing back from the present. Conversely, people distrusted discovery and believed that because some former opinion had prevailed it must forever prevail.

VERSTEGAN

In the same year as Bacon's exhortation to look more closely at matter and weight on the basis of the evidence of logic, Richard Rowlands (1565–1620), a Catholic Englishman whose family came to England from Holland about 1500, published in Antwerp under his family name Verstegan his *Restitution of Decayed Intelligence in Antiquities concerning the Most Noble and Renowned English Nation*, dedicated to James I.[28] In this text that denied the "Englishness" of the English, Verstegan commended the glory, honors, and acts of valor "left to their descending *race*, for them to yeeld their ancetors due grace." Prefixed to the text is a sonnet by Francis Tregian, a noble Cornish Catholic imprisoned by Elizabeth, so it is said, for rejecting her amatory advances, and finally exiled to Madrid after spending twenty-eight years in prison. In these verses the English are encouraged to "learn thy name, thy *race*, thy offspring" in the writing, speaking, and doing, in the registers of antiquity, in a quest for "ancient Nobilitie."

Verstegan's sources were Augustine, Philo, and Josephus, and his division of the world followed the familiar biblical pattern without the more outrageous of Berossus' embellishments. He favored the cosmographies of the Germans, Krantz, and Munster, who had caused deep offense to Angrimus Jonas, the Catholic spokesman for the maligned Icelanders, and he looked to names and words for clues as to origins. The first chapter on the originals of the nations, and consequently of that nation from which Englishmen are undoubtedly descended, begins with the important words: "Englishmen are descended of German *race*, and were heeretofore generaly called Saxons" (1.2).

On the authority of Tacitus, Strabo, and Ptolemy, and acting on the assumption that language is the key to understanding, Verstegan advanced the work of Hotman by putting forward the idea that the Germans were Scythian in origin, having as their first legendary father Tuisto or Tuisco. The Goths, Vandals, Danes, and Normans gave up their names to this German people who had originated in Asia, and the Saxons and Germans together formed the foundation for the English nation: "That our Saxon anceters came out of Germanie, and made their habitation in Britaine, is no question; for that therein all agree, but some not contented to have thé [them] a people *of German race*, wil needs bring them from els where to have come into Germanie, and from Germanie afterwards to have come into Britaine" (2.25). He continued, "I do heer only go about to proove, that our anceters the Saxons were also originally a people of *the German race*" (2.31).

In 1605 this English-Dutch Catholic, looking back at the country of his birth, put forward the staggering claim that the English nation had a common origin not only with the Goths, Vandals, Danes, and Germans, who had been dispersed after the Flood and confused linguistically by the Tower of Babel, but that they had all been swept into an original Germano-Scythian people issuing forth from Asia, and not as Scot suggested from the unnatural union of the Incubi and a group of witches.

Verstegan was not content, however, to rely upon the evidence of the Bible and on unsubstantiated speculation. He sought verification from ambassadors he had employed in Italy to check with Persian ambassadors to see whether they could find any affinity between Duytsh (German) and Persian. Alas, he could find only a half dozen words, although some people had pointed out to him that there was a greater probability that Irish and Hebrew were more closely connected. Verstegan thought that this hardly helped the Irish to be better Hebrews! To resolve the difficulty Verstegan turned, as Acosta had done, to the migration of peoples. If the Germans came out of Asia, how did they get to Germany? Where did they come from? Was it Asia, Africa, Macedonia, Denmark, or Britain? "So as wee may bee moved to compassion, to see our poor anceters thus led up and down the world, by a sorte of blynd guydes" (2.25). Verstegan rejected the tall stories that Britain was once occupied by giants who had been chased out by savage men. He also rejected the Brutus story included in Holinshed and agreed with Caesar's judgment that the "races and descents" of the Isle of Albion, first mentioned in Berossus and Annius, were "altogether uncertain and obscure" (4.111). But Verstegan thought that the inconsistencies in the stories of the Flood, and the geographical oddities needed to be looked at more closely on a factual basis. It is true that the Germans migrating from Asia would have been faced with insuperable difficulties in navigating the Mediterranean and the North Sea, and the channel between England and France would have prevented migration of men and animals. How then was it that wolves managed to cross into England? Nobody "would ever transporte of that *race* for the goodness of the breed" (4.111). The evidence he put forward was the evidence of archaeological excavation— the revelations of fossils, bones, shells, fishes, fir trees in the earth in Holland, and a sea elephant in Brabant—which proved that where there is now sea there was once land. He decided that these geographical complications were all too much to set aside his original proposition that the Saxon ancestors were merely and originally a people of Germany, and that it was honorable for Englishmen to be descended from them for the following reasons: (1) they have been the only possessors of their country; (2) they were never subdued by anyone; and (3) they have kept themselves unmixed with foreign people and their language unmixed with foreign tongues. Building a vivid picture of German endurance in battle, supported by descriptions in Tacitus and Josephus, Verstegan clearly wanted the English nation to have been derived from Germany.

» Conclusion: The Idea of Race

In the sixteenth century dynastic ambitions and religious issues were of such great consequence that there was little room for the growth of a conscious idea of race as we understand it today. The political and philosophical sheet anchors of the ancient polity had held sufficiently in the teeth of the Reformation storm to contain the worst effects of witchcraft, sorcery, and popular religion. Men either found their way ashore on rafts of practical ethics and new natural conceptions of human society, or they stayed with the battered bulk of the Aristotelian ship of state.

Foxe used the term "race" in the sense of an ancient order and course of kings and bishops stretching back into antiquity, refreshed and revived by a stream or race of legitimate authority issuing from the founding rock at Rome. This noble order was authoritative and justified from authors, monuments, and written authorities; it is the legal order we see in the Spanish colonization of South America, where later the idea of race did not make such headway in the face of Las Casas's political theories as it did in the North.

The early volumes of Hakluyt show very little movement from the basic notion of a Greco-Roman and Christian political order in the Aristotelian and Ciceronian sense. The world continued to be divided into the antitheses of *nomos* and *physis*, political and barbarous, virtuous and vicious, *agora* and battlefield, public and private, kings and tyrants, liberty and license.

But, after the accounts of the voyages to Guinea in the 1560s and to North America in the 1570s by discoverers and navigators, we come face to face with a wondrous void, and the accounts of barbarity, incivility, and licentiousness proliferate, especially where there is privateering. Best's popularization of the Hamitic heresy out of Berossus and Annius was a huge success in England as well as in France and Germany, and he, together with Holinshed and the chroniclers and dramatists, opened the door wide to the search for hidden causes of difference in mankind. They found them in witchcraft, sorcery, astrology, and natural infection of the humoral blood as well as in a wide variety of natural explanations in climate, language, and geography.

With Acosta, Purchas, and Charron we see the beginnings of a systematic and schematic analysis of differences in men according to geographical location, with a greater emphasis upon migration and human disposition as original causes. Their views led to a gradual turning of attention toward the idea that the ancient royal race, which at once excluded Arthurian legend and exotic fable, may now contain within it those who may not be noble by birth, or by the bearing of arms, and yet may possibly be so by achievement and worldly success. But no fundamental amendment was made to the exclusive idea of a race of kings, bishops, and nobles, and nothing changed the multiplicity of meanings for the same word in a variety of other unrelated contexts, until after Bacon's reasoned reconciliation of biblical exegesis with the advancement of knowledge about nature based on the logical analysis of place and language.

Richard Verstegan's attempt to build on Hotman's legal argument that the ancient constitution was to be found in some time other than the first beginning in Rome resulted in greater emphasis on the writing, speaking, and doing of an "ancient nobility"—a race—but the difference was now that it had its origin in a common German and Saxon source, which may be better known by factual inquiry.

As Eric Voegelin has contended, these attempts to establish anatomical, physiological, geographical, and astrological relationships between man and man, and man and beast, did not produce a fully developed idea of race, since there was no proper anthropology, natural history, or biology to support it.

When the idea of race appeared in the works just discussed, it could only be considered as "an occasional element."

Voegelin's analysis agrees with that of Theophile Simar, librarian of the Academy of Science in Belgium after World War I, who argues that although anthropological influences were not of paramount importance in forming a doctrine of race in the eighteenth century, nevertheless they provided a platform for, and propagated an idea of, the dogma of the *bonté de la nature*, which he traces back to the mystical Christianism and new Platonism of the Middle Ages and to the falsification and idealization of the savage in the state of innocence (which he lays at the feet of Las Casas), to the exaltation of the German virtues of sobriety, patriarchy, and purity in Lutheranism and Protestantism, and to Hotman's and Verstegan's search for an elect German *gens*, an aboriginal people who had conquered the known world in a dimly remembered past constructed from the fragments of Tacitus' *Germania* and the arcana of Hermetic and Cabalist writings.

Both Voegelin and Simar depend on the important assumption that until the eighteenth century the identity of the person (insofar as a person had any identity at all), and his membership of an order of things, was essentially "political" in the sense that I have used the term throughout this book. As I have shown, the body idea associated with *polis* leads back to Plato's *Timaeus* and *Republic*, and to Aristotle's *Politics*, in which individuals and groups were seen as having no identity apart from a *polis* and were regarded as having no status unless they were seen to be citizens of a legitimate Greco-Roman order: others were simply *barbaros*.

In the course of time these body ideas had been absorbed into a new ecclesiastical Christian order and with Augustine's *magnum opus* relinquished some but not all of the political symbols to create a new identity and to bind its members to a new kind of order. Citizens came to be perceived as citizens, not by virtue of their membership of the *polis* evidenced through the skills and attitudes required in participation in the activity of politics, but as willing partners in the Sacrament, which brought membership of the "mystical body of the faithful in Christ." It is important to note that in both the political and the ecclesiastical a people (*populus*) was bound together, and assumed its identity, through law and through faith; it did not assume its identity through biology and secular history, or through an autonomous moral order independent of political and religious reality. Without these elements, without the formation of a different notion of "species" linked to something called a *Volk*, there could be no idea of race.

The Racialization of the West

» «

Mors sola fatetur
Quantula sint hominum corpuscula

Death alone discloses
how very small are the
puny bodies of men

—*Juvenal*

The First Stage in the Development of an Idea of Race, 1684–1815

In the first six chapters of this book I have deliberately labored the point that there is very little evidence of a conscious idea of race until after the Reformation. The time has now come to identify three main stages during which the idea emerged as an original and imaginative contribution to modernity, rather than as a muddled remnant of antiquity. This chapter considers the stage from 1684 to 1815, when major writers dealt explicitly with race as an organizing idea and came to understand it as an ethnic grouping rather than as a race and order or course of things or events, as described in previous chapters. The remaining stages are 1815–70, when the map of Europe was reconstructed to restore things to their legitimate prerevolutionary "natural" origins, and 1870–1914, the high point in the idea of race, and what followed thereafter.

The first stage involves three complicated changes. The first and most important has to do with methodology—the setting aside of the metaphysical and theological scheme of things for a more logical description and classification that ordered humankind in terms of physiological and mental criteria based on observable "facts" and tested evidence. The important departure point here was the adoption and adaption of Aristotle's ideas of *genus* and *species* (the essences of things) and his classification of the physical world. This methodological change, triggered by René Descartes, Thomas Hobbes, and John Locke during the seventeenth century, created a useful way in which things could be divided into material *classes, genera,* and *species,* thus enabling natural historians to divide and subdivide material things into general orders more systematically than had been possible before. This new method was considered to be as applicable to primates as to plants, and especially to humankind, where from 1684 we begin to see increasing use of the terms "race," "espèces," and "ethnic groups" to describe the ordering of the many different varieties. The lion's share of the story of the varieties must surely be reserved for Johann Friedrich Blumenbach (1752–1840) and those of his predecessors who contributed to the secularization of Aristotle's method, as we shall see later, and the eventual substitution, in place of the uncertain stories of Shem, Ham, and Japhet, the man-brute dichotomy, and the biblical tripartite division of the world, of a competing hypothesis based on what Blumenbach termed his "pentagist (five-part) arrangement" that ordered humankind in terms of anatomy, climate, and pigmentation in a new and more rational science of physical anthropology.

This reconstruction was initially detached and scholarly. Rational analysis was allied with physical anthropology within an existing concept of the unity of species. It did not lead to an immediate renunciation of Aristotle's formulation of the antique idea of state contained in the *Politics* or to a complete break in the classical tradition of thinking politically. But it did raise the question of the legitimate basis for governance and right order according to the newly published criteria of natural history. If the ancient political order by which monarchs justified their title to rule was no longer legally satisfactory and sufficient according to the old tenets, and not in conformity with the new, then what was? In France, Comte Henri de Boulanvilliers and Abbé Jean-Baptiste Dubos tested Hobbes's natural theory of the right of conquest in the light of the contention argued earlier by Hotman and Verstegan that the true origins of authority and title to rule rested in the German strain of a Franco-Gallic *gentis* rooted somewhere in the fifth century A.D. and not in the histories of politics and philosophy of the Greco-Roman period. In 1748 Montesquieu published his *Spirit of the Laws,* which turned away from the search for an ancient constitution hidden in a remote Greco-Roman past toward an interest in the natural origins for the legitimization of present politics. Although he did not identify "races" of people, he put forward a theory of legal inheritance based on three sets of formularies or capitularies, developing through three stages from the political to the feudal to a period in which neither was operative. Montesquieu termed these stages "races," thus giving credence to the notion of natural origins and proposing that the northern barbarians were no longer a lesser people wandering in a northern void—the barbarians of the Greco-Roman era—but very important actors in the working out of the races of time and law. Looking wistfully across the English Channel, Montesquieu saw the epitome of the beautiful system of Germanic government formulated legally into races and containing within the capitularies and formularies the truly free peoples of the natural world.

However, this tortuous struggle to rearrange the world according to rationalist principles left many loose ends. Writers continued to hark back to the old brute-monster themes and to the distinctions between civility and viciousness, except that the emphasis was now placed upon testing whether civilized man could be distinguished from the wild man according to the evidence of natural history rather than of the Bible and ancient authorities. In the early stages of this anthropological inquiry writers were unable to rid themselves of the powerful story of Ham's delinquency, and they simply reworked the tripartite division, giving it scientific plausibility by substituting Northerlings, Middlers, and Southerlings for the sons of Japhet, Shem, and Ham within an overall unity of species. Disputes and discrepancies were bridged by the introduction of a new factor, part material and part spiritual, called the *nisus formativus* (an energy or formative force) that was used as a reference point (like phlogiston) to account for the natural degeneration and regeneration of all humankind and for all causes which for the moment appeared to be hidden. At the same time intensive efforts were made to diminish the influence of written biblical and classical political authorities and to justify natural and intellectual origins in terms of evidence adduced from geographical centers of influence other than the traditional ones of Israel and Jerusalem, Greece and Rome. It is during this period that intellectuals began to turn their attention to evidence derived from the histories of the other natural peoples (termed *Völker*), to the languages of the Caucasus, the final resting place of the Ark, to Franco-Gallia, the home of the barbarian peoples, and to the mysteries of the Indus.

Second, to satisfy the stringent requirements of the new methodology, a new relationship had to be established among body structure, bodily endowment, and mind, and here the argument was advanced that all three had a bearing on something new called "national character." During this period the sixteenth-century notion of nobility was revived to augment the powerful argument that custom and law depended on natural history and that each nation had a hidden but noble natural past that could be legitimized by the new scientific and historical processes. In this discussion the status of the Negro and the Jew, and the natural variations in the principles and practices of governance as between Northern and Southern Europe, presented very real difficulties. The revolutionaries and the romantics, unable to justify title to rule in ancient, inherited, noble constitutions, seized upon Montesquieu's "racial" alternative, looking to the formularies of the Franks and Gauls for a natural justification for change of governance and for weaknesses in the claims of the Jew, the Moor, and the Negro.

Third, at the end of the eighteenth century, the combination of physical anthropology, literary criticism, and history brought to prominence, yet again, the writings of Aristotle. This time, however, it was not his work on politics and political theory and on nature that made the running, but his writings on physiognomy and art, which from Augustine to the Reformation had been treated at arm's length as philodoxical and heretical. Now they became genuine philosophies or sciences of body and spirit. Immanuel Kant, using Aristotle, reintroduced and legitimized the schema of the Cabalists and heightened awareness of the characteristic features of face and expression so as to distinguish national physiognomies and caricatures and to give character to the species by setting material man in an ethical and moral context. Other writers linked literary criticism to anthropology, thus giving rise to notions of personal quality—termed "genius"—which were assumed to reside in blood. Out of the search for true national origins in the blood of romantic pasts came a social order that put a premium on this dynamic personal quality, which people were assumed to carry forward as a formative force in something called a *race,* which realized itself in language, purity of blood, and a rational Reformation Christianity divorced from its authorized biblical and classical political sources and working itself out in the natural processes of the history of the dynamic Germanic peoples. This whole process was assumed to be driven by a progressive history with the *Volk* becoming a major *cultural* force in the world. Natural cultures were given for the first time a primitive status and a spirit (*Volk* spirit) of their own, independent of antique political arrangements, and history became the story of the names and cultures of the primitive *Volk* acting under the influence of milieu and art. In the works of Immanuel Kant and Johann Gottlieb Fichte this emphasis upon personal quality, character, "*gen*-ius," and blood made the moral world more important than the immediate practical realities of the tawdry political world. With Johann Gottfried von Herder the histories of ancient Greco-Roman politics and states no longer existed *sui generis* but now had to be seen in the wider context of the religious, mystical, poetic, technological, and artistic achievements of a naturally self-determining *Volk* divisible into races—the ordinary common people of a history that had become "cultural" and rational.

» *Analytical Foundations and the Germans in the Woods*

I have taken 1684 as the arbitrary starting point for this section because it was then that François Bernier, whose work we shall consider later, published his "Nouvelle division de la terre par les differents espèces ou races qui l'habitent." This text treated human beings mainly in terms of racial and ethnic divisions arising from differences in their observable characteristics, and it marks a significant methodological departure from the old way of seeing humankind in terms of the age-old distinctions between Christian and heathen, man and brute, political *virtù* and religious faith. The two writers who provided the foundation for this methodological change were Thomas Hobbes (1588–1679) and John Locke (1632–1704).

HOBBES

In *The Origins of Totalitarianism,* Hannah Arendt argued that the theorist who contributed most to the break in the tradition of classical political thinking and who provided political thought with the essential methodological prerequisites for eighteenth-century racial doctrines was Thomas Hobbes.[1] Arendt suggested that Hobbes's thought rests upon two important new notions about the nature of man. The first was the notion of self-preservation, which arose from his belief, eloquently and baldly expressed in *The Leviathan* (1651),[2] that the natural condition of mankind is a condition of equality derived from a known disposition to war.

Hobbes argued that the differences between man and man are not very great physically or mentally. The puniest individual, biding his time, can eliminate the strongest adversary, and however learned a man may be, his science is rooted in his own conceit: "For such is the nature of men, that howsoever they may acknowledge many others to be more witty, or more eloquent, or more learned; Yet they will hardly believe there be many so wise as themselves: For they see their own wit at hand, and other mens at a distance" (1.13.184).

And so, with this physical and mental equality of conceit, Hobbes believed that there was an equality of hope for achieving power and mastery by guile and force: "And therefore if any two men desire the same thing, which neverthelesse they cannot both enjoy, they both become enemies; and in the way to their End, (which is principally their owne conservation, and sometimes their delectation only,) endeavour to destroy, or subdue one an other" (1.13.184).

Hobbes worked from the principle that, however much we may wish it to be otherwise, the condition in which men live, unless a civil society contains them, is a condition of war, every man against every man. Although we may speculate about whether such a condition of war has always existed, Hobbes acknowledged, it is a present reality. In this condition of war "every man has a Right to every thing; even to one anothers body. And, therefore, as long as this naturall Right of every man to every thing endureth, there can be no security to any man, (how strong or wise soever he may be,) of living out the time, which Nature ordinarily alloweth men to live"(1.14.190).

For Arendt Hobbes's emphasis on conservation of self provided a new understanding of the world in which force and fraud actually become the two cardinal principles. Contracts made without force to back them up were void (1.14.197). In her view Hobbes announced to the modern world that human beings were free to do what they will with those who live outside the realm of known agreements and understandings of *civis*. The monsters, the brutes, the beasts, and all those who live in apolitical voids (*physis*) will be treated according to self-interest, and not in accordance with the general ruling that Bartolomé de Las Casas had painfully argued at Valladolid in 1550/51. For Hobbes it was a fundamental law of nature that "every man ought to endeavour Peace, as farre as he has hope of obtaining it; and when he cannot obtain it, that he may seek, and use, all helps, and advantages of Warre" (1.14.190). And from this fundamental law is derived a second: "That a man be willing, when others are so too, as farre-forth, as for Peace, and defence of himselfe he shall think it necessary, to lay down this right to all things; and be contented with so much liberty against other men, as he would allow other men against himself" (1.14.190).

Arendt argues that the enunciation of these laws of nature, based on the principles of self-preservation and self-interest, opened up new worlds for occupation and conquest—geographical, physiological, biological, psychological, and economic—without regard for the political elements that had dominated the thought of Church and State in Western Europe since Aristotle and Augustine. Furthermore, these laws of nature had the effect of establishing a second prerequisite for carrying forward new ideas about race, particularly those of George Best and Richard Verstegan: the legitimizing of the right of conquest. The barbarian, the heathen ethnic, and those existing in a prepolitical state of nature were no longer considered as part of an existing order of things, as described in Aristotle's *Politics,* or as part of the spiritual body of the faithful in Christ, as described by Augustine. In Hobbes those unprotected by an existing commonwealth were fit for conquest. The laws that Machiavelli had fixed as the fragile bastions in the defense of the people (*populus*) against the tyranny of the prince were nothing more than applications of force. Hobbes's conviction that debate without force was mere word spinning had the effect of making the English colonies and plantations "voyds by warre" and all the native peoples found in them not citizens, not even subjects, but enemies: "For words are wise mens counters, they do but reckon by them: but they are the mony of fooles, that value them by the authority of an Aristotle, a Cicero, or a Thomas, or any other Doctor whatsoever, if but a man" (1.4.106).[3]

Hobbes referred to race only in the earlier sense of winning a race (2.14.194). In *The Elements of Law* (1650) he used the metaphor of the race, or running course, as an important aid to remembrance of the essential passions of man.[4] For him race was a competitive event we are all compelled to run from birth to death. His two references to the native peoples of North and South America illustrate examples concerning law and contract at home. Like Raleigh before him, he commended plantation and colonization, urging his countrymen not to exterminate the people they found when they landed, who were not without morality and had some skills of cultivation and contract. Unlike the Elizabethan writers, he did not resort to the legend of Noah or the curse of Ham for an explanation of the brutish state of the newly discovered peoples and the geographical division of the world. Hobbes pursued the advancement of knowledge with a second, more important, methodological departure. Mounting a logical attack on the occult—the conjuration of the Hermetists and Cabalists, the metaphorical expressions of an idolatrous Roman Church, and the demonology of heathen poets like Hesiod—he undermined the metaphysical essences of Aristotle's moral philosophy: "And I beleeve that scarce anything can be more absurdly said in naturall Philosophy, than that which is now called Aristotles Metaphysiques; nor more repugnant to Government, than much of that hee hath said in his Politiques: nor more ignorantly than a great part of his Ethiques" (4.46.687). As Arendt points out, Aristotle was the base on which ideas concerning humanity and the conduct of politics *qua* politics had operated for two thousand years. Not only did Hobbes establish the right of conquest, but he rejected Aristotle's principle that law should govern, not men.

LOCKE

In establishing the right of conquest for entirely new situations and rejecting both conjuration and the political philosophy of the Old Philosophers, Hobbes noticed how much human understanding of the world depended on the ideas of so-called wise men, many of whom he considered to be fools. His contemporary John Locke (1632–1704) made the same observation. In *An Essay Concerning Human Understanding* (1690) Locke set out to examine what objects the human mind was, or was not, fitted to deal with.[5]

Locke considered that words on their own mean nothing. It was only when they are communicated between men, who think that they stand, not simply for imagined things, but for the reality of things as they are, that both sounds and ideas take on a meaning. Ideas become general when they are understood as representing many particular things. But it is the mind that establishes these understandings. *Genus* and *species* are no more than abstract ideas that enable actual things to be sorted out more sensibly (3.3. no. 9.27–31.412). Locke concluded that the "real essence of Man" never did exist and never could exist. Thus the abstract constructs of Plato and Aristotle, although perfectly legitimate within their own terms of reference, were both unintelligible and fruitless.

For Locke, Scholastic arguments about monstrous production in nature and the relationship of the malformed fetus to the "essence" of the species were also hopeless lines of inquiry. The world was full of creatures that varied in shape, language, and reason. To understand them a sorting of their observed qualities was required. This was the work of man, and it might best be prosecuted, as Francis Bacon and Thomas Blundeville had shown, by seeking proofs in reason and demonstration. Locke pleaded the case that we "quit the common notion of Species and Essences, if we will truly look into the Nature of Things, and examine them, by what our Faculties can discover in them *as they exist,* and not by groundless Fancies, that have been taken up about them" (4.4. no. 16.4–8.573). Truth is not to be found in the self-evident propositions of the Schoolmen, but by revelation from God through the voice of reason (4.7. no. 314–18.599).

Locke took as his example the English child's understanding of the idea of man:

> First, a Child having framed the Idea of Man, it is probable, that his idea is just like that Picture, which the Painter makes of visible Appearances joyned together; and such a Complication of Ideas together in his understanding, makes up the single complex Idea which he calls Man, whereof white or Flesh-colour in England being one, the child can demonstrate to you, that a Negro is not a Man, because white-colour was one of the constant simple ideas of the complex idea he calls Man: And therefore he can demonstrate by the Principle, *It is impossible for the same thing to be, and not to be, that a Negro is not a Man;* the foundation of his Certainty being not that universal Proposition, which, perhaps, he never heard nor thought of, but the clear distinct Perception he hath of his own simple Ideas of Black and White, which he cannot be persuaded to take, nor can ever mistake one for another, whether he knows that Maxim or no: And to this Child, or any one who hath such an Idea, which he calls Man, can you never demonstrate that a Man hath a Soul, because his Idea of Man includes no such Notion or Idea of it. And therefore to him, the Principle of What is, is, proves not this matter; but it depends upon Collection and Observation by which he is to make his complex Idea called Man. (4.7. no. 16.31.606–607)

Where there were irregularities, Locke encouraged further intensive inquiry according to the tenets of the new learning (3.6. no. 12.446–47, 3.6. no. 22.23.450–51). Only through the collection, observation, and sorting of data would true knowledge be advanced.

Locke's inquiry into the exact nature of the species, coupled with Hobbes's emphasis on the right of conquest and rejection of the essences of Aristotle's political philosophy, led to the conclusion that species and essences and maxims were nothing more than the names attached by man as conveniences for conversation or discourse about them. This fundamental alteration in the perception of *genus* and *species* heralded an increasing interest in the phenomena of natural history.

BOULANVILLIERS AND DUBOS

According to Jacques Barzun, two major theories arising from the work of both Hobbes and Locke eventually paved the way for the transformation of history into an "endless spectacle" of conflict between two competing "racial" systems.[6] The first was expressed by Comte Henri de Boulanvilliers (1658–

1722), who sought Frankish justifications of legitimate origin going back to Charlemagne's coronation as king of the Franks. Boulanvilliers argued that the absolute monarchy of Louis XIV was not legitimate because it was no longer based on the ancient political notion of *imperium,* which the Frankish kings and the nobility had reestablished when they had together first conquered Gaul. Therefore, Louis XIV's kingship and the aristocracy supporting it had descended from polity into despotism; what was needed was a restoration of the aristocratic freedoms born again in the German forests after the collapse of a Rome that had become a tyranny. Claims of Germanic origins had first been advanced by François Hotman in the sixteenth century. Hotman had speculated that the Franks had freed the Gauls from Roman tyranny and that the monarchy was created by an elective principle that permitted the removal of a tyrant by consent of the people. Theorists like Raphael Holinshed, Pierre Charron, and Richard Verstegan had also speculated about the natural Germanic origins of the English nation. But Boulanvilliers arrived at a different conclusion. Instead of sticking closely to the old argument, as Hotman had done, that good governance was dependent on the perpetuation of the tripartite Roman Republican model of counterbalanced monarchy, aristocracy, and mixed polity and that the elective principle and consent were necessary prerequisites for it, Boulanvilliers advanced the view that it was not consent that had reestablished *imperium* and aristocratic freedom but the conquest of the Gauls by the Franks according to Hobbesian right of conquest.

The second theory was put forward by Abbé Jean-Baptiste Dubos (1670–1742), who in *Histoire critique de l'établissement de la monarchie française dans les Gaules* (1734) countered the argument that Frankish rule was a cataclysmic change with a picture of a peaceful transition from Roman rule.[7] Dubos based his history on an examination of titles, documents, and honors bestowed on the Franks by the Romans during a process of legitimization. Dubos saw Clovis, the Frankish king, stepping into the shoes of the Roman emperor, ruling Romans and Franks alike according to the old "political" traditions. The Franks and Gallo-Romans had mixed from the beginning, and one had not conquered the other. Dubos perceived the remnant of Gallo-Roman government in the existing order of things in France. Freedom was inherited from the German nobles who overthrew the king and aristocracy by virtue of a natural right derived from a Gallo-Roman source.

MONTESQUIEU

Both Boulanvilliers and Dubos sought, in different ways, to justify the title to rule by some means other than traditional political theory. Both were indebted to Hobbes and Locke, and both are studiously ignored in modern racial analysis. A full account of the dispute appears in the work of the Gascon Charles Louis de la Brède, better known as Charles de Secondat, baron de Montesquieu (1689–1755). His *Spirit of the Laws,* published in Geneva in 1748,[8] was not well received by those engaged in this dispute, but it was praised in England, perhaps because Montesquieu exclaimed: "In perusing the admirable treatise of Tacitus *On the Manners of the Germans,* we find it is from that nation the English have borrowed the idea of their political government. This beautiful system was invented first in the woods" (11.10.74).

Montesquieu had visited England in the autumn of 1729 and was impressed by its political institutions. But he was not impressed by the Hobbesian argument concerning the right of conquest as the foundation for sovereignty: "The natural impulse or desire which Hobbes attributes to mankind of subduing one another is far from being well founded. The idea of empire and dominion is so complex, and depends on so many other notions, that it could never be the first which occurred to the human understanding" (p. 2).

Montesquieu looked instead to a form of government—a right ordering of people—that most conformed to nature and agreed with the disposition of the people in whose favor it was established (pp. 2–3). His view was that law should be consonant with human reason and with existing political and civil realities as well as with climate, soil, occupation, religion, and the custom and manners of the inhabitants. Each form of government will be conducted according to different principles, he argued, and different species of government will require different remedies on the part of the legislator, producing punishments to fit the crime as well as specific forms of judgment and procedure. Montesquieu recognized that "every man invested with power is apt to abuse it" (p. 69) and that arbitrary power corrupted governments of all kinds.

The Abuse of Power   Montesquieu recognized that the right of conquest arose from the right of war and following its spirit. The conqueror acquires rights over the conquered by virtue of "the law of nature, which makes everything tend to the preservation of the species; the law of natural reason which teaches us to do to others as we would have done to ourselves; the law that forms political societies, whose duration nature has not limited; and in fine, the law derived from the nature of the thing itself" (pp. 62–3). Yet the conqueror ought not to reduce the conquered people to slavery, "though servitude may happen sometimes to be a necessary means of preservation" (pp. 62–3).

Montesquieu did not suffer the illusion that political liberty came about easily and without effort. Nor did it consist of unlimited natural freedom: "In governments, that is, in societies directed by laws, liberty can consist only in the power of doing what we ought to will, and in not being constrained to do what we ought not to will" (p. 85). On Cicero's authority, he connected political liberty with the nonabuse of power, which he found only, and not always, in moderate governments.

The Concept of Political Liberty   For Montesquieu the one nation in the world that had political liberty as the direct end of its constitution (and again not always) was England. In England the division of governmental powers required that an account of administration be given to the people. In examining the origins of the "spirit" of English law, Montesquieu pointed to Tacitus' description of how the Germans lived in the fields, not in towns, and assembled, even when they had been ordered to be dispersed by the Romans, to deliberate on public affairs. This "recourse to representatives" (p. 75), said Montesquieu, was the core element of Gothic government. It combined Greek and Roman elements of political rule—private households exercising their voices in public assemblies as citizens before the law—with the prince's prerogative, the privileges of nobility and clergy, and the civil liberties of the people by letters of enfranchisement. Here was the best species of constitution imagined by man.

The Influence of Climate   At this very point, however, Montesquieu parted company with Roman and Greek political thought to introduce a new methodological element: the influences of climate upon "the temper of the mind" and the "passions of the heart." His analysis of climate and temperature were familiar to those who had read Michel Montaigne, Pierre Charron, and Jean Bodin: "If we travel towards the North, we meet with people who have few vices, many virtues, and a great share of frankness and sincerity. If we draw near the South, we fancy ourselves entirely removed from the verge of morality; here the strongest passions are productive of all manner of crimes, each man endeavoring, let the means be what they will, to indulge his inordinate desires" (pp. 102–4). Differences still depended on the influences of hot and cold air, the elasticity of fibers, and moisture in the blood. But, in relating climate to the laws of civil slavery, Montesquieu put forward new arguments implying that slavery could be justified on economic grounds (sugar), moral grounds (pity), and natural grounds (black faces and flat noses):

> It is hardly to be believed that God, who is a wise Being, should place a soul, especially a good soul, in such a black ugly body. It is so natural to look upon colour as the criterion of human nature, that the Asiatics, among whom eunuchs are employed, always deprive the blacks of their resemblance to us by a more opprobrious distinction [castration]. . . . It is impossible for us to suppose these creatures to be men, because, allowing them to be men, a suspicion would follow that we ourselves are not Christians. (p. 110)

Throughout Books 16 and 17, Montesquieu continued to explore the relation of domestic slavery and political servitude to climate. He praised Scandinavia: "Namely, this country's having been the source of the liberties of Europe—that is, of almost all the freedom which at present subsists amongst mankind. . . . Jornandes the Goth called the north of Europe the forge of the human race [*humani generis officinam*]. I should rather call it the forge where those weapons were framed which broke the chains of southern nations" (pp. 123–4).

The Spirit of Law In relating the spirit of law to climate and soil, Montesquieu used the word "race" for the first time. His use of the term is curious and must be considered at length. At the heart of Montesquieu's argument was the relationship between two ancient formularies that—for good reason—have long since ceased to occupy us, but that were a major stepping-stone in the emergence of the idea of race. These formularies were derived from Salic law, which Hotman had discussed at length to justify female inheritance of the throne.

The perplexities of Salic law seem obscure today, but not so in the twelve hundred years from Clovis, who first compiled the laws of the Salian Franks in the sixth century, to Montesquieu, who found them pivotal in the eighteenth. Little is known of the customary law codes of the Germans before their contact with the Romans, though following Tacitus and Ammianus they are usually divided into four groups: the Gothic (Visigothic, Burgundian, and

Ostrogothic), the Frankish (Salic, Ripuarian, Chamavian, and Thuringian), the Saxon (Saxon, Anglo-Saxon, Frisian, and perhaps Lombardic), and Bavarian (Alemannic and Barvarian). Although the so-called Salic law was believed to have been part of Clovis's *Lex Salica,* it was not an element of the fundamental law of the Merovingian and Carolingian rulers and later of the Holy Roman Empire.

However, what we do know is that the Salic laws laid down the codes of procedure and rights of the chief tribe of the barbarian Franks, who were in contention with the Romans from the third century to the fifth century, when they overcame Roman power and authority and established their own kingdom. Although these compilations are obscure and their precise origins uncertain, they are important for our purposes because they provide an important insight into enduring principles of inheritance of peoples gathered together in villages and tribes, chieftainships and hundreds, and governing in accordance with the rules of a successful chief on horseback moving among his kin, rather than the principles and practices of settled political life enunciated earlier in this book by Aristotle, Cicero, and Augustine.

The rule of the Salic law that attracted most attention was that which entitled women to inherit private movable property, such as arms, cattle, horses, and slaves, yet precluded them from inheritance of land and homes, and hence succession to the throne. This rule of succession was prominently enforced by the Valois and the Bourbons in France, introduced to support the cause of Philip V in Spain, and used decisively in the claim of Edward III to the French throne that served as a pretext to the Hundred Years' War.

For the purposes of Montesquieu's analysis, however, it is important to know that he argued that during the conquest of vast tracts of land by the barbarians, the Salic law was not absolutely kept and in his view was sometimes "silenced" when a man left his land to daughters (pp. 129–32). In support of this argument he cited two formularies. The first ancient formulary is that in which according to Salic law daughters were excluded by males: i.e., when females stood in competition to their brother (*first race*), and the second formulary is that which proves the daughter succeeded to the prejudice of the grandson—therefore, *only* excluded by son—(*second race*). Montesquieu recounted this obscure legal argument to show that if there had been a general prohibition on inheritance of land by females, then the histories, formularies, and charters of France that continually mention the lands and possessions of females would have been inexplicable. What was essential, therefore, was not an advertance to classical Greco-Roman political theory to explain the difference between *politikos* and barbarian, freeman and slave, but a closer examination and understanding of that which had been silenced in the complex stages, or races, of the history of the Salic laws from the third century. Although he thereby introduced the notion of two "races," he offered no theoretical formulation until he looked for historical evidence that the Salic and Ripuarian Franks joined together under Clovis to compile their own laws and to collect the customs of the Bavarians and Germans in written form. He believed it likely that the Thuringian code was given by Theodoric and that all these laws—Salic, Ripuarian, Bavarian, and others—were rooted in Germany. The Franks struck out the elements inconsistent with Christianity but preserved the character and spirit of the German laws. These Franks, claimed Montesquieu, were the *first race*. The *second race* consisted of the Visigoths, Lombards, and Burgundians, who had experienced interference from the authority of the bishops. In fact the code of the Visigoths included laws that were ridiculous and foolish and could be held responsible for the excesses of the Inquisition.

Frankish Origins   Montesquieu attacked Dubos's argument that the Franks and Gallo-Romans had mixed from the beginning, saying that Dubos's sources were suspect (pp. 232–3). His alternative history focused on Charles the Bald, who in A.D. 864 at Pistes required a clear distinction between countries where cases were decided by Roman law and those under Germanic law. In France, Germanic law fell away as feudalism disintegrated, and here Montesquieu reintroduced the idea of races.

The Races of Time   Having made the technical distinction between Roman law and the laws of the Franks by introducing the notion of stages or races, Montesquieu then showed how the races changed historically. Under the first race, or period of time, one law in France was authorized and observed strictly in accordance with Roman "political" principles. Under the second race—the period of the rise of the petty lordships and hereditary fiefs—there was not only a breakdown of vestigial Roman administration but, by the end of this stage, a neglect of Salic, Burgundian, and Visigothic laws. The third stage came when kings, lords, and bishops were unable to assemble together and when the kings no longer had deputies in the provinces to cover the administration of the laws.

Montesquieu's use of the word "race" in this context made reference to races of time, or stages in a legal formulation, and his meaning was not so very different from that of John Foxe. But Montesquieu went one step further: to justify title to rule by reference to a theory of race conceived in terms of these legal divisions. His extremely important contribution was to consolidate a new theory of "racial" origins for the legitimization of politics *qua* politics and for the overthrow of existing unjust regimes like Louis XIV's. Montesquieu grounded his arguments "racially" in the historical transitions made manifest in the struggle between Frankish law and Roman law. Although he did not identify the Franks and Romans as races of men, he gave credibility and momentum to the notion that the European barbarians were not aimless wanderers in an outside, a northern void, but an important part of the races of time and law, firmly rooted in climate, land, relief, and soil.

Montesquieu's discourse on the spirit of the laws had the effect of detaching the traditional inquiry into Church law and the theological formulation of it from existing politics and law, which began to be seen not as sure avenues to the good life and good government, but as unnatural and irrational expressions of an immutable sovereign political order that could only be restored to proper order by a rigorous philosophical analysis of the nature of soul or mind, or by a more prosaic root-and-branch examination of the obligation to land, Christian and feudal notions of property, and a revolutionary move to a money economy and the satisfaction of individual economic interest.

» The Emergence of Anthropology

In 1619 René Descartes pronounced that the universe was a material mechanism—a vast system explicable mathematically by the power of human reason. With Francis Bacon's reasoned reconciliation of biblical exegesis and advancing knowledge about nature, Isaac Newton's rules governing cause and effect, and Thomas Hobbes's gloomy destruction of Aristotle's metaphysics and politics, we see the beginnings of a more systematic approach to understanding species and monstrous production by the logical analysis of place, climate, legal capitularies (races), and language.

PRECURSORS TO BLUMENBACH

The year after Locke published his *Essay Concerning Human Understanding,* John Ray (also Wray, 1627–1705) published his popular work, *The Wisdom of God*

Manifested in the Works of Creation (1691), which was soon followed by *Miscellaneous Discourse Concerning the Dissolution and Changes of the World* (1692). Locke had already praised Ray's fine precision in applying the Aristotelian method to the findings of Francis Willughby's botanical voyages of discovery to England and Europe. First published in 1673, by 1682 these findings had been transformed from a major catalogue or table of plants into a general history— *Methodus Plantorum Nova* (1682)—of the whole organic world of plants and animals. Regarded as the father of natural history, Ray was the first to classify animals in a scheme grounded in nature. His work contributed directly to the works of Georges-Louis Leclerc, Comte de Buffon; the Jussieu brothers; and Georges Dagobert, Baron Cuvier.

Surveying these developments a century later, Johann Friedrich Blumenbach (1752–1840), the father of modern "skin and bones" anthropology, pointed to at least a dozen attempts to divide humankind in a more logical way than had been possible in the sixteenth and early seventeenth centuries. Among the first was that of François Bernier (1625–88), who in 1684, in "Nouvelle division de la terre par les differents espèces ou races qui l'habitent," published anonymously in Paris in *Journal des Scavans,* had proposed four or five "espèces ou races" on the basis of geography, color, and physical traits. These were:

Europe (excluding Lapland), South Asia, North Africa, and America: people who shared similar climates and complexions

Africa proper: people who had thick lips, flat noses, black skin, and a scanty beard

Asia proper: people who had white skin, broad shoulders, flat faces, little eyes and no beard

Lapps: people who were ugly, squat, small, and animal-like

Blumenbach also acknowledged the contribution of the Swedish naturalist and professor of botany at Uppsala, Carolus Linnaeus (1707–78), who had rigorously attended to classification, order, and method in the sorting out of things. Although a devout Christian, Linnaeus doubted the biblical account of the division of the world. His interest in natural objects and his research into the customs and habits of the Lapps led him in his first edition of *Systema Naturae* (1735) to adapt Aristotle's ideas of *genus* and *species* very much along the lines suggested by Locke. Eventually he worked out an arrangement by which class, *genus*, and *species* could be used as convenient tools to postulate a general order of primates in which man was no longer considered to be apart from the animal kingdom, operating in a realm according to moral principles, but a part of a natural order, arranged in the following manner:

Homo ferus: wild, savage, cruel man

Europaeus albus: ingenious, white, sanguine, governed by law

Americanus rubescus: happy with his lot, liberty loving, tanned and irascible, governed by custom

Asiaticus luridus: yellow, melancholy, governed by opinion

Afer niger: crafty, lazy, careless, black, governed by the arbitrary will of the master

Blumenbach recognized Linnaeus' novel division of humankind into White European, Red American, Dark Asiatic, and Black Negro by color, but felt the work was logically flawed by Linnaeus' assertion that man classed *in* nature alongside the lemur and the bat was directly related to the monkey and ape: "It is wonderful how little the most foolish ape differs from the wisest man."[9] In *Fauna Suecica* (1746), Linnaeus classified the population of Sweden by hair, eye, and stature, according to three divisions of Goths, Finns, and Lapps.

Blumenbach was more comfortable with the analysis of Georges-Louis Leclerc, Comte de Buffon (1707–88), disciple of John Locke, who had also classified humankind in physiological terms while avoiding, insofar as possible, both the theological and the mythological biblical schema and the works of the Schoolmen.

Buffon's classification was sixfold:

Lapp Polar

Tartar

South Asian

European

Ethiopian

American

Although his views changed over time, Buffon did not believe in the permanence of species and did not emphasize classification so much as the examination of individual detail. Variations in humankind, he said, depend on climate, habitation, and diet; he also drew attention to the significance of language. He attempted to separate reflection upon natural things from metaphysical and religious ideas, and while, like Linnaeus, he followed the Aristotelian method, he disagreed with Linnaeus' attempt to capture nature within a single classification system, arguing that science was not about certitude but about probability derived from the immense variety to be found in nature.

Buffon's work is more descriptive of individual things, and distinctions between things and words, than the work of Linnaeus. Hence it was neither so tightly constrained and methodical, nor did it carry forward Linnaeus' fixed identities of physical and mental traits. Buffon's perspective may have been influenced by the bitter disputes about method he observed at close hand when he translated Stephen Hales's *Vegetable Statics* (1727) into French in 1735, and by Newton's *Method of Fluxion,* in which Newton contested the invention of calculus with Gottfried Wilhelm Leibniz. It may also have had something to do with the overwhelming popularity of the first three volumes of his own great work, *Histoire naturelle, générale et particulière,* which was published a year after Montesquieu's work on the races as formularies, and covered a vast territory, eventually running to forty-four volumes, on minerals, birds, epochs, reptiles, fish, crustacea, and man. Buffon shared with Blumenbach the clear separation of man from the apes on grounds of man's articulated language, upon which the Lockean distinction between animality and humanity also rested. For Buffon, man was a creature of reason, and the variety between man and man was explained by climate or the mode of living. This distinction between language and milieu stirred up by Locke, Bernier, Buffon, Montesquieu, and Linnaeus greatly occupied Blumenbach and later anthropologists and philologists.

BLUMENBACH

Blumenbach claimed that governor of Virginia, Nathanial Powell (d. 1622) was the first to study the skull in *A New Collection of Voyages,* published in eight volumes in 1767, which examined three divisions based on the white, red, and black sons of Noah (2:273). At the age of ten Blumenbach had been introduced to the study of skeletons at the university at Gotha, where his father was professor. He then went to Göttingen, where he became acquainted with the work of the Swiss anatomist and botanist Albrecht von Haller (1708–77), who had been appointed to the chair of medicine there in 1736. Blumenbach devoted himself to working out a definitive account of the varieties of humankind based on a rigorous commitment to Aristotelian method, as influenced by the contributions of Locke, Linnaeus, and Buffon. His grand idea was the unity of the human species. On September 16, 1775, he published *De Generis Humani Varietate Natura*,[10] for which he is regarded as the father of anthropology.

The Natural Variety of Mankind   As Eric Voegelin has pointed out, in this first edition of 1775 Blumenbach used the traditional term *varietas* to describe the marvelous diversity of humankind, but by the third edition in 1795 the term, although not eliminated entirely, was overshadowed by *gens* and *gentilitius,* which Voegelin takes to mean "race" and "racial." Voegelin also argues vehemently that Blumenbach restricted the meaning of *varietas* to the physical characteristics of man and did not extend it to psychological and characterological traits. His dispositions, therefore, are more like the old humoral descriptions of the "outside peoples" than with the more precise psychological characteristics of a later period. Blumenbach uses the old system of "having such and such a character" (Germans are overorganized, English are underprincipled. . . .) rather than the more systematized sets of individual characteristics derived from the rational analysis of "personality." Blumenbach's *facies gentilitia* should not be taken to be anything but the plastic formation of what Voegelin chooses to call "a racial face type."[11]

Voegelin's caution reminds us not to presuppose the enlargement of a biological category to a mental and historical category before it actually happened. We should be equally careful not to assume that Montesquieu, Blumenbach, Buffon, and Linnaeus had rid themselves of the physical and mental baggage of the Middle Ages or that their reflections on physiological and anatomical data necessarily anticipated a racial disposition.

In the first edition of 1775 Blumenbach initially proposed four varieties of humankind—the inhabitants of Europe, Asia, Africa, and that part of America nearest Europe. Although he noted differences in color, he based his classification largely on the formation of the head. Using his collection of eighty-two skulls, he studied facial angles and laid down fundamental rules for the examination of skulls. After further investigation of eastern Asia and America, he decided that a division of humankind into five varieties was "more consonant to nature" (1st ed., p. 99). He insisted that his varieties were not fixed, immutable descriptions but were liable to discrepancy and subject to further investigation. These varieties were:

1 The largest, the primeval variety: Here Blumenbach placed the inhabitants of the whole of Europe, including the Lapps, whom he was unable to separate from Europeans on grounds of appearance and a language that seemed to have a Finnish origin. He included that part of West Asia this side of Obi, the Caspian Sea, Mount Taurus, and the Ganges, as well as North Africa, Greenland, and the Esquimo in America, whom he saw as distinct from the other inhabitants of America and believed were derived from the Finns.

2 The rest of Asia: Here Blumenbach placed those who live beyond the Ganges, beyond the Caspian Sea and Obi toward Nova Zemlya. These people were brownish in color, verging on olive, with straight faces, narrow eyelids, and scanty hair. He subdivided them into two varieties:

> Northern: The people of China, Korea, Tonkin, Pegu, Siam, and Ava, who were characterized by monosyllabic languages, depravity, and perfidiousness of spirit and manners;

> Southern: The Ostiaks, Siberians, Tunguses, Mantchoos, Tartars, Calmucks, and Japanese.

3 Africa: The inhabitants were black men, who were muscular and had a prominent upper jaw, swelling lips, turned-up nose, and very black curly hair.

4 The rest of America: The inhabitants were copper colored, had a thin habit of body, and scanty hair.

5 The new southern world: The people of Sunda, Molucca, Philippines, and the Pacific archipeligo divided into Otaheitans, New Zealanders, Friendly Isles, Easter Isles, and Marquesas, who were elegant and mild of disposition, and the New Caledonians, Tanna, and New Hebridians, who were blacker and more curly haired, more distrustful, and ferocious.

Not until the third edition of 1795 did Blumenbach reflect fully on the history of these tentative divisions of humankind. He acknowledged the original contribution of Bernier, Leibniz (who introduced the word *Rasse* into German), Buffon, and Powell. Here he presented a revised arrangement of the five principal varieties, introducing the term "Caucasian," which he derived from the name of the peoples who occupied the southern slopes of the Georgian region (and which is now widely and speciously used by immigration services worldwide):

Caucasian (described in the 1781 edition for the first time)

Mongolian (described in the 1781 edition as *Asiatic*)

Ethiopian

American

Malay

In this classification Blumenbach stated that the Caucasian was the most beautiful and preeminent because of the convergence in shape of skull and beauty toward the mean primeval type. On both sides of the mean there were ultimate extremes—the Mongolian, Ethiopian, and indeed other primeval Europeans occupying lands from the west side of the Ganges to Greenland and North America—who diverged from that mean. The American was the transitional passage from Caucasian to Mongolian, and the Malay the transitional passage from Caucasian to Ethiopian. Both were of inferior rank.[12]

Again Blumenbach conceded that these classifications overlapped and should not be taken as fixed and immutable. Indeed, in his introductory remarks addressed to Sir Joseph Banks, president of the Royal Society, he opposed entirely the view of the three kingdoms of nature following one upon the other like steps in a scale or couplings in a chain. This view of a Great Chain of Being, which Arthur Lovejoy refers to as "the sacred phrase" of the eighteenth century analogous to the blessed word "evolution" in the late nineteenth, Blumenbach said was no longer tenable.[13]

Monsters and Wild Men   To arrive at this classification of varieties of man, Blumenbach had first to address the old problem of monstrosity: the relationship between the wild brute and man, between ape and man in nature, between natural causes and hidden causes, between physical evidence and linguistic resonances. He opened his first edition with the fundamental question left unanswered by Linnaeus: are men, and have the men of all times and of every variety, been of one and the same, or clearly of more than one, species?

Blumenbach rejected entirely the disgusting stories put about by Plutarch and Vergil of the sexual relationships between Indian women and the larger apes, and he regarded as utterly barren the disputes raging around him about the endowments of mind, reason, and speech of brutes. Anyone with a modicum of learning about the endowments of mind and body structures must see, he stated, the significant differences between man and beast without need for reference to biblical exegesis, physico-theology, or hidden causes.

What, then, are the characteristics of man? Blumenbach believed that man was destitute of instincts—congenital faculties for protection from external injury and food foraging. Man is born naked and, dependent on society and education, gradually acquires reason. Beasts do not leave the company of other beasts by reason. What distinguishes man is speech; his is the voice of reason rather than the sound of instinctual affection. What permits man to move from the realm of the bestial to the realm of man is speech. Blumenbach provided supporting medical evidence for his contention that man is different from the brute, using his own work on comparative anatomy, especially on the larynx and uvula in apes, and the work of Edward Tyson (1650–1708) on the pygmy. In addition, his dissection, measurement, and analysis of the brain of a mandril had convinced him that the orangutan was not closely allied to man. On this evidence he rejected Linnaeus' opinion that man was not distinguishable from the ape. On the contrary, Blumenbach thought that a glance at man easily shows how much he differs from the rest of animals; analysis by reference to a fixed criterion was unnecessary. Indeed the Supreme Power had avoided giving distinct and persistent characters to the human body in exactly the same measurable proportion because man's noblest part, reason, far excelled that of all other animals and made man the masterpiece of nature.

Blumenbach also investigated the accounts of so-called wild men who were believed to be half-beast, half-man—the Hessian boy, Zell girl, Champagne girl, and Peter Hamelin—and proved that these were human beings. Their dental records differed from those of animals; they possessed characteristic human laughter; and the females had hymens and periodic menstrual fluxes. Blumenbach's close analysis of hair, breasts, circumcision, testicles, teeth, deformed ears, penes, and nails showed that arguments claiming plural origins of the species were more often than not based on causes which turned out to be nothing more than common diseases such as skin ailments and albinism. The monsters, men with tails, pygmies, and giants were, affirmed Blumenbach, tales of the fablers.

In the third edition of *De Generis Humani Varietate Natura,* Blumenbach attacked directly those who had seen the gradation of nature as nicely articulated steps and those who had ranked things artificially, according to incorrect methodology, especially Lord Monboddo, James Burnett (1714–99), who in his massive *Ancient Metaphysics* (1779–99) and *The Origins and Progress of Language* (1773) had stressed the natural transition from animal to man and had included man in the same species as the orangutan. The enthusiasm displayed by Lord Monboddo, Jean-Jacques Rousseau, and John Arbuthnot for the stories of wild men was similarly dismissed as nonsense. Blumenbach urged a consistent use of the Linnaean and Newtonian methodology supported by sound natural historical evidence from Herodotus' *Histories* and Hippocrates' *Airs, Waters and Places* and from his own collection of eighty-two skulls, all of which demonstrated significant differences in ape and man. Where there were confusions and doubts in the division into varieties or species, Blumenbach urged extreme caution and fell back upon two Newtonian rules: (1) that the same causes should be assigned to account for natural effects of the same kind; and (2) that we ought not to admit more causes of natural things than what are sufficient to explain the phenomenon: "We must therefore assign the same causes for the bodily diversity of the races of mankind to which we assign a similar diversity of body in other *domestic* animals which are widely scattered over the world" (190–91).

The Unity of Species   This analysis left Blumenbach with two further un-answered questions: the problem of Creation and change, and the biblical explanation of the tripartite division of the world, particularly the plight of Ham—the Negro. The term Negro was first used by the Spanish and Por-tuguese in the sixteenth century simply to describe in a nonpejorative way the black peoples of West Africa. Purchas used it in much the same way to describe Ethiopians. It was not until the eighteenth century that it was used to imply some kind of physical or mental inferiority, or as a standard mea-surement of beauty and ugliness. Blumenbach wrote at a time when Negroes and Native Americans were considered half-animals, whose physical qualities were not inferior to those of the European but who had lacked opportunity for the development of faculties.[14]

In the first edition Blumenbach had argued that differences in body struc-ture and skin color could be explained by reference to climate. While he argued a strong case for the rigorous employment of the Linnaean and New-tonian methodology in analyzing the human body and meticulously examined scores of individual samples of skulls, bones, and tissue, he continued to hold a biological theory derived from antiquity. He conceived of the body in Hip-pocratian and Galenist terms, as composed of leaking moisture and nutriment. He set physiognomy to one side as a vast study outside his present terms of reference. Later we shall see how Immanuel Kant, Christoph Nicolai, and Franz Xaver Messerschmidt took up this neglected aspect of his study and rehabilitated it in modern guise.

Blumenbach suggested that the plurality of the species allegedly contained in the scriptural account and in widely published works such as Griffith

Hughes's *Natural History of Barbados* (1750), Oliver Goldsmith's *History of the Earth and Animated Nature* (1773), and Henry Home's *Sketches of the History of Man* (1774), which proclaimed the Ethiopian as a different species of man, was "very arbitrary indeed":

> For although there seems to be so great a difference between widely separate nations, that you might easily take the inhabitants of the Cape of Good Hope, the Greenlanders, and the Circassians for so many different species of man, yet when the matter is thoroughly considered, you see that all do so run into one another, and that one variety of mankind does so sensibly pass into the other, that you cannot mark out the limits between them. (98.99)

In a detailed analysis of the Negro, who some had claimed should be placed behind rather than alongside the Caucasian because of an obtuse mental capacity and a distinctive difference in color, Blumenbach asserted his investigations had uncovered no bodily character peculiar to the Negro that could not be found in other peoples. He dismissed out of hand the assertion that Ethiopians were close to apes. Even by the standard of the Greek ideal of physical beauty, which so preoccupied his literary colleagues, Blumenbach affirmed that simple observation would identify as many ugly Europeans as ugly Negroes. He concluded that Negroes were naturally tender of heart, had considerable powers of calculation and aptitude for music, and were not inferior to any other race of mankind when taken all together (307.8). For Blumenbach all varieties and differences overlapped and merged into one another and had to be viewed according to the species, which was one and the same— a unity.

Blumenbach insisted that three rules had to be followed in considering evidence of the variety of mankind: (1) that the human species stands alone; (2) that no "fact" should be admitted without a supporting document, that is, anatomical data; and (3) that no natural scientist should pass from one explanation to another without heeding intermediate terms and shadings. Where there were doubts about such matters as the comparability of skulls and bone structures, Blumenbach thought that almost always they could be resolved by pressing harder on Newtonian method in the examination of the evidence available rather than by falling back on hearsay evidence or the legend of Noah.

The Nisus Formativus *and Degeneration*   Given the persistence of interest in arbitrary divisions of humankind, Blumenbach returned in his third
edition to that account which held that at the dawn of Creation no animal or
plant was generated but that was already formed in the shape of undeveloped
germs. Rejecting this proposition as unsound, he proposed a curious energy—the *nisus formativus*—which he regarded not as a cause so much as a
perpetual and consistent effect that could be deduced *a posteriori* from the
very constancy and universality of phenomena (p. 194). This mysterious energy
was affected by stimuli, such as climate, mode of life, and hybrid generation.
He described it in *On the Formative Force and Its Influence on Generation and Reproduction* (1780), *On the Formative Force and on the Operation of Generation* (1781),
On the Force of Nutrition (1781), and *Contributions to Natural History* (1806). His
nisus formativus became a "life force" in the works of Immanuel Kant, Johann
Fichte, Friedrich Schelling, and Johann von Goethe, as we shall see. Blumenbach introduced the *nisus formativus* only after he had pushed the causes of
degeneration to their limit in his analysis of the corporeal diversity of man
and had explored the true causes of natural phenomena as far as sound Newtonian methodology would take him. For Blumenbach the plurality of the
species could not be tenable before all possible variables within the idea of
the unity of species had been examined and all causes of degeneration to
explain the diversity of mankind had been thoroughly investigated (p. 192).

   Blumenbach considered the causes and ways by which mankind had degenerated as a species, pointing to chemistry, bile, climate, face, and skin as
natural causes for differences in color. He criticized the works of the Dutch
anatomist Petrus Camper (1722–89) on facial angles. Camper's dissertation
on the real differences in the traits of the face among men of different countries (1781) gave an account of facial angle, which he used as a cranial characteristic. Blumenbach's *norma verticalis,* however, took the measuring from the
top of the skull suggesting instead a vertical scale for defining characteristics
of skulls looking down from above. More important, he argued that Camper's
reliance upon form and the measurement of facial angles of skulls had neglected not only the capacity of the skull, but the mind and soul of human
beings. Blumenbach also suggested the examination of teeth, breasts, penes,
hands, legs, feet, and stature, primarily to observe differences and similarities
in a wide catalogue of examples. He was clearly confident that painstaking
and exhaustive comparative analysis without reference to the *nisus formativus*
would yield results sufficient to reject any polygenist theory.

The Influence of Blumenbach   In an appreciation published with the London translation of Blumenbach's work in 1865, M. P. J. Flourens (1794–1867), editor of the complete works of Buffon and secretary of the Academy of Sciences, praised Blumenbach's application of Linnaean method. His great contribution, said Flourens, was in the abortive debates about the true origins of the European, the Jew, the Negro, and the wild men, especially his insistence on well-documented evidence and avoidance of extreme judgments about intermediate terms and gradual shadings. "The human race had forgotten its original unity, and Blumenbach restored it," claimed Flourens (p. 58).

Notwithstanding Blumenbach's categorical statements on the unity of the species and his recognition of the Negro as belonging wholly to the family of man, his conclusions were not wholly accepted. Professor K. F. H. Marx, whose memoirs of his colleague at Göttingen also appeared in the London translation, suggested that Blumenbach had not entirely renounced the idea that people were in different stages of physical and moral development:

> How the osseous structure of the skull will approximate nearer and nearer to the form of the beast, when unfortunate exterior circumstances and inferior relations have stood in the way of the development of the higher faculties, might be seen in his collection from the cretin's skull, which, not without meaning, lay side by side with that of the orang-utang; whilst, at a little distance off, the surpassingly beautiful shape of that of a female Georgian attracted everyone's attention. (p. 9)

Despite Blumenbach's evidence from the analysis of skulls that man and beast were distinct and that there was no physical relationship between the Negro and the orangutan, there remained lingering doubts about the subtle divisions within his exploratory classification system. During the last forty years of his long life controversy raged over items he had put squarely on the agenda: degeneration, the formative force, the significance of language and milieu (geography, climate, relief, soil, land), and, perhaps most important of all, the capacity of peoples for progressive physical, moral, and political development.

» *National Character*

Theophile Simar has pointed out that the idea of race cannot easily be detached from the anthropological inquiries of Linnaeus, Buffon, and Blumenbach because it was they who began the painstaking process of classifying and comparing man anatomically alongside the primates and attributing human difference to the laws of nature. Yet he agrees with Voegelin and Arendt that anthropology proper did not of itself give rise to radical ideas because in its eighteenth-century phase it did not depart from the Greco-Roman notion of order or Aristotelian logical arrangement within a unity of species. Race only became "une entité réele agissant et vivant" when it went beyond the new classifications of Hobbes, Locke, Montesquieu, and the physical anthropologists and developed a *will* to individual power based on a biology that distinguished superior and inferior races.[15]

Montesquieu's interest in the spirit of laws extended the scope of inquiry into the nature of good government beyond Aristotle and beyond the constraints imposed by the hierarchy of tradition, revelation, and authority in the Great Chain of Being to explore the nature of soul and mind. Henceforth the discourse would be about soul, spirit, and mind, rather than a fixed hierarchy of tradition, revelation, and authority. While Aristotle had contended that politics could not take place in nature but only when man separated himself from nature, eighteenth-century theorists returned to the natural environment as the source of the rights of man and the basis for rational social action.

The new form of state put in place of the antique forms of *polis* and *respublica* was sometimes conceived of as an autonomous organic sovereign body and sometimes as a clockwork mechanism within a newly invented natural phenomenon called society. Some writers promoted a natural and physiological state, others a state in which the conduct of life would be governed entirely by the economic, administrative, and moral criteria. Still others were content to see some minimum residual functions retained by the political state, so long as the individuals within society were left to their own devices to pursue their individual occupational interests. And in some extreme instances, state and society were abandoned altogether as a workable concept, with the conduct of life to be left to the hidden hand of naked self-interest or autonomous mind. In whatever form it appeared, the new state drew upon the physiological and biological analogies that were becoming popular in the works of the natural historians, anatomists, and physical anthropologists. Society encompassed individuals associated in nature who increasingly entertained ideas that they had natural rights by birth. These were entirely different from the citizens of Greece and Rome, whose status derived from their action in the political arena.

HUME

In the same year that Montesquieu's reflections on climate and physical environment were published, the Scottish philosopher David Hume (1711–76) addressed the problem of the separation of bodily structures and physical causes from the endowments of the mind.[16] His important essay "Of National Characters" opens with the words: "The vulgar are apt to carry all national characters to extremes; and having once established it as a principle, that any people are knavish, or cowardly, or ignorant, they will admit of no exception, but comprehend every individual under the same censure" (3.244). Apart from the jealous love of the inhabitants of southern climes and the drunkenness of northerners, Hume could see no evidence that physical causes acted on the human mind. It was not climate that made manners similar, but congregation together and the communication of virtue and vice. Rational man was a sociable creature who made resemblances by frequent association. It did not follow, however, that nature produced things in like proportion in all places. In every society there were ingredients of indolence and industry, valor and cowardice, humanity and brutality, wisdom and folly that mixed together to give "tincture" to natural instincts. In republican states the desire for the public good and legitimate authority were impressed upon private interest and the ties of nature.

Contesting Montesquieu, Hume boldly asserted that the principal reason for England's beautiful system of governance was that government, not nature, fosters a national character. This character, developed over a long period of time, is shaped by the accidents of battle, negotiation, and marriage, insofar as they bear upon the extent of a government's authority. But Hume also acknowledged that some peoples managed to maintain similitude of manners despite their dispersion, contending that the Jews were notable for fraud and the Armenians for probity. In a footnote he remarked that a small society within a larger one is likely to display a uniform morality because the faults of individuals will draw dishonor upon the whole (3.249).

Those peoples who lived at the Poles, explained Hume, lived in misery and poverty, just as those who lived in the South were indolent. These conditions he attributed to moral causes rather than physical causes, claiming categorically that these peoples "are inferior to the rest of the species and are incapable of higher attainment of the human mind" (3.256). It was this difference in the capacity of the human mind and the comparative influence and frictional relationship between moral and physical causes that Blumenbach's powerful concept of the unity of species was quite unable to accommodate.

In an oft-repeated passage, Hume speculated that Negroes were naturally inferior to whites because they had produced no civilized nation or individual eminent in action, speculation, manufacture, the arts, or the sciences. Negro slaves exhibited no ingenuity, while whites were enterprising self-starters (3.249). Referring to ancient theories of heat inflaming the blood and the passions and to Aristotle's account in the *Politics* (2.9) of Solon's constitution, Hume argued that the Negro lacked political instincts and was unable to enter into those institutional arrangements that created a civil disposition: "You may obtain anything of the NEGROES by offering them strong drink; and may easily prevail with them to sell, not only their children, but their wives and mistresses, for a cask of brandy" (3.257). Hume did, however, disapprove of slavery on economic grounds and believed it was disadvantageous to the happiness of mankind (11.390, 393).

In sum, Hume did not believe that national character and manners were derived from natural causes, preferring instead to assign cause to congregation over a long period of time. Like Locke, he emphasized the effective communication of ideas of virtue and vice through long-standing public arrangements. The foundation for those political arrangements, however, was not in an original contract, and in this he agreed with Boulanvilliers.

Montesquieu had argued that the English had borrowed their idea of political government from a German noble strain and that it was based neither on Boulanvillier's and Hobbes's right of conquest nor on Dubos's natural right inherited from a Gallo-Roman source but on legal transitions (or stages or "races") from political to feudal to the present. Clearly Montesquieu was fundamentally at odds with Hume, who gave precedence to the efficacy of existing government, if only for the sake of stability and order.

LESSING

These opposing views on contract and on the effect—or not—of physical causes upon the human mind stimulated an outpouring of literary analysis and criticism. In Germany, where Blumenbach's immense scholarship in the field of physical anthropology and natural history had not been matched by a similar achievement in literature or art, the conflict was particularly fierce, especially in relation to the unfinished items on Blumenbach's agenda concerning degeneration, the formative force or energy, the ideal of beauty and ugliness within the unity of species, and the impact of language and milieu upon the capacity for moral and physical development.

In the eighteenth century German writers had generally followed the French rationalists' turgid notes on literary taste laid down in 1730 by Johann Christoph Gottsched's *Kritische Dichtkunst für die Deutschen*. Even though Gottsched (1700–66) was challenged by Friedrich Gottlieb Klopstock (1724–1803), a poet who tried to establish independence for German literature by reviving an interest in the poetry of the Germanic heroes, it was not until Gotthold Ephraim Lessing's (1729–81) *Briefe, die neueste Literatur betreffend* (1754) which attacked the suppression of German genius by French literature, that German writers were urged to investigate Germanic characterization.[17] Following Montesquieu's penchant for Germanic-English forms of government, Lessing promoted William Shakespeare as a model for literary style and taste. There followed in the years between 1759 and 1765 a controversial and stimulating debate about literature and the classics involving Lessing as well as Christoph Nicolai and Moses Mendelssohn.

In *Laocoön,* an essay on literary criticism published in 1766 and running to many editions thereafter, Lessing delineated new judgments in painting, poetry, and the plastic arts, using Aristotle's *Metaphysics* as the touchstone. Throughout the work runs the theme that German literature and its concepts of beauty and ugliness, whether subject to the tests of the amateur, the philosopher, or the literary critic, are shallow in judgment and false in taste.

In considering the ugliness and beauty of forms, Lessing drew upon numerous exemplars from Greco-Roman literature, poetry, painting, and sculpture and from Germanic medieval and Renaissance sources. He noticed that some things, such as scars, harelips, prominent nostrils, or the absence of eyebrows, were not offensive to the common senses of smell, taste, and touch, yet produced a fascinating "inward sensation" of disgust. But not all peoples found the same things disgusting:

> Everyone knows how filthy the Hottentots are and how many things they consider beautiful and elegant and sacred which with us awaken disgust and aversion. A flattened cartilage of a nose, flabby breasts hanging down to the navel, the whole body smeared with a cosmetic of goat's fat and soot gone rotten in the sun, the hair dripping with grease, arms and legs bound about with fresh entrails—let one think of this as the object of an ardent, reverent, tender love; let one hear this exalted language of gravity and admiration and refrain from laughter. (pp. 93–94)

In a debate over the evidence of miracles in the Bible, Lessing defended the right of free criticism of the Bible and the autonomy of Christianity as a living and conquering power in itself. He argued that Christianity was a dynamic formative force that had existed *sui generis* as a living, conquering power before the New Testament was ever written. For this shocking idea, his works were confiscated, and he turned instead to the stage and to Shakespearean drama. In *Nathan der Weise* (1779) he dramatized the creeds of Nathan the Jew (probably modeled after Moses Mendelssohn), Saladin the Muslim, and the Christian Knight Templar as ideas of noble character and used the stage as the platform for his message of the importance of characterization, a new Christianity, and the need for independence and tolerance.

In this dramatic poem Lessing advanced the idea, already explored in *Die Juden* (1749), that the Jew had noble character and that each religion, each dogma, was itself an expression of mankind marching on to higher and more noble moral forms. In these dramatic poems in *Hamburg Dramaturgy* (1962) and in *Laocoön* Lessing created an entirely new critical interest in the operation of personal character in history: "To act with a purpose is what raises man above the brutes, to invent with a purpose, to imitate with a purpose, is that which distinguishes genius from the petty artists who only invent to invent, imitate to imitate" (*Hamburg Dramaturgy*, p. 99). He used the imaginative discovery of Greco-Roman models of beauty and ugliness in art, literature, and poetry to draw attention to a noble German past and to revive an interest, as his friend Moses Mendelssohn had done in his movement to bring anomic Jews back into the mainstream of German intellectual life, in literary criticism and an ideal personal and national character. After Lessing, the Jew, the Muslim, the Negro, the brute are not what they are because they are "extrapolitical"—the *ethnos*—in the antique sense of Hume's static and regressive discussion of national character. They are now what they are because of something to do with their personal moral character. Some, like the Negroes in America, are fixed in it, and bear a lasting burden of "inferiority"; others, like the Germanic peoples, and for that matter the intellectual court Jews, rise to higher and more noble forms of freedom.

KANT

Immanuel Kant (1724–1804), the grandson of a Scot, the intellectual descendant of David Hume, and the inspiration of Houston Stewart Chamberlain, the consummate race thinker, first published his *On the Different Races of Men* in 1775. This tract on nature contested Blumenbach's thesis by proposing a physico-theological order of things. Kant's *Anthropology from a Pragmatic Point of View,* completed in 1798, subjected the concepts of personal, sexual, national, and moral character to a much closer philosophical investigation with the intention of discerning man's inner self—the inner self tentatively and dramatically explored by Lessing—from the exterior physical self.[18] Unlike Hume, Kant used the word "character" in two senses: "Having a certain physical character is the distinguishing mark of man as a being belonging to the world of sense, or nature: having character simply characterizes man as a rational being, one endowed with freedom" (p. 151).

The distinction is between character arising out of sense impression and physicality and character arising out of thought. For Kant physical character was derived from the ordinary feelings of pleasure and displeasure. A man's nature had more to do with the way he was affected by others than with the appetitive power, where life manifests itself not merely in feeling but also in outward activity. From a physiological point of view temperament was understood by Kant to be physical constitution and physical complexion, the ebbing and flowing of the humors; from a mental point of view, temperament was understood to be the emotional and appetitive capacities of the soul (p. 152).

Temperament   Temperaments ascribed to the soul were subdivided into temperaments of feeling and activity, each connected with the heightening and slackening (*intensio et remissio*) of something we have already encountered in Blumenbach's work—the vital force. According to Kant, there are four simple temperaments—the sanguine, melancholy, choleric, and phlegmatic—types Linnaeus also used in his systematic ordering of mankind in *Systema Naturae* (1735) and which continue to be working hypotheses in many contemporary "theories" of race.

These temperaments of feeling were further subdivided into the sanguine temperament of the light-blooded man (*des Leichtblutigen*), and the melancholy temperament of the grave and heavy-blooded man (*des Schwerblutigen*). The temperaments of activity were subdivided between the choleric temperament of the hot-blooded man (*des Warmblutigen*), and the phlegmatic temperament of the cold-blooded man (*des Kaltblutigen*). Kant did not think that there was such a thing as a composite temperament.

Thus far Kant's philosophical analysis separated the physical from the mental, the body from the soul, and "typed" temperaments from one another under the influence of a physico-theological life force or energy. From a historical point of view it is worth noting that the physical basis for Kant's analysis owed much to the humoral doctrine of Hippocrates and Galen, and particularly to the revival of Platonism in the Cabalist writings of the Middle Ages.

Character   For Kant what nature makes of man logically belongs to temperament, where the subject is for the most part passive, but what man makes of *himself* (and here we are reminded of Lessing) has to do with the character he has as the property of *Will*—the force by which he binds himself to principles he has prescribed to himself irrevocably by his own reason. Character is a ceremony of making a vow to oneself "solemnly in a moment of transformation" from Instinct to Reason, "like the beginning of an epoch": "In short, the sole proof of a man's consciousness affords him that he has character is his having made it his supreme maxim to be truthful, both in his admissions to himself and in his conduct toward every other man" (p. 160).

Kant's philosophical analysis of temperament and character is extremely relevant to the emerging idea of race because it introduced an entirely new idea: that the art of judging what lies within the man is part of characterization and physiognomy has something important to say about that.

This line of reasoning is a fundamental departure from Aristotle, who held that a civic disposition appeared when men departed the realm of the private and barbarous and entered into a political relationship by virtue of their capacity to *do* politics, to speak in a public realm, to cut across the monotonous cycle of natural necessity, and to have a respect for the law and a desire to change the law for the general good of the *polis*. Physiognomical and characterological criteria were important only insofar as they shed a dim light upon the realm of necessity, in which man shared his uncertain fate with other men. For Aristotle it is contestable that physiognomy has something important to say about what man is. For Kant the connection is incontestable.

> From the fact that a watch has a fine case, we cannot judge positively that the movement inside is also good (says a famous watchmaker); but if the case is poorly made, we can be reasonably sure that the movement is not worth much either. For the craftsman will hardly discredit a piece of work he has made carefully by neglecting the exterior, which costs him the least trouble. But it would be absurd to conclude, by the analogy between the human craftsman and the inscrutable creator of nature, that the same thing holds for Him: that, for example, he has joined a handsome body to a good soul in order to commend

the man he created to other men and bring him into favor—or that, on the other hand, he wants to scare one man away from another (by *hic niger est, hunc tu Romane caveto*). If we are looking for a ground for regarding these two heterogeneous things (body and soul) as united in man to the same end, this will not do. For taste, which is a merely subjective ground for one man's being pleased or displeased with other men (according to whether they are handsome or ugly) cannot serve as a guiding principle to Wisdom, which has the existence of a man with certain natural qualities objectively as its end (which is, for us, quite incomprehensible). (pp. 160–61)

While Kant expressed some skepticism about the ideas of Johann Lavater (1741–1801), the mystic friend of Goethe who contended that character could be determined from facial characteristics, he proceeded to divide up the physiognomy into the following novel categories, which have come to occupy an important place in a wide variety of modern hypotheses about the existence or nonexistence of race:

Structure: Comparing the ideal Grecian profile (the prototype) with actual examples of modern faces, Kant suggested a measure of conformity to rule and conformity to mean in determining an overall concept of Beauty. He argued that extrapolating mental qualities from facial structure permitted no more than "an uncertain interpretation." (p. 164)

Features: Kant contended that a face which is a caricature, a distortion, or a mimicry, despite its ugliness, can conceal a good nature.

Expression: Expression is the facial features put into play from an emotional agitation of more or less strength, and frequently repeated expressions become permanent facial characteristics. Thus national traits can be impressed on a whole people. (p. 161)

From this analysis, Kant concluded that there is a national physiognomy and marks (not unlike those proposed by Agrippa and the Cabalists) can "characterize" entire societies. While he did not wholeheartedly embrace physiognomy, he gave enormous encouragement to the idea that marks, signs, capacities, gestures, and expressions imprint themselves on the ordinary social and moral life of a people. This notion went far beyond Hume's *ad hoc* reflections on national character, preparing the way for Houston Stewart Chamberlain's soulful alliance of Teutonic temperament, activity, facial structure, features, and expression with the will of Reformation Christianity in the creation of the race-state.

National Character   After discussing the character of the sexes, Kant considered the character of nations. Here it is important to note that although he broadened Aristotle's cautious treatment of physiognomy, he confined his definition of a nation to *gens* and his definition of a people to *populus*. The multitude of people assembled within a tract of land who recognized themselves as united into a civil whole by a common origin is a nation. Those who exempt themselves from the laws are unruly crowds, the rabble, the *vulgus*. Having no volition to be part of a civil whole, they are excluded from the status of citizenship. Apart from this exclusion from civility by will, Kant's idea of nation is the political notion contained in the works of Aristotle, Cicero, and Machiavelli; it has certainly not yet been transformed into the notion of co-terminous natural nation found in the writers of the late nineteenth century.

Kant's investigations of the national character of the French and the English disputed Hume's argument that if each person in a nation assumes his own character then the nation itself has no character. While Hume conceived of a nation as comprised of individuals, Kant believed that affectation of a character by an individual is precisely the *common* character of the people to which he belongs. The Englishman is contemptuous, arrogant, and rude to foreigners because he thinks he is self-sufficient in all things and can dispense with being pleasant to others. The Frenchman is distinguished by a taste for conversation and by courtesy, vivacity, and spirit of freedom. The English character is insular; the French character is continental. The less civilized races, like the Spaniards, Italians, Germans, and Russians were produced by the mixture of races that were originally different: "This much we can judge with probability: that a mixture of races (by extensive conquest) which gradually extinguishes their characters, is not beneficial to the human race—all so-called philanthropy notwithstanding" (p. 182). While in the fusion of races nature aims at assimilation, nature also has a tendency to diversify to infinity members of the same stock and even of the same clan, in both bodily and spiritual traits. The mating of dissimilar individuals revives fertility, keeping life going without repetition. Kant's view of the races is one which accepts the natural tendency of like to be attracted to like, and yet he sees a law of nature resisting the constant and progressive approach toward a uniform portrait or likeness.

The Character of the Species   Kant said nothing more about the character of the races, but had much to say about the character of the species. As a species, man has a character that he himself creates. Endowed with the capacity for reason, he preserves himself and his species through training and instruction for domestic life and government. Man is distinguished by his technical predisposition for manipulating things, by his pragmatic predisposition for using other men skillfully, and by his moral predisposition for adhering to principle in his treatment of himself and others. These levels—the technical, the pragmatic, and the moral—distinguish man from the other inhabitants of the earth, and they are progressive, the means by which the human race improves throughout the generations. Man's highest attainment is the moral level, when he sees himself as subject to the law of duty and is conscious that his choice is free.

But man must be educated to the good. He must cultivate himself, civilize himself, and make himself moral by the arts and sciences. He must struggle against yielding passively to comfort and well-being. And "the scientific progress of the species is never more than fragmentary (according to time), and has no guarantee against regression, with which it is always threatened by intervals of revolutionary barbarism" (p. 187).

Kant saw Jean-Jacques Rousseau's portrayal of the human species when it ventured forth from the state of nature as a pessimistic one and certainly not one which had been wholly resolved by Rousseau's work. He did not believe that Rousseau intended a return to an idyllic state of nature so much as a look back at what had happened to corrupt man's essentially good nature when he had left nature for culture—when he had become civilized and when he had become moral.

Kant rejected Rousseau's idea that man in nature was noble and that education damaged the species. Such a view held few promises for a brighter future. Rather, Kant believed that the innate evil propensity of the species was restrained by human reason but perhaps not entirely eradicated. A civil constitution artificially raises the propensity to good, but even under a civil constitution animality makes itself manifest and hostility always threatens to break forth. Education alone could ensure a constant working toward the good. The human race can and should create its own fortune, but that it *will* do so we cannot infer except from experience and history:

We can therefore say: the first characteristic of the human species is man's power, as a rational being, to acquire character as such for his own person as well as for the society in which nature has placed him. This characteristic already presupposes a propitious natural predisposition and a tendency to the good in him;

for evil is really without character (since it involves conflict with itself and does not permit any permanent principle within itself). (p. 189)

In the case of rational animals, every creature achieves its destiny through the appropriate development of all the predispositions of its nature, so that at least the species, if not every individual, fulfills nature's purpose; in the case of irrational animals, each individual attains its destiny by the wisdom of nature. Only as a species does man achieve the development of good out of evil. Men are rational beings who, though wicked, are still resourceful and have a moral predisposition. As their culture advances, they feel more indignant about the injuries inflicted by egoism and become more ready to subject the private interest to the public interest.

The moral predisposition within—the innate demand of reason—counteracts the tendency to egoism and evil:

> So it presents the human species, not as evil, but as a species of rational beings that strives, in the face of obstacles, to rise out of evil in constant progress towards the good. In this, our volition is generally good; but we find it hard to accomplish what we will, because we cannot expect the end to be attained by the free accord of *individuals,* but only by a progressive organization of citizens of the earth into and towards the species, as a system held together by cosmopolitan bonds. (p. 193)

Kant attempted to set man in an ethical and moral, as well as a physical, context. Questioning Rousseau's notion of the noble savage and the social contract as the means for achieving a civil society, he sought to elevate politics as an activity arising out of the purposes of soul. His thought had the effect of creating an autonomous moral and aesthetic world in which egotistical freedom progressively and historically strove to rid itself of the influences of political writers and political arenas of past eras and of the rational laws of eighteenth-century physical anthropology. Given that there actually existed a crude state of nature in which force, power, anarchy, despotism, and barbarism could not be ignored, the aim should be toward a higher moral order for the species.

THE GERMAN AND ENGLISH ROMANTICS

In providing a philosophical justification for the species in a higher moral order made manifest in national character, Kant inspired a host of writers at the end of the eighteenth century to inquire further into the practicalities of present politics. The best known were Schiller, Goethe, Fichte, and Hegel, all of whom explored ideas pertinent to national character, morality, and mortality.

Friedrich Schiller (1759–1805), lyric poet and dramatist, was inspired by Rousseau's appeal to the spirit of nature and rejection of existing political arrangements to insist on freedom and the nobility of spirit. Initiating German romanticism and *Sturm und Drang* with *Die Räuber* (1779) and, after the French Revolution, with *Wilhelm Tell* (1804), Schiller celebrated the idea of the natural state—truly free peoples bound together not by artificial laws but by a natural parentage and natural boundaries.[19] Here anthropology was linked to philosophy, literature, and language. The hunt that Hotman and Verstegan began on foot was now equipped with the lively horse of national character, personality, and moral purpose, and the search was on for the "true" natural origins of the Germanic peoples of Europe.

Schiller's influence rapidly spread to England through the work of Samuel Taylor Coleridge (1772–1834), who visited Germany in 1798 to study physiology, anatomy, and metaphysics and later translated Schiller. His *Biographia Literaria* (1808–15) included essays on metaphysical, romantic, and literary themes that gave prominence to natural, soulful origins rather than to the existing politics of actual historical states described in the works of Edmund Burke and David Hume. Coleridge's friend and colleague, William Wordsworth (1770–1850), was also interested in metaphysical themes. Like Sir Walter Scott (1771–1832), he created a poetic vision of countryside and freedom that was essentially English in character:

> "In our halls is hung armoury of the invincible Knights of old:
>
> We must be free or die, who speak the tongue that Shakespeare spake;
>
> The faith and morals hold which Milton held.—
>
> In every thing we are sprung of Earth's first blood, have titles manifold."

As a young man, Johann Wolfgang von Goethe (1749–1832) delved into books on astrology, alchemy, and the occult. He later became interested in the symbols of Germanic identity that were opposed to French rationalism and to the pedantry of Gottsched. With *Die Leiden des jungen Werthers* (1774), he attracted wide attention to the idea that the world belonged to the strong as well as to the sentimental. He understood genius (from *gens*) as something that one *was,* not something that one could have. His friend, Johann Gottfried von Herder, taught him the significance of Gothic architecture and inspired in him an enthusiasm for Shakespeare and *Volklied.* With other German romantics, he attempted to restore the loss of faith that had occurred in the mechanistic philosophies of the Enlightenment with a personal identity derived from nation.

But it was Kant's pupil Johann Gottlieb Fichte (1762–1814) who most directly examined the relationship of the personal, the nation, and blood. Of the French Revolution he wrote: "Things have become the subject of conversation of which no one had dreamed. Talk of the rights of man, of liberty and equality, of the limits of royal power, has taken the place of fashions and adventures. We are beginning to learn."[20]

In his principal work, *Wissenschaftslehre* (1794), Fichte wrote of the thinking self (ego) as being the only reality, which in defining itself and its limits created as its opposite the non-ego, the world of experience, which was the medium through which ego asserted its freedom. In *Die Geschlossene Handelsstaat (The Exclusive Commercial State,* 1800) and in *Die Grundzuge des Gegenwartigen Zeitalters (Characteristics of the Present Age,* 1804–05), a series of lectures delivered in Berlin after his dismissal from Jena for atheism, and in the winter of 1807–08 in his *Reden an die deutsche Nation,* he saw reason as ruling human affairs and men free to choose the methods by which they acted reasonably. Fichte looked to education to overcome selfishness and individualism so that people could live in a natural social intercourse in a state that is, as Holland Rose calls it, "an artistic institution intended to direct all individual powers towards the life of the race and to transfuse them therein."[21] Failing individual compliance to reason, as Kant had hoped for, Fichte had a national state on standby to compel people toward *Kultur* (civilization), toward moral and social order in race, language, and nation.[22] The world would belong to those German peoples who realized life to its full by virtue of the personal qualities they had in them through blood. Geography and climate had given the Germans incomparable biological qualities.

Fichte's disciple, Friedrich Wilhelm Joseph von Schelling (1775–1854), professor at Jena, Würzburg, Munich, and Berlin, later reversed Fichte's ideas, arguing that the universe, not the ego, is the ultimate reality. In *Ideen zu einer Philosophie der Natur* (1797), he portrayed nature as a single living organism working toward self-consciousness, a faculty dormant in inanimate objects and fully awake only in man. Nature is obedient to the laws of human intelligence, he claimed, and man's being is an "intellectual intuition" of the world he creates.

Fichte's contemporary Georg Wilhelm Friedrich Hegel (1770–1831), disciple of Kant and successor to Fichte's chair at Berlin in 1818, went on to demonstrate that the rational spirit of the world was becoming more real, in historical process working from despotism to freedom. What Hegel saw for the first time was the emergence of the Germanic world in which *all* people were capable of freedom. Citizenship was not confined to the *populus* of the small Greek city-state. The state exemplified the spirit of the *Volk*. In the historical destiny of the Germans in the woods, as against those of the Latins and the Orientals, lay the potential for the development of political institutions through the Christian ideal of salvation.

Until the time of Kant, Schiller, Goethe, Fichte, and Hegel, the Greco-Roman antique state had formed the basis for philosophizing about Western civilization. Human beings were assumed to have diverse interests and beliefs and to inhabit a mortal world of historical experience in which choices were made, and bargains struck, to achieve a balance between the conflicting forces of good and bad, fortune and *virtù,* public and private, individual and collective. The ancient polity embraced all good citizens and, through the exercise of the law, gave them the opportunity to curb arbitrary government and the abuse of power. What Fichte put in the place of this classical model of social order was an order that relied neither upon political citizenship nor upon membership in the body of the faithful in Christ but that emphasized personal character carried in the blood. The Germanic race was a nation realizing itself in language and the purity of blood, not through the crude machinations of traditional politics and political constitutions.

BURKE

Hannah Arendt has suggested that during this important period Edmund Burke (1729–97) contributed to an essentially English view of race by emphasizing entailed inheritance as the basis for English liberty. Burke extended feudal privilege from the few to the whole English people, so that they became "a nobility among nations." In Burke's thought there is a belief in the temper and character of a people that is unalterable, a pedigree that cannot be falsified. Freedom flows through the veins to form character, and the ties of inheritance are "as strong as links of iron."[23] In this respect Burke has much in common with Hume, Kant, and Fichte. But in his *Reflections on the Revolution in France*

(1790), *Two Speeches on Conciliation with America* (1774, 1775), and *Two Letters on the Irish Question* (1778, 1792)[24] Burke consistently warned of the price to be paid for abandoning fact and practicality for "mischievous theory" and "imagination" such as displayed in the works of Coleridge, Wordsworth, Schiller, and Fichte. Burke's central point was that constitutions were transmitted not by artificial manufacture, but by "the people": "All government, indeed every human benefit and enjoyment, every virtue, and every prudent act is founded on compromise and barter. We balance inconveniences; we give and take; we remit some rights, that we may enjoy others; and we choose rather to be happy citizens, than subtle disputants" (*Two Speeches on Conciliation with America*, p. 180).

Burke contended that whatever the name of the government, whether it be a republic or a monarchy, whether it be in Ireland, Wales, Chester, or Durham, or in the remote American colonies, the ultimate test was whether the people were "disarmed by Statute" or by military force and what control was exercised by the public assembly over the possible abuse of power by any one of its constituent elements. Burke declared that it was not to the Republic of Plato, the Utopia of Thomas More, or the Oceana of James Harrington that we should look for solutions of government, because these works depended on the "delusions of geometric accuracy" or metaphysical speculation. What he extracted from the works of "the great master Aristotle" were the essential facts about the activity of politics and the essential requirements for any form of political rule to exist at all (*Two Speeches on Conciliation with America*, p. 181).

For Burke, political acts are distinguishable from all other kinds of acts. They are concerned with the establishment of rights of citizenship, not abstract metaphysical rights, in public places (parliaments). The civil rights arising from political acts are arrived at not by theorizing or imagining, or indeed by efficient administration, but through a long process of argument, conciliation, and compromise in the light of past judgments, and in the context of time, circumstance, and event. Politics is about bringing into the public domain with magnanimity those things that were "without the pale," so that under the law those acts that may easily be regarded as rebellious, or, as he called them, a libel, affront, or derogation, may be given sanctuary as a "petition of grievance" (p. 162).

On January 3, 1792, Burke responded to a letter from Sir Hercules Langrishe, MP, raising the important question of the place of Roman Catholics within the state. If the state was Protestant at the time of the Glorious Revolution, and the Crown was Protestant, what right did Roman Catholics have to share in the benefits of the state? Would concession and compromise lead inevitably to takeover? Burke tackled the question, as he had the American question, by reference to the ancient constitution that had declared itself in acts of Parliament in such matters as representation, taxation, supply, and the raising of revenue. For Burke these were the pillars of theory, and not abstractions about rights. The treatment of the Catholics in Ireland, therefore, should be related to the realities of time, circumstance, and event—to property, franchise, and education. With awful prescience Burke argued that the temptation would always be to follow the easy path of dividing the nation into two separate bodies without common interest, sympathy, and connection, a division that would result in one group emerging as the possessor and the other becoming, in the course of time, "drawers of water and cutters of turf." The democratic solution was not an option when it reduced "the people" to "mobs" or "camps"; what was required was a clear understanding of the ambiguous term "state" and what it could do under the existing terms of the ancient constitution, its laws and political ways, to remedy the defects and difficulties that were acknowledged to arise from the present state of affairs. Essentially the Irish question was a practical problem requiring an understanding not only of the rights, privileges, laws, and immunities of the state but also the claims of the Irish. Burke started from the simple proposition that all mankind is worthy of liberal and honorable condition and that through politics mankind must seek to avoid the debasement of human nature by oppressive and absolutist single-issue state action or—equally insidious—the specter of sedition and self-determining democracy, which undermines all moderate action.

HERDER

While Burke emphasized the efficacy of political solutions, he seems to have stood alone against the voices of Kant, Schiller, Goethe, Coleridge, Wordsworth, Fichte, and Hegel, who posed an alternative description of nations based on the assumption that innate mental qualities—temperament, character, inward sensation, and genius—may be revealed in literature and the lineaments of the face. R. G. Collingwood regards Johann Gottfried von Herder as the first to bring these ideas together, "the first thinker to recognise in a systematic way that there are differences between different kinds of men, and that human nature is not uniform but diversified." In Herder, the pupil of Kant and the inspiration of Schiller, "There is still no conception of a people's character as having been made what it is by that people's historical experience; on the contrary, its historical experience is regarded as a mere result of its fixed character." Collingwood regards Herder rather than Blumenbach as the true father of modern anthropology, mixing physical and cultural elements to originate a systematic racial theory that assimilates most of the disparate and confused elements analyzed in this chapter. Herder perceived the differences between the social and political institutions of different races as derived from innate psychological qualities, not from the experience of history. Once culture becomes an expression of race, it is an easy step to relate its improvement to breeding and then, states Collingwood, "there is no escaping the Nazi marriage laws."[25] If Collingwood's thesis holds, it should be a matter of grave concern to us that the orthodoxy of modern liberal "race relations," designed to remedy the horrors of Nazi sterilization acts, continues to be heavily indebted to Herder's mixture of physical anthropology with cultural anthropology. The displacement of political differentiation as a way of understanding the world *in* history by economic, social, physical, and psychological differentiation *outside* history is the racial burden that most of us carry away from this period in the ideologies of Western, democratic, self-determining national societies.

The Volk *and the* Völker *in History*   Johann Gottfried von Herder (1744–1803) first studied medicine and later became interested in theology. Influenced by Kant's method and Rousseau's view of nature, he proposed in *Fragmente über die neuere deutsche Literatur* (1767) a cycle of growth in history according to which states, language, literature, and institutions have a youth, a prime, and a decline. He rediscovered the old folk poetry of Germany and published an anthology called *Stimmer der Völker* (1778–79). His *Über den Ursprung der Sprache* (1772) examined the relation between language and human nature. He also wrote *Aucheine Philosophie der Geschichtezur Bildung der Menschheit* (1774), and *Ursachen des gesunkenen Geschmacks bei den verschiednen Völkern, da er geblühet* (1775).

Herder's *Ideen zur Philosophie der Geschichte der Menschheit*, published in thirty-three volumes from 1784 to 1791, is a bookish, literary, aesthetic, and philosophical account of historical experience that focused on a new factor—*Kultur*—in the history of mankind.[26] Herder introduced the idea that this "culture" was a fundamental organizing idea of civilization and race. Shifting the emphasis of history away from polities and the particular forms of states, away from parochial French concerns and rationalist systems, Herder promoted the religious, mystical, poetic, technological, and artistic achievements of Europe.

Herder's concept of history drew on William Harvey's theory of the circulation of the blood, Caspar Friedrich Wolff's theory of generation published in *Theoria generationes* (1759) and Blumenbach's reflections on the *nisus formativus* to propose an idea of a life cycle on a world scale. The relationship of the individual to the *Volk*—a people bound together organically by language, religion, education, inherited tradition, folk songs, ritual, and speech—was not contractual and political but spiritual. A natural inclination to humanness, *Humanitat,* arose not from the state organization, or politics, or the oppressive Catholic Church, but came through the uplifting spirit of music, literature, art, and science. Indeed, the state as conceived in its classical form by Aristotle and Cicero was a destructive force that crushed the true culture and spirit of the *Volk*.

In Herder's work the human mind did not progress from strength to strength as in French rationalist thought. In the state of nature, the *Völker* were not bestial, as the filthy Hottentot appeared to the eye of Lessing, nor were they outsiders who could be civilized by Greco-Roman politics. Each *Volk* was a self-contained entity with an individuality and character of its own. In Herder's analysis the *Völker* grew in time, space, and character in peculiar geographical circumstances. After Herder, the history of the world became the history of the names and cultures of these *Völker.*

The Variety of the Human Form   Notwithstanding the varieties of the human form on earth, Herder maintained that humankind was a single species. Yet no two human beings were perfectly alike. Quoting the preface to Buffon's *Natural History,* Herder stated, "No man is exactly similar to another in his internal structure: the course of the nerves and blood vessels differs in millions and millions of cases, so that amid the variations of these delicate parts, we are scarcely able to discover in what they agree" (7.1.4). Yet Herder insisted that the human species was one and distinct from animal species. "In fact apes and men never were one and the same genus and I wished to rectify the slight remains of the old fable, that in some place or other upon the Earth they lived in community, and enjoyed no barren intercourse. . . . But thou, O man, honour thyself: neither the pongo not the gibbon is thy brother: the American and the Negro are" (7.1.6–7).

To explain visible Negroid characteristics, Herder did not turn to climate or to the influence of the sun but to hereditary succession and the process of degeneration. Like Blumenbach, he rejected the idea of distinct races: "In short, there are neither four or five races, nor exclusive varieties, on this Earth. Complexions run into each other: forms follow the genetic character and upon the whole, all are at last but shades of the same great picture, extending through all ages, and over all parts of the Earth" (7.1.7). Variations in mutation and propagation were external appearances only; the essential internal form of Man, even when forbidding on the outside, remained intact and human: "For the external figure of man is but the case of his internal mechanism, a consistent whole, in which every letter forms a part of the word indeed, but only the whole word has a determinate signification" (7.4.26).

While Herder cautioned against making judgments about people from the face and counseled extreme care in divining the inner self from the outer expression, he seemed to expect that a science of character would some day be arrived at through the alphabet of the face. We do not have to wait long for the first steps to be taken in the development of such a science derived from the hypotheses of Kant's national character, Lessing's discourse on beauty and ugliness in art, and Herder's *Kultur.*

» Conclusion: From Populus to Volk

The writers examined in this chapter still influence our thought. Hobbes provided a philosophical foundation for the right of conquest. Montesquieu laid the foundation for geopolitical and environmentalist hypotheses of race. Locke grounded Aristotle's notion of *genus* and *species* in observable phenomenon, opening the way for the physical anthropologists of the eighteenth century to classify mankind into some kind of animal kingdom. Scientific inquiry and the scientific method, applied by Bernier, Buffon, and Blumenbach, introduced and legitimized the idea that some variable formative force, moved by degenerative and regenerative processes of maturation and mixture, mutilation and milieus, accounted for observable differences between brute and man, Caucasian and Negro.

In the works of English and German romantics, these ideas were broadly linked to the idea that character, and the psychic and physical expression of it, could be distinguished in the structures and features of the face and expression and that the individual races displaying this noble character were descended from ancient noble peoples. In the unfolding of history, some races were advanced and others were retarded. Thus civilization was perceived to advance not through the public debate of speech-gifted men and the reconciliation of differing claims and interests in law but through the genius and character of the *Völker* naturally and biologically working as an energetic formative force in the blood of races and expressing themselves as *Kultur.* Burke's attempt to reassert the political ideas of Aristotle was to no avail. The idea of *populus* gave way to the idea of *Volk.* Yet despite the upheavals of the French, American, Industrial, and Agricultural Revolutions, these ideas of race continued to be debated against the broad backdrop of political ideas which for the time being drew upon classical sources for ideas of state, society, and humanity and political and constitutional process, which had not yielded entirely to the new order. The diverse associationist, physical anthropological, moral, and cultural hypotheses of 1684–1815 had not yet been cobbled together into a coherent theory that the whole history of mankind was the history of race or of any one race.

The Search for Historical and Biological Origins, 1815–1870

The contributions of Blumenbach, Kant, Lessing, Goethe, Fichte, and Herder to the idea of race would have been as naught without the work of the great German historian Barthold G. Niebuhr. In 1813 Niebuhr combined ethnography and chorography with narrative history and philology and the natural history of climate and constitutions to bring about a fundamental reinterpretation of the Greco-Roman past. Before Niebuhr, the *Politics* of Aristotle had occupied a central place in the analysis of states, and although it had yielded some ground to the formidable challenges mounted during the Reformation and the Enlightenment, it had not been discarded entirely in the quest for origins and the justification of title to rule. After Niebuhr a new kind of natural history more closely related to his physics and to Blumenbach's physical anthropology had the effect of "naturalizing" the interpretation of the *Politics*. This reinterpretation provided a new way by which the idea of the Germanic nation glimpsed in the works of Hotman, Verstegan, Montesquieu, Hume, Burke, Lessing, Goethe, Kant, and Herder could be fully realized in a modern form that made the nation and the state co-terminous. It also provided firm basis in thought for other self-determining nations to claim legitimacy and title to rule for themselves, often to the detriment of neighbors they had associated with politically for centuries.

In addition to Niebuhr, four major writers made fundamental philological and etymological contributions to the developing idea of race during the years from 1815 to 1870. They introduced the popular notion that the origins of state and nation were rooted in the pasts of Franks and Gauls, Anglo-Saxons, and Celts. In England, John Mitchell Kemble argued that blood, race, ennoblement, rank, Germanic land settlement, and a notion of freedom and civil society derived from masculine personality and family stretching back to the fifth century A.D. had made the English what they were. In France, Hippolyte Adolphe Taine associated the spirit of the French national character with the superiority of the North over the South. Ernest Joseph Renan elevated the national history of the Celts, who, though dispossessed by the Industrial Revolution, were blessed with the fixed disposition, condition, and character of a race remaining pure from all admixture.

Finally, Jules Michelet saw the Revolution of France bestowing on all nations new political and social ideas that all ennobled the *Völker,* the peasantry, in opposition to the bourgeois vulgarity and fabricated antiquity of the utilitarian Anglo-Saxon English.

These writers provide perceptions of race that have endured—race as territory, race as environment and time, race as poetry, race as revolution, and race as class. None was untouched by the important developments in natural history and physical anthropology during this period. In a reopening of the debate Blumenbach thought he had settled, scientific inquiry into the relationship between the orangutan and man, between monster and man, between Caucasian and Negro, argued at one extreme the unity of mankind and at the other a bewildering variety of hypotheses of creation, degeneration, transformation, environment, and culture. Eventually two competing pre-Darwinian ethnological hypotheses were formulated: "race is nothing" and "race is everything." Both hypotheses permeated the frantic search for legitimate origins in races and classes prior to the Franco-Prussian War and came in the end to find a defense of their position by leaning on the new explanation of social evolution, conjointly invented by Charles Darwin and Herbert Spencer.

» *Race and History*

For there to be a self-conscious understanding of the idea of race, there had to be a history of the ordinary, natural peoples that was at the very least as scientifically accurate and as technically competent as Ray's inquiries into plants and Blumenbach's into the physical composition of animals and men. No such integrated critical history of the races existed until the beginning of the nineteenth century when in Germany and France two writers sought to present for the independent judgment of academia histories that were no longer tied to the official chronicles and histories of State and Church.

NIEBUHR

Barthold Georg Niebuhr (1776–1831), a Prussian diplomat and historian, was credited by Arthur de Gobineau, France's chief advocate of northern white superiority, with providing those who were searching for the hidden causes of Europe's midcentury upheavals with "an analytical tool of marvelous delicacy and novelty."[1] That tool was the interpretation of texts before the "tribunal of history," which Niebuhr had shaped first in his *Lectures on Ancient Ethnography and Geography* published in the transactions of the Berlin Academy in 1812–13, and more elaborately in *The History of Rome* from 1828 onwards.[2]

A New Approach to History   In lectures delivered at the University of Berlin in 1812–13, Niebuhr announced his intention to do what had not been done before—to join Enlightenment ethnography and chorography with narrative history. He believed that without the ability to interpret the past through a combination of philology and a knowledge of constitutions, political divisions (and especially a knowledge of what was *not* a political division), soil, and climate, the historian's work would amount to nothing more than "a sounding brass and a tinkling cymbal; he would be in the same condition which we find the wretched grammarians of old" (Prelim Obs., p. 2).

Niebuhr believed that the move toward a new German approach to historical interpretation began in the seventeenth century with the work of Richard Bentley (1662–1742), who, in common with Bacon, Hobbes, and Locke, had seen the power of words and developed the art of reasoned literary criticism of the past. Perizonius (Jacob Voorbroek, 1651–1715), the Dutch classical scholar, had been the first to move away from mere compilation and chronicle. Johann Heinrich Voss (1751–1826) had examined the geographical knowledge of the ancients. Niebuhr also drew attention to the works of Philip Cluver, professor at Leiden, one of the early founders of philology; to Palmerius (Paulmier de Grentemesnil), who found out about a "buried" dead Greece; to the English for bringing India, Egypt, and Asia Minor into the embrace of history; and to Jean-Baptiste Bourguignon d'Anville (1697–1782), a geographer who transformed charts and maps, and the first to deal with antiquity geographically.

Niebuhr's *History of Rome* was a kind of autopsy of eighteenth-century historiography. It carefully set to one side the histories of Greco-Roman political life, which had been the sheet anchors of the chroniclers of past eras, and presented an alternative history different both in method and in content. Emphasizing the part played by philology in understanding the past, Niebuhr traced an unbroken line from those aspects of Greek and Roman literature that were not political—that literature drew from the imagination of Lessing, Kant, Goethe, and Herder and inspired and nourished the idea of a noble past from exemplars of beauty and ugliness in Greek art and poetry, personal and national character, and intellectual life. Examining the foundations of the ancient Roman people and state (*res-publica*), Niebuhr acknowledged Polybius', Machiavelli's, and Burke's consideration of the political dimension of the Roman state and people but claimed they had overlooked "the dark shades in character." "The order of the history of the world," he wrote, was to "fuse the numberless original races together, and to exterminate such as cannot be amalgamated" (1:xxix). Above all, Niebuhr sought a fundamental reconstruction of the past. History would no longer be conceived of in classical terms as a moral conflict between the antitheses of virtue and vice, patrician and plebeian, public and private, *agora* and battlefield, *politikos* and *barbaros,* civility and barbarism, form and substance, reality and appearance; it would be seen anew in terms of the temper and character of the *Volk*.

The Role of Race and Blood   In this new view Rome was not a set of political ideas and practices but a natural collection of close affections, common names, and "kindred blood and colour" (1.78). Niebuhr interpreted the disputes between patrician and plebeian as arising from original differences of race and blood. He also saw the conflict between the Latins and the Etruscans as arising from race, and in his account of the early history of Rome he referred to tribal divisions as racial divisions. The Latins themselves, he concluded, were "formed by the inter-mixture of different tribes" (1:78). Niebuhr believed there were differences in blood and referred to "the power of the Tuscan *blood* [his italics] when searching for evidence of Latin blood in the tribes" (1:290).

It is interesting in this context that Niebuhr resuscitated the ancient Hebrew argument contained in Josephus' *Contra Apion* that there was nothing original in Greek historiography and little to recommend Greek politics and philosophy as distinctive activities. Quoting the taunt thrown at Apion— "Apion belonged to a people who had kept themselves unmixed; and from him the contempt for such as were without ancestry is intelligible; in Greeks it was sheer malice" (1.6,n. 1)—Niebuhr thereby implied *sotto voce* a malicious racial antipathy on the part of the Greeks that, as we saw earlier, cannot be adduced from their writings.

Moreover, despite his admiration for Burke and the English system of government, Niebuhr undermined the authority of the activity of politics by extracting from the Prolegomena of the *Politics* those passages that emphasize the similarities in natural transitions from individual to household to *polis*. Yet he omitted those parts of the political theory in Books 1–3 that distinguish the political state from a natural state, which we earlier discussed at great length. In my view the problem for Niebuhr was that he wanted the state to be created by human action, not the spontaneous creation of nature as the Physiocrats had argued, and yet the political theories of Aristotle were a major obstacle to a theory of race based on the temper and character of the *Volk* as perceived by Kant. Niebuhr's way out of the dilemma was to "naturalize" the interpretation of the *Politics* by subtly removing the political elements from classical political theory—the nature of citizenship, the emphasis upon speech and law, the transitions from private to public, the part played by leisure and knowledge, the prior claim of the general association over the household, the preeminence of *nomos* over *physis*.

Out of this brilliant historical autopsy and synthesis of the ideas floating through Verstegan, Hotman, Montesquieu, Hume, Blumenbach, Lessing, Goethe, Kant, and Herder came a conception of the German nation founded upon German letters and art, German nobility, German national genius and psychic character, German culture, and German race. Niebuhr's statement is unequivocal:

> Of the German nation, however, with regard to such of its races as did not forsake their home, or did not drop their character while living among the Romanesque nations they had conquered, we may assert that for the war which they waged during centuries against Rome, they have in aftertimes been more than rewarded by the benefits accruing from the union of the world under Rome; and that without this and the fruits that ripened in it we should hardly have ceased to be barbarians. It was not by the forms which our ancestors at the diffusion of letters imported from thence and from classical ground, that the noble peculiarities of our national genius, peculiarities for which nothing can compensate, were smothered; those forms were not irreconcilable with them: but secondhand artificial spiritless Frenchified forms and tastes and ideas, such as even in earlier time had crept in amongst us and overlaid those which were

homesprung, these are the things that for a long time have made us lukewarm and unnatural. And so, while the nations look back on the Romans as holding a place among their progenitors, we too have no slight personal interest in their story. (1:31–32)

THIERRY

Niebuhr's theory of racial domination was impatient with "the wretched grammarians of old" and was particularly averse to "secondhand artificial spiritless Frenchified forms and tastes and ideas." In France the temper and character of the people was also of great concern to his contemporary Augustin Thierry (1795–1856), who as student of Abel-François Villemain was well-versed in the arguments of Rousseau, Montesquieu, and Voltaire and had collaborated from 1813 with Henri de Saint-Simon and Auguste Comte. For Thierry political liberty—the *liberté par excellence* of the Franks and the *droit de cité Romaine* of the Gauls—was not to be found within the *ecclesia* of the Roman Catholic Church or the *res-publica* of the absolutist French state. Like Niebuhr, Thierry looked for different origins. In 1817 he discovered the Hobbesian right of conquest from the works of David Hume and turned his attention to the Germanic tribes, whose conquering spirit had taken them to Gaul, Italy, Britain, and the Iberian Peninsula. After publishing many articles in the journal *Censeur Europeen,* in *Histoire de la conquête de l'Angleterre par les Normands* (1821–25) he turned to a new kind of history that would include the people, the towns, and the provinces of France. His historiography of French liberty was based on an analysis of aboriginal "types"—usurpers of liberty and property like the Church, and impediments to liberty like the nobility. By 1840 Thierry's wavering faith in constitutional monarchy and his historical support for this political liberty of the dispossessed Third Estate was expressed in a history of France that included the traditions of the national mass and the Gallo-Roman affiliation by blood, law, language, and ideas, all as immortalized in the magnificent conquest of the English by the Normans.[3]

Niebuhr's transformation of the history of the Greco-Roman world from a history of politics and political ideas into a history of races, and Thierry's elevation of the role played by provincial people in France and in contemporary Europe into a racial history of Frankish and Gaulish "types" were major contributions to historiography. They set the stage for a vision of a Europe once occupied by a primitive people, innocent and pure, enjoying a cultural civilization superior to that of Greece and Rome. These were the Aryans, the Celts, and the Teutons, who were thought to have shared a common origin and came bearing the marks of the valiant fighting men celebrated in poetry and song during the Middle Ages. Their origins could be determined more accurately as races.

Therefore, from 1813 to the publication of Darwin's *Origin of Species* in 1859, the inquiry proceeded in two closely interrelated directions. First, a search for new insights into the fundamentals of speech and language, and the construction of a genealogy of languages, elaborated on the historical theme of race and race mixture.[4] Following Niebuhr and Thierry, the origins of good government were also to be found in the "other Rome," and title to rule could be established by conquest. Second, the criteria of comparative anatomy and natural history, as well as the new sciences of physical anthropology and ethnology, were applied in a new approach to the interpretation of the past.

THE GENEALOGY OF LANGUAGE AND THE MODERN RACE-STATE

In *The History of Rome* Niebuhr had referred to the English, who brought into the embrace of history the pasts of India, Egypt, and Asia Minor. Undoubtedly the major contributor here is Sir William Jones (1746–94), a brilliant Oriental scholar who did extensive original research on the gods of Greece, Italy, and India; on the Hindus, Arabs, Tartars, Persians, and Chinese; and on the history of Asia. Fluent in thirteen languages and acquainted with twenty-eight others, Jones was the first Englishman to master Sanskrit. In 1786 he drew attention to its affinity with Greek and Latin, even to the extent of claiming that the Pythagorian and Platonic theories were derived from the Indian sages.

Jones's claims set the direction for an intense search for origins through the genealogy of language. The common root was termed "Indo-European," and scholars put forth various views about its source in Central Asia, the valley of Oxus and Iaxarte, and the slopes of the Indu Kush. At the 1847 meeting of the British Association, Christian Bunsen, Niebuhr's former secretary, who had studied Hebrew, Arabic, Persian, and Norse, read a paper entitled "On the Results of the Recent Egyptian Researches in Reference to Asiatic and African Ethnology, and the Classification of Languages," in which he put forward the exciting proposition that the methods and classification systems developed in physical anthropology could be applied to the scientific study of language. The search for the origins of the Indo-Europeans continued through the century and ranged from Finland to the Urals.[5]

Jones's studies of India, distinguished by his understanding of Hindu and Muslim laws and custom, were the first intimation that ancient peoples other than the Hebrews, Greeks, and Romans had a past and that the past could be legitimized outside of biblical and Greco-Roman sources. Through the analysis of an Indo-European language, he perceived India as having an affinity with Europe. The historian and political journalist August Ludwig von Schlozer (1735–1809) applied the same method to the study of Russian, Finnish, and Hungarian. He was, according to Herbert Butterfield, the first to group people according to language and the first to use the term "Semitic." In his *Briefweschsel* (10 vols., 1776–82) and *Staatsanzeigen* (18 vols., 1782–93) von Schlozer discovered the significance of Herder's concept of *Volk* and *Volkseele* in the writing of histories of these natural peoples that could be understood by popular audiences. He also laid the foundations for statistical science.[6] His work provided the historical starting point for the much later transmogrification of the old religious idea of anti-Jewishness into the modern racial concept of antisemitism and for the working out of the new idea of *Volkstaat*.

Also at Göttingen, Friedrich von Schlegel (1772–1829) produced in his *Über die Sprache und Weisheit der Indier* (1808) a grammar with novel insights into languages and the genealogy of languages that drew on an analogy with anatomy. In *History of Ancient and Medieval Literature* (1815) he ascribed the decline of Rome to a grievous loss of language and soul. Unlike Burke, who saw the potential for political revival in the *Politics* of Aristotle, Schlegel described a formative force that enabled the best in Roman civilization to harmonize with German vigor. That force was Christianity, which, as Lessing had recognized, in the hands of the peoples of the North was the driving principle of modern history. For Schlegel the antique pagan state was corrupt not only in practice but also in form. Its political nature needed to be replaced by a modern national state reassembling all those who spoke the same language, observed the same customs, and share the same culture.

Schlegel was indebted to Fichte's trilogy of race, language, and nation, which also reappeared in the works of Madame de Staël and Friedrich List and their followers. In *De l'Allemagne* (1810), Germaine de Staël (1766–1817) took up Schlegel's notion that the mixture of the German races with the corrupted population of the Roman Empire had, through the formative force of Christianity, produced the regeneration of Europe. Her enthusiasm for German romanticism reached England through Coleridge and Wordsworth, who had visited Göttingen in 1798 and done much to turn the attention of the English toward German metaphysical and spiritual themes and to encourage an interest in the literary criticism of Lessing and Goethe. In 1817 Thomas Carlyle (1795–1881) was introduced to Madame de Staël's work. In essays on Goethe and Schiller, and in his masterful *French Revolution* (1837), Carlyle accepted Burke's hypothesis that the state evolved from an ancient constitution accommodating to change, but he advanced the powerful supplementary argument that the state was not so much the outcome of the actions of politicians and orators as the product of the courageous moral struggle prosecuted by men of upstanding aristocratic, Christian, and military bearing.[7]

Political diversity within a state, therefore, was not an asset, a sure foundation for the good state, as Burke, Machiavelli, and Aristotle perceived it; diversity was a source of everlasting corruption impeding the progress of man. The only hope Carlyle could see for the regeneration of European life, literature, and language was in the revival of the chivalrous Germanic racial elements in Christianity. On these grounds Carlyle gave preeminence to the literature of England, Germany, Holland, and Denmark in the reassembly of a national state based on kith, kin, and language, and preeminence to the Teutonic peoples in the struggle against the unworthy Latins and Slavs.

The treatment of the Latin and Slavic peoples also played an important part in the works of Friedrich List (1781–1846), a founder of political economy who also articulated Fichte's trilogy of race, language, and nation. List believed that those who spoke one language ought to be reassembled into one nation because they observed the same customs and belonged to the same race. Race was a creation of nature transmitted by biology. Political formations, on the other hand, were artificial diplomatic combinations embracing diverse entities that impeded economic progress. The forms in which they appeared were transitory and ran counter to nature. What was required was a national economic union autonomously based on the linkages of language. In *Das nationale System der Politischen Ökonomie (The National System of Political Economy* 1841) List argued for a single economic unit (*Zollverein*) that would bring together under a single natural authority all those who formed one race.

It is significant that List viewed the Aristotelian political entity as artifical and the racial state as natural. He saw the nation not as a quantity of exchange values but as a unity of language, manners, historical development, culture, and constitution in which full productive potential could be realized. His dream of reuniting the Germanic peoples (including the English commercial and colonial peoples) in a closed economic entity protected by Prussian military might would realize not only Fichte's trilogy but also Schlegel's romantic combination of language, soul, and culture.

Other early philologists made important contributions to the developing literature on the relation of language and culture. Karl Otfried Müller (1797–1840), professor of ancient literature at Göttingen from 1817 to 1839, promoted the study of Greek life and examined the sources of Greek myths. From the evidence of the language, art, and archaeology of ancient Greece, he argued that classical Greece had a historically distinct identity not deriving from Asian origins. His *Geschichte hellenischer Stämme und Städt* (2 vols., 1820, 1824) and *Prolegomen Zueiner Wiesenschaftlichen Mythologie* (1825) encouraged those who believed the Greeks did come from the East to inquire with equal enthusiasm into the precise origins of language and peoples through painstaking research into comparative grammar. Among them was Ernst Curtius (1814–96), Müller's friend and colleague at Göttingen who accompanied him in his excavation work in Greece. Curtius's *History of Greece* (1857) argued on the evidence of language that the Indo-Europeans had indeed come from Asia. Curtius's brother, Georg (1820–85) produced an influential comparative grammar that established linguistic connections between Greece and the Indo-Europeans.

Also at Göttingen at this time were the Grimm brothers, Jakob and Wilhelm, who extended Goethe's work on poetry and song with a general inquiry into the romantic folklore of the German people. Jakob Grimm (1785–1863) in *Deutsche Grammatik* (1819–37) and *Deutsche Mythologie* (1835) laid sound foundations for systematic philological study and was a powerful influence on the work of his brilliant pupil, the English philologist J. M. Kemble, whose work we shall consider later. Wilhelm Grimm (1786–1859) suggested that German folklore was the remnant of Indo-Germanic tradition.

At the same time Franz Bopp (1791–1867) built on Schlegel's investigation of the languages of India. In a thorough and systematic study of the Sanskrit texts, he used grammar and composition to interrelate languages and their parentages. His work culminated in a series of publications, *Vergleichende Grammatik,* from 1833 to 1852, which described, compared, and enunciated laws of languages from grammatical form and encouraged an interest in the Teutonic, Celtic, Albanian, Greek, Polynesian, Indo-European, and Caucasian language forms.

Not all philological development took place at Göttingen. In England, James Cowles Prichard (1786–1848), friend of Bunsen and follower of Blumenbach in the field of physical anthropology, allied the study of the physical and natural history of mankind to the study of philology. His *Eastern Origins of the Celtic Nations* (1831) created an interest in the Celtic peoples, who, he held, were allied to the Slavonians, Germans, and Pelasgians (Greek and Latin) by language, thus forming a fourth European branch of Asian stock. His *Natural History of Man* (1843) reiterated the unity of man, arguing that all races demonstrated the same inner nature. Prichard is considered to be the founder of English anthropology and ethnology.

At Cambridge Connop Thirlwall (1797–1875) collaborated with Julius Charles Hare to translate Niebuhr's seminal *History of Rome.* This work caused great controversy and led to Hare's *Vindication of Niebuhr* (1829), which gave impetus and purpose to German history and scholarship at Cambridge. Thirlwall's scholarly *History of Greece* (8 vols., 1835–44), as well as that of his friend, George Grote (1794–1871)—also titled *History of Greece* (12 vols., 1846–56)— idealized the Greek *polis* and fostered the image of a pure Greece derived from the aesthetics of Plato and Aristotle rather than from the contingencies of politics and political life described in the *Politics.* Both writers also introduced Niebuhr's idea of race conflict into England.

The early history of philology attached tremendous importance to tracing the origins of languages of known and forgotten peoples. These studies were not simply esoteric; they had in mind the idea of societies no longer wholly bound by the political nexus of Aristotle but by a pure and discoverable natural racial origin, stretching back in time and place, that ought to serve as the basis for the unit of governance. Their work addressed the technical problem of reassembling those peoples, separated by the revolutions of the late eighteenth century and the settlement at Vienna in 1815, who were possessed of one language, one soul, and one race. They sought to replace the political ordering with a natural ordering. And their ideas on the subject of race continue to cast a shadow over late twentieth-century notions of mass democracy and self-determination.

KEMBLE

For twenty years John Mitchell Kemble in England and Jakob Grimm at Göttingen corresponded on Anglo-Saxon studies and Indo-European etymology. Kemble's *Saxons in England* (1849) gleaned much from German developments in philology,[8] and from the full accessibility granted to historians for the first time in 1840 of the Ancient Laws and Ecclesiastical Institutes of the Anglo Saxons. His intention was to critique Thierry's analysis of the Norman conquest, which he believed had succumbed to the romantic enthusiasm that had also inspired Sir Walter Scott's factually inaccurate but beautifully written tales such as *Ivanhoe, The Lady of the Lake,* and *The Lay of the Last Minstrel.*

Germanic Settlement   Kemble inquired more deeply into the successive waves of Celtic, Teutonic, and Slavonic migration, termed by the Germans *Völkerwanderung* after Herder, about which there was very little direct historical evidence. Examining the well-established principles of Germanic settlement observed in the possession of land and rank, Kemble argued that the first principle and rudiments of English law were to be found in the system introduced by the German conquerors into every state founded on the ruins of Roman power. That system involved, first, the idea of consecrated land—a mark—protected by the gods and reserved for public use, and, second, a community of families or households through which free men voluntarily associated to establish a system of cultivation that secured a fair distribution of service and support. The consecrated land became the clearings in the forest where the first public assemblies were held. In time two or three marks joined to form a *scir* (shire), a federal bond intended to ensure right between one mark and another, between man and man. The *scir* was the machinery for governing, and the district in which it existed naturally conformed to geography.

In the Germanic model men were qualified by birth and blood connection to occupy the land. A man's pedigree did not depend on money; nor was it the city that regulated the form of life but the country. Germanic settlement was, therefore, characterized by common property in land and the connection between the individual and the soil.

It followed from this argument that freedom and status were derived from landholding. Kemble's historical thesis rested upon the assumption that the freeman and the noble in the Teutonic scheme were the guarantors of society's foundation and that their sons were the progenitors of the state by virtue of their union as free heads of households to secure civil rights under the law. Kemble used a Lockean argument for the establishment of civil society and state, seeing it as a voluntary giving up of the power to do wrong and the adoption of a means to counteract the natural tendency to evil. Although Kemble quoted Aristotle in support of his contention that a man does not exist except as a member of a state (1:126), he failed to understand that his Germanic state, based in blood and the possession of land, was the very antithesis of Aristotle's formulation of the conditions necessary for political life to exist at all. (The same was true of Niebuhr.) In the Germanic settlement governance did not grow out of public discussion, reconciliation, compromise, and law (1:134–35). The position of the noble arose not out of something he had done or was capable of doing, *qua* citizen. Nobility and kingdoms lay in blood and race.

The Family and Anglo-Saxon Character   Underlying all these assumptions was Kemble's belief that the family was the ennobling device in its highest form in a Christian brotherhood—One Father and One King. The endearing ties of blood relations supported by disciplined military relations arose out of the Germanic house, which was a holy shrine, and the bond of marriage cemented the family system. These Germanic values united all the northern races—the Germans, Scandinavians, Frisians, and Angles. They could be seen in the "folcland" of England and in the myths of the Norse gods. The godlike and heroic sons of Woden were the ancestors of the races qualified to reign. Their stories, said Kemble, had "something to do with making us what we are" (1:427).

In beautiful language, Kemble spelled out what the Anglo-Saxon became in the popular literature and hymns of later generations (1:433–35). The Anglo-Saxon was at one with nature in a far deeper sense than can be bestowed by scientific understanding, "for he knows what science haughtily refuses to contemplate or, it may be, is unable to appreciate" (1:433). Apprehensive of the contribution of science and technology to the true understanding of mankind, Kemble attempted to restore a sense of mystery and belief (1.435).

Responses to Kemble   Kemble's interpretation of the past still has a strong and largely unexamined hold on English pedagogy. Although in *Ethnology of the British Islands* (1852) Robert Gordon Latham, editor of Prichard's *Eastern Origins of the Celtic Nations,* argued from the evidence of Prichard and sparse fragments of Tacitus that the area and population of the Teutonic tribes had been exaggerated and that many tribes supposed to be Teutonic may actually have been Slavonic, his position was soon opposed by James A. Froude (1818–94), friend of Carlyle and follower of Kemble and Niebuhr. In his brilliant and controversial *History of England from 1529 to the Death of Elizabeth* (12 vols., 1858–70), Froude produced a pre-Darwinist conception of English history that made everlastingly popular the idea that the Reformation and the dissolution of the monasteries were decisive in purging Germanic England of Roman influences and that Henry VIII and Elizabeth I were therefore the saviors of a unique "island race."

Froude's work sparked a controversy over the nature of history and morality in the *Edinburgh Review* and the *Saturday Review.* Support for the "race is everything" hypothesis against Latham's more skeptical approach came from Charles Kingsley, Regius Professor of Modern History at Cambridge, poet and novelist, and follower of Carlyle, Coleridge, and Thomas Arnold, who in *The Roman and the Teuton* (1864) allied ethnology with sociology and class with race to show that the practice of enslaving captives would render pure Teutonic blood among the lower classes of the tribe the exception rather than the rule and that a mixed blood in the upper classes would also be produced by the custom of chiefs choosing companions in arms from among the most valiant:

> Only by some actual superiority of the upper classes to the lower can I explain the deep respect for rank and blood, which distinguishes, and perhaps will always distinguish, the Teutonic peoples. Had there been anything like a primeval equality among our race, a hereditary aristocracy could never have arisen, or if arising for a while, never could have remained as a fact which all believed in, from the lowest to the highest. Just, or unjust, the institution [hereditary aristocracy] represented, I verily believe, an ethnological fact.[9]

We shall see later how after the publication of Darwin's *Origin* these inchoate race-class ideas resurface in an evolutionary form in the works of E. A. Freeman, J. R. Green, and especially Matthew Arnold and Ludwig Gumplowicz. For the moment it is important to recognize that in the works of Carlyle, and particularly of Kemble, there was a fundamental Niebuhrian reconstitution of England's past stressing Germanic origins in a system of land settlement that was sacred, mysterious, and inviolate. Kemble put a premium upon birth, kith, and kin and saw the English island people as a nobility emerging from the ruins of Roman power. Froude appended to this view the idea that English owed their freedom to the Reformation and to the royal race of Henry VIII and Elizabeth I, who would henceforth become the compelling markers of English racial history.

TAINE

In France, Thierry's reconstruction of the past was not entirely insulated from these English developments, where they were used to mount a frontal assault upon monarchy, the rights of man, and the Gallo-Roman origins of French government. Hippolyte Adolphe Taine (1828–93) began his career as a brilliant university scholar, acquiring a command of Edmund Burke, Alexis de Tocqueville, G. W. F. Hegel (in the German), Johann Gottfried von Herder, Jules Michelet, François Guizot, Thomas Carlyle, John Stuart Mill, Immanuel Kant, and Benedict de Spinoza. In 1851 Taine was appointed professor of philosophy at Toulon but chose to go to Nevers, where he refused to sign a document declaring his agreement with the government's handling of the 1851 coup. Thereafter his university career came to an end, and he experienced a complete mental breakdown. In 1854, the year of the publication of the comte de Gobineau's work supporting the "race is all" hypothesis, he became interested in the French Revolution, and in 1855–56 he made the acquaintance of Joseph Ernest Renan. He published articles on nineteenth-century philosophers in *Revue de l'instruction publique* and began work on a history of English literature up to Lord Byron. In December 1863, the year of the publication of Renan's *Vie de Jésus,* he published his *Histoire de la littérature anglaise,* which was sent to the Academy for consideration, where it was vehemently attacked by Mgr. Félix Dupanloup, the bishop of Orléans, who had recruited Renan into the Roman Catholic Church when he was a young man and later bitterly opposed him for his wayward views. Taine's work was defended by Guizot, but the prize was not awarded. Taine continued to lecture, and after the Franco-Prussian War he worked on his *Origines de la France contemporaine,* which was published from 1875 through 1893, and is generally considered to be his greatest work.[10]

Taine used the scientific method to study the humanities through philosophy and literature. He interpreted the French Revolution as an attempt to remove absolutist monarchy that ended in tyranny because the idea of popular sovereignty results either in anarchy when used against the established form of political rule or in tyranny when used to support popular regimes. Taine applied Montesquieu's notion about the abuse of power to the Jacobins, whose obsessions with fixed ideas like the notions of the rights of man, popular sovereignty, and social contract had abused rationality. Like Montesquieu, Taine believed that the origin of good government and the right ordering of things lay with things German. The Restoration at Vienna had been made in ignorance of the positive facts of history from which societies were born. Nations were not chosen; they exist. All that was good in existing nations came from reason, and the humane world was a product of reason, of science, and of rational men thinking and making judgments for the irrational mass. But these rational men, the great writers, were not isolated phenomena; they were the result of race, milieu, and moment.

This trinity of race, milieu, and moment appeared in Taine's *Histoire de la littérature anglaise,* in which he attempted to identify the English national character through its literature. Race, he believed, was an internal temperament that "will out," no matter what the external influences. He understood milieu as a general state of mind shaped by external pressure such as the form of government, the organization of the Papacy, the conditions of religion, as well as by climatic conditions, which account for the most fundamental differences between those who dwell in the enervating South and those from the invigorating North. Moment, for Taine, was change—not the cyclical change of Polybius and Machiavelli but a progressive building upon the experiences of the past.

For Taine, instincts and aptitudes—the character of the mind as well as the body—were transmitted by the blood from age to age. To bring about any real change in character there had to be a change in the blood, either by migration or by invasion.

In Taine we rediscover the idea of race described in Kant as a set of characteristics transmitted in the blood but now viewed as a major cause in the affairs of man. It is clear that Taine believed the German mind towered over the aptitude given to the Latins. For him, Macaulay and Byron were the classical Latin class of writers who proceeded by transition, enumeration, and summary. Carlyle and Michelet, on the other hand, were Germanic revealers and romantic poets. For Taine Shakespeare became the ideal Germanic type and the English Renaissance marked the rebirth of the Saxon genius in English literature.

RENAN

Thierry's integration of blood, mass, language, law, and ideas was also an important element in the search for a new genealogy for the peoples of Western Europe dispossessed by the Agricultural and Industrial Revolutions and by the Restoration at Vienna following the French Revolution and its aftermath. People who had once depended on a sense of belonging to land and to dynastic states based upon long-established political principles now looked to race either to reestablish their title to land and political life or to explain their disturbed existence. Joseph Ernest Renan (1823–92), recruited into the Church by Abbé Dupanloup but renouncing his priestly studies after reading Goethe's *Faust,* in 1845 held that the delicacy of Brittany, his birthplace, was to be preferred to the vulgarity of everything portrayed in Thierry's accounts.

The Celts   In his *Poesie des races celtiques* (1857) Renan proposed a wide affinity among the Bretons, Welsh, Scots, Cornish, and Gaels of northern Scotland and Ireland—the Celts—who, by virtue of their seclusion, purity of blood, and inviolability of national character, had avoided the intrusion and confusion of the civilized world.[11] These ignored and isolated peoples, "where the race has remained pure from all admixture of alien blood," had changed the current of Western civilization with their poetry and their genius. Yet Renan saw this world of soul revealed in Kant, Hegel, and Herder being whittled away by the onward march of uniform civilization. Only in Ireland could "the native . . . produce the titles of his descent, and designate with certainty, even in the darkest prehistoric ages, the race from which he has sprung" (1.5).

For Renan the Celts were a race of family life and fireside joys. "In no other race," he wrote, "has the bond of blood been stronger, or has it created more duties, or attached man to his fellow with so much breadth and depth" (1.6). The Celts did not appear to have any aptitude for political life because the spirit of the family had prevented the development of more complex social organizations: "Thus the Celtic race has worn itself out in resistance to its time, and in defence of desperate causes" (1.7). The Celts' history was one long lament recalling exiles from flights across the sea. It consisted of poetic memory, sentimental songs of joy, elegies, and national melodies, and it was female—discovered in the ideal and vision of the women who wholly dominated it. The literature of the Celts was sparkling and bright, portraying a vivid impression of forest, mountain, and stone. Arthur, the hero, was less a political leader than the head of an order of equality, a round table at which sat men of valor and outstanding talents. The court was presided over by a woman, Gwinevere; its ideals were beauty, modesty, and love. In all these things the Celts were entirely different from the Latins and Germans, whose literature was full of vengeance and in whose world woman was nothing.

Renan's renunciation of Latin politics and Teutonic literature turned toward a new kind of religion, a new morality created by intellectuals and illustrated and decorated by poetic feeling based on reason. His heroes are souls in search of the truth and beauty, not politics:

> All noble, dedicated souls, abandoning the earth to all those who find it to their liking, and indifferent to the forms of government, the names of ministers and their actions, will take refuge in the heights of human nature and brimming with enthusiasm for the true and beautiful will create a power which will come down to earth to overthrow the shoddy structure of politics, and in turn become a law for mankind.[12]

Science and Philosophy   Renan's *L'Avenir de la science,* written to counteract the revulsion he felt toward the excesses of the 1848 insurrection, was not published until 1890 on the advice of Michelet and Thierry. It put forward the idea that philosophy and science were born of the union of philology and historical sympathy and that the philosopher was equipped to take over the role played by the Church in the spiritual leadership of humankind. Through scholarly dedication—the pursuit of the Platonic idea of truth, knowledge, and goodness—political machinations such as France had witnessed in the June insurrection would be overcome. This faith in a new science and philosophy, as opposed to the theory and practice of politics, expressed itself in three historical stages.

The first stage was one in which myths and religious literature were created. This is the world of imagining, the world of the demigods, of dream enactment, and scholars must return to these myths for a proper understanding of the creative forces in human nature. History must, in other words, be sympathetic to the rediscovery of myth. The second stage was the evolution of consciousness, which heralded the age of analysis and scientific curiosity. In this stage man became conscious of self and broke with the mythological age. The third stage was *la réflexion complèt*—a synthesis of complete understanding, an imaginative insight consisting of a scientific temper and a religious sense of oneness with nature.

In these three stages Renan traced the scientific organization of mankind, the conscious organization of a society whose goal, shaped by Enlightenment thought, will be to put man beyond the reach of material want. The role of the scientist and philosopher will be to teach wisdom to a wiser humanity. The dead will live on in the memories of the poets and the sages and in the achievements of the race.

This synthesis combined science and philosophy, the poetry of the legendary past with analytical self-consciousness. In this view, and especially in the distinction between ideal science and positive science, Renan was much influenced by his friend Marcellin Berthelot (1827–1907), distinguished chemist and secretary to the Academy of Sciences.

Renan's other works include *General History of the Semitic Language* (1847) and *Histoire générale et systeme compare des langues semitiques* (1863), which Hannah Arendt claims first opposed "Semites" and "Aryans" as a decisive *division du genre humain.*[13] Analyzing religion from a historical rather than a theological point of view, Renan's *Vie de Jésus*, the first of a multivolume history of Christianity, became his best-known book. Here Renan purged Jesus of his Jewishness and made him a historical figure no longer bound by old Judaic law; he now belonged to humanity and to the Christian *Volk*. Renan also wrote a *Histoire du peuple d'Israel* (1887–93). He argued that religious systems undergo profound revolutions, and the religion of antiquity was a religion of state, family, art, and morality raised to a high poetic expression. "Humanity accepts no chains other than those which it has put upon itself," he stated in *Intolerance of Skepticism.*[14]

MICHELET

Renan's contemporary Jules Michelet (1798–1874), the great historian of the romantic school, read Scott's *Lay of the Last Minstrel* and *Lady of the Lake,* and studied the popular poetry of Moldavia, Transylvania, Andelusia, Romania, Persia, and the Scottish borders. In *Le Peuple* (1846), he saw the France of revolution bestowing its newly formed political and social ideas on all nations of Europe and carrying French life to all corners of the globe.[15] Unlike Renan, he did not contain the idea of race within the nation. To Michelet, France was the great Gallic cauldron into which the life of the world was poured and out of which it flowed, and from that life *every race,* even the German, would be renewed. The central force of this life was the people: "It is said that the Revolution suppressed the nobility, but in fact it did just the opposite; it made nobles of thirty-four million Frenchmen. When one of the nobility who emigrated during the Revolution was boasting of the glory of his ancestors, a peasant who had won on the field of battle replied, 'I myself am an ancestor!'" (1.1.34).

For Michelet, the people were the peasants, whose manners and expressions he observed. "How many things half effaced in the manners of our people, seemingly inexplicable and devoid of all reason and sense, I have learned to see as being in harmony with primitive inspirations, and as being nothing else but the wisdom of a forgotten world" (2.2.110). He agreed with Renan that civilization had overtaken the peasantry, breaking their ties with the land and oppressing them with a mass of labor laws. Their laments and sad elegies recorded their degeneration by huge collective forces they did not understand. He did not dispute their commonplace vulgarity. But he also perceived in them the sparkle of life: "Yet, this depression, this degeneration, is only superficial. The foundation is intact. This race still has wine in its blood; even in those who seem most burned out you will find a spark" (2.2.112). "Man is born noble, and he dies noble," Michelet asserted. "It takes the work of a lifetime to become coarse and ignoble and to produce inequality between men" (2.4.123).

Michelet looked across the Channel at the English, not for confirmation of the Germanic strain in government, not for a pedigree of right ordering of public affairs in a legitimate past as Montesquieu had done, not to emulate English literature, not to celebrate the Celts as Renan had done but for evidence of a bastard mediocrity that had striven to preserve tradition by manufacturing antiquity in a utilitarian, bourgeois fashion. The French, he asserted, are the very opposite: "What distinguishes our people from them [is] . . . common sense" (2.2.113). The French character had immense advantages for action and economy in words, and although the people's instincts were being eroded by bourgeois forms of ownership and values, the old French peasant still entertained heroic ideas better than those of any prophet of antiquity. It follows that the instinct of the simple is the instinct of genius, and the man of genius is he who has a rapport with the child and with the people. The birth of the genius is the model of the birth of society. In Michelet there is a belief in the people rising up anew.

But for Michelet the people had to be pure, and he praised "the rough vigour of our mountaineers and the inhabitants of our least racially mixed provinces" (2.9.15). This elevation of purity produced a drive for unity: "One people! One country! One France! Never, never, I beg you must we become two nations! Without unity we perish. How is it that you fail to see this?" (3. preface .21). Those whom he saw as threatening the unity of France were other Jews. "Let that be my contribution for the future," Michelet exclaimed, "not to have attained but to have marked the aim of history, to have given it a name that no one had conceived. Thierry called it narration, and Guizot analysis. I have named it resurrection, and this name will last" (3. preface .21).

STATE AND NATION

With all these investigations into origins and new formulations of the national principle, the antique political model had not yet been rejected out of hand. Although Niebuhr saw a genuine division of blood and a new genealogy, he also reaffirmed his belief in the forms of Montesquieu and Burke. Thierry pursued his wavering faith in constitutional monarchy and liberty in an affiliation of Gallo-Roman blood, law, language, and ideas. Renan, while seeking a home for the little people in the Celtic twilight with scarcely any enthusiasm for the activity of politics, later rejected the elevation of the race into principle in politics and fixed his gaze on the achievement of moral consciousness in each individual nation through the pursuit of truth and goodness. Michelet resurrected the Rousseauist civilization of the noble French peasant and extended it outward to all humankind to counter the inhumane civilization pursued by the English and Americans. Kemble wistfully looked for the foundation of the state in a childlike Germanic dream world that predated the crash of the piston. Taine revived the flagging notion that abuse of power was prevalent in governments of dogma and saw in the geometric relationship of race, milieu, and moment evidence that the right psychological characteristics for countering it were Germanic, not Greek or Roman. All these writers clung for the moment to ideas of state and nation that were mainly co-existent. The state and the nation had not yet become co-terminous and co-extensive with the single, exclusive idea of race.

» Race and Natural History

Entwined with the changes taking place in history and philology were exciting reinterpretations of the past according to the criteria of comparative anatomy and the emerging studies of anthropology and ethnology. Until Blumenbach the inquiry into the relationship between monster and man, pygmy and man, wild man and man, had been conducted on the basis of uncertain anatomical evidence and constrained by astrological, theological, philosophical, literary, and political influences of the age. With Linnaeus and Blumenbach, man was treated for the first time as part of an animal kingdom apart from other influences, and the guiding idea became the unity of species, specifically mankind. Blumenbach's appeal was to the tenets of a disinterested science pursuing only the truth. His work left a number of unanswered questions for his colleagues in the natural sciences to examine further with the same rigor that he had applied. What, precisely, was the relationship between the orangutan and man, between the Caucasian and the Negro? Had the relationship between the monster and man finally been put to rest? Was the *norma verticalis* or Camper's angle of jaw the more accurate measurement of skull formation? What precisely was the *nisus formativus,* the formative force that was behind all nature?

LAMARCK AND CUVIER

In 1809 Jean Baptiste, Chevalier Lamarck (1744–1829) published his *Philosophie zoologique.* Under the influence of his friend Vicq d'Azyr (1748–94), who with Blumenbach had made great strides in the systematic and accurate study of limbs and brains, and Destutt de Tracy, the editor of his works and originator of the term "ideology," Lamarck transformed philosophy by dividing it into two branches—moral and natural. He was also influenced by Cabanis, who argued that psychology could be explained only in terms of biology, and Marie-François-Xavier Bichat (1771–1802), who in 1800 had studied in detail the degenerative change that took place in the cadaver between life and death (an idea that later greatly interested the comte de Gobineau) and was the first to put forward the idea that the organs of the body were formed through differentiation of simple functional units. Lamarck contended that the species was not fixed, as Blumenbach and Georges Cuvier (1769–1832) had argued, and that some environmental influence must have had an impact upon its development. He observed that modification, growth, and atrophy occurred in the process that took place from simpler forms to more complex forms as organs were used, or disused, and their characteristics were transmitted to offspring. The blacksmith's muscular arm was the outcome of the inheritance of countless generations of work in the smithy, transmitted from one generation to another in improved visible characteristics of strength and dexterity.

In *Le Règne animal distribué d'après son organization* (1817) Lamarck's opponent, the distinguished anatomist Cuvier, had welded together the Aristotelian concept of species with the doctrine of special creation and produced a more acceptable "natural" conception of unity of type. Cuvier conceived of animals being classified on the basis of structural characteristics that they held in common as autochthones. This concept of material species, essentially the idea of fixity of type, postulated a universe that had been created, not by transformation or transmutation as Lamarck had argued, but by periodic catastrophic physical changes that had brought one form of life to an end and replaced it with another.

Support for Lamarck came from Étienne Geoffrey Saint-Hilaire (1772–1844), a zoologist who had been on Napoleon's Egyptian expedition and brought back mummified animals, some thousands of years old, that showed little appreciable difference from contemporaneous specimens. Cuvier used the evidence in support of fixity of type, but Geoffroy Saint-Hilaire argued that some forms had remained the same from the beginning of time. This dispute about creation and the origins of the universe was to occupy science for the first half of the nineteenth century, made manifest in the confused struggles between monogenists and polygenists and between those who argued "race is everything" against "race is nothing."

The dispute in France was so contentious that it was carried into the French Academy, where it was resolved in favor of Cuvier's fixity of type. In England strong support for the monogenist side came from James Cowles Prichard, the English anthropologist and ethnologist who, as we have seen, combined his considerable ability in philology with work on the physical aspects of a unified species put forward by Blumenbach while at the same time examining the psychological characteristics and continuing "types" he saw preserved in a bewildering individual variety. Sir William Lawrence's lectures at the Royal College of Surgeons, published as *Comparative Anatomy, Physiology, Zoology and the History of Man* (1816–18), also took a monogenist line, but Lawrence (1783–1867) was concerned mainly with environmental influences affecting the transmission of characteristics from generation to generation. He related the shape of the lips and noses of Negroes to the practice of mothers' carrying babies on their backs while laboring in the fields. He also advocated, at this very early stage, that more attention should be paid to breeding of human beings. His ideas caused an outcry among theologians, to the extent that he was refused copyright for his work and had to suppress its publication.

Blumenbach's monogenist argument and the idea of fixity of species and descent from a single pair were not accepted by all natural scientists in the early nineteenth century. As Leon Poliakov has pointed out, Dürer, Vesalius, Paracelsus, Hume, Voltaire, and others had previously tested theological authority with alternative polygenic accounts based either upon biblical exegesis or upon Hermetic or Cabalistic manipulation of the heresies of Ham and the Tower of Babel, most of which were abusive of the newly discovered peoples and traded in the demonology and numerology of the secret texts.[16] But, leaving aside for a moment the monsters, the brutes, and the Negroes, there could be no anthropology or ethnology at all of "all the natural peoples" (the *Völker*) without a close alliance between physical science and historical science. In *Des caracteres physiologiques des races humaines* (1829), W. F. Edwards pointed out that this connection was clearly lacking, and in 1839 he coined the term "ethnological" to describe it for the Paris Society. This alliance could not possibly have come about before Thierry, following Niebuhr, introduced "race" into history and created a wide and convenient bridge into philological inquiry. Following the contributions of Niebuhr and Thierry and the abolition of slavery in the British Empire in 1833, the inquiry into natural origins and race took on a new meaning and momentum, not so much in relation to the plight of the slave abroad, but more particularly in relation to the problems associated with natural boundaries and "the races of Europe" following the confusion of the Restoration in 1815. Who exactly were the English, the French, and the German peoples? What were their true natural and geographic origins? What was the hidden mechanism that would enable a sufficient and satisfactory explanation to be given to these difficult questions?

RITTER AND THE ENVIRONMENTALISTS

As Theophile Simar has pointed out,[17] following Niebuhr's lectures a vigorous new movement began in Germany with the work of Karl Ritter (1779–1859), professor of geography at the University of Berlin, director of studies at the Prussian Military School, and friend of Alexander von Humboldt, who in ten volumes, *Die Erdkunde im Verhältnis zur Natur und zur Geschichte des Menschen,* written from 1822 to 1859, brought together the study of history and geography. Ritter modified the influence of milieu proclaimed by Montesquieu in the eighteenth century and developed by the environmentalists of the early nineteenth century. He not only provided a scientific foundation for the later analysis of the environment but also moved toward the more romantic view held by Herder—that the development of constitutions and states depended on geographical conditions ordained by God. Opposing Hume and Burke, Ritter claimed that constructive reason played no part in the elaboration of a national constitution, but this development took shape in the moving and countermoving of the unconscious and silent power of nature.

Following Ritter, Gustav Klemm (1802–67), librarian of the city of Dresden, synthesized the enthnographic accounts of the peoples in a Hegelian historical development from savagery, through domestication, to freedom based on the cultural development of the passive and active races. He viewed culture as the pursuit of the spirit rather than the pursuit of politics. His *Allgemeine Kultur: Geschichte der Menschheit* (1843–52) drew on the work of Kant and Hegel.

Klemm also drew on the work of Karl Gustav Carus (1789–1869), the physiologist, comparative anatomist, and psychologist, who wrote profusely on *Naturphilosophie* and the capacity of great men for spiritual development. Carus, a follower of Friedrich Schelling and a friend of Goethe, was also an art critic and landscape painter. He believed that inherited tendency was a proof that the cell had a certain psychic life and that individual differences were less marked in lower than in higher organisms.

In 1857 H. T. Buckle (1821–62) published *Introduction to the History of Civilisation in England,* which emphasized the importance of environmental influences—climate, food, soil, and the general aspects of nature—according to the teachings of Bodin and Montesquieu but drew also upon the methods of the newly invented Comtian "sociology" and employed statistical analysis to piece together the history of civilization according to laws of society. Buckle went further than Ritter in arguing for the primacy of environmental influences. He postulated that if climate, soil, food, and milieu were the prime causes of intellectual progress, then literature, religion, politics, and government were the products, not the causes, of civilization.

Ritter, Klemm, Carus, Buckle, and Friedrich Christoph Schlosser (1776–1881), who wrote popular histories of the German peoples, were formidable influences on the late-nineteenth- and early-twentieth-century race thinkers.

CRANIOLOGY AND CEPHOLOGY

In 1840 Anders Retzius (1796–1860), critic of Blumenbach, introduced his cephalic index to the Academy of Sciences in Stockholm. He used the term "brachycephalic" to describe broad-headed peoples and "dolichocephalic" to describe narrow-headed peoples, thus extending the work of Dürer and Camper, as well as Blumenbach, on the facial angle. Two years later Herbert Spencer made his epic statement that "everything had its laws" and that in the change from simple to complex there were laws applicable not only to natural life but also to political life, as witnessed in the principle of the "survival of the fittest." The search for anthropological laws continued in an anonymous work on *The Vestiges of the Natural History of Creation* (1844), some forty years later found to be the work of Robert Chambers (1802–71), a writer on Scottish history and on science who applied the principles of slow progressive development and growth to demonstrate the orderly succession of general laws in the universe. In direct contradiction to theories that postulated a cataclysmic beginning for the universe, Chambers argued that the operation of general laws could be observed in vestigial remnants such as polydactylism. Darwin's colleague, Alfred Russel Wallace (1823–1913), regarded Chambers's work as an important transition in the development of the idea of evolution.

Retzius's work on the cephalic index also interested Paul Broca (1824–80), craniologist and brain surgeon in Paris, who discovered the seat of articulate speech in the left side of the frontal region of the brain (the convolution of Broca) and was one of the founders of the Societé d'Anthropologie de Paris in 1859, and later of L'Ecole d'Anthropologie. Broca, like Lamarck at the beginning of the century, acknowledged the importance of the work of Bichat and Cabanis, but he also saw the significance of language and philology. Like Müller and Renan, he recognized the problem arising from the confusion of philological analysis with scientific analysis and in his early works expressed wariness about the use of the general term "Aryan" to describe Indo-Europeans. Broca concentrated his attention upon the development of better instruments to measure more reliably the material that was actually available, particularly that which he had acquired during his appointment in 1847 to the commission investigating cemeteries. He invented the goniometer, stereograph, and occipital crochet for the measurement of the skull and used the cephalic index to inquire more deeply into the composition of existing populations. He was primarily interested in finding proofs regarding the single or separate origins of mankind. Broca originated methods of classifying hair and skin color, and he established brain and skull ratios. As a polygenist who favored a division between Aryan influences and Hebrew influences and opposed the mixing of the two races, he held that although the outward conditions of man might change, there were, nevertheless, enduring human types and that if these types were transferred to a different landscape their natural character would be resistant to change. It should be possible, he thought, with sufficient cranial evidence, to ascertain the true origins of the French.

Taken together, these ideas stimulated an interest in vestigialism as an alternative to creationism and transformism, perhaps best illustrated in the use of cephalic measurement in the exhumation of the remains of a skull discovered at Neanderthal in Prussia in 1856, in which T. H. Huxley (1825–95) and Rudolf Karl Virchow (1821–1902) were consultants. Huxley used the analysis as an opportunity to condemn the vestigialism of Chambers, and later at the Oxford Conference of the British Association in 1860 he mounted a staunch "agnostic" (a term he coined) defense of the Darwinist evolutionary line against Bishop William Wilberforce's continuing support for biblical exegesis. Huxley's *Races, Species and Their Origins* (1860) and *Methods and Results of Ethnology* (1865), in which he attempted to avoid talking of "races" by using the term "stocks," recognized the discovery at Neanderthal as human but closer to the ape than to Australoid man. He continued the defense of science as a better basis for education on these matters than the humanities—a view opposed by Theodor Waitz and Matthew Arnold.

Huxley's colleague Virchow, the Pomeranian craniologist and somatic anthropologist, who had in 1851 worked on cretinism, took a more guarded line, particularly after the publication of Darwin's *Origin,* which he regarded only as one possible hypothesis. Virchow advocated, instead, the exclusive concentration upon cellular pathological evidence and the archaeological and anatomical clues that the remnants of the skull might possibly reveal. He was regarded as one of the most significant physicians of the nineteenth century. In 1848 he investigated the great epidemic of Upper Silesia and recommended political, economic, and social reform to the Prussian government. After 1849 he worked upon cellular pathology, and in his analysis the examination of the microscopic unit took on a new significance. A co-founder of the German Anthropological Society in 1869, Virchow was responsible for the survey of schoolchildren that recorded hair and eye color, skin, and skull shape. He concluded that there was no pure German race, only a mixture of morpho-logical types.

Renan, and later Max Müller, were early popularizers of Virchow's theory of the separation of philology from natural history. All these writers were instrumental in the formation of the sciences of cephalometry, craniology, and biometry, upon which much of the late-nineteenth- and twentieth-century writings on race were based, and we ignore them at our peril.

HUMBOLDT

All these new ideas—monogenism, polygenism, transformism, creationism, vestigialism, culturism, and environmentalism—were competing hypotheses in the attempt to construct a self-sufficient idea of race. Philological expla-nations and natural historical explanations often intermixed and borrowed one from the other, and it was extremely difficult to separate both from political context. These multiple ideas of race continued to be held within an overall concept of the antique state as amended by eighteenth-century notions of self-determining nationhood. Yet contemporary events were increasingly expressed in terms of natural and racial antecedents. The argument was en-gaged in a fierce religious and political conflict between those who held to Blumenbach's idea of the unity of species and Cuvier's unity of type against Lamarck's fixity of species and differentiation of function. This argument, which may be expressed in terms of a "race is nothing" hypothesis versus a "race is everything" hypothesis, overshadowed both the philological and the natural historical inquiries to the extent that each area of study was divided. Alexander von Humboldt (1769–1859), the Prussian naturalist who died in the year of the publication of Darwin's *Origin,* spent the last years of his life writing a physical description of the universe. This important text, *Kosmos* (1845–62), surveyed the state of physical anthropology from Blumenbach to Darwin and is a major contribution to the critical analysis of the idea of race.[18]

Humboldt opened his discourse with this statement: "The most impor-tant questions in the history of civilisation are connected with the descent of the races, the community of language, and the greater or lesser persistency in the original direction of the intellect and disposition" (1.351). He believed that man had managed to escape the influence of climate and soil by the activities of mind, organization, and adaption, and that the much-contested problem of the community of origin, which had been attributed to environmental influences by Ritter and Buckle, could be examined in connection with the parentage and affinity of races alongside the science of language.

Humboldt argued that the first vivid impressions of people were derived from the senses and directed primarily toward color and form. Differences described in newly discovered peoples were held to be different characteristics, not mere variation, and so as evidence of distinct aboriginal species. But this assumption, based on impressions, was incorrect. Committed to the notion of the unity of humanity and understanding differences as varieties, not subspecies, Humboldt shared with Herder a vision of intermediated gradations in everything, including the tint of the skin and the form of the skull. Employing sharp powers of observation and analogies derived from the history of varieties in animals, wild and domesticated, and variations and limits in fecundity of hybrids, Humboldt diminished the polygenist argument made in favor of the diversity of the species. He cited studies on the pelvis and on the brain of the Negro and the European to show that Western views were often derived from sense impressions, as Locke had suggested. He also cited Johannes Müller (1801–58), the anatomist and professor at Berlin, who had argued that if mankind were not a single species the descendants of mixed breeds would not have been fruitful. Humboldt concluded, therefore, that mankind was distributed in varieties that people had come to designate vaguely as "races." The points of departure for these races could not be determined, especially when one took into account the remarkable extremes of color and form, the locations from which people were assumed to have come, and the changes that had taken place in migration over long periods of time.

Humboldt accepted, however, that languages were important in recognizing the similarity or diversity of races, and he regarded the descent of language from a common origin to be the connecting thread that linked together physical and mental powers and dispositions in a thousand varied forms. Here he acknowledged the work of Theodor Waitz (1821–64), who in *Anthropologie der Naturvölker* (1859) had argued that the character of language was more stable than racial or ethnological qualities and a more reliable guide to historical continuity. Comparative philology was a more exact science, therefore, than physical anthropology or craniology.

Above all, Humboldt warned that in this brilliant new field of ideal speculation and controversy people needed to guard against "historical illusion." The fact of the matter was that foreign invasion, the long association of some peoples, foreign religious influences, and families of languages all contributed to the immensely complicated physical and historical problem of what is a true origin. Humboldt returned to the unity of the human species, categorically refuting the assumption of superior and inferior races (which he, interestingly, attributed to Aristotle's *Politics*): "All are alike designed for freedom; for that freedom which in ruder conditions of society belongs to individuals only, but, where states are formed, and political institutions enjoyed, belongs of right to the whole community" (1.335–36).

Humboldt did not go on to discuss the conditions under which a state existing as a whole community enjoying political institutions might possibly exist in the new circumstances. In supporting the "race is nothing" hypothesis, he simply put the important question of real politics and political expediency to one side, preferring to stress, as did Niebuhr, Herder, and Buckle, pasts that were apolitical and made naturally legitimate by an appeal to the final authority of the common humanity of the *Völker* and to the influences of geography. Humboldt summarized it brilliantly in this politically naive quotation from his brother Wilhelm von Humboldt (1767–1835), the classifier of languages and author of a text on the Kawi language of Java:

> If there is the one idea which contributes more than any other to the often contested but still more misunderstood, perfectibility of the human species— it is the idea of our common humanity; tending to remove the hostile barriers which prejudices and partial views of every kind have raised between men; and to cause all mankind, without distinction of religion, nation or colour, to be regarded as one great fraternity, aspiring towards one common aim, the free development of their moral faculties. This is the ultimate and highest objective of society; it is also the direction implanted in man's nature, leading towards the indefinite expansion of his inner being. (1.356)

GOBINEAU

But by what means? How would that noble mission be accomplished? Count Arthur de Gobineau (1816–82), writing at the same time as Humboldt and greatly indebted to the scholarship of Niebuhr, Thierry, Karl Müller, Ritter, Carus, and Klemm, was not satisfied with such a nebulous statement of aims and objectives, nor was he content to return to the tenets of classical Aristotelian and Machiavellian political theory for an answer to the awful problems of his age. He dedicated his *Essai sur l'inégalité des races humaines* (1853–55) to George V, king of Hanover, saying that he had been forced to seek the hidden causes of the terrible upheavals of his age in a "historical chemistry"—a synthesis with which he hoped to find "the master key to the enigma."[19] The editor of the English version of Nietzsche's work, Dr. Oscar Levy, introduced the translation of Gobineau's *The Inequality of the Human Races* (1915) to a First World War English public as a prophecy of evil and disaster in the Hebrew tradition from a man of poetic insight who had a remedy for the ills afflicting modern industrial society—the slave morality of Europe, the corruption of the Church, and the widespread propagation of debilitating semitic values. Such enthusiasm some sixty years after the first publication of Gobineau's work indicates that it is deserving of close attention.

Race in History   Gobineau returned to the works of Barthold Georg Niebuhr, whose *History of Rome* had moved away from historical compilation toward philology and had explicated for the first time the foundations of the ancient Roman people and state: the character of the people, the history of wars, the state of literature, and the deeds of great men. Gobineau responded to this work with enthusiasm: "An analytical tool of marvellous delicacy has made a Rome, unknown to Livy, rise before us under the hands of Niebuhr" (p. xii). With Niebuhr it had become possible to reconstruct the pasts of vanished peoples from art, portraits, and costumes rather than from politics. Gobineau's colossal truth was this: "that the racial question overshadows all other problems of history, that it holds the key to them all, and that the inequality of the races from whose fusion a people is formed is enough to explain the whole course of its destiny" (p. xiv). He was convinced "that everything great, noble and fruitful in the works of man on this earth, in science, art, and civilization, derives from a single starting point, is the development of a single germ and the result of a single thought; it belongs to one family alone, the different branches of which have reigned in all the civilized countries of the universe" (p. xv).

Gobineau looked for truths about the past based not upon the intellectual contributions of the philosophers, whom he acknowledged had made a great contribution to civilization, but upon the principles of natural history that caused great civilizations like Rome to collapse. The failings of the modern rationalists, and for that matter the founding fathers of the Revolution, were that they placed great emphasis in their historical narratives upon classical notions of virtue and vice and saw in the collapse of governments and civilizations a corruption of values or institutions thought to be eternally grounded in a particular kind of political life. Gobineau believed that this interpretation was the cardinal error: governments have no influence whatsoever on the life of civilizations, he maintained, and corruption was no longer a valid, scientific explanation for the fall of Rome.

The Degeneration of Society   Gobineau turned to Prichard's *Natural History of Man* and to Karl Friedrich Philip von Martius's (1794–1868) and Johann Baptist von Spix's (1781–1826) *Reise in Brasilien in den Jahren* (1823–31) for confirmation of malady and disease in natural organisms, and he applied the analysis not to the body politic but to society. The first major proposition of his work, drawn from the facts of history, histology, anatomy, and physiology, was that the true cause of the life and death of a people was a shift in the share of blood and inheritance into different hands. "The word *degenerate*," Gobineau explained, "when applied to a people, means (as it ought to mean) that the people has no longer the same blood in its veins, continual adulterations having gradually affected the quality of that blood" (p. 25). Barzun sees this proposition as Gobineau's adoption of a principle, first enunciated by Montesquieu, that the interpretation of history should be properly seen as conflict between races.[20]

Prichard had argued scientifically that civilization was independent of climate, geography, and the wants of man, and Carus had demonstrated the scientific principle of inherited tendency, that the cell had a psychic life, and that individual differences were less marked in lower organisms than in higher organisms. And while François-Pierre-Guillaume Guizot had called civilization an event, for Gobineau civilization was a series of events linked logically by the interaction of ideas. From this foundation, which is a complete rejection of Buckle's conceptions of civilization, as well as the classical concept of Christian and European civilization entertained by Humboldt and Guizot, Gobineau constructed his second proposition: that climate and geography had little influence on the progress and stagnation of a people and that a nation's place on the scale of civilization did not come from the fertility or infertility of the country: "In other words, a nation does not derive its value from its position; it never has and it never will. On the contrary, it is the people which has always given—and will always give—to the land its moral, economic, and political value" (p. 61). Here Gobineau promoted the exact opposite of the "race is nothing" hypothesis seen in the works of Buckle, Herder, and the Humboldts. Gobineau defined civilization as "a state of relative stability, where the mass of men try to satisfy their wants by peaceful means, and are refined in their conduct and intelligence" (p. 91). He believed that civilization was characterized by an instinctual impression of well-being and by the unity, cooperation, and sociability of peoples as well as a hatred of violence. Most important, modern civilization was not superior to previous civilizations.

The Rejection of Politics   With the history of European man seen as a fight between two races (now expressed in biological terms), and the true cause of the life and death of a people seen as a shift in the share of blood, it is not surprising that Gobineau was pessimistic about the capacity of the Negro and Cherokees to be brought to civilization by governmental institutions of the kind set up by the framers of the United States Constitution. He clearly regarded these North American peoples as brutes occupying the lower strata of society and asserted that their enslavement exemplified his principle of natural inequality. It would take generations to civilize them, he believed, and then only by dinning it in like teaching a dog new tricks. Politics and political science would be of little consequence in achieving civilization, because both were in bondage to the instinctual impressions of the masses: "Theories of government can never rise to the rank of accepted truths" (p. 103), Gobineau argued.

In Gobineau we see an outright revulsion against any genealogy rooted in a Greco-Roman political tradition and a complete rejection of Las Casas's Aristotelian interpretation of the brutishness and viciousness of the act of enslavement. For Gobineau nationality was based not on the good administration of good laws grounded upon classical political theory; the health of a people and its system of government were assumed to have no impact whatsoever upon the course of events. The true health of a people and the cause of life and death were to be found, as Kant and Lessing had observed, in an "inner constitution." In Gobineau's works and in the works of his followers there was no place for the great "political" writers. Even Claude Adrien Helvetius (1715–71), who in *De l'esprit* (1758) had argued that external organizational utility and self-interest distinguished men from beasts and that "culture" was the formative element in nationality, was rejected out of hand. Rather, Gobineau relied upon Bichat, the inspiration of Lamarck and the inventor of degenerative change, who "did not seek to discover the great mystery of existence by studying the human subject from the outside; the key to the riddle, he saw, lay within" (p. 24).

Nationality   Like so many modern concepts that see state, nation, and race as co-terminous, Gobineau's concept of nationality owed more to anatomy, histology, and physiology than to political theory. His notion was of a human body—an organic mass, not an aggregation of individual parts—incessantly being transformed year on year, so that it retained few original elements, but there the analogy stopped. There was one significant difference between the nation and the human body: a nation did not preserve its form. Nation and society have difficulty in moving from a rudimentary type of organization to a more complex one, and the leap is made only by a gifted race. It would be difficult, Gobineau believed, for tribal forms to break free from their pure-blooded impotence to assume the form of nationality.

Here is this same disjunction between antique political origins and newly discovered natural origins found also in the work of Niebuhr and then in Humboldt and Herder. But with Gobineau the idea moves into an entirely new world in the second half of the nineteenth century. Gobineau did not believe that politics had changed much since Greece and Rome and held there had been no improvement in political machinery or manners. There was so much more to learn from the natural forms of social organization employed by bees and insects *en masse* and by the comparisons of groups than there was from the study of individual men and their spent political theories.

The Unity of Species   In *The Inequality of the Human Races* Gobineau pursued this interest in social organization and comparative groupings, but he was ambivalent about the pre-Darwinist controversy on genealogy, seeming to have difficulty accepting the claims of those who argued no single origin for humanity and postulated many genealogies. At first he adhered to the unity of origin theory, but when confronted with Camper's analysis of the traits of the face and with the work of Christian Meiners, the multiplicity theorist, who in *Grundriss der Geschichte der Menschheit* had argued on the basis of beauty and ugliness that there could not have been a single origin, Gobineau wavered. But he returned again to Prichard, to Blumenbach's measuring technique, and to Pickering's *Races of Man* to compare differences in busts, pelvises, and color. He did not accept Humboldt's view of the infinite gradation of color from white to black or the belief that human families create hybrids, unlike plants and animals that produce from allied species. He believed in permanent racial differences on the basis of the changing mixture of blood of the old and new, which takes place regardless of environment and government.

Gobineau's one major difficulty was the biblical authority of Genesis, which he had to address to solve the fertility problem. Accepting Adam as the ancestor of the white race, the heresy of the Ham story, and the old division of the known world into three parts to Shem, Ham, and Japhet, he was left with a number of questions to be resolved. For his solution, he went not to history or political theory but to Cuvier's scientific discussion of the unity of type of dogs and hybrid breeds, to *Arabian Nights,* and to Blumenbach's celebrated "Caucasian" type:

> Unhappily, modern science has been able to provide no clue to the labyrinth of the various opinions. No likely hypothesis has succeeded in lightening this darkness, and in all probability the human races are as different from their common ancestor, if they have one, as they are from one another. I will therefore assume without discussion the principle of unity; and my only task, in the narrow and limited field to which I am confining myself, is to explain the actual deviation from the primitive type. (p. 119)

While he could not prove or disprove the validity of the unitarian hypothesis, and preferred to leave it open, Gobineau continued throughout the text to nibble away at it by producing examples of separate stocks and branches. He encouraged, for example, a more scientific approach to the weakest links in an iron chain in line with the geological theory and practice of Sir Charles Lyell (1797–1875) (pp. 134–35). In footnotes to the works of Sir John Barrow, FRS (1764–1848), whose *Travels in China* (1804) and *Travels in the Interior of South Africa* (1806) had remarked on similarities between the Hottentots and the Chinese, Gobineau actively promoted the idea that climate, habit, locality, and environment were insignificant and that the incommunicability of civilization had prevented the fusion of racially distinct groups.

It is this uncritical acceptance of the Adamic account of Creation and division that led Houston Stewart Chamberlain some fifty years later to describe Gobineau's work as belonging to "the hybrid class of scientific phantasmagorias" (p. 267). For Chamberlain it was flawed because it failed to anticipate the Darwinist process of evolution and hence had not achieved an integrated "scientific" idea of race. Chamberlain found it reprehensible because it was based on the assumption that originally "pure" races crossed with each other in the course of history and thus became less pure and less noble. For Chamberlain this was not a tenable assumption.[21] What an Aryan is and what a Semite is cannot be decided either by the scientist or the philologist. Races are but "inventions of study" and *not* primeval peoples: "One of the most fatal errors of our time is that which impels us to give too great weight in our judgments to the so-called 'results' of science. Knowledge can certainly have an illuminating effect, but it is not always so, and especially for this reason that knowledge always stands upon tottering feet" (p. 267).

THE AMERICAN EXPERIENCE

Gobineau's references to the Negro and the Cherokee have to be seen in the light of developments taking place in North America during the period leading up to Chief Justice Roger B. Taney's ruling in *Dred Scott v. Sandford* (1857) that slaves were property, not citizens, and had no standing to sue in court. The idea of freedom and equality enshrined in the U.S. Constitution was theoretically in conflict with chattel slavery but did not present much of a "political" problem until the 1830s because the Constitution had not envisaged that the Negro should, or ever could, be part of the natural societies envisioned by Hobbes, Locke, and Montesquieu. The Constitution had created a minimalist residual political state (and even that was deplored by Gobineau!) mainly driven by natural rights theory, Reformation Christianity, and doctrines of civil and economic rights. Although some states had under the pressures of good Christian works and egalitarian natural rights doctrines moved toward emancipation after 1787, and after 1808 the country ceased to import slaves from Africa, the Negro was considered neither to be part of the political state nor entitled to enjoy the benefits of the novel "natural" co-existent state that had been set up to gain independence for the colonies from the correspondingly unnatural and unequal monarchical English state. Until the 1830s the Negro in North America was considered to be a slave by right of conquest, by empirical observation of natural difference, and by biblical exegesis; he was not a man by virtue of his membership as a good citizen of an Aristotelian, Ciceronian, or Machiavellian *res-publica*. The *Dred Scott* ruling sealed this status.

While during the Civil War Abraham Lincoln argued that the guarantee of equality enshrined in the Declaration of Independence extended to all men, and that all were entitled to "certain unalienable rights," among which were "Life, Liberty, and the pursuit of Happiness," his modest attempt to reintroduce the elements of political discourse and political reality into a state perversely based on the primacy of individual, natural rights and mass democracy was later frustrated by the ruling in *Plessy v. Ferguson* (1896), which held that segregation of black people and white people was constitutional. The case legitimized the "separate but equal" doctrine, which owed more to nineteenth century biological, social, and economic theory than it did to antique political theory.

Here we can see American law and practice implementing the Niebuhrian Germanic racialization of history that was taking place generally throughout Western Europe from 1815 onward. Not only did the Negro continue to be excluded from enjoying civil, economic, and discredited political rights as a citizen, but the judgments as to his entitlement to those rights issuing forth from the pens of European intellectuals supported American practice. The writers we have examined were more interested in theorizing about the color, size, intellect, moral development, social capacity, psychic personality, and character of the European (his essential racial nature) than about the basic political conditions necessary for the establishment of a peaceable and secure state that included all the people and confirmed and encouraged their status as citizens *qua* citizens (their essential political nature).

Thus Gobineau's pre-Darwinist synthesis provided an important gloss upon a debate that hitherto had been about slavery. Not only were the institutional arrangements of government and politics in states generally useless in making any indentation upon uncivilized peoples, but the Negro in particular in the United States and elsewhere was racially fixed in his slavery. While he believed that some Negroes were more intelligent than peasants and half the middle class of France, Gobineau refused to say that every Negro was a fool, because it would mean that every European was intelligent: "Heaven keep me from such a paradox" (p. 180). Just as the peasant was in the grip of the mass instinctual impression of his type, so was the Negro in America, and no government could possibly extricate them from this grip by political means.

Some eighty years after Blumenbach's classification of the varieties or races of mankind within a unity of species, there was still no agreement as to mankind's true historical, philological, or natural origins. Despite the emancipation acts, the ban on importation of slaves in 1808, and the abolition of slavery, despite the revolutionary attempts to accommodate the peoples of Europe within settled governmental arrangements in the aftermath of the great revolutions of the eighteenth century, there remained no consistent synthesis to explain, remedy, or reconcile the turmoil of temper and character, kith and kin, the blood, law, and language of the common people.

The monogenist, polygenist, creationist, vestigialist, transformist, and environmentalist ideas within the emerging studies of ethnology and anthropology had failed to provide Gobineau with an adequate explanation for the continuing social decadence and disorder he saw around him. In these circumstances insistence upon notions of common humanity and the unity of species was simply not good enough. What Gobineau provided was a "proof" that government and politics were of little significance in determining social existence. His achievement was to mobilize anatomy, histology, and physiology to provide an adequate explanation for the Fall of Man. He created a social anatomy of the degeneration and regeneration of the races in place of politics properly conducted and shifted the involvement of the people away from participation in *res-publica* toward an interest they all shared *en masse,* like bees in a hive, in the more easily recognizable Lamarckian traits of blood and inheritance. Henceforth the dispossessed peoples of Europe, as well as the Negro in America, had their abject condition confirmed and reinforced by a scientific analysis based on fixed inherited characteristics and function.

As Richard Dawkins has shown, the hypotheses of Lamarck and Cabanis, upon which Gobineau's theory rested, supported an idea of change that stressed the principles of inheritance of acquired characteristics and their use and disuse (the blacksmith's muscular arm).[22] On the other hand, William Paley's (1743–1805) *Natural Theology; or, Evidence of the Existence and Attributes of the Deity Collected from the Appearances of Nature* (1802) was based upon a science that still accepted a formative force or design behind all nature—a view strenuously denied, as we have seen, by David Hume, but supported by Blumenbach and Linnaeus and later by Kant, Herder, and the Humboldts. None of the hypotheses we have so far considered, however, had wrenched entirely free from biblical exegesis. Somewhere in the natural racial explanation there still lurked the Fall, the mark of Cain, and the delinquency of Ham.

DARWIN AND SPENCER

When Gobineau's discourse on the inequalities of the human races was published in 1854, it created little stir. It was only after the Civil War in America and the Franco-Prussian War that Gobineau's ideas attracted attention. Dawkins argues that the three accounts of the natural world—by divine intervention or some other energetic force, by ascent of the ladder of the antique Great Chain of Being, or by the cumulative transmission of fixed inherited characteristics—provided no explanation for the natural processes of life consistent enough for them to be translated into a convincing scientific theory. What they all lacked was a *mechanical* explanation to overcome the material sticking points in the various competing arguments. That explanation was provided by Charles Darwin's (1809–1882) *Origin of Species* (1859), which introduced the idea of an "evolution" of material things that was gradual, cumulative, painfully slow, and natural.

Not only did Darwin provide an important historical stepping off point for the evolutionary sciences of physical anthropology, anatomy, and biology, but he also created a new science of social evolution in which the account of Niebuhr could now be viewed as a natural organic evolutionary history combining ethnology, topography, chorography, and philology acting together in a series of co-terminous natural events, thus enabling for the first time an idea of evolving "self-determining" races to emerge. Wedded to Herbert Spencer's (1820–1903) earlier doctrine of laissez-faire in *The Proper Sphere of Government* (1842), which recognized that everything in nature had its laws and should be left to its own devices, Darwin's work led people to believe that evolution was as much a characteristic of political and economic life as it was of the natural world of flora and fauna. Henceforth the condition of human society depended for explanation more on the principles of natural selection and evolution than upon the quality of political life and its traditional institutions. As Spencer prophetically put it in his *Social Statics* (1851):

> There seems no getting people to accept the truth, which nevertheless is conspicuous enough, that the welfare of a society and the justice of its arrangements are at bottom dependent on the characters of its members; and that improvement in character which results from carrying on peaceful industry under the restraints imposed by an orderly social life. The belief, not only of the socialists but also of those so-called Liberals who are diligently preparing the way for them is that by due skill an ill-working humanity may be framed into well-working institutions. It is a delusion. The defective natures of citizens will show themselves in the bad acting of whatever social structure they are arranged into. There is no political alchemy by which you can get golden conduct out of leaden instincts.[23]

Benjamin Kidd, whose *Principles of Western Civilisation* (1902) and *Science of Power* (1918) provided the framework of reference for Arendt's later critique of race thinking, saw the dawning of this new Darwinian era of social evolution as the most profound and significant departure from all that had gone before in the science of man. Before Darwin the controlling principles of the science of man had been those of the political philosophers operating within a vaguely defined, but authoritative, political and ecclesiastical framework. After Darwin the principle of natural selection introduced into the explanation of the differences in the races made evolution both natural and social. The science of civilization became the doctrine of efficiency. As Kidd argued, what ended with Darwin was the conception of political society that saw human existence as an aggregation of contingent interests and thoughts of individuals thrown together by a colligated past and in which the principal task was deemed to be the understanding of that past, and then accommodating its diverse elements within some kind of authoritative co-existent and reciprocal political arrangement that actually worked. Faith in God and allegiance to the classical notion of the political life were not enough. One optimistic Harvard modernist has described the processes of social evolution that Wallace, Darwin, and Spencer created as "a glimpse of an underlying symmetry and logic in social relationships which, when more fully comprehended by ourselves, should revitalize our political understanding and provide the intellectual support for a science and medicine."[24] It is that ominous glimpse that we carry forward into the next chapter.

» *Conclusion: Race Is In, Politics Is Out*

We can glimpse the symmetry and logic of the new social relationship termed "race" only by working our way through the seminal texts of those historians and scientists who were preoccupied, if not obsessed, with it, from the end of the eighteenth century to the Franco-Prussian War. A diligent study of this voluminous material has demonstrated that there are three major hypotheses contending for ascendancy: Locke/Linnaeus/Blumenbach, who observed that race is a fact and may be categorized scientifically but cautioned that we should not be too firm about its boundaries; Kant, who put race all down to soul, character, and temperament inherited in the blood; and Hegel, who saw race as part of the long developmental process of history moving toward greater rationality. Their successors played historical and scientific tunes upon these philosophical themes, mixing the philosophical with the historical, the scientific, and the aesthetic to produce a potent racial brew. During this period the foundations were laid for eight or more derivative hypotheses upon which the commonplaces of modern racial analyses are shakily based. These are:

Hobbes: Race is nothing more than the right of conquest of one man over another, because nature is a war of every man against every man.

Locke: Race has to do with sensation, with the association of the familiar and the unfamiliar, with attraction and repulsion.

Herder: Race is the ethnic *Kultur* of the ordinary people (*Volk*).

Humboldt: Race is a bewildering variety of different anthropological qualities under the single umbrella of a common, rational humanity in the cosmos.

Marx: Race is merely the manifestation of the class conflict arising from inherent inequalities in the economic mode of production.

Comte: Race has to do with the three stages of historical development of consciousness from myth to reality and oneness with nature.

Gobineau: Race has to do with the degenerative biology of the masses.

Spencer: Every social and economic institution has its natural laws; only the fittest survive.

Darwin: Race has to do with biological evolution.

In those writers examined closely in this chapter politics and political thought have been bypassed by the more alluring idea that true origins of states and nations, and the foundation for their legitimacy, are in natural or linguistic criteria. During this period the stages of the race idea were beginning to be clarified in anthropology and sociology; the grammar of race was created in the folklore and poetry of the ordinary peoples; the major "ethnic groupings" of Europe and the surrounding states were legitimized in the concepts of Anglo-Saxon, Celt, Hebrew, and Indo-European; the ideas of *Volk* and *Völkerwanderung* were democratized; the idea of an alternative to Greco-Roman civilization was proposed; and the foundations were laid for comparative anatomy, comparative geography, and comparative cephology. All these changes, expressed variously in degenerative and regenerative terms, penetrated the language of politics and changed not only its form but its nature. In the half century following Darwin the language of politics and politicians was suborned by race.

What burst upon the scene in 1842 and 1859 through the works of Spencer and Darwin was a movement that treated political activity as subject to the same rules of evolution that applied to the natural biological world and thus provided a scientific basis for decrying all those aspects of the Greco-

Roman polity and Christian civilization that were out of step with modernity. It also permitted "society" to be viewed as a natural entity in a state of war in the classic Hobbesian sense, in which power and force in the hands of the classes or the races, scientifically applied, would lead inevitably to the progressive ends of something termed "industrial civilization." From the middle of the nineteenth century all aspects of legal right, feeling, justice, treaty, compromise, settlement, conciliation, arbitration—the essential components of political society—were eclipsed, and then obliterated, by a doctrine of force that saw each matter primarily in terms of its natural evolutionary course. This doctrine would finally express itself in the language of biological necessity, managerial efficiency, and effectiveness in a science of eugenics.

The Rise of the Race-State and the Invention of Antisemitism, 1870–1900

9

In an entirely rational world it would be reasonable to suppose that Darwin's principles of natural selection and evolution had resolved once and for all the disputes over inheritance that had raged in science during the first half of the nineteenth century. In fact, from 1850 to 1870, when the English were still suffering the humiliating effects of the Crimean War and bedeviled by the Irish, Canada, and India questions, the disagreement about the racial consequences of Darwin's hypothesis became more intense, especially among those who persisted in sustaining Blumenbach's "race is nothing" case against the contrary view of the Lamarckian Gobinists.

In *Social Statics* (1851), Herbert Spencer put forward the cardinal principle that the progressive advance observable in flora and fauna was also observable in the development of human society from simple to complex forms. His application of the analogies of the natural world to the analysis of the political arena and his abandonment of Aristotelian political theory in favor of the imperatives of survival of the fittest fueled the fires of controversy between the parties to the dispute. Spencer had traced out the move away from military forms of rule to a new industrial society in which laissez-faire was the driving formative force in the marketplace at home and in the wider sphere of international cooperation and free trade abroad. Seen in that light, economic disparity in a rapidly urbanizing England could be reinterpreted according to a new social evolutionist economic doctrine that cautioned against the interference of politics and the state in matters considered to be essentially natural and rational.

Pivotal to both sides of the dispute was the condition of the poor at home, migration, and the status of the Negro and the so-called backward races in the colonies as well as the enslaved peoples in America and the West Indies. If evolution and natural selection were the principles of natural existence and therefore applicable to social life, it must be true that the poor and the Negro were in their natural condition because of some deficiency in their physical and intellectual capacity. Both sides to the dispute—the evolutionists and the creationists, the "race is nothing" theorists and the "race is everything" theorists—mustered whatever forces were available to support their respective arguments. Notable was the persistence of the argument that the peoples living in simple ways were in such a state because of the original corruption of Ham or some "scientific" variant of it.

» *The English Genius*

In 1860 at the Oxford Conference of the British Association, T. H. Huxley brought the dispute to a head with his now-famous contestation with Bishop William Wilberforce over the biblical account of Creation. In declaring support for the Darwinian hypothesis, Huxley and Spencer stimulated an angry public controversy over that issue. Huxley elaborated on his argument in *Elements of Comparative Anatomy* (1864) and later introduced the word "agnostic" to describe his scientific position. It is during this period that John Langdon Down (1828–96) wrote on the "ethnic" classification of idiots, and Dr. James Hunt (1833–69), in his celebrated *Lectures on Man* (1863), rejected Blumenbach's hypothesis of the unity of species through comparative analysis of the cranial capacity of the Negro and the European. Hunt's conclusion was that human "types" began with the Negro and ended (progressively) with the superior Germans. His paper "On the Negro's Place in Nature" (1863), read before the British Association meetings at Nottingham and Newcastle, argued that there was a far greater difference in intelligence between a Negro and a European than there was between a gorilla and a chimpanzee and that the Negro was a distinct and inferior species. The *Anthropological Review* of January 1870 reported Hunt's death as the death of "the best Man in Europe."[1]

It is also during the period preceding the Franco-Prussian War that Francis Galton, grandson of the eminent physician Erasmus Darwin and friend of Spencer and Huxley, concluded that evolution provided a more satisfactory and sufficient explanation for existence than the old explanation contained in the Adamic account. Instead of looking for theories of inheritance in history, philosophy, and the humanities, he too switched his attention to the analysis of the relationship between social position and ability drawn from the evidence of hereditary data, which he first published in article form in 1865—the same year Gregor Mendel put forward the hypothesis that the character of sweet peas was determined by the transmission of hereditary characters from one generation to another according to the laws of segregation and assortment. In *Hereditary Genius* (1869) Galton proposed that a science of society based on the breeding of hereditable characters might bring greater benefit to mankind than all the antics of the residents of Westminster.

The scientific debate of 1850–70 provides a foundation in the literature for a formidable scientific "hereditarism" that developed after the Franco-Prussian War and from which—led by Anglo-German and American writers—Europe took its scientific and social vocabulary. In England this scientific literature was much influenced by the writings celebrating Anglo-Germanic history discussed in the previous chapter. Before 1870 this literature was illuminated by the seminal works of Sir Charles Wentworth Dilke, Matthew Arnold, and Walter Bagehot, and afterwards by the masterpieces of E. A. Freeman, William Stubbs, and J. R. Green. Their ideas are deeply ingrained in the commonplaces of English racial thought.

DILKE

In 1866 Luke Owen Pike, in *The English and Their Origins: A Prologue to Authentic English History,* examined the physical and psychical evidence of the true origins of the English in the light of the new theory of evolution and the cranial evidence that had so recently become available. Pike noted the disjunction between the "race is everything" hypothesis of people like John Knox and Benjamin Disraeli, and the "race is nothing" hypothesis of Johann Blumenbach, Alexander von Humboldt, and H. T. Buckle and commented (as we have done) on the yawning gap that had opened up between the two since the publication of the work of Darwin and Spencer.

In that same year Sir Charles Wentworth Dilke, Bart., MP (1843–1911), had begun his travels into the English-speaking world to record his reflections on English settlement. In the New World, he was intrigued by the conditions he observed in the poorer quarters of New York, where he perceived the vigor of the English race driving out cheap labor, absorbing the Germans and the Celts, extirpating the Red Indian, and checking the advance of the Chinese. In *Greater Britain,* published in 1869, Dilke introduced the metaphor of the "upturned bowl" to depict America as a giant cauldron into which the streams of the races ran and fused together to destroy physical type and eccentricity, "and the fusion must be in the English mould." In the rival colonies in Australia Dilke saw the influx of landless colored labor from India, Malaya, and China as the degradation of the labor that both morally and economically already ran the new populations of Queensland and New South Wales, as well as the southern states of the United States. The transfer of these propertyless peoples to temperate climates meant that they did twice the work of Englishmen at half the cost. "It looks as though the cheaper will starve out the dearer race, as rabbits drive out stronger but hungrier hares."[2]

In *The Victorian Illusion* (1928), E. H. Dance argued that Dilke introduced into English literature and politics the idea that the British had a moral, apolitical claim over the United States and the rest of the inhabited world by virtue of a natural membership in "Saxondom"—a term he introduced. This justification was buttressed by an entitlement to rule derived from the economic laws of nature. Dilke's affirmation that "nature seems to intend the English for a race of officers, to direct and guide the cheap labour of the Eastern peoples" (192) not only established a truism of national character but also represented a turning away in the literature from Adam Smith's individualistic vision toward an ideal internal and external economic community more dependent on the kith and kin of a Germanic economic brotherhood (an enlargement of Kemble's "folcland") and much more receptive to the ideas of a metapolitics of race such as that found in Friedrich List's *National System of Political Economy.*

Faced with the tremendous economic, scientific, and technological questions that were thrusting themselves into politics and religion, Dance held that English politicians were quite unable to interpret the changes except in terms of a natural national character rooted in the Celtic intransigence and the Anglo-Saxon stubbornness of Dilke's "Greater Britain." As a consequence, when addressing the immense difficulties of Irish land tenure and religion, French settlement in Quebec, and the administration of India, English politicians invoked the new principles of social evolution, inheritance, national character, economic self-determination, and the subordination of the minority to the majority, thus derogating the antique politics and political theory of Burke and Aristotle. As a result, Parliament became a place for busy opportunistic politics of little quality and substance, and the action moved to Whitehall and Downing Street. "Of all the arts and sciences," Dance concluded, "it is in its politics alone that the age appears most truly 'Victorian'—if by 'Victorianism' we mean a pettifogging narrowness of outlook—a losing of the end in the means."[3]

ARNOLD

This "pettifogging narrowness of outlook," and the failure to develop a new and effective form of political society in England, was also noticed by Matthew Arnold in *Culture and Anarchy* and *Friendship's Garland,* published in serial form from February 1866 to November 1870.[4] Arnold (1822–88), the son of Thomas Arnold (1795–1842), Regius Professor of Modern History at Oxford, follower of Niebuhr, and godson of Kemble, was attracted by the works of Goethe, Carlyle, and Max Müller. He identified two forces at work in the ever-changing economic processes of history. The first was the characteristic of energy, which was driving in the direction of practice and was defined as a sense of obligation, duty, self-control, work, earnestness. It was always to be distinguished from the second characteristic: the force of intelligence, which was driving after ideas based on right practice with an indefatigable impulse to know. These formative forces of energy and intelligence were seen as "rivals dividing the empire of the world between them" (p. 163), not naturally by necessity but as exhibited by man and his history.

Arnold gave to these powerful forces the names of the two "races" of men who had supplied the most signal and splendid manifestation of them, the Hebraic and the Hellenist. He saw the world moving between these two points of influence, with both having the same end—"man's perfection and salvation" (*Culture and Anarchy*, p. 165). Both had striven for the love of God: the Greek through right thinking; the Hebrew through right acting. "The governing idea of Hellenism is spontaneity of consciousness," Arnold explained, "that of Hebraism, strictness of conscience" (*Culture and Anarchy*, p. 165).

Both racial forces had contributed to the development of man, although not according to Spencerian laws of development. Like Froude, Arnold saw the great historical event in England as the Protestant Reformation, which he portrayed as a Hebraizing and Hellenizing watershed that saw the reentry of a renewed and purged Hebraism and the reintroduction of Hellenistic right thinking and consciousness in the rediscovery of nature:

> Science has now made visible to everybody the great and pregnant elements of difference which lie in race, and in how signal a manner they have made the genius and history of an Indo-European people vary from those of a Semitic people. Hellenism is of Indo-European growth, Hebraism of Semitic growth; and we English, a nation of Indo-European stock, seem to belong naturally to the movement of Hellenism. (p. 173)

Although Arnold's original contribution was to knit together the genius and history of the Hebrew people and to seek a rapprochement between them in the long processes of history, nevertheless he was keenly aware of the fundamental separation between the two "races" by virtue of the profound and irreconcilable differences in their natures:

> Who, I say, will believe, when he considers the matter, that where the feminine nature, the feminine ideal, and our relations to them, are brought into question, the delicate and apprehensive genius of the Indo-European race, the race which invented the Muses, and chivalry, and the Madonna, is to find its last word on this question in the institutions of a Semitic people, whose wisest King had seven hundred wives and three hundred concubines? (p. 208)

Arnold's separation of the two races was sexual and natural and moral, and their reconciliation would work through the *Zeitgeist* and *Volksgeist,* not through politics. As P. J. Keating points out, Arnold's practical interest in politics had more to do with his recognition of the onward move of events after Waterloo and the Treaty of Vienna and the abject failure of the English to adapt, as the French had done, than with the implementation of political reform.[5] The problem as Arnold perceived it was that the English were trapped in the aristocratic prerevolutionary class system (as illustrated in the works of Charles Kingsley and Robert Gordon Latham), which favored the status quo, while the historical reality in Europe, and particularly in France, was that the masses were on the move. The Victorian divisions in England were based on a conflict among the working-class poor (the crude, the raw, the illiterate), the middle classes (the philistines, the self-seekers), and the aristocrats (the "barbarians" who had isolated themselves in their country retreats and no longer provided a model inspiring intelligence, morality, and responsibility as had their forefathers). Arnold turned to the middle classes, not as a support for the working classes in a political alliance, but to mobilize a business consciousness that would help achieve the liberty of the individual through a national system of political economy.

Arnold's notion of state, still a powerful force in English thought a century later, was not political; it rested upon the assumption that politics is an unwanted and idle activity, that parliaments are little more than chat shops, capable of achieving nothing to alleviate poverty and the deep-seated malaise of society. In Arnold's model the state rose above class as an educational center of excellence, and salvation was found not in politics but in a romantic culture of a middle-class *Völkerpsychologie,* which supported in an English context Niebuhr's and Kemble's racialization of history.

BAGEHOT

The role of natural society as an entity comprised of classes and races, sometimes acting together and sometimes in opposition but always in a progressive, rational order, together with the derogation of political theory and practice, was the subject of Walter Bagehot's *Physics and Politics,* published in 1872.[6] Bagehot (1826–77) contrasted the study of man according to the new methods of natural science, in which the emphasis was on inheritance and natural selection, with the traditional approach adopted in political philosophy. Trying to imagine what life might have been like without nation and without *nomos,* he perceived that man's greatest need was to create a political society in which argument and discourse might proceed freely.

Bagehot argued that the social evolutionists and those who were seeking a middle-class consciousness in the romantic ideals of the late eighteenth and early nineteenth century had failed to distinguish heredity in nature and the animal kingdom from the inheritance of "the collective tissue of civilisation," which was comprised of political ideas and ideals and legal practice (p. 2). The chief offender here was Sir Henry J. S. Maine (1822–88), whose *Patriarchal Theory* (1861) had fostered an erroneous belief in primogeniture and the principles of kinship in blood in a misleading account of Greek and Roman political society. Bagehot believed, with some justification, that the literature on the state since Niebuhr had extrapolated from Aristotle those passages that favored the explanation of the origins of the *polis* as arising wholly from natural criteria and had neglected passages on the constitution of civil and political society. Maine and other nineteenth-century theorists had failed to recognize the significance of the *nomocratic* state. "The first ascent of civilisation was at a steep gradient," reflected Bagehot, "although when now we look down upon it, it seems almost nothing" (p. 21). For Bagehot, formulations of the state based on the natural criteria of inheritance and social evolution, such as could be observed in the principles enshrined in the French and American Revo-lutions and in the programs of the Social Darwinists, were based on the dual error of conceiving everything in the classical past as reprehensible and naively assuming that the transition from status, place, custom, and family to political life was an easy, natural process. In fact, the legal fiber of Western civilization had not come easily, and it hung on a fine thread. It had come from the ancients, and especially from Aristotle, who had no notion of scientific prog-ress and viewed trade not as the fount of energy but as a potential source of corruption.

What is especially interesting and relevant about Bagehot's restoration of classical political theory is its emphasis on rule by law as the beginning of European civilization. Bagehot countered the view of Niebuhr, Kemble, and Maine that civilization was rooted in nature, kith and kin, and blood (*physis*).

The dichotomy he thus opened between physics and politics was to have enormous implications for all that followed after 1870. Those who took the line of Niebuhr, Kemble, and Maine found an inevitable logic in the self-determining co-terminous and co-extensive race-state. On the basis of the new folk science they set aside Aristotle's *nomocratic* state and the political process of compromise and reciprocity between diverse citizens in public places.

Bagehot did not carry his analysis of the realms of physics and politics beyond the point of maintaining a clear distinction between the two. He did not argue, as the eugenicists did a generation later, that physics should absorb all politics, nor did he regard science as irrelevant to the understanding of man. He simply recognized that two great forces of race making and nation making had been set loose upon the world and that the modern nations invented in the eighteenth century probably had some root in an original diversity of race. He did not accept the idea of purity of race, nor did he believe that there was much evidence of race in the ancient world. Invasion, conquest, and adoption had confused the simple notion of common ancestry and descent so that the modern race and nation makers "made an artificial unity in default of a real unity" (p. 67). Modern civilization and governance could not have been unilinearly descended from Aryan or Germanic origins, Bagehot concluded. "The theory which makes government by discussion the exclusive patrimony of a single race is on the face of it untenable" (p. 182).

Bagehot clearly perceived Social Darwinism as a lamentable and retro-grade step when introduced into politics, a revival of the Hobbesian right of conquest in scientific guise in political affairs as well as in the marketplace. For all his ambivalence about race itself, Bagehot saw race making in whatever form as a reversion from political association to the barbarism of natural society and, above all else, as a dangerous intellectual idea in the hands of the ill-informed, especially so when physics was confused with politics. Alas, Bagehot's brilliant analysis of the historical distinction between political philosophy and evolutionary science produced no countertheory of real politics to bridge the yawning gap. He failed to curb the derogation of political theory or to check the spread of the idea that governance by discussion was the exclusive preserve of those descended from the Germans in the woods.

After the Franco-Prussian War J. R. Green's (1837–83) *Short History of the English People* (1874), William Stubbs's (1825–1901) *Constitutional History of England* (1874–78), and E. A. Freeman's (1823–92) *History of the Norman Conquest of England* (1867–79) sustained the idea of kinship in blood as the basis of civilization. Freeman pinpointed the origin of the free man, the man of action, as in the land between the Elbe and Ems. Green, the first English historian to write a history of "the people," drew on place names to describe branches of the Teutonic family and throughout his text referred constantly to "races," using Shakespeare's Caliban, Montaigne's *Essais,* and Hakluyt's *Principal Voyages* as sources for "the one purely German nation that arose on the wreck of Rome." "A state is accidental," he wrote in his introduction. "It can be made or unmade, and is no real thing to me. But a nation is very real to me. That you can neither make nor destroy." Similarly, Stubbs saw the English as a people of German descent in the main constituents of blood, character, and language and in possession of the elements of a Germanic civilization, including Germanic institutions. "This descent is not a matter of inference. It is a recorded fact of history, which those characteristics bear out to the fullest degree of certainty" (1.11) he claimed. He used Caesar and Tacitus as well as Niebuhr, Kemble, and the Grimms to trace a fifth-century Germanic migration led by Aryan kings and including Saxons, who were unconquered by the Franks and untainted by Roman manners.[7]

SEELEY

Arnold's treatment of the state as an entity rising above the realities of existing politics coupled to Kemble's idea of the relationship between Anglo-Saxon and "Heathendom," which later led to Dilke's coining of the term "Saxondom," was taken up by Sir J. R. Seeley in his popular work *The Expansion of*

England (1883) and in his series of lectures at Cambridge in 1885 and 1886. Seeley asked the question, In what direction and toward what goal had the English state been advancing and progressing? For Seeley the simple and obvious fact was that the English name was being extended, as Dilke had recognized earlier, into other countries of the globe, constituting the foundation for the concept of a "Greater Britain." The diffusion of "our race" and the expansion of "our State" were celebrated in his oft-quoted aphorism: "We seem, as it were, to have conquered and peopled half the world in a fit of absence of mind."[8]

Like Dilke, Seeley saw the history of England as encompassing alien races ruled by the right of conquest. Unlike other empires, the British Empire lacked an essentially military character. The English state in India, for example, needed only minimal force to maintain it, for natives in India were low in the ethnological scale. The English people had also created another empire—the empire in America lost in revolution yet retaining the English character and race.

English expansion was, in fact, not just the export of blood but the real enlargement of the English state—English political life carried over the seas to create a new basis for property ownership and to extend trade. England was becoming "cramped for room," and Seeley envisioned a "boundless room for expansion" in the lands governed by the queen. "If there is pauperism in Wiltshire and Dorsetshire," he explained, "this is but complementary to unowned wealth in Australia; on the one side there are men without property, on the other there is property wanting for men" (p. 60).

For Seeley, the Charter of Virginia (1606) marked the beginning of the move of the epicenter of civilization. A new world was being formed abroad. Colonial affairs were no longer a footnote to history but the rearrangement of history in terms of development and advance of civilization. Thus, although the American Revolution might seem like the end of a Greater Britain, it was really a new beginning. In fact, it was a watershed event, "pregnant in consequences," not only because it transferred the inherited traditions, character, and language of England to America but, more important, because it was driven by the Anglo-Saxon race, upon which the destiny of humanity and the planet depended (p. 150). The expansion of England could be explained only in terms of the heroic qualities of the English race and their natural genius for government.

SAXONDOM

Together these English contributions propounded a complex idea of race. English scientists and historians introduced into the understanding of the Germanic English a racial explanation that owed much to the processes of evolution and natural selection in the affairs of man. For the majority it signaled a release from the Burkean idea of politics *qua* politics and allowed for the substitution of the powerful *Volk* idea of "Saxondom," which forged an inheritance by race with those who had gone from the homeland, the folcland, to settle the economically promising lands of America, Canada, Australasia, and southern Africa. It also transformed the Protestant Revolution into a unique but popular racial event that welded together the genius of the English and all Saxon peoples, whose dominance confirmed the principles of natural inheritance.

Scientific hereditarism, a reaffirmation of the Niebuhrian racialization of history, and a romantic middle-class consciousness of Hebraism and Hellenism—these ideas would resonate in Germany and France after Bismarck's famous victory.

» The Franco-Prussian War: Scientific Explanations

In the winter of 1807–08, after the defeat of Prussia by Napoleon, Fichte had written *Reden an die deutsche Nation* to revive the spirit of the German people and to instill in them a belief that they were naturally elected by God to membership in a state driven by *Kultur* and expressed in the moral order flowing from race, language, and nation. Now, following the Franco-Prussian War, conditions were reversed: France had fallen, and Prussia was in the ascendancy. The justification and vindication of both victory and defeat were expressed racially in three main ways—in terms of the new sciences, in terms of history, and in a struggle to reconcile philology, science, and aesthetics in the facts of sociology and the synthesis of history and philosophy.

Chancellor Otto von Bismarck had justified the war in ethnological terms. The initiative and energy once shown by the Latin peoples for politics now reposed in the peoples of the North, he claimed. The Germans were charged with a dynamic mission for the good of man. The failed democratic revolution in France demonstrated that the Latins were a spent race. The future belonged to the Aryans.

QUATREFAGES

At the Paris Museum of Natural History, Jean-Louis Armand de Quatrefages (1810–92), a zoologist and professor of anthropology, set out to counter the application of anthropology to the practice of politics. His *Prussian State Ethnologically Considered* (1871) proposed that every political division based on ethnology produced an absurdity. Not only was this application a source of gross error, but its inevitable logic would lead to the inevitability of war. "Thanks to the idea of the antagonism of the *races*, set going and worked with Machiavellian skill," he exclaimed, "the whole of Germany rose. In the name of Pan-Germanism, they declared they would reign over the Latin races."[9]

He endeavored to counter Bismarck's arguments by showing that the Prussians, who had acted barbarically during the war, were not really a truly German people, but Finns or Slavo-Finns. Every care was needed to distinguish species, variety, and races. The true German was a mixture of French elements of Celtic, Gallic, and German blood.

Quatrefages was partially supported in his anthropological attack upon Bismarck's views by Paul Broca's pupil Paul Topinard (1830–1911), a Darwinist anthropometrist, who suggested in *L'Anthropologie* (1876) that, judged by the evidence of skull sizes, the French were not Aryans by blood after all, but a mixture of races. In a sense, these defensive works were little more than a working out of the old ideas of Boulanvilliers and Dubos in an anthropological context. Others who contributed to the debate include Numa Denis Fustel de Coulanges (1830–89), professor of medical history at the Sorbonne, who attempted to reduce the significance of the influence of Germanic (Frankish) elements in France by pointing to the blending of the Celtic and Teutonic stocks of genius. Maurice Barrès (1862–1923), novelist and nationalist politician, later erected upon this Celtic myth the notion of the noble blood of the Celtic ancestors coursing through the veins of the French, denying what he perceived as the racial degradation of blood mixture with Germans.

HAECKEL

A powerful counterargument derived from the works of Ritter, Carus, Klemm, Buckle, and Waitz, who, as we have seen, had attached themselves before

Darwin's *Origin* to a spiritual scientific world view that embraced the shaping of the life of the individual according to the principles of geography and nature, was mounted by Ernst Haeckel (1834–1919), a prominent popularizer of the works of Darwin in Europe. Haeckel had avidly read accounts of Darwin's voyages and had been much influenced by Matthias Schleiden's (1804–81) *Die Pflanze und ihr Leben* (1848). He gave up medicine for anatomy and embryology and later studied Johannes Müller's (1801–58) anatomical works on the concurrence of causes and conditions in scientific zoology. His *Generelle Morphologie der Organismen* (1866) related his studies of cell nuclei to Darwin's theory of evolution and applied Darwinist theories to the natural kingdom. Extending beyond the bounds of biology, Haeckel proposed a science-based *Weltanschauung* postulating a monistic universe influenced by heritable Lamarckian characters and plasma related to environment, nature, and space arranged geographically according to fundamental biogenetic laws. He drew up the first genealogical tables along anthropological lines, and his early work was popularly disseminated in *Naturliche Schopfungs-Geschichte (The Natural History of Creation)* published in 1868.

Haeckel's *Anthropogonie oder Entwickelangs geschichte des Menschens (Evolution of Man)*, first published in 1874 and running to numerous editions in both German and English, postulated an embryological basis for evolution, with ontogeny as the science of the development of the individual organism, anthropology as the science of the evolution of man, and phylogeny as the science of the human stem. This sophisticated romantic science of race evolution, supported by the science of paleontology, posited the ascent of man from the lower ranks of the animal world to the higher in opposition to the theory of the descent of man from an Adam, supported by uncertain biblical evidence. Not only was this ascent from biogenetic origins observable physiologically, asserted Haeckel; it was also true that psychic life was evolving from lower to higher, as evidenced by comparing the social and political arrangements of ants and insects to those of mankind:

> If we are evolutionists at all, and grant the causal connection of ontogenesis and phylogenesis, we are forced to admit this thesis: The human soul or psyche, as a function of the medullary tube, has developed along with it; and just as the brain and spinal cord now develop from the simple medullary tube in every human individual, so the human mind or psychic life of the whole human race has been gradually evolved from the lower vertebrate soul.[10]

Haeckel argued that the process of evolution is neither democratic nor socialistic; it is aristocratic. His views on heredity and acquired traits were immensely influential in forming a popular view of "man making himself"—from sperm to death—and in confirming the physiological and psychic natural history of man's biogenic ancestry to "prove" who were the winners and the losers in class and race.

Haeckel's views were shared, for instance, by Cesare Lombroso (1835–1909), whose major work, *L'uomo delinquente* (1876), described the atavistic criminal as a biological throwback. This atavistic criminal could be identified from somatological and psychic racial stigmata, and his inborn delinquency was natural not to contemporary mankind but to primitive races.

GALTON, WEISMANN, PEARSON, AND RATZEL

By this time Herbert Spencer had gone beyond his 1851 analysis of social statics to apply the principles of natural selection to the political world. His *Man versus the State* (1884) attacked both bureaucratic corporate action and "the divine rights of parliaments," establishing an intellectual liaison with Carlyle and Arnold in an extremely popular Germanic-English antipathy toward the intrusions of politics in the construction of state. Francis Galton (1822–1911) embarked on a much more radical departure with his *Inquiries into the Human Faculty* (1883), which described the human hereditary process and introduced the term "eugenics."[11] Later his *Natural Inheritance* (1889) used the number theory developed by the German mathematician Carl Friedrich Gauss (1777–1855) to analyze randomly sampled populations in terms of their deviation from the mean distribution according to weight, height, and other physical quantities, such as the sizes of noses and skulls. Using comparisons of parent and child along the lines suggested in 1865 by Gregor Mendel, Galton sought to establish the hypothesis that the same hereditary influences occurred in the development of man, that hereditary characters were transmitted from one generation to another according to laws of segregation and assortment and to the Darwinian laws of the natural selection. With elaborate statistical tables, analysis of characters, dependent and independent variables, and a wealth of data incorporating the theory and method of mathematical probability and related to regression and correlation coefficients rather than to first causes, Galton concluded through analysis of measurable quantities that genius is inherited and passed on in blood relationships.

This idea of evolution clashed head-on with the science-based cellular monistic account of the universe introduced by Haeckel in the 1860s and 1870s. The controversy was intensified by August Weismann (1834–1914), who in his early *Studies in the Theory of Descent* (1882), published before Galton's study on the human faculty, opposed the Lamarckian doctrine of acquired traits and put in its place the hypothesis of "germ plasm," which was supposed to be impermeable to environmental influences. August Weismann later published *Keimplasm. Eine Theorie der Vererbung,* translated as *The Germ Plasm: A Theory of Heredity* (1893), and *The Evolution Theory* (1904). His work helped to propagate the idea of hereditarism, which held that environmental reform could have little effect over the long term because germ plasm remained the same.

In the same period, Galton's compatriot Karl Pearson (1857–1936) was introduced to the study of inheritance at Cambridge, Berlin, and Heidelberg by way of law and mathematics. As a student in Germany in the late 1880s he, too, became captivated by Goethe and German metaphysics. He also became acquainted with the works of Ernst Mach (1838–1916), the Austrian physicist and philosopher who was attempting to reinstate sensationalist and empiric thought in the face of organic germ plasm theory. In his early collection of essays on free thought in 1888, Pearson did not embrace the Spencerian economic version of Social Darwinism but turned more directly to the political aspects of Fichte's teaching. Pearson was especially interested in those aspects of Fichte's state that had been developed by Friedrich List in the 1840s. But whereas List's rationale for an Anglo-German commercial alliance was based on the argument that those who spoke a common language belong to the same race and so ought to form a nation, Pearson used numbers and biology to achieve the same end. Just as List had argued that the state was an artificial creation and race a natural one, and that political formations were artificial diplomatic creations that ran counter to the natural order of things, so Pearson came to argue with the German environmentalists that the nation and the state should be built upon a biological formation rather than an economic one.

The response of the political geographer Friedrich Ratzel (1844–1904), disciple of Haeckel, was that reason had nothing to do with national constitutions and that it ought to stand aside before the unconscious forces of nature. In the *Anthropo-geographie* (1882–91) and *Völkerkunde* (1885–86), Ratzel developed the idea of *Lebensraum,* which would have a great influence on the study of political geography and geopolitics in a later period. Ratzel returned to Kemble's argument that each people had an organic life derived from habitation, and change had to do with the first occupation or abandonment of land. Aggrandizement was the major characteristic of that change, and the mission of state and the race consisted in aggrandizing itself and its relationships. As we shall see, Ratzel's work projects us into the post-Nietzschean stage of progressive scientific hereditarism and the environmentalism of the *Völker.*

LAPOUGE

In a series of lectures at the University of Montpelier in 1888–89, published as *Les selections sociales* (1896), G. Vacher de Lapouge (1854–1936) warned against concluding that a community of culture, inherited from a common language, formed the basis of race among the Latin nations. Race was connected to nation and state, both of which were spiritual notions, not political notions. The qualities necessary for the stability of nation and state were derived from physical constitution of the race, which arose from the crossing of racial groups. Nature and natural selection were powerful forces that could not be altered. All optimism expressed by contemporaries about education and political reform as correctives for the ravages of war and the irresolution of French governance was misplaced and futile.

The true conditions of France, said Lapouge, had resulted from the dilution of the higher-class dolichocephalic Frankish elements during the French Revolution and their subsequent replacement by the increasing brachycephalic lower-class elements. Using statistical analysis, Lapouge had studied seventeenth- and eighteenth-century Montpelier skulls, concentrating on the superiority of the blond, dolichocephalic types. Following Gobineau, he divided Europe into races:

> European man: tall, blond, dolichocephalic, with black eyes; almost extinct
>
> Alpine man: Mediterranean, small, brachycephalic, with brown or black eyes, a hybrid
>
> Homo contractus: corresponding to the Alpine man, but small, dolichocephalic, with brown eyes

Lapouge assigned all the higher characteristics to the European man, reproducing within a so-called disinterested science many of the historical, literary, and philological images of the romantic Aryan and integrating them into the hypothesis of class struggle. The European was adventurous, audacious, intelligent, with a tendency to genius. He was logical and of few words, Protestant in religion, and in intense need of work and progress, a fighter, a seeker after profit and possessions, personally linked to the spiritual interests of his nation and race, and ready to sacrifice himself for the highest destiny.

In contrast to the dynamic European man, the Alpine brachycephalic was frugal and hardworking, but less economical. He was prudent and not lacking in courage, but he had no stomach for war. He had the Latin love of land and the soil, was distrustful, a spinner of words, a man of tradition and what is commonly called good sense. Progress to him was not necessary; he exhibited patience, loved uniformity, and was Catholic. He was interested in his family and all those around him but had no vision of the marks of the country, boundaries, and frontiers. In politics there was for the Alpine but one hope—the protection of the state.

As Theophile Simar points out, Lapouge was applying the romantic Anglo-Saxon approach apparent in the literary works of Hippolyte Taine to the field of anthropology and race.[12] Simar argues that Lapouge was quick to spot the error in confusing country of origin with language and in recognizing races as an order of zoology and little else. Lapouge saw that there was no such thing as a Latin race or a German race. But, he made the cardinal error when, having affirmed that the zoological order was different from the political order of state and nation (both moral concepts) he clandestinely reintroduced Gobinist qualities into his social analysis of extant European, Alpine, and Mediterranean races. At this early stage his explanation of race was a class-race explanation with social change coming about through the scientific processes of selection and degeneration stirred up by the democratic and plutocratic forces of the French Revolution rather than by race alone. In his later works, however, Lapouge shifted his ground and exhibited an acute distrust of the Revolution, which he described as a plutocracy in disguise. The crossing of peoples had diminished the power of the aristocrats and provided an entry point for the more persistent biological character of the Jews, who had reduced the bourgeoisie to misery by their greed. In the volatile new democracies, an anti-democratic, anti-semitic Lapouge saw only an acceleration of the process of self-destruction. With frightening prescience he announced: "I am convinced that in the next century people will slaughter each other by the million because of a difference of a degree or two in the cephalic index. It is by this sign, which has replaced the Biblical shibboleth and lin-

guistic affinities, that men will be identified. . . . And the last sentimental-
ists will be able to witness the most massive exterminations of peoples."[13]
[*L'Aryen, son role social*, Paris 1800, pps. 22 and 464, and L'Anthropologie et la
science politique, Revue d'Anthropologie, 15 May 1887, p. 15.]

» *The Franco-Prussian War and German History*

In the immediate aftermath of the Franco-Prussian War, three major treatises
confronted Chancellor Bismarck's account of victory as the triumph of the
virile Germanic peoples over the effete Latins, not simply in the war but in
the denial of the French Revolution and the democratic mentality fostered by
Thierry and Anglo-Saxon writers in racial history during the period from 1815
to 1870. These three texts were Friedrich Wilhelm Nietzsche's *Geburt der
Tragödie aus dem Geist der Musik* (1872); Ludwig Gumplowicz's *Rasse und Stat*
(1875) and his *Der Rassenkampf* (1883); and Ernest Renan's retraction of his
early ethnic work and his wistful reinstatement of the political idea in *Qu'est
ce qui un nation?* (1882). All three are replete with references to the ideas of
scientific Darwinist evolution, romantic class-consciousness, Lamarckian hereditarism, and degenerative histology that we considered above.

Bismarck's position owed much to the foundation work in the early part
of the century of the historians Niebuhr and Ranke and to the great Prussian
school of Johann Gustav Droysen, Heinrich von Sybel, and Heinrich von
Treitschke. Droysen, who benefited after the publication of Darwin's *Origin*
from his evolutionary view of the world and from the opening of the archives
of the German, British, and French states, placed God and history at the center
of a Prussian stage, emphasizing the authority of a regenerative Lutheran
monarchical state imbued with the Germanic ethical ideas of Hegel, Humboldt, and Herder. Sybel similarly profited from access to the archives, and
his *History of the French Revolution* (1867–79) portrayed the revolution, like Burke
and Taine, as undermining the ideals of the Reformation and the Protestant
monarchical and constitutional state, thereby releasing the floodgates of popular excess. His *Die Begründung des deutschen Reiches durch Wilhelm I (The Founding
of the German Empire),* published from 1890 to 1898, resurrected the idea of
the Holy Roman Empire in a German Empire guided by history and a strong
national state rooted in the Niebuhrian forces of nature.[14]

NIETZSCHE

In 1872 Friedrich Wilhelm Nietzsche (1844–1900), professor of philology at Basel, published *Die Geburt der Tragödie aus dem Geist der Musik*.[15] Its preface was addressed to his friend Richard Wagner (1813–83), who in 1849 had been forced into exile in Zurich, where he worked upon a theory of opera and drama. In prose and music Wagner portrayed the relationship among art, revolution, and the future. His magnificent operas, drawn from romantic poems in Middle High German of the twelfth century, celebrated the *Volk* now realized as a new type of man and a new moral order flowing from the artistry of race, language, and nation. This *Volk* is not Carlyle's stolid, cold man of Christian morality and military bearing, not the leaden Anglo-Saxon of Kemble, Froude, Green, and Freeman, but a natural, sexual being possessed of a dynamic and magnetic intellectual will—the will that informed Fichte's *Reden an die deutsche Nation,* the will inspired by Arthur Schopenhauer's (1788–1860) new Germanic Christianism of renunciation, and the Aryan will threatened by the Jew in Gobineau's Lamarckian degenerative histology and physiology.

In the wake of the Franco-Prussian War and in light of the writings of historians and natural scientists, Nietzsche claimed that he, too, had to face up to a serious German problem, "right in the centre of German hopes, as a vortex and turning point." This was the problem of modernity. In a brilliant synthesis, Nietzsche brought together the philological, anthropological, and historical arguments of the past century: the Prussian historians, and particularly Treitschke, were distasteful and wretched; Niebuhr's disengagement from the Greek world of politics was only a partial separation and needed to be projected into the future with a clean break; Carlyle and Darwin were scholarly oxen; J. S. Mill was a liberal blockhead; Hobbes, Locke, Hume, Spencer, and Buckle were vulgar sensationalist Englishmen who had been taken in by the modernity of scientific thought and degraded the value of philosophy; Renan was a disastrous calamity; Rousseau's concept of the common man was likened to a buffoon on a high wire suspended over an abyss at the bottom of which was certain death—for both the philosopher and the buffoon. For Nietzsche, the search for origins was a deceit, and the concepts of state, nobility, and order upon which modernity rested were a sham. What was required was a complete philosophical reappraisal.

Greek Tragedy versus Modern Barbarism   Returning to the seminal texts of Greece, Nietzsche considered those aspects in opposition to the search for origins and the aims of Social Darwinism and utilitarianism. He noticed at once the historical distinction of Greek and barbarian—the distinction we examined in the opening chapters as distinctions of politics and philosophy— but saw it in terms of two art impulses: the Apollonian art of sculpture and the Dionysian art of music, which ran counter to and yet parallel to one another and came together, through will, to form Attic tragedy.

For Nietzsche, the Greeks embodied what Schopenhauer had considered to be the criterion of philosophical ability: the ability to be aesthetically sensitive. Apollo was for them "the glorious divine image of the *principium individuationis*" (p. 45), sitting alone in a boat on a tempestuous sea seized by terror. In Dionysus it was intoxication, the narcotic draft of song and dance, that enabled the Greeks to express themselves not as artists but as members of a higher community enchanted, ecstatic, and unmediated—as works of art themselves.

The Greek world was, therefore, an expression of the energies of art in which the Dionysian Greek was separated from the Dionysian barbarian not by his ability to do politics but by his Apollonian resistance to cruelty and sexual licentiousness. The reconciliation between the Apollonian and Dionysian opposites of dream experience and intoxication came about not by political regulation, reconciliation, speech, argument, and accommodation but naturally through the symbolic power of music, rhythm, dynamics, and harmony in collective release.

What held the Greeks together, then, was not politics and philosophy but the knowledge and feeling of "terror and horror of existence" (pp. 43–4)— a realization that was not political in the sense that we have described it throughout this book but derived from the struggle for control between two hostile principles realized and revealed to the Greeks in the Olympian divine order of joy: "In the Greeks the 'will' wished to contemplate itself in the transfiguration of genius and the world of art; in order to glorify themselves, its creatures had to feel themselves worthy of glory; they had to behold themselves again in a higher sphere, without this perfect world of contemplation acting as a command or a reproach" (p. 44).

The nub of Nietzsche's argument was that the origins of tragedy were in the tragic chorus, which was not a crowd of thoughtless spectators but a public intensely connected with the act of viewing a work of art. The chorus was in an ideal domain above the actual paths of mortals. The effect of Dionysian tragedy was this: "The state and society and quite generally the gulfs between man and man give way to an overwhelming feeling of unity leading back to the very heart of nature" (p. 59). In Nietzsche's analysis, the Dionysian state literally annihilated the ordinary bounds and limits of political existence as it was conceived by Bismarck and Treitschke.

Nietzsche saw the problem of modernity not simply as the Niebuhrian detachment from the world the Greeks knew but primarily as the loss of life and true culture in the urge toward mass democracy that had resulted from what he regarded as a poor copy and caricature of the Greeks. The science of his age, with its insatiable search for knowledge and causal connection, was both optimistic and suicidal. It had not produced greater insight, only heightened the need for art: "Our eyes strengthened and refreshed by our contemplation of the Greeks, let us look at the highest spheres of the world around us; then we shall see how the hunger for insatiable and optimistic knowledge that in Socrates appears exemplary has turned into tragic resignation and destitute need for art" (p. 98).

The Hope for Renovation and Purification   At this point Nietzsche found a new hope for the future in German genius as it acted to interpret Greek tragedy. The modern world, entangled in the culture of Socratic science and Prussian educational method, was not only exhausted and bankrupt but was creating a class of barbaric slaves ready to avenge. Myth was paralyzed by logic. But if myth and poetry were being driven out by the advance of science, the hope for their restoration lay in music. The fact was—as Kant had recognized—that all the riddles of the universe could not be known. What was required was a new culture of tragedy, based on "the wisdom to live resolutely and fully" (p. 121), and a new German art of Kantian metaphysical culture surmised from Greek analogies. Through the "fire magic of music" (p. 124) there was hope for the renovation and purification of the German spirit.

Nietzsche believed that the state and patriotism could not live without the fully developed individual personality, and he perceived that the Greeks achieved this self-sufficiency through the prophylactic, prepolitical power of tragedy. The basis for the rebirth of the German myth was the German Reformation, born of primordial Lutheran spiritual power, and it must be constantly held up to the myths of Greek tragedy. Only then could the necessary and fundamental connection among people, myth, custom, tragedy, state, and artistic drive be restored, superseding the poverty of contemporary, secular, historical, critical analysis (p. 138).

In a stirring finale to *Geburt der Tragödie,* Nietzsche called for the "bringing back" of all things German into the mythical home: "And if the German should hesitantly look around for a leader who might bring him back again into his long lost home whose ways and paths he scarcely knows anymore, let him merely listen to the ecstatically luring call of the Dionysian bird that hovers above him and wants to point the way for him" (p. 139).

Thus, in this early work Nietzsche expressed the need for a complete break with the politics of Greece, the associationist thinking of the English sensationalists, and the superficial constitutional forms of modern mass democracy and education being paraded about after the Franco-Prussian War. He was deeply skeptical both about modern culture and the ability of science to justify anything. His conception of state was born out of the conflict between the impulses of art in nature and dependent upon a reorientation of the present secular world toward a higher metaphysical culture, to be realized through the regeneration of German myths of primordial Lutheran power. At this early stage Nietzsche's highly original thought contained little that directly related to the thought of Bismarck, Sybel, and Treitschke, or that of Hobbes, Locke, Spencer, Arnold, and Galton, except the terror of entropy and the magnetism of dream.

GUMPLOWICZ

Like Quatrefages, Ernst Haeckel's pupil, Ludwig Gumplowicz (1838–1909), professor of political science and sociology at Graz, also opposed the importing of scientific principles into the field of social analysis. He shared neither his master's views on *Weltanschauung,* nor Spencer's prosaic account of change; nor was he inclined to accept the normlessness of Nietzsche's dream world. Instead, in his early work on *Rasse und Staat* (1875), Gumplowicz reiterated in Lamarckian-Darwinist evolutionary terms the basis for the foundation of the state as the Hobbesian right of conquest of one people by another, thus bringing about the conditions necessary for the fundamental recomposition and reconstitution of the classes and castes, groups that in his work he equated with races.[16]

The Emergence of Class   In *Rasse und Staat* Gumplowicz used the conquest and occupation of land given up by the vanquished feudal regime to explain the emergence of a warlike nobility in opposition to the monarch, with whom in time the nobles accommodated themselves by force. By the same token he attributed the emergence of a middle class, with its claims to rights, to the monarch's mobilization of the *Volk* in opposition to the nobility. In *Der Rassenkampf: Soziologie Untersuchungen* (1883) Gumplowicz described three classes: the first class consisted of those with military and political supremacy and the possession of land; the second class corresponded to the industrial, commercial, and banking elite (including the Jews); the third class was the common people.[17]

Rather than going down the Darwinist anthropological road, Gumplowicz had revived the old Franco-Gallian race-class argument of the late eighteenth century and placed it in the new context of industrial civilization. To explain social change, he utilized Herder's concept of the *Volk* in place of *populus,* Spencer's theory of social transition, and a Lamarckian evolution. Aligning Machiavelli's construct of naked power in *The Prince* with Hobbes's right of conquest, he put forward a natural class-race theory of state based upon the natural criteria of kith and kin. He believed that he had simultaneously disposed, once and for all, of Noachic settlement and Greco-Roman political theory, which, in his view, had already been abandoned by Western industrial society.

Race as Reality   Gumplowicz's evolutionary theory as expressed in *Der Russenkampf* (1883) and in *Grundriss des Soziologie (1885)* was not wholly Darwinian, however, and it was certainly not anthropological. He did not accept the natural superiority of one group over another, either physically or intellectually, and believed it was a mistake to mix an anthropological concept with a sociological concept. His theory of race, therefore, is a sociological theory based upon the fundamental idea that there is a group basis to social life, that the reality of existence is that when they are not isolated social groups have a tendency to mix, and that when heterogeneously arranged they inevitably come into conflict over land or competing interests. In other words, there are no distinct anthropological races or ethnic groups born out of biology, cephology, phrenology, and physiognomy but only social groups—identified as ethnic groups in the real world—and it is the business of sociology to study them.

This aspect of Gumplowicz's thinking was carried across the Atlantic to play an important part in the founding of American sociology, particularly in the cultural anthropology of Lewis H. Morgan's (1818–81) *Ancient Society: Researches in the Lines of Human Progress from Savagery through Barbarism to Civilization*

(1877) and in the sociology classes taught at Yale University by William Graham Sumner (1840–1910), which will be examined more thoroughly in the next chapter. Albrecht Wirth's (1866–1936) *Rasse und Volk* (1914) also drew upon Gumplowicz in maintaining that races were fashioned by mixture and isolation over long periods of time and fixed in their appropriate civilization. Too quick a change in culture, social structure, and religion would bring disastrous consequences, he argued. In France, too, Ferdinand Bruntiere (1849–1906) carried forward the work of Gumplowicz by arguing that races and the struggle of the races for domination were the central facts of historical development.

Race Conflict and the State   This thesis of civilization, law, and right being born of the conflict, amalgamation, and assimilation of races—a thesis still tacitly accepted in American racial theory—was later expanded in *Der Rassenkampf* along the lines already examined in Boulanvilliers and Gobineau but within a Comtian rather than a Marxian analytical framework. In this work, Gumplowicz proposed a system of philosophy and history based on the three sequential stages of Rudolf Rocholl's *Philosophie der Geschichte* (1878): the theological stage (God), which gave way to the idealist and rationalist stage (Man), and finally to the positivist and naturalistic stage (Nature). Gumplowicz described the theological stage as focusing on the works of the divine and the providential and trusting that all the enigmas of human destiny, will, and supernatural design would be resolved by appeal to God. The rationalist stage was concerned with the history of man and his evolution through the human spirit as it progressed through time. Finally the naturalist stage envisioned man in the fatal circle of the laws of nature, fixed for all time, forever researching and analyzing the nature of those laws.

Gumplowicz held that this third, naturalistic stage did not require a biological or evolutionary theory to explain the state. The reality was that social groups met, crossed, and mixed and that there was a group basis to social life that, for whatever reason, had become racial. The driving force behind social change was conflict between heterogeneous groups when they strayed into unfamiliar territory or when one or another interest was threatened. Homogeneous groups tend toward solidarity; two or more solidarities encountering one another produced conflict. It was an unavoidable fact that man was a material phenomenon joined to the forces of nature with all other forces of nature. The birth of states was analogous to all other births, subject to biological and social laws pertaining to races. While he acknowledged the cautions of Blumenbach, Humboldt, and Prichard regarding racial classification and supported Newton's and Locke's passion for precision in observation, Gumplowicz recognized that race as an idea had a strong hold on social groups. Even though it could be shown that race was irrational, that physiognomical analysis was poverty-stricken, that the lines between "types" elided, it could also be demonstrated from the observation of groups that differences in language, religion, education, food, and hygiene existed and that it was possible to study them sociologically.

Therefore, it followed that historical knowledge depended on the analysis of what really existed in the composition of the social elements as well as on biological and anthropological classifications. Gumplowicz adopted Adolf Bastian's notion of race psychology manifest in folk thought (*Völkergedanke*) but believed Bastian (1826–1905) was mistaken in assuming that there was a natural development from kinship alignments to the political state. Instead, said Gumplowicz, the state was a social phenomenon consisting of social elements behaving according to social laws. Its activities emanated from the ruling class. Differences in the histories of states were due to differing local and ethnic conditions and to differentials in the application of force. Gumplowicz was firmly of the view that modern efforts to perpetuate the antique Aristotelian form of the state had made the theory of state endless and fruitless (p. 199). The state is nothing more than "a settled folk"; no further association is needed to make it one, and it is superfluous to mention constitutions: "A State is the organised control of the minority over the majority. This is the only true and universal definition; it is fitting in every case" (p. 200).

It followed from this view, and not from Nietzsche's hypothesis, that Aristotle's definition of the state was wholly inadmissible in sociological analysis. Indeed, in sociology the state was an industrial organization economically determined, and social progress was the outcome of industrial progress. The history of European politics turned upon the struggle of the lower classes for participation in legislation; it had nothing to do with the moral and political principles of the ancient world. The growth of the state depended on conquest and the eternal laws of nature, the workings of which could be discovered by mathematical analysis of the variables.

In this analytical framework the understanding of the social laws of the prime factors—ethnic and social groups—was of paramount importance, as distinct from the understanding of individuals, who escaped all scientific calculation. As for the arbitrary and insipid notions of natural rights embodied in the doctrines of the French and American Revolutions, these were based upon pure imagination. Man is not free; he is not even reasonable. The only rights are those that come from the state; there are no others. The only choices in life are between inequality and anarchy. Abstract concepts of justice, such as one finds in Plato, and scholastic Aristotelian formulations are all redundant, "dead and buried," said Gumplowicz (p. 263). If the abstract influences of milieu and principle are no longer of any consequence, then what is left to resolve social conflict? "Race-war," was Gumplowicz's answer, "for such is its inexorable animosity that each group that is able, tends to become exclusive like a caste, to form a consanguinous circle. In short, it becomes a race" (p. 27).

With Gumplowicz, the politics of Aristotle are finally redundant. The story of civilization and culture is retold according to the realities of conquest and race war. New spheres of law, morality, and economic life had appeared to bring about new forms of organization and new classes of men. These changes were manifested in the artists, technicians, savants, and luminaries, and most certainly not in politicians and classical political processes and constitutions. That which is the totality of these visible moral, juridical, economic, and aesthetic advances is born in the state and rendered possible by it. Culture is produced not by the pedestrian compromises and settlements of politics and ordinary political life but by the war and the conflict of the races.

The work of Gumplowicz casts its Comtian shadow more surely over the race relations theory of the twentieth century than do the "theories" of Blumenbach, Lamarck, Kant, Hegel, Niebuhr, Gobineau, and the Social Darwinists. Here was the restatement of the Frankish title to rule naturally by Hobbesian right of conquest. What Montesquieu had set aside as cause in his original formulation of the races in the eighteenth century was adopted as the guiding principle of the new industrial race-class state in a race-class war of conflicting ethnic groups. Words like "assimilation" and "integration" became the commonplaces of the new cultural milieu.

RENAN, AGAIN

Taken together, the explanations of Nietzsche and Gumplowicz provided little succour for the French, who after four years of tortuous legal argument had managed to put together a Republican parliamentary regime in 1875. Even then it was stalked by the threat of military coup, business opportunism, and an intractable conflict between Church and State over education. As we saw in the previous chapter, Ernest Renan appealed to reconstruction, resurrection, restoration, redemption, and reassembly and to the achievement of the full potential of the Celtic race through the self-conscious analysis of science and philosophy, poetry, and soul. But after his break with the Church following the publication of his *Vie de Jésus* in 1863, and in the aftermath of war, when Prussia was pressing hard on France over the claim to Alsace and Lorraine, Renan sought to reestablish the politics that Nietzsche and Gumplowicz had already renounced.

The Separation of Ethnography and Politics   Before the publication of the monumental *Histoire du peuple d'Israel* (1887) and the delayed *L'Avenir de la science* (1888), first written in the 1840s, Renan gave his celebrated lecture *Qu'est ce qui un nation?* at the Sorbonne on March 11, 1882.[18] Now, with the optimism of his early works brought face to face with the realities of real politics, he rejected the confusion of race with nation and linguistic groups, disposed of the Franco-Gallian racial origin for the French nation as historically unproven, denied the primordial existence of races in antiquity before the emergence of ethnology in modern times, and abjured against the confusion of philology, psychology, zoology, and biology in the understanding of history (pp. 62, 67, 71). "Race, as we historians understand it," he concluded, "is then something that makes and unmakes itself. The study of race is of capital importance to the student who occupies himself with the history of mankind. It has no application in politics. The instinctive consciousness which presided over the construction of the map of Europe took no account of race; and the greatest European nations are nations of essentially mixed blood" (p. 74).

This view was altogether a different view from Renan's earlier writings. He now believed the Germans would live to regret their ethnographic claim to Alsace-Lorraine: "You exploit it today on other people; some day you may see it turned against yourself" (p. 74), he said. He also warned that one day the Slavs would come to rummage around in the entrails of history trying to find the selfsame connections in their remote past. It was good for people to know how to forget, Renan concluded, as well as how to remember.

Although ethnography was a worthy study, it had no political application. Natural fluctuations in academic understanding—of patriotism, of kith and kin—might lead in the course of time to an Anglo-Saxon fighting a war only to discover that he was a Celt after all, and then ten years later being told that he was really a Slav. Race is not all, and philology is not all: both exist in the wider sphere of humanity and Western civilization.

The Nature of Nations   What, then, is nation? At this late stage in his life, Renan looked back wistfully to Renaissance man, who was not French, German, or Italian but a contributor to the education of the human mind and to devotees of it. While religion, community of interest, and geography were important, they were a not significant basis for nationality. What mattered was the living soul. The past was rich in heritage, and the present was rich in consent. A nation is a will to live together and to go on living together— a will to preserve an undivided inheritance. It is also the outcome of the past and the present, an understanding that "our ancestors made us what we are." It is a belief in common glories in the past and a common will in the present: "We have done great things and we shall do them again," Renan reflected, and "we love in proportion to the sacrifices we have consented to make, to the sufferings we have endured." "A nation's existence is—if you will pardon the metaphor—a daily plebiscite, as the individual's existence is a perpetual affirmation of life" (p. 81).

For Renan the will of the nation was the only legitimate criterion. He eliminated race, language, geography, community of interest, and religion based on metaphysical and theological abstraction, reducing all to will. Wills change, as the times change; nations change; Renan even foresaw a European confederation (p. 32). But for the time being the nation is the guarantor of liberty, a civilizing element on behalf of humanity, the aggregation of races, language, religions, and geography, of men of warm heart and moral consciousness who recognize the legitimacy of common consent.

Renan's new view had been inspired in part by his exposure to the work of Thomas Reid (1710–96) of the Scottish "commonsense" school, which had rejected Hume's skepticism, particularly that part of it which relied too heavily on Locke. Renan's early work had celebrated a Celtic people insulated from the admixture of alien blood and separated from political life. With their poetry and genius and natural isolation, they had renounced political and religious influences and retreated into soulful truth and beauty. This view was quite different from Taine's Anglo-Saxon trinity of race, milieu, and moment, in which race persisted in the blood and its character will "out" whatever the physical environment, whatever the state of mind. And it is a view that finally ended in an academic lecture on the potential of a victory of human culture

(*Humanität*) over philology and ethnology, in the partial reinstatement of the political way in a civilizing concept of nation based on will. But it was all too late and all too ambivalent in the face of what was coming out of academia in England and Germany.

MÜLLER

In the same year that Lapouge began his anthropological lectures denying a basis in language for race and Renan finally published his *L'Avenir de la science,* the German philologist F. Max Müller (1823–1900) published his *Biographies of Words: The Home of the Aryas* (1888).[19] At the time he was Gifford lecturer at Glasgow University, where he was among those who cultivated interest in the hymns of the Rig-Veda and asserted a relationship between moral ideas and ethnicity. In this text Müller reflected that ethnology had ceased to be a true science in the way it had been conceived by Prichard and Waitz at the beginning of the century; it was now little more than a collection of amusing anecdotes and paradoxes. Languages were mixed, readily adopting foreign words, idioms, and grammatical forms, and it was dangerous to transfer terms having a proper and well-defined meaning in one country to similar objects in others.

Thus attempts to find in language, or in blood, the cradle of the races were in vain. There could be no mathematical certainty or plausible supposition, because what was under study was not a common beehive, as in Spencer's analogy, but human beings subject to the uncertain relationships of language and blood, to the fluctuating influences of continuity and change in war and peace. No race at present could safely be called unmixed. "Aryan, in scientific language," Müller concluded, "is utterly inapplicable to race. It means language and nothing but language; and if we speak of Aryan race at all, we should know that it means no more than x + Aryan speech" (pp. 89–90). "Scholars, however," Müller continued, "who know how thin the ice really is on which they have to skate, are not inclined to go beyond mere conjecture, and they tremble whenever they see their own fragile arguments handled so daringly by their muscular colleagues, the palaeontonologists and cranioscopists" (p. 109).

But having denied race in blood and pointed out that many Jews had forgotten Hebrew and learned English, German, and French, Müller was still left with a spiritual principle derived from history contained in will. Will, said Müller, bestowed upon the individual—"the living soul of the nation and race"—through "the imposition of hands," whether of parents or of foreign masters, the Aryan blessing and gave him unbroken succession beginning with the first apostles of that noble speech, continuing into the present in every part of the globe.

In the sharing of a common but ambivalent interest in the will of the nation, sustained by literature and by anthropology, Renan and Müller unwittingly prepared the way for a renewed interest, post-Darwin and post-Nietzsche, in the arcana of character, nobility, and inheritance in nature. This interest in will was further exploited, as we shall see, during the 1890s and into the early twentieth century.

» The Synthesis of History and Philosophy

Beginning after midcentury, the English search for origins had led to a rejection of the political state. In its place arose a romantic consciousness of the spiritual forces of race and a scientific hereditarism that both explained and justified the advance of Anglo-Saxon civilization in all corners of the world. At the same time, in the aftermath of the Franco-Prussian War, the French sought to explain defeat and the Germans to vindicate victory through evolutionist arguments about inheritance and theories introducing anthropo-geography, environment, cephology, germ plasm theory, and folk science. Nietzsche dismissed the politics of the antique state for the formative forces of art, music, and aesthetics, while Gumplowicz revived the idea of race-class, both in a new historical landscape of apolitical civic entropy. Bagehot, Renan, and Müller were ambivalent, but their musings came far too late either to reinstate Blumenbach's unity of species or to revitalize the political way. Whatever uncertainties remained were finally eclipsed by the powerful appeals of two of the greatest writers of the nineteenth century—Heinrich von Treitschke and Friedrich Nietzsche.

TREITSCHKE

In *Deutsche Geschichte,* published in seven volumes from 1879 onward, and in lectures on the science of politics published after his death, Heinrich von Treitschke (1834–96) set out to analyze the history of Germany in the nineteenth century as a process of political unification.[20] Treitschke edited the *Preussische Jahrbucher,* which was dedicated to a Prussian-led reunification of

Germany. After Germany's victory over Denmark in 1864, he became a supporter of Bismarck. He was appointed to an assistant professorship of political science at Freiburg, then at Kiel, Heidelberg, and finally at Berlin in 1874. After the Franco-Prussian War, he was elected to the Reichstag, but he soon turned against liberalism to became an advocate of strong monarchy supported by an anonymous bureaucracy. Like Bismarck, he feared too much enthusiasm for radical democracy and ancient constitutionality, both associated with chaos and disorder, ineffectiveness and delay.

Treitschke's history is a romantic account of the German nation starting with the Peace of Westphalia and ending in 1848. Its aim was the elevation of German self-consciousness and the justification of German self-determination; it was not intended to be impartial. As William Harbutt Dawson, the editor of the English translation, summarizes, Treitschke "with a defiant pride and a high disdain . . . struck the word apology out of the German vocabulary; his role and his mission were to be those of his country's vindication" (1:viii).

Disunity and Weakness   In the opening chapters Treitschke laid out the history of a forgotten Germany as an illustrious civilization formerly split asunder by disunity and horrible confusion. Although with appalling loss Germany had secured Protestantism for Europe throughout the Thirty Years' War and had remained a citadel containing the very fiber of Protestantism, it had been left to suffer all the disadvantages of an imperfect confederation and the narrow views of particularism:

> The political state, however, which was responsible for this general contempt of Germany, was everywhere regarded as the essential safeguard of European peace, and our people, whose reputation for national arrogance had once been as bad as is that of the British today, repeated in parrot phrases the accusations of their jealous neighbours, and accustomed themselves to look upon their fatherland with the eyes of a stranger. (1:25)

But while Germany had become effete and cosmopolitan, it had not forgotten the *Völkerwanderung* of an active-minded race. As they spread themselves across Europe, the Germans had retained the Teutonic idea of state in contradistinction to the Latin political state. In time the epicenter shifted to the northeast, to the stock of those who dwelled beyond the Elbe, and a new North German tribe arose from the mixing of Lower Saxon stock with the old Wendish indigenes. These were hard people, who saw themselves as a dominant race and regarded the Slavs with contempt. They lived in a frontier land of the mark, which Elector Frederick William took in hand and gave purpose and will against a foreign world, particularly against the political concept of state. Treitschke saw in the Elector Frederick a parallel to William and the Norman Conquest of England, and he extolled Frederick's *virtù* for putting an end to the dualism of opposing political parties seeking to reconcile their differences and for creating a well-disciplined citizen army. Frederick brought back the renowned German mercenaries scattered across Europe, educated the people, reformed the economy, and created a force that had not been there since ancient times. And yet it was a Spartan policy, without art. Frederick's dictum "Negotiations without weapons are like music without instruments" (1:57) summed up his emphasis on despotic military methods. His policy had not gained full acceptance in the minds of the nobility or the common people.

Treitschke acknowledged that until the great revolutions of the eighteenth century, conditions were not favorable to the reform of Germany. While Frederick seemed to pave the way for national reform, he relied too heavily upon the noble and military classes and had not taken sufficient account of the new merchant, industrialist, and leaseholder classes.

The Epoch of Poetry and Language   Beginning about 1750, however, a new formative energy was released through poetry and literature. The works of Leibniz, Bach, Handel, Goethe, Kant, Schiller, Herder, Lessing, Fichte, the Grimm brothers, Bopp, Niebuhr, Humboldt, and Ritter released a new, free, secular culture and reintroduced the German people into the circle of civilized nations. This poetry was internalized, and it enabled the petty states to roll back the pervasive influences of the French Enlightenment and particularly the rationalism of Voltaire.

This unique process, which was German to the core, began with the work of Leibniz, who introduced the word *Rasse* into German. Through science and literature, through *Sturm und Drang,* through Lessing's restoration of German literature, through Herder's discovery of art and culture, through Schiller's reawakening of the simple energy of the ancestors, through Kant's discovery of the categorical imperative and immense contributions to cognition and ethics, through Prussian military science and English practicality, the German nation had reached a dramatic turning point. That turning point, which Treitschke marked as Fichte's *Reden an die deutsche Nation,* was a turning point of a mind. The antique political state that had so long safeguarded European peace was no longer sufficient and satisfactory. Through will, hope was restored to the German people with these words: "A new German race must be brought to life." (See 1.99 et seq for Treitschke's detailed history of the significance of the New Literature.)

The Aryan and the Semitic Sensibility   But it was not simply in art, literature, and lyric poetry that Treitschke saw the dynamics of the new Germany. In the contributions of the German writers on science and geography he found what he called "the mental currents of the age" (2:303). These currents stood in opposition to French radicalism, which he saw as ambivalent and obstructive to progress and change.

But an even greater impediment to change was the loss of cultural energy that Treitschke ascribed to the emergence, since the French and American Revolutions, of a literary Jewry with the express purpose of concealing its long-standing hatred of Christianity. A countermovement led by Ludwig Börne (1786–1837), a German journalist of Jewish origin (his original name was Löb Baruch) who had been a leader of Young Germany, was undermining the purity of Kant, Goethe, and Lessing. In his "cultureless" railing and abuse of fatherland conducted from afar in an imprecise language—the reference is to Börne's *Briefe aus Paris* (1830–33)—and with a vulgar Orientalist wit, Börne had revealed the contrast between Aryan and Semitic sensibilities. Treitschke identified Börne and other "semi-Jewish writers" as members of an opposing race that was "our national misfortune." "These Jews [are] without a country, vaunting themselves as a nation within a nation" (4:557), he wrote. It is this misfortune that I shall consider in the final section of this chapter.

The State and Race War   The definition of state in *Deutsche Geschichte* had much in common with that advanced by Gumplowicz in *Rasse und Staat* and *Der Rassenkampf,* both published after the euphoric Prussian victory. For both writers German unification achieved through antique political forms and practices was ruled out because of their connection to enthusiasm for constitutional democracy. Treitschke argued that the cosmopolitanism and egalitarianism of the French and American revolutionaries, as well as the individualism of the English utilitarians like J. S. Mill, Jeremy Bentham, and Adam Smith, who argued for commonality of material interest and greater uniformity of morals, customs, and institutions through the hidden hand of market forces, would be ineffectual. For Treitschke, as for Gumplowicz, the essence of state power was force, at the center of which was the Hobbesian right of conquest made manifest in war. Gumplowicz focused on the conflict between contending social groups, which was working itself out in the opposition of the lower and the higher race-classes in the new industrial civilization, while Treitschke focused on the state as a person conceived of as unified will prevailing against foreign and alien wills. But both entertained the powerful idea of a race war. For Treitschke the state was a living Leviathan of personality intensively lifting individuals of Kantian character to a higher civilization. At the core of his reasoning, therefore, was the romantic displacement of traditional politics by persons endowed with an artistic inner temperament that oriented the individual toward a natural goal. It was this consciousness of self that held nations together, and the more Herder's concept of culture was realized and implemented, the more the sense of national identity would be developed—and the more the Gumplowiczian friction between nations would occur, with a high probability of race-class war.

NIETZSCHE, AGAIN

When Nietzsche wrote *Die Geburt der Tragödie* in 1872, he had declared his open opposition to precisely the same points that Treitschke had raised in the *Deutsche Geschichte:* to the sexual and monetary elements of Social Darwinism and utilitarianism, to Rousseau's doctrine of the democratic *moi commun,* and to the historical misinterpretations of the English historians like Carlyle. But, as we have already seen, Nietzsche went further, expressing his revulsion from the German historians, and especially from Sybel and Treitschke. Although he shared their historical perspective of the release of the individual personality as conceived in the works of the late-eighteenth-century German philosophers and saw the origins of the state in history as a Niebuhrian fight between two races for mastery, he believed that the present Kantian character traits existing in English, French, German, or Jewish "types" were poor replicas of the true idea of noble character of the future. Only a conception of a new nobility could triumph over crude democracy and shatter all established boundaries of classical political theory, even those that Treitschke was parading in his "pathologically estranged" version of German nationalism. Indeed, in the *Macht Staat* (the power state) politics *qua* politics had not simply been submerged by the Gumplowiczian and Treitschkean "war of everyman against everyman" in the established Hobbesian sense, but these blockheads, screamers, and "rabbit shooters" (change agents) had failed abysmally to see that the destiny of their new formulations lay in oblivion as another kind of war emerged—the war of and for minds.[21]

The Overman   After an emotional crisis in 1879, Nietzsche relinquished his chair of philology at Basel. In 1885, he published forty copies of *Also Sprach Zarathustra*.[22] Here, in a literary form reminiscent of the *Aeneid,* he developed his theory of the superman, or Overman. Openly contemptuous of Hume, Locke, Rousseau, J. S. Mill, Carlyle, Darwin, and Galton, and particularly of Treitschke and the German historians, Nietzsche turned to the seventh-century-B.C. founder of the Persian religion, Zarathustra, and to the Zend-Avesta, its Bible, to consider the conflict between the God of Light and Good and the God of Darkness and Evil.

In the prologue Nietzsche constructed an allegory in which all existing conceptions of state, church, justice, history, philosophy, *Kultur,* art, and poetry were dismantled one by one and annihilated as frivolous deceptions. All reformulations or emendations of state, political or otherwise, he proclaimed, were lies (pp. 76, 77). In his philosophical reconstruction of the idea in the allegories of self-overcoming and the will to power and in the dream of self-redemption, Nietzsche unharnessed all past efforts of man to release himself from bondage. Man could not become free by becoming his own redeemer through the traditional avenues of political life or through the recommendations of the new intellectual elite. He could only become free by recognizing his own mortality in the riddle of eternal recurrence, which revealed that life and its old habitual moral values were fallacious and bankrupt. "I shall return eternally to this identical and selfsame life," Nietzsche proclaimed, "in the greatest things and in the smallest, to teach once more the eternal recurrence of all things" (3.2.238). In the fear and terror of existence without a supposition of God, man was on his own. What was required to put things right was a new nobility with a will for the future.

In this analysis the new nobility were the begetters and sowers of the future. They were neither the old nobles who were habituated to serving princes nor the shopkeepers. They gazed outward rather than backward. "You shall be fugitives from all fatherlands and fore-fatherlands" (3.12.221),

Nietzsche exhorted. The greatest danger for the future was with the good and the just who held on to old values, who taught false security, and who sailed toward false shores.

The following year Nietzsche published *Jenseits von Gut und Böse* (1886), which interpreted *Also Sprach Zarathustra* for the benefit of the "rabbit shooters" and "fire dogs" (racketeering revolutionaries) who had not understood his allegory of the natural history of morals.[23] Here Nietzsche reflected on the disintegration and race mixture that had been occurring since the end of the seventeenth century and had been described in such glowing Germanic terms in Treitschke's release of will.

Nietzsche's starting point was a Lamarckian assumption that human beings have in their bodies "the heritage of multiple origins," which they carry in their blood from generation to generation. But instead of approaching race positively, as the Comtians did, Nietzsche regarded it, like all other questions, from the negative standpoint: "It is simply not possible that a human being should *not* have the qualities and preferences of his parents and ancestors in his body, whatever appearances may suggest to the contrary. That is the problem of race" (p. 404).

The question of race was not that qualities and preferences were transferred from generation to generation, or that "later types" would be, on average, weaker human beings than "earlier types." That was the deception of origins practiced by the exponents of modern education and *Kultur.* The truth was that nature could not be expelled, and both the polygenists and the monogenists had failed to understand that *all* was appearance. Only when human beings inherited, or cultivated, self-control and self-outwitting, only when they understood that monstrosity *is,* would "magical, incomprehensible, and unfathomable ones arise" (p. 302).

Nietzsche perceived more clearly than his contemporaries that in his own time Europe had been plunged into semibarbarism by the very mixture of classes and races identified clearly for the first time in the eighteenth century. What he found so disturbing was that for the first time history was open to "modern souls." Every taste, every culture, every past was open to scrutiny. "We ourselves are," he concluded "a kind of chaos" (p. 341).

Not only that, but Nietzsche saw the European "present man"—the nineteenth-century interpreter of the past—as part of a great physiological process expressing itself in the concepts of civilization and progress or, in political terms, in democratization:

> The Europeans are becoming more similar to each other; they become more
> and more detached from the conditions under which races originate that are
> tied to some climate or class; they become increasingly independent of any
> *determinate* milieu that would like to inscribe itself for centuries in body and soul
> with the same demands. Thus an essentially supra-national and nomadic type
> of man is gradually coming up, a type that possesses, physiologically speaking,
> a maximum of the art and power of adaption as its typical distinction. (p. 366)

In this democratic movement appeared the "evolving European," locked
in a process that was leading to the leveling and mediocritization of man,
turning him into a useful, multipurpose herd animal. In such conditions only
the mediocre had any chance of continuing their type; the conditions that
had first fixed the noble traits and characteristics of types were in the past.
The luxury and abundance of industrial civilization, and its temporary, fleeting
nature, would bring about the inevitable corruption of the old and produce
the conditions likely "to give birth to exceptional human beings of the most
dangerous and attractive quality"—a future nobility of dazzling human potential (p. 366).

The Nation and the Will   It followed that the unrest after the Franco-
Prussian War had come about because of the inheritance in blood of diverse
standards and values and the movement and countermovement of spiritual
values. Abroad in the world there were hybrids of body and hybrids of will
that were causing a general loss of independence. The respectable but vulgar,
brutal, and clumsy English skeptics were but a spiritual expression of a physical condition called nervous exhaustion, a sickliness caused by a paralysis of
will when sudden and decisive crossing of races and classes hitherto separated
took place. Nietzsche regarded the strength of will in the French and the
German as little better, and in the Italian virtually nonexistent. The Russian
was "waiting menacingly to be discharged" (p. 321). As a good European, he
thought that unless Europe strengthened its will it would succumb to this
Slavic threat: "The time for petty politics is over: the very next century will
bring the fight for the dominion of the earth—the *compulsion* to large-scale
politics" (p. 321).

As for nationalism, that was the "pathological estrangement" and "nerve
fever" whipped up by Sybel and Treitschke from genuine studies of European
art, literature, and poetry (p. 386). The idea of nation was a modern invention;

it was neither a race nor a type. There may be races and types within it—
most notably the Jews, who had resisted the corruption of modernity and the
skepticism and exhaustion of values brought about by the English, by Darwin,
Mill, and Spencer. Of all peoples, Nietzsche perceived that the Jews had endured the worst possible conditions over long periods of time and had survived. This process had stiffened them: "The Jews, however, are beyond any
doubt the strongest, toughest and purest race now living in Europe" (p. 377).
If the Jews had wanted to they could have achieved mastery over Europe, but
Nietzsche was certain that they were not working toward that end, nor plan-
ning for it. He saw their main objective as the ending of the life of the Wandering Jew and believed they should be accommodated within Europe. "To
that end," he proposed, "it might be useful and fair to expel the anti-Semitic
screamers from the country" (p. 378).

Contrary to popular opinion, Nietzsche did not express support for the
antisemitism that was beginning to appear in Germany in the 1870s and 1880s.
He accepted as fact that the Germans were not terribly well disposed toward
the Jews, but the problem as he saw it had less to do with excess of feeling
than with the difficulty encountered when a "weaker race" (the Germans)
had to absorb a "stronger race" (the Jews). In that respect it was partly a
problem of digestion of numbers. Nietzsche even argued that a dose of Jewish
nobility would do a powerful amount of good for the Prussian command
structure!

In contrast to the toughness and tenacity of the Jews, the French had all
the heroic trappings of will without any notion of what was necessary for the
attainment of true nobility. The Germans were complacently profound, wal-
lowing in German soul, German beer, German music, German taste, and
German honesty (p. 369). The English were little better than the Germans,
lacking in philosophy, dance, and rhythm. All that you could get from the
English, he pretended to lament, were the moral grunts of Methodism and
the Salvation Army: "Finally listen to them sing! But I am asking too much"
(p. 380).

Although Nietzsche denied a relationship conceptually and actually in
blood between the Goths, Vandals, and other Germanic tribes and "us Germans," he nevertheless adhered to Niebuhr's fundamental concept that conflict
in history was a conflict between the races. Yet this view was subsumed in
his more important recognition that all life was appearance—a chance, a risk,

an uncertainty, a throw of the dice. What man makes of himself at the center of the vortex was the nub of all future change.

For Nietzsche, both science and politics were poverty-stricken; both were unreliable. The great departure point in the modern world was the self-realization of the emptiness of all political values. Man must will himself forward by becoming his own redeemer, overcoming redemption, reconciliation, compromise, discourse, argument, and debate. Nietzsche's contemplation of the transfiguration of individual genius and the world of art saw race as an example of estrangement and "nerve fever," a consequence of the general departure from noble ideals. Race was not a prescription for a forward-looking society; for Nietzsche it was a pathological state.

» *Antisemitism: A New Formative Force*

It is commonly believed that Nietzsche, following from Machiavelli, was the theoretician of "the master race," just as Kant, Hegel, and Luther were its historical progenitors. But Hannah Arendt, Sir Ernest Barker, and Nietzsche's editor Walter Kaufmann contest this point. Nietzsche did not contribute to the glorification of the *Herrenmensch* or the concept of *Lebensraum,* which were closer to the hearts of Ritter, Haeckel, Ratzel, Gumplowicz, and Treitschke, and the Prussian historians, whom, as we have seen, Nietzsche despised.[24]

In her monumental *Origins of Totalitarianism* Arendt argues that antisemitism did not emerge with the search for the true origins of the Franks and the Gauls, the Germans, the English, and the French. While some have perceived antisemitism as linked to an exaggerated nationalism and xenophobia, in which the Jews were the scapegoats, victims to be expelled in modern repetition of what had happened at Barcelona in 1492, Arendt's analysis is more complex. She explains that for two thousand years the Jews were kept apart from state and politics in the West. Until the 1870s they were a well-defined, self-preserving group (*nomoi*) with rights and liberties given in return for service to the state. Yet their apolitical position left them vulnerable and exposed. Especially with the emergence of the modern secular state, Jews had become increasingly visible, closely identified with government and authority through their roles in state finance. At the same time they attracted suspicion, as liberal and radical movements believed them to be denying opportunity to the newly discovered *Volk*. This suspicion was expressed as anti-Jewish feeling, but not as antisemitism, which Arendt regards as a distinctively different historical phenomenon. In order for one to be transmogrified into the other, there had to be something more popular, more able to capture the imagination than the boring questions of legitimate inheritance and generation hitherto expressed by the anthropologists and the philologists, and some explanation more convincing than that which held that antisemitism was an exaggerated form of the persecution that had taken place throughout the Middle Ages.

Arendt's suggestion is that antisemitism began in the 1870s in the aftermath of the Franco-Prussian War and was essentially a French phenomenon during the 1880s and 1890s. Race thinking in its antisemitic form appeared when there was a fundamental collapse of political thinking, when men ceased to use the hard categories of politics in the antique sense and put in their place ideas that flowed from new, unhistorical concepts of the social realm recently discovered by historians, anthropologists, sociologists, psychologists, and biologists. With the introduction of autonomous entities such as "society" and "the commercial world" came the decay of real politics and the political state.

The key historical turning points in the emergence of a doctrine of race, therefore, for Arendt, as well as for Theophile Simar and G. L. Mosse, were the defeat of Napoleon in 1805, the influences of Darwin from 1859 onward, and the defeat of France in 1871, which I have dealt with in some detail above. But for Arendt there could be no fully developed intellectual idea of race, and no idea of antisemitism, until the romanticism of the late eighteenth century, with its emphasis upon noble personal character, had been wedded to the Darwinist and Gobinist movements of the nineteenth century—movements that in their different ways saw the prerequisite for a new natural nobility in primitive tribal origins, and not in the realities of politics properly conducted according to classical rules. The suggestion here is that there was no fundamental historical movement of racial and antisemitic ideas until after 1880, and, more important, that it is a mistake to see antisemitism as, for instance, Leon Poliakov does in his vast *Histoire de l'antisémitise*, as an omnipresent historical idea, or as Norman Cohn does in his *Warrant for Genocide,* as a new form of political antisemitism, a simple variant on the anti-Jewish antipathies of the Middle Ages and a case study in collective psychopathology.[25]

MOMMSEN

As we have seen, in England the escape from political reality began to take shape early with Dilke's reflections on the export of the masses to distant lands, the invention of "Saxondom," the application of the notion of the survival of the fittest to a spurious Hebraic and Hellenist division of mankind, and the creation of a popular national history that treated as a certain fact the direct connection between Reformation Christianity and the blood bond of the Teutonic peoples.

Similarly in Germany, from 1862 to 1875, Theodor Mommsen (1817–1903) in his *Römische Geschichte* (1854–56) advanced an immensely popular historical-physiological theory of the past in which race played a critically important part. Mommsen idealized Goethe and was a disciple of Niebuhr. He was awarded the Nobel Prize for literature in 1902. Writing on the Roman constitution and criminal law, he reinterpreted the collapse of the Roman *respublica* as arising historically from a necessary act that had guaranteed the survival of peace, true freedom, and civilization of one race over another. For Mommsen the "other Rome" was not the political Rome of Cicero and Machiavelli; it was the Rome of serene empire that had rejected the classical notions of political virtue and morality of the republican period and justified the destruction of an alien Carthage solely on grounds of reason of state. This Rome, and not the "political" Rome of the Republic, stood vindicated from the strictures of the antique moralists by what it had achieved for Western civilization.

In Nietzsche's early work on the rebirth of German myth and artistic drive addressed to Wagner, and in Mommsen's justification of the preemptive amoral strike, we see novel elements being added to the Hobbesian right of conquest in the conditions then prevailing in the post-Darwinian and post-Gobinist era. As Poliakov, Simar, and Mosse have shown, the idea of antisemitism has to be seen in the light of fundamental changes in the perception of the Jew that began with the development of the modern national *Volk* states and *Volk* churches after 1859. In 1863 Renan, in his *Vie de Jésus*, had recast Jesus as less Jewish than Christian, a historical figure who belonged to the *Volk*.

Renan's was an anticlericalist intellectual reinterpretation of Christ's Jewish life. A more popular interpretation appeared in the antisemitic catechism of the emigre I. Zollschan, who in *Das Rassenproblem* (1870) allowed the Jew to be seen as a different species—a Semite—no longer separated within humanity by a difference in religion and randomly persecuted for it by the traditional methods of the medieval church, but now by the technical and administrative apparatus of the modern State.[26]

Moreover, Marx and the syndicalists had encouraged within their theoretical economic discussions a belief that the Jew was an extra-economic force, a threat to rational economic systems. From the 1850s religious persecution acquired an economic edge as states produced long series of forgeries and fabrications stretching back to the French Revolution blaming the upheavals of the past on the Freemasons and Jews, who were together seen as the root cause of revolution. Herman Goedsche (1815–78) popularized the idea of a Jewish conspiracy in his novel *Biarritz* (1867), thus laying the foundation for the conversion of a fictional account into an allegedly accurate historical record.

In Russia, where there were large numbers of Jews, the Tsarist regime dealt cruelly with them throughout the nineteenth century. After 1850 the Jews were subjected to increasing privation and restriction culminating in pogroms in 1871 and expulsion in 1881. In Germany, organized resistance to the infiltration of Jews from Russia, and to the Semitic threat within, came from William Marr (1818–1904), who was himself alleged to be a Jew, with the publication in 1867 of the pamphlet *Der Sieg des Judentums uberdas Germanentum* (The Victory of Jewry over Teutonism). This was followed by other antisemitic pamphlets, catechisms, and newspapers. In 1879 Marr founded the Anti Semitic League, which was influential in Germany, Rumania, Austro-Hungary, and France, and in 1882 Karl Lueger founded an antisemitic movement which eventually gained seats.

In France the formation of the newspaper *L'Anti-Semitique* during the period 1870–79, and the important work of Eugen Dühring (1833–1921) in *Cursus der Philosophie als streng wissenschaftlicher Weltanschauung und Lebensgestaltung* (1875) reinforced the idea that the Jew was not someone of a different religion but a different species of man and that Jewishness was a social problem practically insoluble in bourgeois society without the positivist driving force of state socialism. After his expulsion from the University of Berlin for slander in 1877, Dühring took up the more virulent theme of race war in 1880 in *Die Judenfrage als Frage des Rassencharakters und seiner Schädlichkeiten für Völkerexistenz, Sitten und Kultur* (The Jewish Question as a Problem of Racial Character and Its Damage to the Existence of Peoples, Morals, and Culture). Going through five editions by

1901, the work saw the *Volksgeist* as the prerequisite for a stable society and sound economics and the extirpation of the Jew as a necessary expedient.

DRUMONT

The publication of Nietzsche's *Jenseits von Gut und Böse* in 1886 coincided with the publication in France of Edouard Drumont's (1814–1917) two volumes on *La France Juive,* which provided the intellectual foundation for the antisemitic movement in the Action Française of the Third Republic.[27] Drumont was a journalist and founder of *Libre Parole.* During the formative period of anti-semitism, he wrote the preface to August Rohling's *Talmud-Jude* (1871), which had sought to reveal the immorality of the teachings of the Talmud. Drumont explained France's defeat in the Franco-Prussian War not, as Bismarck and Treitschke had argued, as the triumph of the dynamic Germanic Northerners over the Latinized French, but as brought about within France by Jews— particularly Rothschild and Gerson Bleichröder—who were bent on plun- dering France. He proposed that together the French and the Germans— Aryan peoples—had fallen victim to Jewish high finance. Acting on this hy- pothesis he conducted an ethnographic, physiological comparison of Semite and Aryan, representing the two races as separate and antithetical entities.

Drumont's main source was Maximilien Paul Émile Littré (1801–81), lexi- cographer, positivist, disciple of Comte, who in *Paroles de philosophie positive* (1859) had argued that Sanskrit philology provided evidence that the Romans were Aryans and that the Latin language had a direct relationship with the Greek, Persian, and Sanskrit. As Drumont employed the word, "Aryan" de- noted someone noble, high-minded, and of the superior branch of the white race that had its beginnings in Iran and spread out as branches to become Greeks, Romans, Celts, Ario-Slavs, and Ario-Germans. Unlike Gumplowicz, who favored more overtly Darwinist applications, Drumont developed Littré's theme that European Christians were direct descendants of the Romans and by virtue of this descent were "seized of the rights of their progenitors" (p. 89).

Furthermore, when subjected to the tests of linguistic science, European Christians also turned out to be Aryans. In contrast to the Semitic race, which derived from Aramaic, Hebrew, and Arab sources in Mesopotamia, "the Aryan or Indo-European race is the only one to uphold the principles of justice, to experience freedom and to value beauty" (p. 90). The conflict between Aryan and Semite had existed since the dawn of history, and the Carthaginian, Saracen, and Trojan wars were all attempts to enslave the Aryan race. Now the Jew had once again emerged in the forefront, as "dangerous invasion has given way to silent, progressive and slow encroachment" (p. 92).

Drumont's characterization of the Aryan of humble origin, with roots deep in Roman civilization, in the *gens,* in the feudal family, was expressed as Ignatius Loyola, the Jesuit. The slow development of the Aryan talent, its illustrious inventiveness, its intellectual, monastic, poetic bravery, its spirit of adventure, contrasted with the instant transformation that characterized Semitic peoples, who could never rise to even a semblance of civilization: "The Rothschilds, in spite of their billions, look like hawkers of second hand clothes; their wives, with all the diamonds of Golconda, will always look like haberdashers, dressed up not for Sunday, but for the sabbath" (p. 100).

Here the Semite is portrayed as the businessman, the commercial interest symbolized earlier in Gumplowicz's second banker class, and in the syndicalism inspired by Charles Fourier, Alphonse Toussenel, and Pierre Joseph Proudhon and the antipathies of Karl Marx and Friedrich Engels. He is the born trader dealing in every imaginable commodity for the sake of money and advantage. He has no creative ability, no inventiveness. He strips the first class of property, land, custom, and religion.

Drumont's work gave prominence in modernity to the notion of "the invisible Jew," elements of which were evident in the episodes immediately preceding the Expulsion from Spain in 1492. He represented the Jews as observing principles of solidarity in an alliance that was inexorably secret and universal, symbolized as two hands clasped beneath a halo. Hinting that Jews were the bearers of disease, Drumont set the rumor and innuendo of the fourteenth century in a modern context, pointing to statistical data on the incidence of sickness and mental illness:

> The question of understanding why the Jews stink has only preoccupied a number of well intentioned people. In the Middle Ages it was felt that they could be purified of this odour by baptizing them. Bail claims that this feature is due to natural causes, and that there are still black men in Guinea who emit an unbearable odour. Banazzini, in his *Traite des Artisans,* attributes the evil smell of the Jews to their lack of hygiene and their immoderate taste for goat's milk and cheese. (p. 108)

The warning of Renan and Müller that it was dangerous to introduce ethnographic claims of this kind into politics, and their advice that the study of history, zoology, and politics should be kept separate, went unheeded. Anthropology was wantonly mixed with class and race, with history and philology, to produce out of the old Gallo-Roman argument a virulent Franco-Saxon anthropological amendment that would soon wreak havoc among the Jews.

THE TOTAL STATE

Arendt argues that three powerful forces in the new French Republic constructed a bridge to the future total state. The first was Boulangisme, or the reconstruction of military power in alliance with action in the streets—an alliance predicted with some accuracy by Edmund Burke in *Reflections on the Revolution in France*. Appointed minister of war in 1886, General Georges Ernest Boulanger (1837–91) recognized the potential of the mob in circumventing parliamentary authority in his quest to root out the inefficiency and corruption in the army, and he almost brought the new republic to its knees. Second, the republic's attempt to remove the influence of Roman Catholicism from education revived again the arcane Gallo-Roman arguments over title to rule and generation, and especially those of Jacques Bénigne Bossuet (1627–1704), who had maintained the superiority of the national (self-determining) church over Rome. Third, during the Panama scandal the popular press bypassed parliamentary and judicial procedures to mobilize an ill-informed public opinion and transform a religious anti-Jewish feeling into antisemitism. These forces came together in the Dreyfus case (1894), which Arendt labels "more than a bizarre imperfectly solved crime . . . a prelude to Nazism—with its hero not Dreyfus but Clemenceau."[28]

Arendt perceived in the Panama scandal the emergence of a relationship between business and politics in which Parliament ceased to be a public arena in which members dispassionately represented the interests of citizens and balanced out as best they could the general interests of the state against the selfish interests of individuals. Here she follows closely the general arguments of Walter Bagehot, E. H. Dance, and Benjamin Kidd: that the coming of the new civilization had seriously undermined real political consciousness and replaced it with a managerial and business consciousness. In alliance with their civil servants, French members of Parliament in the Third Republic had become businessmen and administrators themselves, acting in their own private and corrupt interests to milk funds from the middle classes through public loans backed by the guarantee of Parliament and the state, ostensibly to support the ill-fated Panama Company.

Although there were no Jews among the bribed members of Parliament or on the board of the Panama Company, there were two Jews in the chamber who distributed funds to members and Jewish middlemen—financial new-comers, who had displaced the old court Jews of the eighteenth and early nineteenth centuries—and did not play the game according to the traditional rules. As a consequence, Jews generally became more suspect than they had ever been before. Arendt argues that an added dimension appeared when Jacques Reinach, one of the members of Parliament, released his list of "re-mittance men," not before a public assembly with full opportunity for reply to detailed accusation, but in dribs and drabs for maximum effect in Dru-mont's newspaper *Libre Parole,* which publicized lists of culprits in tantalizing serial installments somewhat like the practice of modern tabloids. This appeal to the masses by the racketeers so despised by Nietzsche—the gutter press—signaled not only the emergence of antisemitism as a dangerous new force in Western political life but the beginnings of totalitarian rule. Now the Jews were *anomic,* experiencing for the first time Nietzsche's new civilization with-out the protection of antique notions of state, law, justice, reason, and citi-zenship. In short, they were no longer the political responsibility of any church or state, and because the state was no longer playing the public game according to its own political rules, they (and others in similar situations) were in double jeopardy to bureaucracy and a self-determining mass democracy of the mod-ern natural state.

For Arendt the Dreyfus case was the culmination of the Jews' effort to find their place in a caste-ridden entity—the army—which at the time, under the influence of Boulangisme, was struggling to assert itself as an independent interest group outside the political nation. When the Jews, and particularly "anti-Semitic Jews" like Dreyfus, went for places in the army, they were re-sisted by the caste spirit with the support of the Jesuits, who became "their first unappeasable foes."[29] There was no political compromise, no willingness to settle, and in the dissolution of the state machinery in France, and the political disillusion that followed, the Jesuits exploited antisemitism as an ex-citing new concept.

Thus the chaos of the Third Republic produced a mob that took action from Parliament to the streets. Antisemitism was tested on the streets of

France, not in its public assemblies, its parliaments and courts. As a consequence the Jews withdrew from politics into the security of hearth and home, refusing to see that mob action was an issue affecting their basic right to citizenship within a political state. They also failed to see that the street fight was now highly organized and on turf unmarked by traditional political principles. They thereby left themselves wide open to the consequences of Hobbes's state of nature.

Arendt's account of antisemitism in France included German and English contributions to the foundation of race thinking and to elements in totalitarian thinking that have now become commonplace in twentieth-century daily life. Race thinking and totalitarian thinking came together when there was a fundamental collapse in political thinking—when men ceased using the traditional political categories and relationships of Aristotle, Cicero, and Machiavelli. Now the lines between public and private were blurred and the teachings of classical civilization were distorted to meet the specific requirements of ideology. In this new natural social realm (society), people no longer looked to fallible political actors for measured judgments about political reality and no longer saw themselves associating as citizens in a bewildering world of variety and contingency. They became part of "a gigantic nation-wide administration of housekeeping," as Arendt called it in *The Human Condition*,[30] partners in a retrogressive prepolitical set of corrupt business arrangements in which attention turned to naked power (*sui generis*) and the Nietzschean ways in which it could be used to manipulate the ideas that moved the ignorant masses.

» *Conclusion: From Race-State to Race War*

Between 1870 and 1914, antisemitism was invented. The English, searching for their true origins as they engaged in a romantic mission to take their civilization throughout the world, contributed to the ideas of social evolution, hereditarism, and eugenics. In the immediate aftermath of the Franco-Prussian War the Lamarckian-Darwinist, science-based perception of politics and society emerging in France and Germany further derogated the morality of Greco-Roman political life. As Nietzsche reoriented discourse toward modernity, Gumplowicz laid the foundation for the sociological study of social conflict and ethnic groups engaged in a race-class war. Finally history, biology, and will were allied in the influential works of Treitschke and Nietzsche. Treitschke harnessed heredity and will in the service of an apolitical state and mobilized the aesthetic sensibilities and character of an evolving German people engaged in a conflict with the Semites. Nietzsche saw the futility of reconstructing new national models on the wreckage of the old and recognized that the future would be a war of, and for, minds. That war actually began in France, where Drumont drew upon the intellectual resources of philosophy and science to promote, through the popular press, the idea that the Semites were the cause of France's defeat in the Franco-Prussian War.

In the anomie of Nietzsche's Persian allegory, there was little left to protect the Jew. In face of the frailty of existence, the death of God, and the bankruptcy of the political state, there was only a state of civic entropy. It was Treitschke and Gumplowicz who put this antipathy to the political state and political civilization on a firm footing. Proposing the power state as a living Leviathan, they made it a vehicle for war at the service of those embarking upon this new pseudoscientific quest to exclude the Jew from citizenry.

Race is All, 1890–1939

At the end of the nineteenth century, Treitschke's power state and Gumplo-wicz's race-class state combined with Nietzsche's stark description of the frailty of all secular existence to produce the awful conclusion that nothing could succeed in the new industrial state but force. All classical formulations of political and constitutional life could not prevent the fall into the abyss of death. What could not be settled in the *agora* could only be mastered by the will to power, by the Overman—self-overcoming man making himself sci-entifically, technologically, and industrially without recourse to politics and religion. Treitschke, Gumplowicz, and Nietzsche hang over us as we interpret the events leading up to the Second World War. Their ideas continue to form an important part of the rich vocabulary we use to describe the race relations of our own day.

As we have seen in previous chapters, the Darwinian era marked a pro-found departure from all that had gone before in the science of man. The principles of political philosophy that had once guided human affairs were now replaced by the principles of natural selection and the processes of social evolution set in an ideological frame of reference. Hannah Arendt, following Benjamin Kidd, has interpreted these new processes of social evolution as placing much less emphasis upon the human past than upon an ideal future. What Herbert Spencer, Charles Darwin, Francis Galton, and Karl Pearson and their social evolutionist followers had introduced into political life was *the future* as an ideal toward which people traveled through struggle against the forms and beliefs of a redundant past. Now parliaments and political com-promise as ways of fixing the affairs of state succumbed to theories of social order based on the interference or noninterference of the state in the affairs of individuals, allowing the full force of evolutionary and psychological struggle to be realized ideologically in the economic realms, so that industrial production and industrial struggle began to dominate all aspects of thought.

Race thinking was not the sole invention of the Nazis. With deep roots in Enlightenment and nineteenth-century thought and in the antisemitic movement of 1870–1900, race thinking was but one innovative aspect of a more general post-Nietzschean phenomenon shared by all the denizens of the Western world. It was as much the preserve of the English, the French, the Americans, the Canadians, and, from Arendt's point of view, the Jews, as it was of the Germans, and it is that disturbing route that I shall now travel.

» The Roots of Nazism

By the end of the nineteenth century it was accepted that man may be recognized for what he is from the instant and immediate signs of his material appearance (aspectus), which may be divined in the eyes, nostrils, and skin, and may be seen to emanate from type to prototype, from macroprosopus to microprosopus, through the action of demons, hidden causes, or intelligent sources. This doctrine had its roots in the Hermetica, the Zohar, Agrippa, Paracelsus, Vesalius, Bodin, and Montesquieu rather than in Aristotle, Cicero, and Machiavelli. It provided the inspiration and the material for a wide variety of writers, not all of them German, who were busily constructing the ethnocentric and racial world picture that Hannah Arendt and Nicholas Goodrick-Clarke, in their different ways, have explored.

In The Occult Roots of Nazism, Goodrick-Clarke has traced out historically the influence of Ernst Haeckel, Otto Ammon, and Ludwig Woltmann upon the lives, doctrines, and cult activities of the Ariosophists, Guido von List and Jorg Lanz von Liebenfels and their followers, who, it is claimed, were seminal influences on Hitler and the Nazi movement. He demonstrates the historical connections between these Aryan cults and the Hermetic and Cabalist writers of the so-called secret texts, which became of very real interest to those seeking to establish a new materialist focus in something called "ethnic background."[1]

During the period from 1890 to 1915, race as an organizing idea claimed precedence over all previous formulations of nation and state. Although the works of many racialist writers of the period are virtually unreadable today without an elementary insight into Niebuhr and Treitschke and their accounts of Western history from 1740 to 1870, they attracted vast audiences in Germany, France, Britain, and the United States, who were greatly excited by racial ideas. On his own admission, Adolf Hitler obtained all of his ideas confirming the singular importance of race from the period immediately preceding 1910. The influence of this literature continues in contemporary understandings of race and ethnicity.

LANGBEHN

Into the Nietzschean abyss and the turmoil of the Treitschkean state of war plunged an anonymous "German," later revealed to be Julius Langbehn (1851–1907), with *Rembrandt als Erzieher* (1890). This book, which attracted the attention of Kaiser Wilhelm II and Chancellor Otto von Bismarck, had a much greater popular success before the First World War than Nietzsche's vehement attack upon the "fire dogs" and "rabbit shooters." In it Nietzsche's argument concerning the art impulses of nature and self-overcoming were supplemented with the more dynamic idea that the life force of *Volk* art mystically revealed the genius of race. This important popular analysis promoted the idea suggested by Lessing at the end of the eighteenth century that art, literature, and politics were the true expression of the divine spirit of Christ working in and through the genius of the "Germans in the woods." Other writers promoted pan-Germanism by exploiting the idea of a Germanic Jesus, among them Klaus Wagner, J. L. Reimer, and Gustav Frenssen.

According to Langbehn's account, Rembrandt, the artistic genius, was the exemplar of the race that inhabited Lower Germany in the great plain between the Rhine and the Elbe. The Low German was intelligent because he was Aryan and the least defiled by race mixture. Racial superiority had, in turn, given rise to an elite social class, and in fact the visible differences in class also depended on race. The minority that directed the state and assumed political, military, and cultural leadership was confirmed in title and right to rule by a combination of race and class.

AMMON

In 1893 Otto Ammon (1842–1916), influential member of Alldeutsche Verband, formed in 1891 to protest the trading of Zanzibar to England in exchange for

Helgoland, published his *Selection naturelle dans l'homme,* and in 1900 he published *Die Gesellschaftsordnung und ihre natürlichen Grundlagen.* Ammon was ambitious for a Germany that stretched from Berlin to Baghdad, but he was not
at all enamored of Lapouge's argument that nation and state had a spiritual
basis or of Marx's ideas of class struggle.

A close follower of Haeckel, Ammon opposed Nietzsche's nihilist portrayal of the new civilization. He saw social anthropology as a useful tool
whereby educated people could engineer changes in society. In his view the
threatening social question was not the debilitation of France by the prepon-
derance of brachycephalic (lower-class) elements, but of Germany by the Jews
and the Jesuits. In this conflict he saw a process of denordicization (*Entnordung*)
at work. Like Langbehn and Gumplowicz, Ammon conceived of the state as
comprised of class relationships that were at the same time blood relationships
and constantly crossing. For Ammon entrepreneurship was the role of the
middle class, and this class was invigorated with new blood as the peasantry
drifted into towns. He corroborated this idea from his measurements of thousands of conscripts of the grand duchy of Baden, claiming to have discovered
proofs of racial difference from the analysis of head forms between city and
country people and the upper and lower classes.

From these conclusions Ammon reconstituted Haeckel's hypothesis of
Weltanschauung—"nature is all"—as a base for the order of society in opposition to the Marxist economic interpretation. According to Ammon, materialism and the principle of the struggle of the classes upon which Marx
had founded his historical theory neglected the psychic element in human
activity and cast doubts upon some interpretations of the Social Darwinist
theory. Ammon sought to demonstrate that social classes exercised an advan-
tageous action at the levels of marriage by the limitation of intermixture and
the effect of "rising" by intermixture. Education and nurture of the favored
classes brought advantages for psychic development, and the greater material
well-being of the favored classes encouraged the lower to copy them. The
implacable law of natural selection demonstrated by Spencer and Darwin,
when applied to the military, commerce, and industry, allowed for the exercise
of leadership roles within a caste and enabled hereditary genius and racial
talent to triumph and to adapt, while the inept were condemned to oblivion.
In Ammon Marx's law of the struggle of the classes was replaced by the law
of the onward march of the racially best and their eventual triumph.

RIPLEY

In the United States, Ammon's work played a prominent part in William Z. Ripley's highly influential *Races of Europe* (1899), which published Ripley's Lowell Institute lectures on physical geography and anthropology at Columbia University in 1896. Ripley had corresponded with Ammon and spoke of his work with warmth and affection: "To him belongs the honour of the discovery of the so-called 'Ammon's law,' that the Teutonic race betrays almost everywhere a marked penchant for city life."[2] Ripley drew heavily upon Haeckel, Ratzel, Waitz, Virchow, Lombroso, Freeman, Pearson, Dilke, Lapouge, Broca, and Joseph Deniker. In this vast work, which was finally published in 1899, Ripley attempted to move beyond considering Europeans as one race, as had been the practice from the time of Linnaeus, Blumenbach, Camper, and Retzius, and to use the works of Ammon, Lapouge, Broca, and Deniker to analyze the multiplicity and diversity of the races of Europe. He recognized the difficulty in the term: "Race, in the present state of things, is an abstract conception, a notion of continuity in discontinuity, of unity in diversity. It is the rehabilitation of a real but directly unattainable thing." Only upon that basis did he put forward three ideal racial types distinguishable in Europe: "They have often dissolved in the common population; each particular trail has gone its own way; so that at the present time, if indeed ever, do we discover a single individual corresponding to our racial type in every detail. It exists for us nevertheless" (pp. 111–12). Having said that, Ripley asserted that all political boundaries were superficial and that nationality was an artificial result of political causes. In this view he presaged Sir Arthur Keith's *Nationality and Race from an Anthropologist's Point of View* (1919), which contended that racial and national boundaries were simply part of nature's evolutionary machinery. For Ripley, underlying causes of family, caste, party affiliation, and religious denomination was race: "Race denotes what man is; all these other things denote what he does."

The central thesis of Ripley's work was that there was not a single European "type" or white race, but three recognizable races—Teutonic, Celtic Alpine, and Mediterranean—which could be distinguished from a close examination of the geographical distribution of head forms, hair color, and stature. He argued that from a scientific point of view this evidence was far more reliable than inferences drawn from social and linguistic data or from vague influences of milieu found in writers like Buckle. Ripley's work was a natural history treatment of concrete "facts" like migration, colonization, and acclimatization that drew on the evidence of Ratzel's anthropo-geography, Pearson's measurements, and Dilke's observations on American and Australian population shifts, along the way bringing in writers on acclimatization and contemporary asides on race hygiene, which he admitted until the early 1890s the German writers had handled with kid gloves.

In his scientific work on physical geography Ripley touched upon the problem of antisemitism in Germany, treating it not so much as a concern of the present as a protest against future evil. He saw Germany's problem of Jewish exiles from Russia as America's problem also, describing them as "a swamp of miserable human beings" (p. 33). Borrowing heavily from Lombroso and Freeman, his plates display a veritable rogues' gallery of Jewish "types" easily recognizable for what they are by what he called their "nostrility," as were the Negroes by their respiratory power, pulse rate, diminished muscular capacity, and lesser endurance.

The theories of Ammon and Ripley dovetailed with the graphic illustrations presented by Joseph Deniker, librarian of the natural history museum in Paris, in his *Races of Man* (1897). Establishing the dolichocephalic, mesocephalic, and brachycephalic measurements and their indices, Deniker not only influenced Houston Stewart Chamberlain, Oswald Spengler, Paul Popenoe and Roswell Hill Johnson, and Adolf Hitler but created a mass view of what the people the indices described were assumed to be like ethnologically, according to the tenets of a detached and truthful science.

GALTON AND PEARSON, AGAIN

In 1883, as we have seen, Francis Galton introduced the term "eugenics," which he later defined as "the study of agencies under social control that may improve or impair the racial qualities of future generations either physically or mentally."[3] Galton also introduced the term "anthropometry" into England, taking it from Alphonse Bertillon, who in 1883 had invented a system of body measurements that included head length, head breadth, length of middle finger, length of left foot, and span of elbow to the middle of the little finger. During these same years Karl Pearson was beginning his studies on inheritance. In 1892 Galton published the second edition of *Hereditary Genius* and Pearson his *Grammar of Science,* a philosophical text propagating the ideas of Immanuel Kant and Ernst Mach. Both texts have to be seen in the context of the debate on denordicization, race psychology and race hygiene, the doctrine of the inheritance of acquired traits, and the impermeability of environmental influence contained in August Weismann's germ plasm theory, which was consolidated in his *Keimplasm. Eine Theorie der Vererbung*, published in 1892. They also have to be seen in the light of Langbehn's provision for the entry of Christ and His genius as the supreme revelation of the life force of the *Volksgeist,* Ammon's reconciliation between class and race, and Gumplowicz's emphasis upon the conduct of social and ethnic groups in conflict. All these ideas mixed together in a pseudoscientific, pseudohistorical potpourri.

From 1893 Pearson's work began to attract attention, particularly his collaboration with Walter F. R. Weldon (1860–1906), Jodrell Professor of Zoology at University College, London, who had been examining shrimps using Galton's sampling techniques to find a different way of fixing "types" or "races" and their evolutionary descent. Pearson assisted Weldon with the statistical analysis, and, until 1906 when Weldon died, they merged the two disciplines of biological research and empirical statistical analysis to form a new science of biometry. From their studies Pearson concluded that physical and psychical characters were inherited and from that argued that Sir Charles Dilke's "Greater Britain" was rapidly deteriorating. Observing that the working classes were multiplying with Malthusian consequences while the well-bred were limiting their families, Pearson advocated a national program to breed intelligence so as to limit, or eliminate, the worst effects of working-class poverty by the efficient and effective management of population—in much the same way as the Taylorists were advocating the management of steel plants in the United States.

WEISMANN AND WOLTMANN

Ranged against this "individual characters" hypothesis was August Friedrich Leopold Weismann's (1834–1914) physiological and biological hypothesis that the force and continuity of heredity was contained in a substance impermeable to environmental and cultural influences, a permanent hereditary substance that appeared as a biological materialization of Blumenbach's *nisus formativus.* Publication of Weismann's *Keimplasm* and *Vortrage über Descendenztheorie (Evolution Theory)* (1904) revived the eighteenth-century scientific debate about the Lamarckian hereditary characters and stimulated again an interest in scientific and historical hereditarism, which held that the reform of the environment could have very little influence in the long term because germ plasm remained unalterable; whatever nurture was applied in the form of government, law, politics, and education would ultimately be defied by nature.

Weismann's hypothesis received the support of Ludwig Woltmann (1871–1907), who in *Politische Anthropologie* (1903) defended Weismann's thesis and opposed English and American notions of individual heredity. Woltmann was a follower of Lapouge, Gumplowicz, and Gobineau and a pupil of Haeckel, founder of *Politisch-Anthropologische Revue,* and co-founder with Alfred Ploetz (1860–1940), the racial biologist who coined the term *Rassenhygiene,* of the *Archiv für Rassen und Gesellschaftsbiologie* in 1904. Woltmann's *Die Germanen in Italien* (1905) and *Die Germanen in Frankreich* (1907) revived a version of Niebuhrian racial inheritance in a cultural, psychological, and characterological context to prove that Italy, France, and Spain were formed from a mixture of Gallo-Roman physiological and psychological elements. He based his arguments on his research on musical talent, which suggested that talent was ethnically inherited.

Woltmann identified social class with race. He also believed that the human race was governed by the same natural and biological laws that governed the zoological and botanical world. He took Gumplowicz's theory of the mysterious laws of nature and hereditary genius, identified certain somatic indices, linked together the psychic and the physical in the way of Haeckel and Adolf Bastian (1826–1905), who from 1860 had studied psychical evidence of the development of *Volk* psychology, and submitted the whole process to the penetrating gaze of statistical proof. The certainty of proof that Max Müller and Ernest Renan could not find in language was now sought in mysterious yet concrete material characters.

Friedrich Ratzel, the environmentalist and anthropo-geographer, was also active in the founding of the *Archiv für Rassen,* whose purpose was to publish the findings of race biology and race psychology. This and other academic journals propagated Ratzel's idea of a race science (*Völkerkunde*), and in 1905 an international society for racial hygiene was established. The society was linked to the German Society for Race Hygiene, the British Eugenics Education Society, founded in 1908, and the Eugenics Record Office established in the United States in 1910, and both the societies and the *Archiv für Rassen* translated and disseminated the works of Galton and Pearson on the national significance of eugenics as a useful science capable of unifying state, nation, and race in the realization of a new industrial civilization.[4]

In parallel with these developments, and with much international exchange of views, Francis Galton, Weldon, and Pearson founded the journal *Biometrika* in 1902, and, from a financial contribution made by Galton, a Research Fellowship in National Eugenics was set up in Britain in the same year that *Archiv für Rassen* was founded in Germany. A Eugenics Record Office was also established to collect and study the pedigrees of the intelligent and expert Fellows of the Royal Society. In 1911 the Galton Eugenics Professorship was established at University College, and a new Department of Applied Statistics was opened to conduct research.

DAVENPORT

In the United States, at the Eugenics Record Office in Cold Spring Harbor on Long Island, Charles B. Davenport (1866–1944) set up a station to study not only the observable characters of organisms (phenotypes) but also the genetic composition of organisms that were not observable or visible. Davenport tracked back the incidence of disease through family records, questionnaires, and public inquiries. In 1911 he published *Heredity in Relation to Genetics,* which demonstrated patterns of heredity in the incidence of abnormality—in Huntington's chorea, hemophilia, albinism, polydactylism—and in human eye, skin, and hair color. Davenport also examined the incidence of feeblemindedness, insanity, epilepsy, alcoholism, and criminality. He also conducted an exhaustive analysis of the effects of miscegenation in the United States.

In his approach, Davenport was much influenced by Galton, Pearson, and Weldon and by the work of William Bateson (1861–1926), who in *Mendel's Principles of Heredity* (1902) and later in *Biological Fact and the Structure of Society* (1912) had put forward a Mendelian nonbiometric, genetic view that argued that notions of equality of opportunity and cooperative political society were not borne out by the Hobbesian natural order of things. Following the publicist J. L. Reimer (b. 1879–?), who had maintained in *Ein Pangermanisches Deutschland* (1905) that a hereditary caste was necessary to safeguard the Germanic state and future civilization against Dilke and Ammon's "swamping," Bateson argued that a hereditary arrangement of classes, in which everyone was doing what he was best suited to do naturally, should be encouraged by governments.

Davenport was not so concerned as Karl Pearson with race-class identities as with American racial-caste identities, which following the scientific format in relation to the eighteenth-century typologies of Linnaeus and Blumenbach and the qualities of Kant. For Davenport, the influx of immigrants to the United States threatened to "swamp" better stock, and his solution was a "negative eugenics" designed to keep out the drunkenness, sexual immorality, imbecility, insanity, and criminality of the Poles, Irish, Italians, and Jews, and internally within the United States to limit the spreading effects of bad germ plasm.

In the Eugenics Record Office *Bulletin* 9, of June 1913, Davenport considered the results obtained by his field workers on inquiries into the feeble-minded and imbecile, the epileptic, and the insane and evaluated the best possible and worst possible chances of what he described as "neuropathic taint" issuing from any one of those obtaining licenses to marry into weak and strong stock. He then went on to consider whether the state laws limiting marriage selection within and between families in any way matched the known biological effects of such unions and concluded that in some cases they were justifiable and in others not. He advocated the continuance of state licenses to control such marriages, and recommended that for complete enforcement of existing laws, and for the better administration of future laws, state eugenics boards should be established. State physicians should issue licenses to marry, and field workers should collect data concerning the long-term effects of these marriages. The state boards would be staffed by trained biologists, who would act as a final court of appeal, and physicians and field workers would make recommendations as to the allocation of licenses to marry on the basis of the biological evidence available on the couple's suitability. Those who were denied a license and defied state restraints by cohabiting and producing a child, should be penalized by the sterilization of the male, Davenport recommended.

It is puzzling that George L. Mosse holds that at this stage the founders of these scholarly societies and laboratories did not consider themselves to be creating anything more than respectable scientific equivalents of Galton's Eugenics Education Society. In Mosse's view the wedding of race hygiene, folk psychology, and mysticism had not yet taken place, and there was considerable ambivalence about their union until after the formation of the Nazi Party and the promulgation of the Nazi Law of June 28, 1933. Nevertheless, as Daniel Kevles has shown, there can be little doubt about the widespread interest in Galton's eugenics, which was seen by many people in high places in Britain and the United States as a promising new instrument for the release of civilization from the uncertainties and contingencies of existing politics.[5]

However well-intentioned these scientific societies and journals may have been at the time of their formation, and however much we may wish to distance their illustrious academic and industrial founders from what happened in the death camps, it has to be remembered that the first experiments on the feebleminded were sanctioned by states in the United States and justified by the U.S. Supreme Court. These acts were performed in knowledge of the antisemitism of the Third Republic, which was further inflamed in 1902 when the czar's secret police forged the *Protocols of the Wise Men of Zion,* a tract purporting to show a world conspiracy by the leaders of Jewry to undermine Western democracy. Although the czar took no notice of it and it was not translated into German until 1919, by rumor and innuendo the bogus *Protocols* encouraged those who wished to perpetuate the fictions of I. Zollschan and Eugen Dühring by scientific and other means that the entry of the Jew posed a conspiratorial racial threat to Western civilization.[6]

In this context it is difficult to ignore the influence of Davenport's advocacy of state laws limiting the marriage of the "unsuitable" and Harry H. Laughlin's essay on "The Legislative and Administrative Aspects of Sterilization," which outlined a means for dealing with the feebleminded and disabled and was also published in the Eugenics Record Office *Bulletin* 10 1914. Von Hoffmann's *Rassenbiologie* (1913) described for Germans the promising advances made in race biology in America and the work of the state institutes in Sweden and Russia devoted to *Rassenbiologie.* When the Nazis were censured by the international scientific community in the 1930s for their eugenic practices, it was no little wonder that these and the works of Pearson and Galton were thrown back in the faces of their critics.

» *Social Darwinism, Sociology, and Race Psychology*

Between 1870 and 1900, the foundations for American sociology were laid, solidly grounded in the works of Darwin and Spencer. The sales of Spencer's books in the United States from 1860 to 1900 exceeded 300,000.[7] Various interpretations of the phenomenon of race owed much to the Anglo-Saxon hypothesis of Carlyle, as well as to Kemble, Freeman, Green, Kingsley, and Dilke, but the old themes of civilization and history as the opposition of the Romano-Celtic and the German races also continued to exercise a powerful influence.

SUMNER

At Harvard John Fiske (1842–1901), a Comtian who later embraced Spencer and was familiar with Humboldt, Goethe, Mill, Buckle, and Huxley, spearheaded the introduction of Darwin's works into the United States, and at Yale William Graham Sumner's lectures on Spencer's *Principles of Sociology* (1876–96) were extremely popular. In *What Social Classes Owe to Each Other* (1883), Sumner (1840–1910) explained that the German idea of the state as an entity having conscience, power, and will sublimated above human limitations was unknown in history. For him the state should perform the functions of army and police and very little else. Nor did he believe the rich ought to take care of the poor, an idea he attributed to English sentimentality stimulated by pressure groups, newspaper proprietors, and caucuses in a new form of "legislation by clamor." In any event "poor" was an elastic term, Sumner stated, a fallacy, and hence could compel no duty. "Every man and woman in society has one big duty," he announced. "That is to take care of his or her own self." Sumner had no patience with what he called "social doctoring," and he advocated a laissez-faire approach that consisted of minding your own business. He believed that class would always exist and that present and future distinctions depended upon the variety of chances that presented themselves to the individual: "Instead of endeavoring to redistribute the acquisitions which had been made between the existing classes, our aim should be to increase, multiply and extend the chances."[8]

In *Folkways* (1906), Sumner pursued a social psychological and culturally deterministic explanation of society following Spencer's developmental schema and examined the folkways and mores that regulated societies through the customs people had adopted historically to satisfy their basic wants and needs. Sumner's vision was not that of a social evolution based on the Germanic military and geopolitical, Darwinist and Hobbesian, elements of survival of the fittest and conquest in war, which Heinrich Driesman (1863–1927) had described in Germany in his *Rasse und Milieu* (1902) and which was stimulating his American compatriots Alfred Thayer Mahan (1840–1914) and Homer Lea (1876–1912) to investigate geopolitical influences. Nor did Sumner owe much to the new evangelical faith in a Germanic Jesus, the laws of blood, and the pan-Germanism being advanced by Friedrich Lange (1828–75) in *Reines Deutschtum* (1902). Lange assumed that warlike qualities were transmitted by heredity and that the Germans were descended from noble conquerors who carried the better blood of humanity and had the right of first place among peoples. Rather, Sumner favored a notion of social evolution that relied upon a comfortable, cooperative, apolitical Comtian society for those ordinary members of the masses who sat arranged in economically free Gumplowiczian social groups somewhere in the middle ground between the privileged elite and the delinquent mob.

In his *War and Other Essays,* first published in 1903, Sumner posed the dilemma: man must enter into civilized organization or die out. The Indians of North America exemplified the dilemma. Sumner did not think that the human race would be civilized except by the extermination of the uncivilized, unless the men of the twentieth century could devise by more knowledge and more reason that which had eluded all previous ages. He foresaw only more force and more bloodshed.

Sumner's works on folkways and mores bore a great resemblance to the ideas of Albrecht Wirth, who although a follower of Gumplowicz and the environmentalists, as we have seen, in arguing that mixture and isolation fashioned the spirit and culture of the race, which remained unalterable, clearly recognized the problems that might arise when change was imposed upon a culture, social structure, and religion by right of conquest. In *Rasse und Volk* (1914) Wirth examined the spirit of race reflected in clothes, arms, utensils, and machines, and he traced its operation in commerce, religion, art, philosophy, and literature as it affected the mental structures of peoples.

Wirth thought that contemporary Western democratic and national ideals, especially those emanating from America, would soon encircle the globe and begin to fashion and cultivate the ideas and ideals of colonial and indigenous peoples. Wirth did not advocate the right of conquest or the imposition of culture upon the mental structures of these peoples, because he believed that too quick a change would bring disastrous consequences. His explanation for social transformation, like Sumner's, relied on a psychological infiltration of the lower spirit by the higher through educative cultural processes rather than through the art of politics.

LE BON

In 1894, the year of the Dreyfus affair, Gustave Le Bon (1847–1930) published *Les Lois psychologiques de l'evolution des peuples,* which achieved enormous popularity, eventually running to seventeen editions and being translated into sixteen languages, even becoming bedside reading for Theodore Roosevelt. In this book Le Bon attractively digested his own voluminous work on human psychology, hygiene and medicine, hypnotism, illusion, hallucination, recurring events, and the crowd mind derived from the works of Friedrich Anton Mesmer, Jean Martin Charcot, and Ambroise-August Liébeault and cleverly allied it to a comparative ethnology drawn from the principles of Gobineau, Comte, Spencer, Adolphe Quetelet, and Darwin and from his expeditions to Algeria and India.

In his early work, *La Vie: Psychologie humaine appliqué a l'hygiene et la medicine* (1872), Le Bon had concluded from hypnotic studies that each people possessed a collective psychology. Combining English sensationalist thinking and the principles of hypnotism, he recognized that when attention is focused on one idea repetitively, the intensity of that idea is heightened and all other sensations are blocked out; ultimately the individual takes for reality the ideas suggested to him.

In *L'Homme et les societes* (1881) Le Bon had developed the ideas of race psychology and crowd mind from the threefold theological, metaphysical, and positivist structures of Comte, from Spencer's developmental process, from Quetelet's statistical method, and from Darwin's evolution. His explication applied principles of natural selection and adaptability to the retention of Lamarckian characters that were useful. The following year he was able to observe mixing of races in his ethnological and photographic travels to Algeria and later in travels to India. Like Dilke and Max Nordau, he was convinced that race mixing would lead to decadence and the decline of civilization. Alfred Fouillée (1838–1912) came to the same conclusion. In a study of the psychology of the French people published in 1898 and in *Esquisse de la psychologie des peuples européens* (1919), he examined the causes of decline in Spain based on cephalic measurements and shifts in the Celt-Slav, Aryan, and Gaullic elements of the population due to celibacy and war.

Criticized on methodological grounds by Renan, Le Bon did not receive the recognition he thought he deserved. After 1886 he concentrated on the problems of race psychology and developed the idea that social classes, linguistic groups, sexes, religions, and races were distinguished by lasting psychological and characterological differences that were threatened by the great danger of assimilation. These speculations captured the imagination of Houston Stewart Chamberlain, Madison Grant, and G. Vacher de Lapouge, particularly his critique of Germanic theory as a false notion based on the purity of race. Although modeled on Gobineau and the persistence of Lamarckian characters, the history of Europe as perceived by Le Bon was the history of the crossing of primary races. He understood the degree of stability of psychological characters as the outcome of such crossing over the centuries. Communal institutions and interests also moved toward unity in the course of twelve hundred years, and every individual born had a spiritual collective relationship with the soul of the *patria*.

Le Bon recognized how seductive the egalitarian idea was for the Boulangist mobs wishing to shatter the basis of antique political societies. Instead of waiting, as Lapouge had been content to do, for the new democratic class to self-destruct in the course of time, Le Bon confronted head-on Taine's specter of revolutionary democratic upheaval with the opposite idea that men are born *unequal* and ought to remain so by the order of nature. Le Bon substituted one materialist hypothesis for another in defense of elite claims to privileges by virtue of birth. He elevated the importance of ancestry and inheritance over immediate parentage and geographical milieu and assigned sovereignty to the influence of character in the life of peoples, even to the extent that it overwhelmed the intelligence and artistic taste called for in Nietzsche's notion of self-overcoming. It was by iterative character, the kind of character described by Lessing, Goethe, and Kant, that peoples persist, and loss of character that led to their enfeeblement. It was by character alone that 60 million English held 250 million Hindus in yoke!

The kind of character of which Le Bon spoke does not appear in the writers of the ancient world. It would later be capitalized on by Houston Stewart Chamberlain, Madison Grant, and particularly Theodore Lothrop Stoddard in his "iron law of inequality." This mental, mystical quality was asserted to be possessed by the Anglo-Saxon race, with its initiative, tenacity, perseverance, energy, inviolability, and respect for law. But crossing of blood would eventually efface the best qualities of character and produce a nondescript "type" in which the physical and mental energy was enfeebled. Le Bon saw in Mexico and Brazil, in Algeria and in India, a decadence, which he compared with the disaster that followed from the Roman Empire's mistakenly treating barbarian invaders as citizens. It followed logically that all countries with large number of *métis* and Jews were for that reason alone condemned to perpetual anarchy.

In the same year that Le Bon published *Les Lois psychologiques de l'evolution des peuples,* Charles H. Pearson (1830–94) published *National Life and Character: A Forecast,* which described the specter of "swamping" by black and yellow races, and the alarming increase in the Jewish population in Russia. Of Australia he warned: "We are guarding the last part of the world in which the higher races can live and increase freely, for the higher civilisation." And he lamented: "It has been our work to organise and create, to carry peace and law and order over the world, that others may enter and enjoy. Yet in some of us the feeling of caste is so strong that we are not sorry to think that we shall have passed away before that day arrives."[9] Pearson called for a national state with compulsory military service to combat the rise of the industrial state and to replace the weakness of the political and ecclesiastical state.

SOMBART

In opposition to this view, yet still adhering to the principle that there were common inherent psychological characteristics congenial to the exercise of economic functions in the new capitalist organization, Werner Sombart (1863–1941), in *Die Juden und das Wirtschaftsleben* (1911), attributed successful commercial development not to the Weberian Protestant ethic but to the positive contribution of the Jews in Western history. Rejecting Ripley's hypothesis of geographical isolation and Chamberlain's explanation of the role of the Jew in history, Sombart drew upon the contributions of the psychological race theorists published in *Archiv für Rassen* and upon the works of Gumplowicz, Ratzel, and Woltmann to argue for racially determined mental dispositions, commonly inherited psychological characteristics, and collective soul. In chapters dealing with Jewish characteristics, the race problem, and the vicissitudes of the Jewish people, he sought to demonstrate that it was genius rooted in a set of specific Jewish psychological characteristics that accounted for the prosperity of modern capitalism. The Jew was not the degenerative creature that Ripley, Chamberlain, and Gobineau had seen threatening Europe. Rather the Jew's teleological view of the world, his intellectualism, energy, mobility, and rationalism were positive features in the development of European history.

With this conflicting emphasis upon character and the psychological laws of evolution that make individuals and social groups naturally unequal and susceptible to persuasion by a hypnotic leader playing upon their sensations and upon their soul, Le Bon had consolidated the Gobinist attack upon the democratic revolutions of the eighteenth century. These views were not accepted by Sombart, and they did not find ready acceptance in the United States where, despite the experimentation introduced by Social Darwinist and Gumplowiczian influences, there was some adherence to the principle that all men were created equal.

THOMAS

At Chicago, following a period of study at Göttingen, William I. Thomas (1863–1947) applied a Lockean associationist psychology to argue that human beings develop a "growing consciousness of kind" as they are attracted and repelled by the solidarities of blood, brotherhood, kinship, dress, speech, social practice, and habit. He demonstrated that there were different sexual conceptions of beauty in skin color, size, length of hair, beard, and face line, which could be altered to exaggerate, accentuate, or even to understate individual characteristics. In that sense Thomas suggested that racial prejudice was a superficial matter: "It is called out primarily by the physical aspect of an unfamiliar people—their color, form and feature of dress—and by their activities and habits in only a secondary way." Since appearance was apprehensible by the senses, it followed that there would be periods of intense and immediate prejudice—which Thomas ascribed to instinctive reaction—that could be dissipated by association, conversion, or slight modification of the stimuli. In time, antipathy could be controlled. "When not complicated by caste-feeling," Thomas concluded, "race prejudice is after all very impermanent, of no more stability, perhaps, than fashion."[10]

That is not to say, however, that Thomas believed that race prejudice could be reasoned with or legislated away, for it was connected with affective processes that were instinctual and arose in the tribal stage of society. Race prejudice, or some analogue of it, would never disappear completely simply because of the diversity of the world in which human beings lived. Yet in Thomas's ideas we can glimpse the beginnings of the renowned "Chicago format," which saw in improved communication, equal job status, and standard systems of education a future remedy for managing and removing by psychological means the existing race and caste prejudices of America.

» Race, Politics, and History

ACTON

When Sir J. R. Seeley, the promoter of "Saxondom," died in 1895, the Regius Chair in Modern History at Cambridge passed to Lord Acton. Until his death in 1902 Acton gave two courses in modern history and the French Revolution that openly challenged the racialization of history. In *Essays on Freedom and Power*, compiled and published after his death, he contested the utilitarian theory of John Stuart Mill that the state and the nation must be co-extensive, co-terminous, and self-determining and that it was in general a necessary condition of free institutions that political boundaries should coincide with those of nationalities. On the contrary, Acton argued that the real test of a state and the best security for its freedom—and, more important, the chief instrument of a humanizing civilization—was when several nations co-existed under the same state.[11]

Acton regarded the French Revolution as a repudiation of the geographical boundaries and the historical events that created them. The revolution had wiped out past administrations, physical identities, classes, corporations, even weights and measures, and had replaced them with natural concepts of state. The postrevolutionary nation postulated by Treitschke was heavily dependent upon perpetuation of fictional, as opposed to historical, notions of equality, and upon a hatred of nobility, feudalism, and church. By "fictional," Acton meant hypothetical, thought up, a nice thing to have, an abstract desirable aim, an idea; by "historical," he meant all those notions of equality under the law that had been tested over long periods of time, and had hammered out the rights of individual human beings in the light of historical experience. Acton argued that the theories of nation extant at the end of the nineteenth century were divisible into two quite distinct kinds—those which tended to diversity (the political) and those which tended to unity (the natural), dismissing existing conditions of life and obedience to the laws of history as impediments to an ideal future.

Although Acton held to a view of "inferior races," he was anxious that future arrangements of governance should be of benefit to those who were in a subject state. Here he suggested that the connection with race was merely natural and physical, whereas the duty to the Aristotelian political state was ethical. One was connected to animality; the other to authority, law, duty, obligation, and rights. When a state equals a nation equals a race, then theoretically all other states within its boundaries would be subject states and the primary urge would be to neutralize, absorb, expel, and destroy the vitality of politics as well as of peoples.

This thesis was in distinct opposition to Niebuhr's portrayal of history as a history of races. For Acton, the history of Western Europe was not the history of conflict between ethnic groups; it was a history of Greco-Roman and catholic politics perpetually seeking to rid itself authoritatively of narrow national and ethnic distinctions and identities and, failing to do so, sinking back into the abyss of naked unregulated power acting under no authority, from which no force on earth could rescue it: "Where political and national boundaries coincide, society ceases to advance and nations relapse into a condition corresponding to that of men renouncing intercourse with their fellow men."

BRYCE

This reminder of the efficacy and morality of political life, which came to be fiercely contested in England, was also taken up in 1903 by Viscount James Bryce in his *Relations of the Advanced and Backward Races of Mankind* and later in his celebrated lecture at the opening of the Skeat and Furnivall Library at London University on *Race Sentiment as a Factor in History* (1915). In the closing passages of his great history of the Holy Roman Empire published in many editions from 1866 through 1897, Bryce had already reflected on how the small states of Europe had been swallowed up into larger ones and how following the Franco-Prussian War the great states had themselves reached the extreme boundaries of race and language. "It is now the passions and interests of peoples rather than princes that are the potent factors in politics," he concluded.[12] In 1897 Bryce welcomed the foundation of the new Prussian state, but he also saw the storm clouds gathering over it because its character was national and military and economic rather than political. He predicted that unless the new Germany was very careful in attending to the basic principles of political life—to those elements that had allowed any kind of political life to exist at all in Western civilization—it would be exposed to "the contagion of social disturbance" arising from its incapacity to deal politically with the dual problem of creating popular elements in its constitution and of overcoming the persistent jealousies and conflicting interests of the different peoples and classes who lived within its boundaries.

Bryce's gloomy prognostication at the beginning of the First World War was that the race conflict that prevailed in Southeastern Europe, and has broken out again as I write, would be eased only by the blending of stocks. Like Acton, he foresaw the awful consequences that might flow from the neglect of the political life. In the context of the late nineteenth and early twentieth centuries, however, Nietzsche's and Treitschke's conception of the state was altogether more appealing.

And while Alfred E. Zimmern (1879–1957) attempted to reinstate the idea of political citizenship and a humanizing civilization in *The Greek Commonwealth* (1911) and J. Holland Rose (1855–1942) in his lectures in 1915 at Christ's College, Cambridge, had pursued much the same idea, little notice was taken of Acton's warning that the political realm should not be confused with the natural and that the co-extensive and co-terminous versions of state then being considered might pose a threat to the co-existent political state that had hitherto been the bedrock of Western civilization. In his reflections on *Nationality as a Factor in History* (1916), Rose specifically rejected the ideas of Ripley and Deniker that the facts of history were analogous to the facts of nature, and that there was a close relationship between racial cephalic material and nationality, but the dominant note throughout the period was that both history and civilization had their true origins in nature and evolution. J. R. Green, William Stubbs, E. A. Freeman, and Matthew Arnold all continued Kemble's theme that the English were derived by blood from a Teutonic race. The origin of the free man and the man of action was to be found in Reformation religion, consanguinity, language, and moral character, summarized Stubbs. Similarly, in *Anglo-Saxon Britain* (1901) Grant A. Allen (1848–99) reiterated these ideas about the Teutonic and Celtic elements in blood and character and asserted that the English arose from these origins.

SIEGFRIED

In the year of Dilke's visit to North America, Canada had achieved a difficult settlement with the British that brought together the *habitants* and *courreurs de bois* of New France (who had lived there for more than three hundred years and knew little of postrevolutionary French thought) with the English, German, Scottish, Irish, Cornish, Swedish Protestant, and Catholic Loyalists who had fled the unwanted democracy of the United States in 1776. The Canadians had negotiated a sovereign political arrangement, covering a vast physical territory much larger than the United States, with an agreement indebted more to the principles and practices of Acton's co-existent antique state than to the utilitarian assumptions of Mill's co-extensive and co-terminous physiocratic ideas.

Andre Siegfried (1875–1959), a French Protestant exiled after the German occupation of Alsace, inserted into the discourse of politics a reinterpretation of the British North America Act (1867), seeing it as reflecting conflicting race sentiment rather than as a difficult exercise in politics. His *Race Question in Canada* (1906) introduced European folk psychology and political anthropology as the means for understanding Canada's recent past. Like Seeley and Charles Pearson in England, and Mahan, Lea, and Theodore Roosevelt in the United States, Siegfried projected a mystical extension of the natural anthropological development of the Anglo-Saxon Frankish world to Canada, where Latin-French race conflict continued as a major theme. After Siegfried, Canada could not be perceived in terms other than those of the co-terminous state. There was the added threat of "swamping" by the United States, with American mass democracy extending its life forms and vital forces of self-determination northward. From this point Canada's history was racialized, and despite valiant attempts from time to time to reestablish a political understanding, principally by the intellectual politician Pierre Trudeau, that Niebuhrian interpretation still hangs over the Canadian state.

WILSON

But it was to the south that the historical ground was being cleared more rapidly to make way for the developing social sciences. Woodrow Wilson's lectures at Princeton University on public administration, contrasting the energy of the American public service system with the tight control of the English, introduced the idea of the comparative study of American and European governments. Wilson (1856–1924) thought that the European should be in the forefront of the study of systems. "Aryan practice may often be freed from doubt by Semitic or Turanian instance but it is Aryan practice we principally wish to know."[13]

The concept of governance Wilson worked out in *The State* (1899) was grounded in the Germanic assumption that the basis for good government was kinship. The state, as he conceived of it, progressed from the patriarchal family to community to state in accordance with the principles enunciated by Freeman, Stubbs, Dilke, Macaulay, Maitland, Kingsley, Waitz, Spencer, Seeley, and Maine. Personal allegiance to the state depended in principle upon the idea of the *comitatus* (the contingent relationship of the leader to the warband), Hobbesian right of conquest, and the inheritance of Teutonic systems and characteristics. American government was an extension and perfection of Germanic-English political arrangements: "The original bond of union and the original sanction for magisterial authority was one and the same thing, namely, real or feigned blood relationship." Wilson's principles faithfully followed Niebuhr's racialization of history, even in interpreting the governments of ancient Greece.

OSBORN

Wilson's thought was in keeping with that of a large number of intellectuals who were advocating the application of the evolution idea to the history of man. Among them was Henry Fairfield Osborn (1857–1935), distinguished vertebrate paleontologist at Princeton and Columbia, who had met Darwin and was a follower of T. H. Huxley. Osborn had studied fossil life in Wyoming and Colorado in 1877 and 1878, and had published some six hundred papers on evolution. In *From the Greeks to Darwin* (1894), he depicted history as a chain of thought stretching from the Greeks to modern times, with Darwin providing the proof stage in speculation, hypothesis, proof, and demonstration: "Before Darwin the theory; after Darwin the factors." Osborn argued and further developed under the influence of Weismann and in association with Madison Grant the powerful idea that political life and ecclesiastical life had blocked scientific understanding for centuries and their removal would bring in a more promising era of scientific reasoning: "If the orthodoxy of Augustine had remained the teaching of the Church, the final establishment of Evolution would have come far earlier than it did."[14]

McDOUGALL

At Harvard, William McDougall, professor of psychology, sought to discredit those who were denying the importance of racial composition and differences of innate endowment. In *Is America Safe for Democracy?* (1921), he also used the "fact" of race to discredit those historians who concentrated upon the obvious truth that race and nation were not coincident; they were, he argued, dragging a red herring to put scientific inquiry off the scent. The fact was that science had undermined the theory that men were equal and had created a new civilization in which the differences of mental qualities would be of paramount importance. Positing a fixed structure of mind, he devised experiments that purported to show marked innate racial differences in the intelligence and performance of Europeans and Negroes. McDougall believed the real reason that America was speeding down the road to destruction was because the capacity of "the parabola of its peoples" for intellectual and moral development was distributed unequally and that there had been in recent times a decline in the quality of its mental constitution: "The great condition of the decline of any civilization is the inadequacy of the qualities of the people who are the bearers of it."[15] Having transported to America a philosophy of physiological psychology in support of the ideas of race "swamping" current in the experimental laboratories at University College and Oxford, McDougall regarded the education and reform promoted by the sociologists at Chicago as useless.

WALLAS

Also in lectures at Harvard, and in his *Human Nature in Politics* (1910), the liberal publicist Graham Wallas (1858–1932) reiterated Seeley's aphorism that the inhabitants of Great Britain conquered half the world in a fit of absence of mind and as a consequence left five-sixths of the population of that vast empire as administered natural peoples without a concept of citizenship. In the absence of politics in India—a politics Wallas clearly recognized as a peculiar practical activity suffering grievously in the West from the useless attention of academic systems analysts and singularly lacking in the understanding of its practical human dimensions—all he could offer was a certain forbearance of the science of eugenics and the improvement of racial type: "For the moment we shrink from the interbreeding of races, but we do so in spite of some conspicuous examples of successful interbreeding in the past, and largely because of our complete ignorance of the conditions on which success depends."[16]

LIPPMANN

Wallas's contemporary, Walter Lippmann (1889–1974), was more forthright in his critique of what was happening around him. Although he shared many of Wallas's views on the nature of politics, he expressed a disdain for the well-meaning but "unmeaning" social analysts like McDougall, who, without any understanding of "statesmanship," were indulging a weak psychology in the service of eugenics.

In his *Preface to Politics* (1913) Lippmann used the Chicago Vice Report of 1911, which sought to eliminate "white slavery" (prostitution) by social intervention, to illustrate the indifference to politics in contemporary society as well as to demonstrate the dangers inherent in overzealousness. He was not optimistic that prostitution, sex, and lust could be eliminated by this means.

In believing that the remedy could be as simple as a change of legal status the authors demonstrated a lack of understanding of the dynamic social forces and human impulses at the heart of "the problem." Contrasting "white slavery" with chattel slavery in America, Lippmann pointed out that the Emancipation Proclamation broke a legal bond, but not a social bond: "The progress of negro emancipation is infinitely slower and it is not accomplished yet. Likewise no Statute can end 'white slavery.'"[17] Lippmann's skepticism did not rule out all action, however. Somewhere between indifference and moral enthusiasm he thought there was room for a political philosophy that illuminated theory and practice, such as he had found in Alfred E. Zimmern's remarkable analysis of citizenship in the Greek commonwealth. Lippmann believed that politics was "the foundation of national vigor through which civilizations mature." What he called for—and did not receive—was a new start for political thinking—not a concrete program, not a new dogma, not rote learning, but a new politics, a new creative interest in, and a new attitude toward, the realities of a difficult human activity. For Lippmann, "The great social adventure of America is no longer the conquest of the wilderness but the absorption of fifty different peoples" (p. 189).

» *The Final Synthesis*

CHAMBERLAIN

At the end of the nineteenth century the ideas current in a variety of arenas— denordicization, eugenics, race-caste-class conflict, folk psychology and crowd mind, and race history—were synthesized in the work of the Anglo-German Houston Stewart Chamberlain (1855–1927). Chamberlain, the son of British admiral William Charles Chamberlain, was educated at the lycée in Versailles, then with a German tutor. Following study in Geneva, he went to Dresden to study Wagnerian philosophy and music, eventually marrying a daughter of Richard Wagner and settling in Germany. In 1892 he published *Das Drama Richard Wagners* and later *The Life of Wagner.*

In his *Grundlagen des neunzehnten Jahrhunderts* first published in German in 1899, Chamberlain played upon all the diverse anxieties then afflicting Europe's industrial powers—militarism, anticlericalism, "pan-isms," extraparliamentary action, the degeneration of political life, the rise of technological and managerial society—in an effort to create an integrated theory of race.

Developing a science-based history of the origins of the nineteenth century, he also sought to reconcile with Social Darwinism all the ideas of genius, character, defilement, psychic heredity, and antisemitism that were current at the century's end. This text is by far the most comprehensive analysis of the "race is everything" hypothesis ever published and the closest thing to a "theory" we yet have or will ever achieve. It is a daunting intellectual work requiring a vast knowledge of Western history and science even to begin to grasp its meaning, and paradoxically it can be understood in an instant by a simpleton in possession of the elementary commonplaces of the National Curriculum. When it was first published it ran to eight editions and sold more than sixty thousand copies. First translated into English in 1912, it was introduced to an English audience by Lord Redesdale as detailing the triumph of the Teuton over the Jew and as a magnificent Kantian bulwark against religious dogma and scientific superstition.[18] It enjoyed enormous support in theological and scientific circles in Britain, the United States, and Germany, and it was not until the hideous excesses of the Nazi regime that the early intellectual adulation turned to execration, or worse still, convenient amnesia. In my view, there is no proper understanding of the currents of thought that drove the eugenics movement from 1904 to 1915 without a careful and painful working through of Chamberlain's version of history and science. To do that we have to confront two modern orthodoxies: the orthodoxy that increasingly interprets the Holocaust as just another example of persecution in a long series of similar happenings, and the orthodoxy that insists upon treating the works of such writers as Chamberlain, Grant, Osborn, and Stoddard as politically incorrect, best forgotten in attempts to deracialize history and deracinate science.

What Is Race?   In Chapter 4 of *Grundlagen* Chamberlain addressed the question, What is race? There is, said Chamberlain, "perhaps no question about which such absolute ignorance prevails among highly cultured, indeed learned, men, as the question of the essence and significance of the idea of 'race'" (p. 259). In all the explanations of the phenomenon he found disconnection and contradiction—as we have done—and from his voluminous reading sought to synthesize the several meanings into a single explanation that would satisfy all. His first attack was upon Rudolf Karl Virchow, who had concluded that there were no pure races, only mixtures of morphological types. These Chamberlain explained by pointing to Darwin's work on do-

mesticated plants and animals, which concluded that continual breeding between types modified and eventually destroyed the preeminent characteristics
of both. Chamberlain extended the examples of greyhounds, poodles, and
Newfoundland dogs to the physiognomy of Englishmen, Sephardim, and Ash-
kenasim, and especially the noses of Germans.

Chamberlain further developed his hypothesis by attacking the work of
Albert Reville, professor of comparative religion at the College de France, who
in *Jesus du Nazareth* (1897) had examined whether Christ was of Aryan descent.
Using the work of Heinrich Ewald (1803–75), Old Testament scholar and
orientalist at Göttingen, Heinrich Graetz, and Ernest Renan, Chamberlain
showed that historically Galilee was of mixed race, colonized by Greeks,
Phoenicians, and Assyrians. The term "Jew" was applicable only to those who
had succeeded in living separately and maintaining their marriage laws and
religious affiliation. Thus in religion and education Christ was a Jew, Chamberlain concluded, but in the narrower sense of race he was not: "The probability that Christ was no Jew, that He had not a drop of genuinely Jewish
blood in his veins, is so great that it is almost equivalent to a certainty" (p.
212).

And so race was not a matter of a temporary loss of common sense, as
argued by Virchow and the associationist psychologists—or simply a rush of
blood, such as we are witnessing as I write in Goražde and Rwanda—but a
fact of history confirmed by Darwinist principles and by the separation of
Christianity from Hebraism through a difference in breeding habits at a particular time and place.

The Determining Features of Race   In common with Niebuhr, Kemble,
Maine, Arnold, Seeley, Michelet, Taine, and Renan, Chamberlain regarded the
section of Aristotle's *Politics* on the natural origins of the state as the central
support for the contention that the races were unequal and that freedom
could be found only in a nation that was true to its nature. The Greco-Roman
distinctions between politics and barbarity, citizenship and *physis*, virtue and
vice, were simply the "surface superficialites" of life. As Nietzsche had argued,
the bond between peoples was not political life as conceived by classical political theory, but anthropology, nobility, and the artistic impulses of soul.

It is necessary to capture the significance of this important textual point,
not simply to confirm the thesis that I have pursued throughout this book
but to emphasize how this matter of interpretation continues to intrude upon

the modern intellectual treatment of the phenomenon of race. The basis for Chamberlain's argument was that the integrity of Western political life was sustained not by Aristotle's distinctions between political and barbarian states but by the distinctions between preeminent souls and commonplace souls, and between freeman and slave. Of predominant importance in this interpretation is the notion that constitutions, laws, and political authority—those entities that make politics possible in any given society—are not as significant as the instinct finding its highest expression in art and culture. This freedom of expression is neither the egoistic utilitarian variety of the English reformers (the head counters), nor the democratic equality of the Rousseauist and Marxist fire dogs, but Kant's daringly, genuinely Germanic definition of personality: "freedom and independence of the mechanism of all nature," "that which elevates man above himself (as part of the world of sense), attaches him to an order of things which only the understanding can conceive, and which has the whole world of sense subject to it" (pp. 549–50).

With an apt quote from Goethe—"Everything is simpler than we can think, and at the same time more complicated than we can comprehend"— Chamberlain used Theodor Mommsen and Ernst Curtius to explain the concept of the mixture of races and Darwin's "laws" on the obliteration of characters by perpetual crossing under controlled conditions to prove that races originated through specific combinations of geographical and historical conditions that "ennobled" the original material through inbreeding and artificial selection. This hypothesis was in direct opposition to Gobineau, who accepted that the world was peopled by Shem, Ham, and Japhet and coupled this fantasy with the idea that the originally "pure" races crossed with each other and with every crossing became less pure and less noble. Renan, too, had said that the fact of race loses significance every day. This theory was, said Chamberlain, a fundamental misunderstanding of the process of evolution: "One of the fatal errors of our time is that which impels us to give too great weight in our judgments to the so-called 'results' of science. Knowledge can certainly have an illuminating effect; but it is not always so, and especially for this reason that knowledge always stands upon tottering feet" (p. 267).

Chamberlain's work, therefore, was not only an assertion of character and personality but an outright rejection of the geographical and environmental conditions that the Comtian Buckle, and also Haeckel and Gumplowicz, had accepted as the *sine qua non* of race. In place of "milieu" Chamberlain introduced the psychic effects of "crossing," drawing his evidence from the West

Indies and the United States, as witnessed in Hesketh Prichard's (1876–1922) *Where Black Rules White* (1900) and in the works of Auguste-Henri Forel (1868–1931), psychiatrist and teacher of Carl Jung.

Race, Nation, and Civilization   In defining the nation, Chamberlain saw race as increasingly significant in its formation and composition: "Race formation, far from decreasing in our nations, must daily increase. . . . The sound and normal evolution of man is therefore not from race to racelessness but on the contrary from racelessness to ever clearer distinctness of race" (p. 296). Here Chamberlain quoted Disraeli: "Race is everything; there is no other truth. And every race must fall which carelessly suffers its blood to become mixed."

Chamberlain's national union "signifies common memory, common hope, common intellectual nourishment; it fixes firmly the existing bond of blood and impels us to make it ever closer" (p. 297). The national hero or genius personified the best in the race. Exemplars were "the lighters of the beacons of the imagination": men like Homer, Plato, Shakespeare, Copernicus, Goethe, Kant, Schlegel, the Grimms, the philologists who researched into the poetry and mythology of the Teutons, and Ranke, who recognized the fundamental opposition of nation to nation in history.

Chamberlain's understanding of race and nation depended much on culture and art. He held that the history of Christian and European civilization could not be attributed to climate, food, and soil, or to general aspects of nature subjected to statistical analysis. History was not Gobineau's series of linked events brought about by the interaction of ideas, sometimes moving and sometimes stagnating. It was certainly not Humboldt's conception of the humanizing of peoples in terms of their customs, laws, and institutions, with *Kultur* acting above civilization. No, the idea of Western civilization and its history could no longer be explained in terms of the old histories of Church and State, which simply justified the old Aristotelian political divisions, the old Augustinian ecclesiastical divisions, and Greco-Roman and Judaic political forms of rule.

The fact of the matter was that in the nineteenth century a new Nietzschean secular civilization had emerged and replaced the old. This new civilization was based on urban life, technical competence, Malthusian population growth, manufacturing industry, mathematical sciences, numeration, algebraic calculation, and dissection and evolution, all of which made the political ideas of the old history and its ossified skeletal institutions of Church and State defunct. It had also made immediately imperative the assertion of power from sources other than the Magna Carta and parliaments.

The New Civilization   Chamberlain saw the great turning point in "our history" as the awakening of the Teutonic spirit with the birth of Christ: "He won from the old human nature a new youth, and thus became the God of the young vigorous Indo-Europeans, and under the sign of the cross there slowly arose upon the ruins of the old world a new culture—a culture at which we have still to toil long and laboriously until some day in the distant future it may deserve the appellation 'Christ-like'" (p. 200). Barbarian and Christian histories achieved synchronization in the sixth century, and consolidation in the thirteenth century with the overthrow of the Greco-Roman and Catholic superstructure: "The awakening of the Teutonic peoples to the consciousness of the all-important vocation as the founders of a completely new civilisation and culture forms this turning point; the year 1200 can be designated the central moment of this awakening" (p. lxv). The barbarian inhabitants of North Europe emerged as the evolution makers.

Chamberlain's powerful idea of civilization, skillfully crafted from Darwinian, Marxian, Kantian, Comtian, and Spencerian sources, legitimized history as a struggle of ideas and the product of one definite "race" of men, one individual "type" under certain elemental conditions. It was a concept independent of all forms of government, all politics, all traditional distinctions between public and private, all classical notions of citizenship. It combined the visible technical, industrial, transport and communication forces with the invisible forces of the revolt of the mind against dogma contained in the contributions of the great Teutonic thinkers. Darwin, Herder, Goethe, and Kant had shaped civilization by compounding circles of abstract ideas into a single idea, word, or person and transient moments into movements.

But the new civilization consisted of more than ideas. It included elements of "man making himself" that Nietzsche and Treitschke had promoted—men rising above sensation and common sense through will to the highest artistic achievement. *Kultur* was the classical philosophy contained in the metaphysical and artistic works of Plato, Homer, and Aristotle in a holy alliance with science under the stimulus of an intensive intellectual and artistic drive toward freedom and self-determination. Central to this idea was the redundancy of Greco-Roman political forms and apparatus made possible by Mommsen's removal of the destruction of Carthage as a moral indictment of Rome and the reiteration of the Niebuhrian "other Rome" as the apotheosis of fatherland and moral, artistic, and intellectual superiority.

Interpreting the emergence of Western civilization as a singular racial event, Chamberlain agreed with Froude that the Reformation was a critical influence. Martin Luther, John Wycliffe, and Jan Hus were the progenitors of the movement that threw off the dead hand of Roman practices and principles and realized the spirit of the Germans in the woods. The Reformation enabled the German, Slavic, and Celtic forces to enter history, and at that "moment . . . we do not find three ethnical souls side by side, but one uniform soul" (p. 516).

The Alien Jew   This racial interpretation of the Reformation posed the Germanic "type" in opposition to its counterpart, the alien Jew. Chamberlain's treatment of the Jew went beyond the reflections of Matthew Arnold on Hebraism and Hellenism but did not follow the obscenely antisemitic path of Drumont. Chamberlain saw the Teutonic *Kultur* weakened and threatened by Hebraism because it had failed to capitalize upon the advances gained when during classical times Rome broke the stranglehold hitherto held by Semitic Asia and reoriented the axis of power to the West. For Chamberlain the Jew was not inferior; he was superior over all other Semitic peoples, racially pure and unified: "Of the Semites only the Jews, as we see, have positively furthered our culture and also shared, as far as their extremely assimilative nature permitted them, in the legacy of antiquity" (p. 256). But the entry of the Jew was the counterpart of the entry of the German. Chamberlain cemented the religious antipathy between Jew and Gentile, Judaic and Christian faith as essentially a matter of racial antipathy. The synoecism of Ezra, which I earlier argued was not a distinction of race but of faith, now came to be seen as a major historical racial event. "Judaism made this law of nature sacred" (p. 255), claimed Chamberlain.

To sustain this racial argument, Chamberlain took Niebuhr's view of the past as a conflict between Etruscan and Latin, as a fight between the races derived from topographical, chorographical, and climatic forces, and added two ingredients from the works of Herder and Renan. In "Bekehrung der Juden," section 7 of his cultural history *Untersuchungen des vergangenen Jahrhunderts zur Beförderung eines geistigen Reiches*, Herder had argued that the Jewish people were Asiatic people alien to Europe and irrevocably bound to the Covenant:

> Herder may be right in his assertion that the Jew is always alien to us, and consequently we to him, and no one will deny that this is to the detriment of our work and culture; yet I think that we are inclined to underestimate our own powers in this respect and, on the other hand, to exaggerate the importance of the Jewish influence. Hand in hand with this goes the perfectly ridiculous and revolting tendency to make the Jew the general scapegoat for all the vices of our time. In reality "the Jewish peril" lies much deeper; the Jew is not responsible for it; we have given rise to it ourselves and must overcome it ourselves. (p. xxviii)

Renan, in his philological history, *Histoire générale et systeme comparé des langues sémitiques* (1863), had been one of the first to claim that the European Jews were members of a Semitic race that was inferior to the Indo-European race, and he argued that a Christianity resting upon the two pillars of Judaism (historical and chronological faith) and Indo-Europeanism (symbolic and metaphysical) could have no future unless it purged itself of Judaic influences. Chamberlain did not subscribe to Renan's notion that Christ was the evolving perfecter of Judaism. The Jewish religion had been arrested in its development; but the Aryan, originally thoughtless, ambitious, and drunken, had asked the question, Whence came I? Then the Aryan had heard mysterious voices and had discovered in himself "immeasurable destinies." In the birth of that faith he had seen the heroes of his race, the supermen, and he willed himself to be like them. Thus the Aryan became the negation of the laws of Judaism.

Chamberlain synthesized these historical speculations with the Darwinian laws of material, inbreeding, natural selection, mixture of blood, and ennoblement to show that the conflict between Teutonic and Semitic was racial and historical. It followed that the antisemitic explanations of people like Drumont were crude and mistaken. What was much more important from Chamberlain's standpoint was that in the eighteenth century everyone knew what a Jew was from the evidence of the Bible. Now the biblical currency had been spent, and the new currency was race not religion: "Race is not an original phenomenon, it is produced; physiologically by characteristic mixture of blood, followed by in-breeding psychically by the influence which long lasting historical and geographical conditions exercise upon that special, specific, physiological foundation" (p. 354).

The threat posed by the Jews, therefore, was racial and was in the blood. It arose by physical presence and physical intermarriage because, as Herder and Goethe, Mommsen and Treitschke, had stated, the Jews comprised a state within a state. But they were more. Though born in the heart of Germany speaking a German tongue, they were not, and would never be, Germanic. Germanicism was in the blood, and this blood made possible the sentiments and capacities of the German spirit. Physiognomy and soul were in the very structure of bones, skin, color, muscular systems, and skull shape. "There is perhaps not a single anatomical fact upon which race has not impressed its special distinguishing stamp" (p. 518), Chamberlain asserted. The Germans—the Celts, Teutons, and Slavs—were the inheritors of the new civilization heralded by the Reformation and personified in the birth of Christ and the Resurrection. Like an electric power Christ had transformed man: "No political revolution can compare with it" (p. 197). Thus the presence of the Jew—the very antithesis of the German—was not only an ever-present threat to this new civilization of the Germanic spirit but, like the traditions represented by the Basque Ignatius Loyola, the bearer of the backward-looking culture, and all who would maintain ancient political arrangements, stood directly in the way of the Germanic impulse to form a co-terminous and co-extensive nation.

GRANT

In exposing the horrors of the Nazi regime, historians and scientists have often neglected the influences of prominent public figures who directly and indirectly contributed to the doctrine of Aryan superiority during its formative years and afterwards denied any connection with it. Before I conclude this section I want to add just a little to Chamberlain's synthesis as it worked itself out in the writings of the early twentieth century.

While Acton, Bryce, and Lippmann were uneasy about the derogation of politics in intellectual circles in Britain and the United States before the Great War, the work of Madison Grant (1865–1937) can be used to illustrate the force of the argument put forward by those who were unashamedly mixing natural and political arguments. Grant was chairman of the New York Zoological Society and trustee of the American Museum of Natural History and the National Geographical Society. Inside the copy of Grant's *The Passing of the Great Race* (1916) in the British Library is the original calling card of Dr. Rupert Blue, surgeon general of the United States Public Health Service, and a letter from him to Henry Wellcome dated March 13, 1918, recalling conversations about the book at Pinehurst, North Carolina, and endorsing it as "interesting reading." The preface to the book is by Henry Fairfield Osborn, who was at the time president of the American Museum of Natural History, chairman of the New York Zoological Society, professor of biology and zoology at Columbia University, and a major influence on museum display in the United States and Britain.

Reflecting on the writing of European history, Osborn affirmed that race had played a far greater part than either language or nationality: "Race implies heredity, and heredity implies all the moral, social and intellectual characteristics and traits which are the springs of politics and government."[19] Osborn believed he had hit upon an important distinction that marked Grant's work—a distinction that is confirmed by a careful reading of it. In recognizing the thrust of heredity as the superior force in history, Grant had come across something more stable than environment, education, and politics. He had put together a picture of a great movement that could be traced back to biometry and germ plasm, to Galton and Weismann, and could be demonstrated scientifically to be a reaction against the syntheses of Hippolyte Taine and Herbert Spencer, who had mistakenly applied the scientific method to the study of literature and language.

According to Osborn, the correct scientific approach to the problem of the past was to treat the history of man wholly as "the heredity history of Europe," a study of peoples influenced by the impulses, tendencies, and predispositions of heredity stretching back over millennia to primitive tribal beginnings. The influence of environment, education, politics, and government was merely immediate, apparent, and temporary, "while heredity has a deep, subtle, and permanent influence on the actions of men" (p. vii).

Osborn's introduction to Grant's book offers an important insight into the way in which distinguished scientists were thinking about race in 1916. The eugenics movement was popular and well regarded in the United States, Britain, and Germany at that time, and Osborn's views were not unusual. He sought to produce a grand theory that would mobilize the modern eugenics movement and multiply the best moral, intellectual, spiritual, and physical forces in support of scientific endeavor, consolidating the principles and premises developed since the publication of Darwin's *Origin.*

In my view it is wrong to regard these writings as temporary aberrations mitigated by a later change of mind. The writings themselves reveal a powerful belief in the ability of modern science and technology to correct the errors of a misguided past. They also reveal a complete ignorance and derogation of the value of political groupings, literature, and language of peoples, which were seen as no more than the outward marks of the onward march of heredity in the world. As Grant himself said: "The great lesson of the science of race is the immutability of somatological or bodily characters, with which is closely associated the immutability of psychical predispositions and impulses" (p. xv).

Among the noteworthy elements of Grant's thinking was the denigration of the principles of self-determination because they encouraged standardization of "type" and a diminution in the influence of genius: "Vox populi, so far from being Vox Dei, thus becomes an unending wail for rights, and never a chant of duty" (p. 8). Other noteworthy elements were his dismissal of philology and language as being nothing more than myth and invention and the categorical denunciation of the Adamic account of inheritance and Hebrew chronology on scientific grounds. But much more important than these intellectual pillars constructed upon Ripley's tripartite division of racial types and Deniker's racial mapping of Europe was Grant's complete rejection of education and environment as capable of changing the lot or disposition of "aberrant types," such as the American Indian and the Negro, or of resisting the effects of "swamping" from the West Indies, South America, and Southern, non-Nordic Europe. The only solutions to these problems were apolitical and scientific—the rigorous application of the South African model of complete segregation of Bantu and white, or sterilization, selective breeding, extension of the laws against miscegenation, and social engineering: "The only possible solution is to establish large colonies for the negroes and to allow them only as labourers, and not as settlers. There must be ultimately a black South Africa and a white South Africa from the Cape to the cataracts of the Nile" (p. 72).

Grant formulated his idea of state and nation not on classical political theory but wholly in terms of a race supported by a ruling group of savants and luminaries who were in full possession of scientific facts, sufficient for them to make policy decisions, based on the best knowledge available about the mental and physical state of the perverts, bastards, cripples, and feeble-minded individuals living in the new intellectual and industrial state. Just as Marx had postulated the inevitability of the onward march of the proletariat, so Grant put forward the onward march of great physical and biological natural families to which we are all supposed to belong. Politics was replaced by the administration of people who were, in truth, physical and psychical racial things.

STODDARD

Just as Grant wished to segregate the races, so his compatriot, Theodore Lothrop Stoddard (1883–1950), in his equally dangerous but highly popular *Revolt against Civilization* (1922) argued the rigorous segregation into "farm colonies" of all clearly defective individuals alive in the United States. Regarding the evolutionary process as quantitative and qualitative, he held that "natural equality" was a delusion. In its place he proposed the "iron law of inequality" derived from Weismann's work on the germ plasm and Bertillon's work on measurement.

Like Grant, Stoddard believed that civilization was fundamentally conditioned by race. He held that the Asians, American Indians, and African Negroes belonged to barbarian stocks and that a superior human stock cultivated from the application of the highest principles of biological knowledge was necessary for the maintenance of society. Stoddard was in no doubt that the glory of Greeks, and of Plato and Aristotle, was that they had been the first to think of race betterment—"in other words, the 'Eugenics' theory of today."[20]

For Stoddard, the germ plasm theory of Weismann had revealed that racial impoverishment was the plague of civilization—a disease, a multiplication of inferiority—that could be observed in the denordicization processes at work as Poles, Russian Jews, South Italians, and French Canadians proliferated. Like Chamberlain, Grant, Osborn, and Davenport, Stoddard saw the solution to the problem of social order not by means of a civic disposition created by way of existing political instruments and articles of governance but through the application of science. Through eugenics, or racial engineering, the insanity, epilepsy, deafness, blindness, and hereditary diseases that were contaminating civilization and tainting it with degeneracy could be eliminated.

GUNTHER

Just how far race thinking had come since 1910, and how thoroughly assumptions about the continuity of physical and psychic traits in a racially determined realm had captured the intellectual imagination, can be seen in Sir Arthur Keith's *Nationality and Race*. First delivered as the Robert Boyle Lectures at Oxford in November of that year, the study examined aspects of denordicization that had attracted a wide following. After the Great War there was in fact a vast outpouring of anthropological, zoological, biological, psychological, and sociological writing. Hans Gunther's extremely popular book on race science (*Rassenkunde*)—*Rassenkunde des deutschen Volkes* (1922)—is usually held to be the major influence on Hitler's eugenic policies, but it is frequently forgotten that he was moving in good company and that his views were not so far removed from others who have escaped the obloquy that was rightly heaped upon him when the horrors of the death camps became known in the 1940s. Gunther (1891–1968) was a professor at Jena and deputy editor of *Zeitschrift für Rassenkunde*. Acknowledging the influence of Galton and Pearson, who had recognized the denordicization of England, he wrote on the bodily characteristics of Nordic, Mediterranean, Alpine, Baltic, Asian, and Oriental peoples and displayed their cephalic measurements in a rogues' gallery of plates. Alpines were portrayed as sneaks, perverts, and petty criminals. Nordics were noble but had been undermined biologically by the democracy of the French Revolution. Gunther elaborated the much-quoted example of the "Juke stock" in the United States. He used this example to advocate a policy of sterilization for such people who perpetuated mental disease and criminality through propagation, quoting the Swedish labor paper *Arbetet:* "It is a false humanity which thinks of the individual at the cost of the race."[21]

WELLS

The "facts" of race were reflected not only in the works of the social scientists. They permeated fiction as well. In England, for example, the immensely popular historian and writer of science fiction H. G. Wells (1866–1946), in "The Lord of the Dynamos" (1927), cast the relationship between two characters in race-class terms. Azumi-zi, the stoker, was portrayed as subhuman: "He was, perhaps, more negroid than anything else. . . . His head too, was broad behind, and low and narrow at the forehead, as if his brain had been twisted round in the reverse way to a European's. He was short of stature, and still shorter of English."[22]

Here was a description bearing little resemblance to the ambivalence of, for example, Rudyard Kipling (1865–1936) in *Kim* (1901) and the *Just So Stories* (1902) or to the demoralizing yet humanizing encounter in Joseph Conrad's (1857–1924) *Nigger of the Narcissus* (1897) between European crew members and native peoples.[23]

APPLIED EUGENICS

The Juke stock example used by Gunther was but one of a wide variety of similar scientific case studies being popularized at the time. Paul Popenoe, editor of the *Journal of Heredity,* the organ of the American Genetic Association, and Roswell Hill Johnson (b. 1877–?), professor at Pittsburgh, had written in *Popular Science Monthly* on the control of human evolution, and in 1920 they coauthored a seminal text on *Applied Eugenics,* published by Macmillan. Their ideas owed much to the work of Galton, Karl Pearson, and Weismann and to the support and enthusiasm for eugenics shown by Alexander Graham Bell in his association with Davenport and Laughlin at the Eugenics Record Office at Cold Spring Harbor. Other support came from the Harriman family, the Carnegie Institution, and the Young Men's Christian Association (YMCA).

The text had the clear aim of making legal, social, and economic adjustments to ensure that a larger proportion of superior racial persons had children and that the inferior had none. Its stated objective was to respond positively to the decimation of population brought about by World War I, which was seen as a calamity falling upon the white race and the potential onset of racial decline. Popenoe and Johnson addressed the problem of the blind, deaf, insane, feebleminded, poor, criminal, and the epileptic in much the same way as the Eugenics Record Office *Bulletin* had done before the war, and displayed statistical analyses of the Jukes, the Kallikaks, Zeroes, Dacks, Ishmaels, Sixties, Hickories, Hill Folk, and Piney Folk as evidence of the workings of deviance and degeneracy in the United States. They called for a popular involvement in a national genealogical audit in line with the biometric findings of the Eugenics Record Office and the Galton Laboratory and the resolutions of the German Society for Race Hygiene and its programs. They advocated sterilization, immigration restriction, tax reform, and population control to regulate the eugenically inferior Negroes and Southern and Eastern Europeans, and to encourage Nordic colonization and repopulation.

At the same time Samuel J. Holmes (b. 1868–?), professor of zoology at the University of California, delivered a series of lectures on the forces modifying the inherited qualities of civilized mankind that were published as *The Trend of the Race* (1921), taking as his starting point the work of Lapouge on the military, political, and religious selection processes. As we have seen, Lapouge believed that as civilization advanced so the evil effects of the various forms of social selection became more intense and had a deleterious influence on race. Holmes claimed that there would be similar debilitating effects on modern civilization from mis-mating. He advocated a reexamination of the egalitarian ideas of Thomas Paine and Rousseau in the light of the recent and abundant evidence of inherited mental, physical, and social ability.

These ideas were not simply theoretical. In *Carrie Buck v. Bell* (1926–27), the U.S. Supreme Court upheld the constitutionality of Virginia's sterilization laws. About half the American states had laws permitting prisons and other institutions to sterilize inmates, and between 1905 and 1972 some seventy thousand American citizens were ruled eligible for sterilization on grounds of feeblemindedness, social inadequacy, and retardation.

HITLER

Great texts have been written about the sources, real or imagined, of Adolf Hitler's *Mein Kampf*, written in prison and published in 1924.[24] Hitler (1889–1945) himself claimed that he was greatly influenced during a period of intensive study from 1909 to 1910 by a diverse range of writers and thinkers to whom he makes reference, including Woodrow Wilson, Friedrich von Schiller, Johann Wolfgang von Goethe, Arthur Schopenhauer, Frederick the Great, William Shakespeare, Houston Stewart Chamberlain, Wilhelm Frick, Georg von Schönerer, Karl Lueger, Karl von Clausewitz, and Otto von Bismarck. Having read the texts of the period, one cannot fail to be struck by the prominence given to a version of cultural history virtually unknown to the ordinary English reader. The concepts Hitler used were complex, and their popular appeal lay with the way in which he manipulated and simplified his material to fit into a comprehensive, hypnotic Le Bon-like whole.

The story Hitler constructed linked biological mixing and crossing to sin, defilement, regression, and sickness. His primary idea was that of "inner experience" linked emotionally, not logically, to a single race. The influence of milieu and soil was minimized; it was the influence of an illuminating Promethean inner nature that was important: "All great cultures of the past perished only because the originally creative race died out from blood poisoning" (p. 262).

For Hitler, this inner experience was the basis of Aryan superiority. In the Aryan, will, dedicated to work as a creative effort, produced a state of mind of purest idealism realized in fulfillment of duty (*Pflichterfüllung*). This dedication was not a flight of fancy, such as pacifism, but an idealism linked to the reality of race.

Culture, State, and Race   Hitler's history had the cultural sweep of Oswald
Spengler (1880–1936), who in *Der Untergang des Abendlandes* (1917–20), and the
pamphlet *Preussentum und Sozialismus* (1922) portrayed the history of all peoples
who have created civilizations as obeying inevitable and constant laws. For
Spengler, the principal cause of the decline of a culture was the extinction or
degeneration of the old nobility. Walter Rathenau (1867–1922), the German
Jewish industrialist and statesman who was assassinated by antisemitic fanat-
ics, had influenced Spengler's thought in portraying the loss of ideals and
"soul" that accompanied industrialization and bureaucratization.

Hitler made a concerted attack on the historical science of political history, which he regarded as parasitic. Political thinking was dilettante, politicians and parliaments were reprehensible, and the old politics of Vienna and
the Austro-Hungarian Empire, in which many nations co-existed within a
state, was a tragic failure. Germanic Aryan history was culture-forming, while
Oriental history was culture-bearing. What separated the culture-formers
from the culture-bearers (in Schiller, the Aryan from the Moor) was a drop
in the racial level caused by a change in the blood.

It has been an important part of my thesis that antiquity gave to Western
civilization an idea of politics and a concept of liberty under the law that were,
in the nineteenth century, increasingly held up to ridicule. Hitler's political
ideas are the antithesis of all that is contained in the Aristotelian, Ciceronian,
and Machiavellian state. His is the apotheosis of the co-terminous and co-
extensive apolitical state bereft of all politics. He replaced the *res-publica* with
Volksgenosse, politics with race. The idea of *Volksgenosse* had to do with the idea
of *Volksgemeinschaft,* society consisting of all the members of the same *Volk*
community as a working association in the service of the *Volk* as an organic
whole. For Hitler the state and politics were not about the reconciliation of
the particular with the general, the private with the public, the natural with
the political, the vicious with the virtuous, as in the Greco-Roman concept
we have pursued throughout this text. Hitler's state was bonded by a culture
of purity of blood and posited on the deepest longing of the triumph of the
German spirit. The words he used to describe the dying cultures were medical, evoking public health concerns: sclerosis, putrefaction, abscess, virus, ba-
cillus, parasite, syphilis, sanitation, and cleansing. The causes of the collapse
of cultures are "profanation of blood": "Blood, sin and desecration of the race
are the original sin in this world and the end of a humanity which surrendered
to it"; "All who are not of good race in this world are chaff" (pp. 226, 269).

The Jew   For Hitler, the Jew was a culture-bearer like the Japanese—bereft of ideas, entirely subject to self-preservation, in possession of no genuine art, architecture, or music. He was not a nomad but a cultural parasite preying on state and nation and parading under the guise of membership of a religious community. In references drawn from Goethe and Schopenhauer, Hitler disposed of the idea that a Jew living in France, England, Germany, or Italy could be a national by language or by exemption of faith. The Jews were a racial people committed to a doctrine of keeping the blood pure, and they were alien to Christianity, to Jesus, and to the Almighty Creator. For proof, Hitler pointed to the *Protocols of the Wise Men of Zion.*

In his description of the history of the Jews, Hitler observed that until the time of Frederick the Great and Goethe, who opposed the marriage between Christian and Jew, the antipathy to the Jews had been on grounds of religion and court privilege. Until that time they were only a foreign people with a different religion. But, with the rise of the idea that to be a German did not mean speaking the German language, the idea also emerged that once a Jew, always a Jew. From the court Jew there developed the idea of "a people's Jew," an ordinary man in the street, which Hitler claimed had institutionalized itself for the purposes of self-preservation in the secret society of Freemasonry and the press, thus creating a state within a state.

Hitler claimed to have gained much of his understanding of the Jew from Karl Lueger (1844–1910), the antisemitic mayor of Vienna, and from the antisemitic press, particularly *Deutsches Volksblatt*. He avidly read *Arbeiter Zeitung,* the central organ of the old Austrian Social Democratic Party, and from that source he claimed that he gained an understanding of the workings of the lying press and of Marxism as a Judaic doctrine. Wherever he went he saw Jews, and every encounter confirmed for him Chamberlain's proposition that intuition is superior to logic. Everywhere he saw prostitution, rape, defilement of blood, and bastardization as evidence of the lowering of the racial level by the Jew.

The Race-Class System and National Resurrection   Drawing heavily upon Karl Marx's analysis of organization of the means of production and on Friedrich List's analysis of national economy, Hitler saw the factory worker as being proletarianized and Judaized by the conversion of the Aryan inner experience through economic and national change. Here he used the lament that the monuments, state buildings, works of art, poetry, and mores of the "other

Rome" had been befouled by modernity (p. 236). The remedy was the elevation of the administrative apparatus of the army and the civil service to bring about a national resurrection. Existing class cleavages were fundamentally related to race, and the lower classes needed to be integrated and uplifted within the nation.

The mechanism for this resurrection was not to be found in political arrangements but in extraparliamentary, apolitical, and technical means—in social engineering.[25] Hitler called for a new spiritual and religious zeal arising out of personality—"One man must step forward" (p. 346)—harnessed to the struggle and faith of a fanatical Christianity. He clearly understood crowd psychology and the manipulation of the masses. Here he used the term *Verhaltungszustand* (a mutual relation of struggle), a term seldom, if ever, used before (p. 160).

» *Conclusion: The Final Solution*

The program of the National Socialist Party of February 25, 1920, established the principle in Article IV that a "citizen" was a member of the German race (*Volksgenosse*). A citizen was a person of German blood and descent without any reference to religious faith, profession, historical status, interest, opinion, or associational membership; thus no Jew could be a citizen, and the article explicitly said so. "No Jew can be a member of the German race": the whole jurisprudence of the National Socialist state, painstakingly constructed from the intellectual arguments about the nature of the natural state and the political state developed since the early nineteenth century, hung upon that principle. Moreover, Article VI of the program ensured the operation of the principle: "Every public function, *of whatever nature it may be*—whether in the Reich, in the States, or in the municipalities—should be confined exclusively to German citizens."[26] These principles were based on the idea that there was a difference in the respective natures of the Jewish and German races, not merely, as Chamberlain had argued, a difference in their values. The principles were justified in the literature by reference to United States and Australian immigration legislation, which divided immigrants into "desirable" and "undesirable."[27]

In his speech at the Reichstag on March 23, 1933, introducing the Enabling Law of the Government of National Recovery, Hitler rejected the idea of monarchical restoration and set out his aim to establish a true national community distributed in functional economic, cultural, social, and political departments of state and nation under a unity of leadership. The clear objective was to suppress communism and to eliminate unemployment and all opposition. These steps were taken in the name of preserving ethnic personality with all its inherent energies and values as the eternal foundation of "our life." "Blood and race will become the source of artistic intuition," claimed Hitler, and education, theater, press, radio, and literature will be the means by which "our" social organisms contribute to the moral cleansing and the maintenance of eternal values.[28]

Two weeks later the Law for the Reconstruction of the Body of Public Functionaries dismissed all communists and Jews, all the inefficient and the untrained, and the following year the Law for the Reconstruction of the Reich abolished the political state altogether and in its place established a National Socialist *Weltanschauung* of one nation, one Reich, one Führer.

The laws implementing moral cleansing were drawn up by the gentle Dr. Wilhelm Frick, described in the propaganda of the time as in the habit of giving musical evenings at his home where one could hear the best chamber music that contemporary German artists could produce. He was applauded for his integrity and upright conduct as upholding the highest traditions of the German public service.

On July 14, 1935, Frick's Law for the Preservation from Hereditarily Diseased Posterity set the sterilization program in train. It stated that all people, institutionalized or not, who suffered from feeblemindedness, epilepsy, blindness, drug or alcohol problems, or physical deformity interfering with locomotion, and all who were physiognomically offensive, were to be sterilized. Between 1934 and 1937 some 225,000 people in Germany were sterilized in what was regarded as a courageous act in the cause of public health by many in the United Kingdom and the United States. When Frick was criticized by the International Congress on Population, he simply referred to the work of Francis Galton and the resolution of the 1934 International Conference on Eugenics in Zurich, which stated:

> Despite the diversities between their political and ideological points of view they are united in the firm conviction that the study of the principles of racial hygiene are of importance—nay indispensable to all civilised countries. The Congress recommends all Governments throughout the world to study the problem of

biological heredity, population and racial hygiene, thus following the example already set by certain countries in Europe and America and to apply for the benefit of their respective nations the results yielded by such study.[29]

The German Ministry of the Interior and the Ministry of Education and Science described a race "as a human group distinguished from other groups by physical, moral and intellectual characteristics sui generis resulting from consanguinous relations between its members."[30] The nearness of the physical relationship between different races appeared more clearly in the proportion in which their respective characteristics harmonized with each other. Therefore, the various races living in Europe possessed certain physical and intellectual characteristics. But race had a purely biological base, while nation had a historical base. A nation was a group unified by ties of blood, common destiny, and common ties of migration, language, and tradition. It followed, therefore, that nobody could be considered to belong to a national community if he or she belonged to a race with no consanguinous relations, cultural or otherwise.

There is a strong belief in this theory that nation once had a tribal consanguinous base and that the fundamental problem of modern times is that race and nation are no longer co-terminous. This argument was certainly in concert with what was being argued in British and American anthropological circles after World War I. It rested on the assumption that the German nation was Nordic and Germanic and a member of the Indo-European family known as Aryans, which included the Roman, Greek, Slav, and Celtic peoples. The theory sought to secure the homogeneity of hereditary qualities inherent in that race by biological transmission. It opposed hybridization and mixture of blood, from which different consequences ensued, including physical and moral disharmony. Essential to this theory was the maintenance of racial purity as a "primordial duty."

On September 15, 1935, the Law for the Protection of the German Race and Honor was introduced at the Annual Congress of the National Socialist Party at Nuremburg. It was to regulate a citizenship conditioned by race. Following a decree circulated by Bernhard Rust, minister of education and science, student of literature, former headmaster, vocational educator, described as a man in touch with the people, special schools were opened for Jews. No Jewish family was allowed to employ an Aryan servant under the age of forty-five. Marriage and sexual intercourse with Jews were prohibited to

Aryans. On October 18, 1935, the policy of racial hygiene was linked to sanitary organization with the Law Relating to Matrimonial Hygiene, which prohibited the marriage between disabled and degenerate persons. On December 13, 1935, medicine was declared a state function, and the medical profession was placed in the service of race hygiene. Race was all!

Reactions, Retractions, and New Orthodoxies, 1920 to the Present

At first there was no outright condemnation of the "race is everything" hypothesis. Sir Ernest Barker in *National Character and the Factors in its Formation* (1927), based on a course of lectures on citizenship given at Glasgow in 1925–26, reflected not unkindly on the contributions of Deniker and Grant. Despite some slight apprehension about the glorification of the Nordic race, he largely accepted the intellectual legitimacy of nineteenth-century Anglo-Saxon theory and John Stuart Mill's argument that the state and the nation must be co-extensive.

> The history of the century since 1915, and of the generation since 1914, will teach us that in some form a nation must be a State, and a State a nation. ... A democratic State which is multi-national will fall asunder into as many democracies as there are nationalities, dissolved by the very fact of will which is the basis of its life—unless, indeed, as we have somehow managed in our island, such a State can be both multi-national and a single nation, and can teach its citizens at one and the same time to glory both in the name of Scotsman or Welshman or Englishman and in the name of Britons.[1]

Barker saw the multinational state as an unusual phenomenon, unlikely to survive the democratic pressures within it that tended toward dissolution. Lord Acton, however, thought that no benefit would accrue to "inferior races" within a state where state and nation were thus unified. On the contrary, for Acton the only hope for true citizenship in a civilized community was logically and historically vested in a theory of nationality that was political in character. Acton shared with Hilaire Belloc (1870–1953) the Catholic view that the civilization of Europe, which predated the industrial civilization of the eighteenth and nineteenth centuries, arose historically through the Church's gathering up the political traditions of the Greco-Roman world and giving them a unity and philosophy—a view also endorsed by W. E. H. Lecky in his *History of European Morals from Augustus to Charlemagne* (1869). Belloc, whose *Crisis of Our Civilization* (1937) identified Christendom as "the capital event in the history of the world," thought that tradition had been threatened by a fundamental change in the nineteenth century from political thinking to sociobiological and economic thinking. Economic change now took precedence in human affairs and in the machinery of government, but, Belloc warned, "The conception is false; political change invariably comes prior to economic change."[2]

Barker was unable to accept these antique views as relevant to the spirit of the collective national state of the interwar years. Instead he openly favored Mill's co-terminous theory, and Renan's more dynamic verdict that the nation was not a physical "fact of blood" but the mental fact of tradition. Even after the nightmare of the Holocaust, Barker was still able to write in a footnote to the fourth edition of *National Character*, published in 1948, that the facts of race did not require amendment. Although Nazi theory and practice had come and gone, "the facts of race remain what they were" (p. 12).

» *The Counterhypotheses*

CHESTERTON

But at the beginning of the 1920s there were a few who began to question the biology of race contained in the eugenics of Galton, Pearson, Laughlin, and Davenport, and the psychology of the innovative social psychologists. In *Eugenics and Other Evils* (1922) G. K. Chesterton mounted an attack upon the moral basis and social application of eugenics, principally upon the works of Wells and Pearson. Chesterton saw eugenics as a delusion, a denial of the reality of human experience, a lunacy outside the parameters of public law: "The madman is not the man who defies the world: he is the man who denies it."[3] He found the eugenist state more sinister than the socialist state, more menacing than Belloc's servile state, and a complete deviation from the antique feudal state upon which the civil liberties of the English and all of Western civilization had historically rested. What England had forgotten (and

Lippmann had remembered!) was that judgments about human beings could be made only by other fallible human beings. Experts were no more qualified in that regard than tramps, laborers, and eccentric rustics. Chesterton was actually happier to lock up the strong-minded than the feebleminded.

Chesterton was prepared to grant that Karl Pearson knew a vast amount and lived in a forest of facts concerning kinship and inheritance, but the problem was that he had not searched the forest or recognized its frontiers. H. G. Wells was "a harsh and horrible Eugenist in great goblin spectacles, who wants to put us all into metallic microscopes and dissect us with metallic tools," but he deserved a medal for being the eugenist who destroyed eugenics, according to Chesterton: "Marry two handsome people whose noses tend to the aquiline, and their baby (for all you know) may be a goblin with a nose like an enormous parrot. Indeed, I actually know a case of this kind" (p. 7). The true facts of heredity were that it existed but that it was subtle, comprised of millions of elements, and it could not be unmade into those elements.

Although totally opposed to Chesterton's idea of politics and to his Catholic apologia after his conversion in 1922, rationalist writers like J. B. S. Haldane (1860–1936), Julian Huxley (1887–1957, grandson of the agnostic T. H. Huxley), Lancelot Hogben (1895–1975), and Herbert Jennings (1868–1947) in the United States also began to express doubt about heredity as promoted by Chamberlain, Grant, and Hitler. Their biological and anthropological perspective focused on a new genetic approach to race that sought to distinguish the rational boundaries of science from the lunatic.

BOAS

In America the German-born anthropologist Franz Boas (1858–1942), in *Anthropology and Modern Life* (1928) and again in *History and Science in Anthropology* (1936), raised very real doubts about race hygiene and mass psychology, stating baldly that "the inference that various populations are composed of individuals belonging to various races is . . . objectively unproved."[4] His pupil and colleague Otto Kleineberg had begun to examine more closely McDougall's hypothesis of fixed structure of mind, demonstrating that his tests were culture laden, and methodologically flawed. Here was a cautious correction of the scientific misdirections of Pearson, Galton, and the Eugenics Record Office. "Eugenics is not a panacea that will cure all ills," Boas warned. "It is rather a dangerous sword that may turn its edge against those who rely on its strength" (p. 119).

At the same time, Boas conceded that there may be a proper field for eugenics in the suppression of those defective classes whose deficiencies can be proved by rigid methods to be due to hereditary causes and in the prevention of those unions that will unavoidably lead to the birth of disease-stricken progeny. For Boas the problem of civilization and race and the dispute about the efficacy of eugenics and the structure of mind could be resolved rationally within the bounds of the scientific community, with better evidence. Pearson, Galton, Spencer, and the *Archiv für Rassen* were only overenthusiastic in the presentation of their case. Boas's single instance of outright condemnation was reserved for Theophile Simar, who in extending the study of race and ethnicity beyond the boundaries of scientific inquiry into a history of philosophy and science had, in Boas's view, completely misunderstood the meaning of racial and national traits.

It is also interesting that in the United States, during the whole of this period of Depression and the New Deal, with few exceptions, the social sciences held the race issue at arm's length. Academics sought to explain and understand race in the scientific language of a detached, value-free economic and social theory drawn mainly from the deep wells of a racialized history of cultural, social, and physical anthropology rather than from the fast-running waters of political reality, which Lippmann had so clearly discerned in 1913.

HUXLEY AND HADDON

It was not until 1936, in the shadow of the sterilization acts in Germany and the United States and under the menace of Hitler's apolitical regime, that Julian Huxley and A. C. Haddon, in *We Europeans,* exposed the idea of race as unscientific. In this important text they steered the discussion away from historical inexactitude to demonstrate the fallacies of hereditarism by means of the new science of genetics. "So far as the interpretation of the inter-relationships of the groups of modern man are concerned the reader should realise that the current conclusions of anthropology are tentative to a far greater degree than are the generally accepted conclusions of most biological sciences. It is just where knowledge is least sure that feeling always runs highest!"[5]

Huxley and Haddon did not, however, entirely neglect the historical aspects of race. In their overview of history from Aristotle to Darwin they produced a catalogue of instances in which scientific discovery moved inexorably through an inventory of more correct "facts" discerned by an improving and more rational methodology. In this analysis race appeared as an invented pseudoscientific term with no definable meaning but nonetheless having a widespread currency in its subjective, impressionistic, variable usages. For Huxley and Haddon anthropology in its modern setting had begun in 1860 and more recently been absorbed into the study of sociology. Like Boas, they expressed disquiet about the current interpretations of descent and inheritance that had come out of these popular evolutionary interpretations of the new civilization and were now being treated as though they were "facts": "With a species in which intercrossing of divergent types is so prevalent as our own, no simple system of classification can ever be devised to represent the diversity of the situation" (pp. 266–67).

Huxley and Haddon's conclusion, at the very apogee of Hitler's race-science policy, was that "race," as a concept, should be avoided and that "the term race as applied to human groups should be dropped from the vocabulary of science" (pp. 107–8). They argued that it was fallacious to believe that race could be a collection of people descended from a single couple, for ancestry converged and diverged, and family trees were social, not genetic, documents. It was also fallacious to believe that language was a criterion for race. No Celtic race, no Aryan race, could be adduced from the fact that people today speak these languages, and the same criteria applied to art, institutions, gestures, habits, traditions, dress, and nations: "None of these can serve as any criterion of racial affinity between peoples" (p. 271). In these brief sentences the historical, philological, and scientific explanations that had kept Europe in turmoil for a century were cast to one side, and an entirely new debate about the genetic basis of race opened up.

The problem then arose of reconciling the absence of race and ethnicity in science with the obvious manifestations of it in national and international affairs. Here Huxley and Haddon turned the argument away from the case put by Grant, Keith, and Stoddard that the idea of nation had a tribal and racial base and reinstated the group theory of Barker as the explanation for changing social organizations. Nations were temporary arrangements comprised of groups of people with a common tract of land bound together in a common state by a common history, common sentiments and traditions, common social organization, and usually a common language. The disputes between them could be explained sociologically in terms of Gumplowiczian conflict theory and Mill's individualistic theory of the co-terminal State. The remedy that was needed to cure the racial mythology was education, rationally

THE RACIALIZATION OF THE WEST

and constructively applied to reveal "the biological realities of the ethnic situation."

FLECK AND BUNCHE

The Europe of 1936 did not yield to Huxley and Haddon's call for international action to renounce the horrors then being perpetrated in the name of science, but their voices were not alone. During the summer of 1934, the fateful year of the neutrality agreement between Chancellor Hitler's Germany and Poland and the full coming to power of the Führer, Ludwig Fleck, in *Genesis and Development of a Scientific Fact,* reflected on the nature of science. He pointed out that in the early eighteenth century Georg Ernst Stahl, the German chemist, believed that the burning of substances and the corrosion of metal in air produced a hypothetical substance Stahl called "phlogiston." One hundred years were spent in measuring the elusive substance before Antoine-Laurent Lavoisier discovered that it did not exist and that the key to understanding combustion was oxygen. In what was ostensibly an exploration of the relationship between blood and syphilis before its "cause" was discovered, Fleck demonstrated that the uncritical acceptance of accumulated progress in scientific knowledge as though it were an "improvement" upon the thought styles of previous generations, as the Comtians had argued, was wrong. He proposed that we may be so mesmerized by the "carnal scourge" of race, and so antagonized by it, that our perception of it becomes no more than a "ritual mechanical action."[6]

Ralph J. Bunche (1904–71), a political scientist who would later be the first black to be a division head in the State Department, also saw race as a compelling sort of social voodoo, and not a very consistent one at that. In 1936, in *A World View of Race,* he wrote, "Race is the great American shibboleth." But he saw class as supplanting race in world affairs: "Race war then will be merely a sideshow to the gigantic class-war which will be waged in the big tent we call the world."[7]

BARZUN

Jacques Barzun (b. 1907), born in France but staying in the United States following studies at Columbia University, expressed similar cautions. As early as 1931, he had with great prescience recognized that the three main groups or types embedded in Ripley and Deniker's analysis of the races of Europe— the Teutonic, Alpine, and Mediterranean—were already stuck in people's minds and unlikely to go away. Moreover, these powerful ideas had not emerged, as was commonly supposed, by a well-marked rational highway but by a dusty and tortuous ancient route illuminated by savants no longer read or remembered. Where these pathways would lead, and with what painful consequences, Barzun considered in his second volume, published in 1937, reprinted in 1965.[8] He suggested the investment of time on various "theories of race" was not only a waste of intellectual effort but also a perpetuation of myth: "Race theories shift their ground, alter their jargon, and mix their claims, but they cannot obliterate the initial vice of desiring to explain much by little and to connect in the life of the group or individual some simple fact with some great significance" (p. 114). Barzun had little patience for labeling and classifying on the basis of insufficient evidence. To him, the nineteenth-century natural scientists and anthropologists, the "objective" historiographers, the psychologists, and philologists of whatever language, were all indulging in what he called "racial lumping." While admitting that he had no answer to the race problem, and no faith in the cures of the race relations schools, he steadfastly argued that the notion of race obliterated the individual: "If we want social peace, this restriction on judgment must become a moral imperative; it must be taught as we teach 'Thou shalt not steal, and Thou shalt not kill.' Part of the common upbringing must consist in showing the danger and the folly of thinking that groups are made up of identically hateful or identically lovable people" (p. xiv).

In the preface to the second edition of his *Race: A Study in Superstition,* Barzun demonstrated that people would eventually come to see how ridiculous and superstitious the idea of race actually was.

It is worth remembering that Barzun's texts were written before the outbreak of war and his outstanding critique of what he called "transmogrified phrenology" certainly did not endear him to those who were promoting racist doctrines in Germany, Britain, France, and the United States. After the war, when he clung to the belief that without political accommodation and a true understanding of the past the valiant attempts by international agencies, governments, and do-gooding sociology to cure the ills of the world by social intervention were foolhardy and doomed to failure, he was, ironically, accused of racism.

If the idea of race is nothing more than transmogrified phrenology, then all that we are left with is what Erik H. Erikson referred to in 1968 as "something as evolutionary sounding as man's division into *pseudo species.*"[9] For whatever reason, human beings share in common a set of prejudgments and pre-conceptions that they belong to a series of such pseudospecies. It stands to reason; it is common sense that race exists; if people believe it, it must be so. Therefore, there is no need for historical disquisition about it. Donald L. Horowitz, in his *Ethnic Groups in Conflict*, has described this human state as a cocktail of false cognition in which some deep longing to belong persists, and Primo Levi, in his moving work on the degradation of man, as "a conviction that lies deep down like some latent infection" which, when allowed to be carried through to its ultimate logical conclusion, leads to the death camp, and, in the obliteration of all political life, threatens us all.[10]

» *The Orthodoxy of Modern Race Relations*

PARK

Into this no-man's-land between "race is everything" and "race is nothing" moved the modern race relations schools of the 1920s and 1930s. The main impetus of this movement was derived from the work of Robert Ezra Park (1864–1944), who in *Race and Culture* (1950) traced his interest in sociology to the reading of Goethe's *Faust* and to his introduction as newspaperman to John Dewey and Franklin Ford, who believed "that with more accurate and adequate reporting of current events the historical process would be appreciably stepped up, and progress would go forward steadily, without the interruption and disorder of depression and violence and at rapid pace."[11] To gain an insight into the function of knowledge called "the news," Park went to Harvard to study philosophy. He wanted to be able to describe society under the influence of news in the precise and universal language of science. Then he studied at the University of Berlin under Georg Simmel (1858–1918), who had published on Goethe and art, and with Max Weber, who had founded the German Sociological Society in 1910. With Wilhelm Windelband (1848–1915), Simmel was the proponent in Germany of a philosophical and historical sociology that attempted to liberate itself from all scientific schools of thought. Both were in the historical tradition of Hegel, Schopenhauer, Nietzsche, Spencer, Comte, and Marx. Park soon tired of their bookishness: "I was looking for something more thrilling than a logical formula" (p. vii), he confessed.

Park discovered his thrilling new interest in the study of the race problem and the Negro in America after meeting Booker T. Washington (1856–1915), the head of Tuskegee Institute who advocated cooperation and self-help as the means for Negro advancement. Park was convinced that the historical process he observed in the steady advance of the Negro in the American South was the process by which civilization had evolved as it drew into its influence a widening circle of races and peoples. Examining and describing this process were the work of the sociologist:

> According to my earliest conception of a sociologist he was to be a kind of super-reporter, like the men who write for *Fortune*. He was to report a little more accurately, and in a manner a little more detached than the average, what my friend Ford called the "Big News." The "Big News" was the long-time trends which recorded what is actually going on rather than what, on the surface of things merely seems to be going on." (pp. viii–ix)

In the introduction to Park's collected papers Everett Cherrington Hughes remarked that the dialectic of Park's life was reform and action as against detached observation, "writing the news of the unique event as against the discovery of the eternal themes and processes of history" (p. xiii). For Park, race relations had been a problem from the Greeks to modern times, and although the Roman world had abolished national and racial distinctions there had been a revival of the race idea in the modern world that required reporting as the "Big News" and not as a dull philosophy of history.

As Peter I. Rose has shown, Park's work firmly established race relations as a standard feature of the sociological curriculum in the United States, as people like Louis Wirth, Robert Redfield, and Everett Cherrington Hughes introduced the first university seminars on the subject, usually in conjunction with the study of economic depression and immigration. After the Second World War these courses on race and ethnic relations multiplied and, as returning war veterans searched for a new identity in the much changed conditions of the 1940s and 1950s, and the civil rights movement began to gather strength, they burgeoned. But race relations remained the province of education, psychology, sociology, and anthropology departments; courses were seldom found in departments of history and politics.[12]

MYRDAL

In 1938, the Swedish economist and sociologist Gunnar Myrdal (1898–1987) was commissioned by the Carnegie Corporation of America to collect information about, analyze, and interpret race relations in the United States for the advancement and diffusion of knowledge. Myrdal was selected because Sweden was assumed to have no tradition of imperialism. *An American Dilemma: The Negro Problem and Modern Democracy,* published in 1944, was written with the assistance of Richard Sterner and Arnold Rose and an army of experts from universities sensitively recruited from Chicago, Howard, North Carolina, the Yale Institute of Human Behavior, Fisk, and Columbia. The preface also credited discussions with Ruth Benedict, Franz Boas, Melville Herskovits, Otto Kleineberg, Robert Linton, Ashley Montagu, Robert Ezra Park, Edward Reuter, Edward Shils, and Louis Wirth. Myrdal paid tribute to the collaborative nature of the enterprise and to the open-mindedness of American academic institutions in permitting him, a foreigner, to write about intimate domestic problems. In the 1962 edition he obdurately refused to go back over old ground and refrained from answering criticisms that had been leveled at his study when it was first published, principally by the Marxist emigré historian Oliver Cromwell Cox and to a lesser extent by Herbert Aptheker, a younger left-wing critic.

Myrdal saw himself as involved in a labor of moral concern, a linking up of the rationalism, liberalism, and optimism of American culture. He perceived American culture as more moralistic than other Western cultures, and also more rational. In the United States, even romanticism and transcendentalism were pragmatic and optimistic:

> American civilization early acquired a flavor of enlightenment which has affected the ordinary American's whole personality and especially his conception of how ideas and ideals ought to 'click' together. He has never developed that particular brand of tired mysticism and romanticism which finds delight in the inextricable confusion in the order of things and in ineffectuality of the human mind. He finds such leanings intellectually perverse.[13]

And so Myrdal turned away from what he called "obscurantism" to "ascertaining social reality as it is" (p. lxxiii), based upon an examination of observable "social facts" grounded in the moral beliefs of ordinary people as reflected in Park's "Big News" and in Bunche's concern for his people. Myrdal's introduction steered clear of single causal factors—economic, biological, or political:

> The social scientist in his effort to lay bare concealed truths and to become

maximally useful in guiding practical and political action, is prudent, when, in the approach to a problem, he sticks as closely as possible to the common man's ideas and formulations, even though he knows that further investigation will carry him into tracts uncharted in the popular consciousness. (p. lxxiv)

For Myrdal, the essential starting point was the examination of the mental constructs of ordinary people, not of intellectuals. The project was an analysis of morals, not an analysis in morals.

From Myrdal's point of view the race problem was determined by the white side, and the Negro's life was a secondary reaction to a life style that had been established by whites. Therefore, Myrdal's book has to be seen not as a description but as an analytical prescription for future social and political action in the mode of Park and the Chicago format. Its aim was scientific investigation, purged of all possible bias, rationally done, properly defining problems and terms, so that a logical foundation could be laid for practical and political conclusions.

Myrdal committed himself unequivocally to the analysis of "broad and general relations and main trends," not to "uniquely historical datum," thereby consolidating the work of the Park school and providing a common, value-free platform upon which the "race is everything" and the "race is nothing" supporters could comfortably stand together. Nevertheless, his emphasis upon broad and general relationships and main trends—the "Big News"—did not entirely rule out history. His Whig version of history claimed for America the most explicitly expressed system of general ideas in reference to interhuman relations as they appeared in written form in the Declaration of Independence, the Preamble to the Constitution, and the Bill of Rights. Myrdal saw the American creed springing from the philosophy of the Enlightenment and triumphing over the aristocratic spirit of the English Crown, Parliament, and British power holding. It was a rationalist creed that drew also from lower-class Protestantism, the English legal system, natural law, American Puritanism, and the doctrine of natural rights as expressed in principles of equality before the law and Christian ideals. Myrdal's diagnosis of the peculiar American problem of race was that the present legal system placed too much emphasis on due process and the letter of the law and not enough upon the spirit of the law. In that sense the ordinary people (the folk), and in particular the Negro folk, had been isolated from the law, the practice of politics, and the institutional arrangements of the Republic. What existed in America, therefore, was not Stoddard's "iron law of inequality," not McDougall's debilitation of the mental constitution of its peoples, but a failure in legislation, administration, and academic endeavor.

COX

The publication in 1948 of Oliver Cromwell Cox's *Caste, Class and Race* subjected both Myrdal and Park to penetrating, even merciless, criticism. These criticisms have often been overlooked, perhaps because of their strident tone, but more likely because Cox declared in his preface that no system could explain the facts of caste and class so consistently as scientific Marxism (as opposed to gospel Marxism). Cox was of the opinion that Myrdal's work provided no new insight and developed no hypothesis or consistent theory of race because it relied upon the historically incorrect interpretation of the caste system in India as having racial origins. Park, the founder of this line of intellectual thought, was guilty of telekinesis in providing such a wide definition of caste that everybody belonged to it. His frame of reference was too broad, and thus his theory was weak. "Probably the crucial fallacy in Park's thinking," claimed Cox, "is his belief that the beginnings of modern race prejudice may be traced back to the immemorial periods of human association."[14]

Marxist Premises Like Park, Cox believed that the social scientist should be "accurate and objective but not neutral" (p. xvi) and that his findings should contribute to public well-being. But he thought his materialist approach—an analysis of primordial and fundamental economic forces—better described the American dilemma than Myrdal and Park's romantic caste hypothesis. Myrdal had adopted the white theory of the caste school of race relations and its procedures without a thorough historical understanding of Hindu society and organization, upon which his explanation of group conflict in the U.S. South had been based. The result of Myrdal's serious historical misunderstanding was to give primary emphasis to sex as an explanation of race relations and to disregard socioeconomic condition (p. 526). Hence, Myrdal's perception of race prejudice had become a personal, psychological matter, and not an institutional and political one.

Cox's criticism of Myrdal and Park hinged on a belief that the modern caste school of race relations in the United States in the 1930s, principally under the leadership of W. Lloyd Warner, John Dollard, and Hortense Powdermaker, posited *völkisch* caste as race. Of special interest to Cox was Warner's argument that the Negroes in the American South were from one caste, and the whites from the other, and that they were unalterably and immutably born into color. Cox regarded this argument as invalid, having more to do with the kind of obscure, impressionistic romanticism current at the end of the eighteenth century and the pre-Lockean "social essences" (endogamy, accommodation, and etiquette) than with the principles of physiology and history that had emerged since that time.[15] Charles Sumner, William I. Thomas, and Sir Herbert Risley had extensively researched India at the end of the nineteenth century, and little had been added to their conclusions on the nature of caste, except perhaps by publicity and false "scientific" prestige (p. 506). Myrdal's was the old racial discourse in new caste bottles: mystical, evasive, and exploitive. His work was nothing more, said Cox, than a powerful piece of propaganda for maintaining the status quo by turning a blind eye to the conflict between two moral systems—socialism and capitalism. What was required, said Cox, was not a scholarly campaign about biology, creation, and cultural capacities, but a powerful, "positive program" for raising the consciousness of workers—black and white—in regard to their common interests: "There will be no more 'crackers' or 'niggers' after a socialist revolution because the social necessity for these types will have been removed" (p. 537).

This vituperative attack upon Myrdal's and Park's work was also visited upon Ruth Benedict, the anthropologist (p. 462). Cox claimed that Benedict's *Race: Science and Politics* (with Gene Weltfish, 1958) had assumed "ethnocentric relationships" in history without asking what, precisely, those relationships were supposed to be. Both Park and Benedict used the word "ethnocentric" as a technical term to describe a "we" feeling, or "a consciousness of kind" feeling—an incipient psychological race feeling based on the work of W. I. Thomas. Cox looked for something more precise, more intellectually challenging, more accurate, and more historical than these loose popular street definitions and abstractions. He claimed that Benedict gave no attention to the materialistic source of her rationalizations. Her conclusion that racism was first formulated in conflict between classes was a tentative one; she saw evidence of racism before it had actually appeared. Behind each bush lurked a Gumplowiczian ethnocentric bear!

Given all of these mocking criticisms, which certainly did not endear him to his contemporaries, it is important not to miss the significance of Cox's own hypothesis as to the meaning, origin, and progress of race relations, for they have something still to contribute to the thesis that race was not a universal idea at least until the Reformation. First, Cox eliminated from his definition all *a priori* associations with ethnocentrism, racism, and intolerance. The fact was, he asserted, that differences between people and peoples arose from multiple sources in history, and it was a mistake to begin with the presupposition of race and ethnocentricity. Second, he argued that race relations did not originate in some "social instinct" of antipathy between peoples caused by some mechanism within the mind that allowed it to classify, automatically and inevitably, every individual that it met (the Park approach). Rejecting what he called "the instinct hypothesis" (p. 322), Cox asserted that race classification had been introduced in history. Third, he proposed that race prejudice and racial exploitation had developed historically among Europeans with the rise of capitalism and nationalism and that, because of the worldwide ramifications of capitalism, all racial antagonism could be traced to the policies and attitudes of leading capitalist peoples—the white people of Europe and North America (p. 322). In this explanation he applied the Marxist perspective.

Cox was patently more disturbed by the avoidance of discussion of this ideological aspect of his work than he was by the academic content of his opponents, whom he treated with disdain. Certainly he was not as subtle as Barzun in dealing with the genuine academic deficiencies he had detected in the Chicago format. Unlike Barzun, who was prepared to offer no solution to the universal political and historical ignorance of his time, being content to stand back and wait for the movement to fail, Cox was forced into action by his ideology. His conclusion was that liberation and modern democracy were most backward in America and, by definition, most developed in that one country, the Soviet Union, where dialectical materialism held sway and which appeared to offer a hope, nay a certainty, that the elimination of economic conflict would result in the end of racial conflict.

All the time Cox was writing, after the Second World War, many people throughout the world were perceiving the beginning of a class struggle for dominance of the capitalist world, and Cox saw the Soviet Union as the natural leader of that new class struggle. In fact we now know that the Soviet Union was not free from "the racial problem," and Cox's explicit appeal, like Park's, was as much to the journalist, the missionary, and the social worker as it was to the scholar. It was also as much opposed to Barzun's academic detachment and disengagement and Lippmann's political realism as were the race relations schools. It is not surprising, therefore, that Cox should come under fire politically and academically for his views, and particularly for his trenchant criticisms of the race relations and caste schools. What is not so clear is why his most valuable contributions to the historical understanding of the idea of race should have been put aside so lightly by academic historians.

The Nature of Caste   Whether or not we accept Cox's scientific Marxism, he made a number of extremely important disciplinary distinctions about history that deserve detailed consideration, and which from the moment of their publication have been ignored by the followers of the race relations schools. His discussions of the perception of Aryan and Dravidian castes as races, of the telescoping of race into caste, and of the identification of the color question as being the root of the varna system were central to his critique.[16]

Cox concluded from his analysis that color in India meant several things—appearance, exterior, color, kind, species, and caste—that were also synonymous with *jati,* meaning "birth," specifically the form of existence determined by birth, position, rank, family, descent, kind, and species. The relationship between Brahmans (white), Kshatriyas (red), Vaisyas (yellow), and Sudras (black) was not a color relationship in the "racial" sense but a metaphor identified with *dharma*—"a way of life virtue complex" (p. 95)—that was acquired by "the mode of livelihood" or "the inherent qualities of nature." His fundamental argument was that the case for color as a dominant factor in the development of caste was not supported by the evidence of historical literature, and that it was foreign scholars who had made it so: "The writers who use the modern ideas of race relations for the purpose of explaining the origin of caste make an uncritical transfer of modern thought to an age which did not know it. The early Indo-Aryans could no more have thought in modern terms of race prejudice than they could have invented the airplane" (p. 91).

If it is the case that race was introduced into India by foreign scholars and that caste was an essentially religious occupational relationship, then this insight has the important implication that there is a fundamental difference between life in a caste system and life in a political system. Life in a *polis* necessarily implied civic relationships that elevated citizenship as the key relationship and the creation of a civil disposition as the ultimate end. A caste system, in which endogamy, priesthood, and functional occupation were the key determinants, was unable to entertain the notion of citizenship as we conceive of it, or the kinds of civic dispositions that stem from it, unless we stretch both definitions to the breaking point and make them meaningless.

Moreover, Cox's commitment to the view that race relations was a phenomenon of modern times, even to the extent of specifying precise dates for its emergence, was not simply a crude historiographical justification of Marxist ideology. It was more than that; it was the reinforcement of the historical viewpoint, supported by many other non-Marxist authorities, including Bernal and Snowden, that Greece, Rome, the Hellenistic empires of Alexander, the Helots of Macedonia, and the Metics did not constitute races as conceived in the modern world. From a strict academic standpoint the *poleis* relationships, estate relationships, and ecclesiastical relationships of the ancient and medieval worlds were not race relationships. Cox labored the point with numerous examples: the Spartiates, the Perioiki, and the Helots were not races but estates; the Metics were alien residents; the Huns, Saracens, Moors, Seljuk Turks, Ottomans, and Tartars were bands of fighting men whose social organization was military.

Christianity, Capitalism, and Racism   According to Cox's account of the origin of the idea of race, a fundamental change began in the eleventh century with the Crusades. The period between the First Crusade and the discovery of America "set a pattern of dealing with non-Christian peoples which was to be continued, minus only its religious characteristics, to this day" (p. 326). Critical events marking the beginning of modern race relations were Pope Alexander VI's Bull of Demarcation (May 3, 1493), and the Treaty of Tordesillas (June 7, 1494), when all heathen people and their resources were put at the disposal of Spain and Portugal. The relationship thus established was "not an abstract, natural immemorial feeling of mutual antipathy between groups, but rather a practical exploitive relationship with its socio-attitudinal facilitation—at that time only nascent race prejudice" (p. 332). Thus for Cox racial antagonism was the modern outcome of economic exploitation, with race prejudice its convenient tool. He depicted the dispute at Valladolid in 1550–51 between the politics of Bartolomé de Las Casas and the administration of Gines de Sepulveda as nothing more than an early logical and legal justification for a particular form of capitalistic economic exploitation. With Sepulveda the victor, the enslavement of the African and the American Indian was an inevitable consequence. "Sepulveda, then, may be thought of as among the first great racists" (p. 335), Cox concluded.

ELLISON

Interestingly, in 1944 the black musician and novelist Ralph Ellison (1914–95) wrote a review of *The American Dilemma* for the *Antioch Review* that was not published until twenty years later, in his brilliant *Shadow and Act* (1964), a collection of essays on childhood influences, jazz, his own feelings, segregation, education, Southern oppression, the role of the church in the life of the Negro, art, and fiction. Ellison mounted a substantive challenge to unspoken conventions of both American democratic social science and ideological Marxism:

> It does not occur to Myrdal that many of the Negro cultural manifestations which he considers merely reflective might also embody a *rejection* of what he considers "higher values." There is a dualism at work here. It is only partially true that Negroes turn away from white patterns because they are refused participation. There is nothing like distance to create objectivity, and exclusion gives rise to counter values.
>
> Men, as Dostoievsky observed, cannot live in revolt. Nor can they live in a state of "reacting." It will take a deeper science than Myrdal's—deep as that might be—to analyze what is happening among the masses of Negroes. Much of it is inarticulate, and Negro scholars have, for the most part, ignored it through clinging, as does Myrdal, to the sterile concept of "race."[17]

» *Postwar Palliatives*

THE UNITED NATIONS

In the shadow of the extermination camps, world leaders met to consider what policies should be adopted to prevent once and for all the excesses of race theory. The United Nations was established to promote collaboration in order to further justice, the rule of law, and human rights and freedoms without distinction of race, sex, language, or religion. At the sixth session of the United Nations Economic and Social Council, it was agreed that a program should be adopted to disseminate scientific facts to remove race prejudice. The director general was instructed to collect and study scientific data and to mount a widespread educational campaign based on these studies. The UN Statement of Race of 1950 referred to this project as "one of the most important contributions in the last century to an understanding of race and racialism."[18] What in fact the United Nations had adopted was the social engineering approach of Park and Myrdal, supported by Cox's Marxist cry for a positive program of action.

On December 12–14, 1949, eminent anthropologists, psychologists, and sociologists met in Paris to define the concept of race and to describe it in clear and easily understandable terms. Among those present were Juan Comas, professor of anthropology at the Mexican School of Anthropology, Maurice Ginsberg from the United Kingdom, Claude Lévi-Strauss from France, and Ashley Montagu from the United States. The final Statement on Race contained fifteen salient points, most of which had been covered in Huxley and Haddon's *We Europeans:* that all men belonged to the same species, *Homo sapiens*; that national, cultural, religious, geographical, and linguistic groups had been falsely termed races; that it would be better to drop the term and use "ethnic groups" in its place; that the "race is everything" hypothesis was untrue.

The statement raised objections as soon as it was published. The main criticism was that the committee was inclined too heavily toward the sociological and had continued to confuse race as a biological "fact" with the idea of race as a social phenomenon. The committee met again from June 4 to June 8, 1951, this time strengthened by the presence of powerful figures representing the international scientific community: L. C. Dunn and Thomas Dobzhansky from Columbia University, J. B. S. Haldane from University College, London, A. E. Mourant of the Lister Institute, Harry L. Shapiro of the American Museum of Natural History, J. C. Trevor from Cambridge University, and Solly Zuckerman from Birmingham University, as well as Julian Huxley, who had a hand in drafting the final statement. Before publication the statement was scrutinized by nearly one hundred anthropologists and geneticists throughout the world. As might be expected, reactions were divided. Carleton S. Coon of the University Museum, Philadelphia, who had continued to back the biological theory that each major race had evolved independently and had been molded in a different fashion to meet the needs of different milieus, that is, separate biological histories, said that the spirit of the statement was in keeping with the times, but he did not approve of slanting data to support a racial theory "since it is just what the Russians are doing, and what Hitler did." A more subtle and chilling criticism came from Walter Scheidt, director of the Anthropologisches Institut of the University of Hamburg, who saw it as a repetition of all the Nazi errors in reverse: "I can have no part in attempts to solve political manifestos, as is the practice in Soviet Russia and now at UNESCO as well."[19]

The policy paper was published together with the qualifications, and it was followed in 1953 by a UNESCO paper by the Reverend Father Yves M.-J. Congar entitled "The Catholic Church and the Race Question." In his foreword Congar, a Dominican whose manuscript had the imprimatur of the ecclesiastical authorities, argued that the problem of race was not one that had a purely scientific bearing, and it would certainly not easily yield to the blandishments of race relations theory. UNESCO's educational campaign to find solutions by bringing scientific findings to the attention of the public was naive; there were too many fundamental philosophical, theological, historical, and scientific deficiencies and discrepancies in its program for it to succeed. Congar also used biblical exegesis to confound racial theory. He attempted to show that Christianity, properly understood epistemologically and historically, ruled out racism, but not its genetic determinants, which had been made the basis for discrimination in history. The accomplishment of such an understanding was obviously going to take a long time, a commodity that was not in abundant supply.

Despite Congar's careful analysis, which might have turned attention toward the political and historical realities treated by Acton, Alfred E. Zimmern, and Barzun before the wars, faith in the human relations and industrial relations approaches to the problem of race and racism persisted well into the 1950s and formed the basis for the legislation that followed in many countries in the 1960s. UNESCO claimed that it was best equipped to lead the campaign to extirpate the outcome of this antirationalist system of thought through education, science, and culture. To this end the agency continued to publish the findings of prominent scientists who endeavored to explain the concept of race in simple language free from propaganda and sentimentality.

Lévi-Strauss in his contribution drew attention to the complexity of cultural history, and recommended amputation of the infection of race and better education. Kenneth Little believed a clear identification of political and class conflict in history and a radical reorganization of international affairs would liberalize attitudes. And Michael Leiris, while acknowledging the need for a Whig emphasis on cultural and economic history, issued a prescient warning against overindulgence in the civilizing mission lest the emerging nations take on the dogma of race themselves as they became competitors in the world of new nations and new alignments. He conceded that while many anthropologists were willing to condemn the arbitrariness of the racial classification systems, and to reject the concept of race as an impossibility, the reality was that people believed in race and that the belief could not be avoided.[20]

Leiris identified a very real problem for contemporary analysts: the failure to distinguish between innate characteristics traceable to the "ethnic" (meaning natural or physical) and those coming from background and upbringing. He put the common cultural, linguistic, and religious criteria for race to one side, leaving investigation solely to the province of physical anthropology, "the only one from which such a concept (essentially biological since it relates to heredity) can have any validity" (p. 92). The components of culture—instinct, experience, learning, symbolizing—were a social legacy quite distinct from biological inquiry.

G. M. Morant, a zoologist, regarded Leiris's distinction between literary evidence and scientific evidence as too broad and artificial. He considered that the literary approach to the past (which we have witnessed throughout this book) had failed to arrive at a solution to the problem of race and urged that scientific treatment of all classes of evidence should be given a chance to see whether it could produce better results. Otto Kleineberg stressed the need for more objective training, more techniques, more proofs, all the while acknowledging the imprecise nature of the tests themselves. Quite obviously so many factors in environment, culture, and history—not to mention the motivation and emotional state of the subject and rapport with the tester—could not be held constant.

Prominent among these essayists was Arnold Rose, professor of sociology at the University of Minnesota and collaborator with Gunnar Myrdal in setting out the race relations approach to the Negro problem in the United States. Rose suggested that practical action should be addressed to the mind of the person who practiced discrimination and that the cause of prejudice sought through the scientific methodologies of the social sciences. He also pointed to the enormous waste accumulating from prejudice in terms of economic and social costs—the damage to the image of the industrial West in Africa and psychological deprivation, encompassing frustration, fear, anxiety, and disrespect for the law. Rose distinguished a number of basic causes for prejudice: personal advantage, ignorance (the tendency to stereotype), racism, and the superiority complex (power, religion, and the perversion of science). He rejected the "dislike of differences" theory, which held that like cleaves to like and that people naturally veer away from that which is different. Instead, he embraced the "frustration aggression" theory, which incorporated the "scapegoat theory"—the idea that someone, some group, is set up for the venting of the deepest feelings of aggression. An adjuct of the "frustration aggression" theory was the "symbolic theory," which accounted for some groups being chosen by the unconscious mind as symbols for things disliked. In this utilitarian way the work of W. I. Thomas was reconciled with that of William McDougall.

From this analysis came a practical program of action by the United Nations, which to a large extent accepted the psychological propositions of the American race relations schools and incorporated them into the mechanisms and structures devised to remove racial prejudice in the world. Both Myrdal and Rose explicitly assumed

> » that an intellectual appreciation by prejudiced people of the harm done to them by race prejudice would educate them into better ways

> » that stereotypes could be broken by the provision of accurate information about "causes"

> » that an intellectual attack should be made whenever biological explanations were applied to social phenomena

> » that penal legislation should be implemented to ensure successful removal of race prejudice

> » that success depended upon the transmission of healthy attitudes through children (mental hygiene)

BENEDICT

This approach was endorsed by Ruth Benedict and Gene Weltfish in *Race: Science and Politics* (1958). Sorting out the morally suspect writers like Gobineau, Broca, Carlyle, Green, Lapouge, Ammon, Quatrefages, Fustel de Coulanges, Chamberlain, and Hitler, they shifted the blame for racism—not race, for that was an objective reality—to politics: "Seen in its perspective of fifty years on [racism] has stemmed not from the sciences—which has repudiated it, and which, indeed, racism has constantly distorted in its pronouncements, but from politics."[21]

At a stroke rational scientific thought as practiced by "the true theorists of race"—Linnaeus, Blumenbach, Cuvier, and Darwin—had been exculpated from complicity in all that had been visited upon humanity from 1684 until the death camps. The blame was conveniently shifted to antirationalist thinking and wicked politicians. Margaret Mead's preface to the book described it as a kind of handbook for those who carried "a pilgrim's staff" in the day-to-day skirmishes over discrimination in schools, churches, employment, and housing (p. xi). It was not so much a carefully worked out history as a guide to action. It was an attack upon what Benedict herself called "the new Calvinism," and it was written from the standpoint that the historian should take sides in the ensuing bedlam: "And the history of the future [sic] will differ according to the decision which we take" (pp. 4–5).

Benedict saw the solution to the American problem as twofold. First, governments must act; they must work to eliminate discrimination through legislation. Second, experts must teach the "facts" of race: "The fatal flaw in most arguments which would leave to the schools the elimination of race conflict is that they propose education *instead* of social engineering. Nothing but hypocrisy can come of such a program" (p. 161).

Of course, we now know that the approach of Park, Myrdal, Rose, and Benedict was the one incorporated in the Equal Employment Opportunity Commission (EEOC) established under the 1964 Civil Rights Act as a means for dealing with the problem of discrimination in employment. The model was transported across the Atlantic by the chairman of Britain's Race Relations Board after a quick visit to the United States in 1966 to become the new orthodoxy for the board and its replacement, the Commission for Racial Equality.

This new orthodoxy was not received without the expression of intellectual disquiet both in science and in history. But despite Huxley and Haddon's reservations about the use of the word "race" and the suggestion in the UNESCO papers that the Linnaean nomenclature denoting the races of mankind was conceptually bankrupt, racial divisions incorporated into the race relations model of public administration continue to be used to this day.

MONTAGU

At the very least these descriptions flew in the face of the description of existence put forward in the early 1950s by Francis Crick, J. D. Watson, Maurice Wilkins, and Rosalind Franklin in their analysis of the structure of deoxyribonucleic acid (DNA) and called into question again the premise that *Homo sapiens* was divisible into a series of generalized "races" recognizable as significant biological entities and describable by the taxonomies of the eighteenth and nineteenth centuries. At the University Seminar on Genetics and the Evolution of Man at Columbia in 1959, the centenary of the publication of Darwin's *Origin,* Ashley Montagu (b. 1905), who had long been publishing in the field of human culture, biology, and physical anthropology, cautioned against biological concepts that continued to toss around notions of type, heredity, blood, culture, nation, personality, intelligence, and achievement: "The process of averaging the characters of a given group, knocking the individuals together, giving them a good stirring, and then serving the resulting omelet as a 'race' is essentially the anthropological process of race making. It may be good cooking, but it is not science, since it serves to confuse rather than clarify."[22]

Like Huxley and Haddon, Montagu could see no clear reason for retaining the term "race," proposing in its place "genogroup" or "ethnic group," so that the door would not be slammed shut on understanding by the persistent misuse of the term by the scientific taxonomists (who ought to know better) and by the man in the street (who could not be expected to know better). These ideas were brought together in a collection of essays published in 1964 under the title *The Concept of Race* in which a number of distinguished physical anthropologists and biologists provided a stimulating intellectual challenge to all those who used the term "race," and even "ethnic," indiscriminately. In his introduction to the collection Montagu suggested that it was not defensible to assume that races exist, to recognize them, to describe them, to systematically classify them, or to treat them as objects of objective reality, as the UNESCO papers had done: "For two centuries anthropologists have been directing attention towards the task of establishing criteria by whose means races of man may be defined. All have taken for granted the one thing which required to be proven, namely that the concept of race corresponded with a reality which could actually be measured and verified and descriptively set out so that it could be seen to be a fact."[23]

Notwithstanding his inclination to regard the concept as extremely uncertain, and perhaps meaningless, Montagu still retained the basic view held by Rose that the roots of racial prejudice were woven into the psychic structure of the person and that the remedy could be found only in liberal education and the study of human relations. Montagu called for a complete reorientation of values in schools, which must become places for the training of humanity: "If mankind is to be saved, it can only be done by replacing the values of industrial technology with those of humanity, of cooperation, of love. It is only when humanity is in control, that technology in the service of humanity will occupy its proper place in the scheme of things. A most important and immediate task is to make people understand this" (p. 165).

VAN DEN BERGHE

P. L. Van den Berghe, an early disciple of Park's Chicago format with a deep appreciation of the contributions to social theory of Marx, Weber, Talcott Parsons, Clyde Kluckhohn, and Claude Lévi-Strauss, candidly recognized in the preface to his *Race and Racism* (1967) how the Park approach may be construed academically as little more than a bandwagon of liberal intellectuals eager to display their moral indignation in an intellectually acceptable way. Van den Berghe was fascinated by the problem of an "objective science" free from ideology and extrinsic values, which had been at the heart of the historical-philosophical approach of Simmel and Windelband before Park's utilitarian modification of it. Van den Berghe's early critique of the dominant trends in the study of race relations in the America of the 1960s was that much of American historiography was at best "ethnocentric" and at worst plain racist, not simply in relation to the Negro and minorities but also in the general tendency to perceive the world as being divided into races and ethnic groupings and in no other way. He concluded, therefore, that the concentration upon immediate problems, academically and governmentally, had produced a lack of sensitivity toward the past that impeded a thorough understanding of contemporary events. Moreover, the great emphasis placed on practice, and the lack of sophistication in comparative methodology—as well as the difficulty of setting heredity and physical environment against intellect and capability—meant that the studies had become detached from a corpus of theoretical sociological knowledge: "Despite a great deal of valuable research the field of race relations has come to resemble a theoretical no-man's land between psychology, sociology and anthropology."[24]

Race scholars, said Van den Berghe, were reluctant to theorize about race relations. Although there can be no general theory of race, race relations must be placed within the total institutional and cultural context of the society to be studied. "A few sociologists like R. E. Park, Gunnar Myrdal, Oliver C. Cox," he conceded, "have from a variety of perspectives related race relations to such basic elements of social or cultural structure as stratification, ideology, the distribution of power, and the system of production; most, however, have adopted a piecemeal rather than a holistic approach" (p. 7).

In his important work, Van den Berghe noticed the deep-seated epistemological antithesis between science and history. Western racism, he believed, was well defined as a historical phenomenon; it had reached its apogee between 1880 and 1920 and had since entered its decline, "although of course its lingering remains are likely to be with us for at least the next three decades" (p. 15).

The historical profile, according to Van den Berghe, was the expression of three factors: capitalist exploitation and colonialism; Darwinian currents of thought and biology, and the egalitarian and libertarian ideas of the Enlightenment, the French Revolution, and the Industrial Revolution. In psychopathological terms racism was not a sickness, as some were arguing, but a convenient rationalization for rewarding behavior. In his optimism that racism was in decline, and that something constructive could be done to accelerate the progress, Van den Berghe turned toward a typology of race relations consisting of a Weberian scheme of paternalistic and competitive ideal types against which a set of independent variables (such as economy, division of labor, mobility, social stratification, numerical ratios, and value conflicts) and dependent variables (race relations, roles and statuses, etiquette, forms of aggression, miscegenation, segregation, psychological syndromes, stereotypes, intensity of prejudice) and forms of control (the government and the legal system) could be compared and contrasted so as to illustrate the utility of his typology and model and move forward toward a more objective science of society.

THE BIOLOGICAL AND SOCIAL SCIENCES AND THE PERSISTENCE OF RACE THINKING

Of course, since the debates of Park, Myrdal, and Cox, and the United Nations statements, as constantly amended and emended, the prospect of racism being banished from the earth has not been realized, and the methods employed for its eradication appear not to have had the result originally intended. Indeed, it may well be argued that, despite the clarity of the Crick-Watson nonracial description of the biological composition of the human organism, which is currently transforming human genetics at a frightening pace, the tendency to see the world in racial terms, and in no other way, is expanding rather than contracting the theoretical wasteland that Van den Berghe noticed between psychology, sociology, and anthropology. Van den Berghe himself has since gingerly traveled down the road of sociobiology and the new systematics; yet even in his important work we cannot help noticing the resonances of the historical impact of Darwin and Spencer after 1870. Others have espoused rational choice theory and thereby summoned up anew the ghost of the right of conquest, the Germans in the woods, and the subjugation of mankind by technique. And yet again, others have fallen back upon the Chicago format, cutting the theory and telling what Ford told Robert Ezra Park to concentrate on—the "Big News"—but this time using the delivery system to eliminate "politically incorrect" words of "race" and "gender" from the language of humankind.

Notwithstanding all this, genuine attempts have been made from time to time to reconcile the multiple theories of race and ethnicity that occupy the cratered no-man's-land between history and politics. Notable among recent efforts was the Conference on Theories of Race and Ethnicity held at St. Catherine's College, Oxford, in March 1984, which contrived to bring about an Aristotelian dialogue among eminent scholars from a limited number of competing theoretical traditions—Marxist, Weberian, Hegelian, Kantian, and Comtian—all of which I have tried to show have confused and uncertain historical and political pedigrees.[25] The hope expressed in the preface to the published findings by John Rex, former director of the Research Unit on Ethnic Relations, was that the irreconcilable conflict of partial equilibrium analysis might be replaced by a sense of complementarity and, despite the recognized difficulties, might in the end bring about a better understanding of race and ethnic relations theory when approached from the perspectives of sociology, social anthropology, sociobiology, and social psychology.

David Mason's somewhat more pessimistic introduction clearly showed that academically the historical divisions and confusions we have noted above have not gone away. There are those who still aspire to the illusion of a "grand theory" of a phenomenon that exists either because we think it exists, or imagine that it exists, or because it is assumed to have an objective "factual" reality in science or history; and there are those whose interest is satisfied only by the complete excision of the word from the dictionary, or by the prospect of fitting together the pieces of a confusing jigsaw for its own sake, or for some uplifting contemporary utilitarian purpose urged on by some pressing contemporary need.

In these important papers Michael Banton's epistemological essay on the differences in Hegelian and Kantian and Marxist assumptions about race traced out the incredible difficulties faced by researchers as well as those who have to validate research coming from different intellectual traditions and different disciplines. Banton concluded "that there are important differences in the selection and definition of *explananda*, and in the criteria of explanation, that cannot be understood apart from their philosophical presuppositons" (p. 62).

What I have tried to show throughout this text is that the *explicanda* and the criteria have also to be placed in a historical context that does not confine itself simply to the fleeting psychological, social, economic, cultural, philological, biological, and anthropological emphases of the Hegelian, Kantian, Herderian, Marxist, Comtian, and Weberian traditions and variations thereof. Some elementary attempt has also been made to distinguish, as Aristotle did, the philosophical presuppositions of what politics is, what are its opportunities, and what are the limits of real political action and citizenship within and between political states and states acknowledged to be inhabited by human beings of many shapes, colors, sizes, opinions, and dispositions. In other words, to paraphrase Banton, in the selection and definition of *explananda,* and in the criteria of explanation, we cannot stand apart from the presuppositions of political philosophy and history that both sit within a Western tradition of inquiry.

I have suggested that beginning with Niebuhr in 1813 a tradition of inquiry was fractured with the brilliant, novel, but absurd hypothesis that the history of the world was not the history of politics properly conducted according to the tenets that applied before the great revolutions of the eighteenth century, but the history of races. In recent times the moral exhortations of Myrdal, both in the United States and in Britain, sit firmly within the Niebuhrian framework of the racialization of history, and even when they do go beyond moral exhortation to action the implementation depends on some rational-mechanical Enlightenment engineering remedy and not upon addressing publicly, in language that all parties understand, the real political interests and issues that actually exist within and between communities. It is not surprising that after the *Brown v. Board of Education of Topeka, Kansas,* desegregation ruling of 1954, which overturned the *Plessy v. Ferguson* decision of 1896, and after Martin Luther King Jr.'s "I Have a Dream" speech of 1963, and the interventionist Civil Rights and Voting Rights Acts of 1964 and 1965, the issue of race and its relationship to citizenship in an increasingly complex and diverse urban and industrial world went off the political agenda. People now speak of racism in a new racist antiracism, in "ethnic newspeak," or not at all. In the United States the Moynihan Report of 1965 and in Britain the Bonham Carter initiatives of 1966 both advocated that the way forward for race relations was in the field of jobs, welfare, and family. The history of race upon which these suppositions were made remained shackled to a Myrdalian model of social engineering and moral reform that I have tried to show had its roots deep in a Germanic *Volk* state, *Volk* culture, and *Volk* psychology, Thatcherite economics, caste-race hypotheses, pseudoscience, and the shibboleths of cultural and physical anthropology. As a consequence, they are bereft of the one ingredient—political imagination—that can release us from the material and intellectual poverty that these well-meaning administrative programs are vainly seeking to achieve.

» *Conclusion: Politics and Political Theory*

With very few exceptions the common feature that we find in most writers on the subject of race from 1813 to our time is the rejection and derogation of the idea of state created politically—the political state that Acton and Zimmern recognized as arising from the politics of individual citizens who are seen to be citizens and not mere producers and consumers of industrial products, from the act of composing the relationship between the public and the private, from laws pertaining to constitutions created in a past and their amendment to meet present and future requirements, and from notions that take into account qualitative as well as quantitative reflections of social, economic, and organizational interest.

The political form of rule places great emphasis upon treaties, charters, constitutions, legal process, embassages, diplomacy, negotiation, and settlement to bring about change and to rearrange rights, duties, and obligations. It is built upon a concept of citizenship that does not regard membership of the general public association as dependent upon a single criterion, such as physiological, mental, economic, and leadership capacity, but upon the more complex notion that a citizen of a political community may speak, act, and argue to protect his or her interest when it is threatened by the abuse or neglect of power. Moreover, wherever there are political forms, there is a deep conviction that things should be done legally and politically without violence, vengeance, expulsion, incarceration, or death. By the same token the political state is seen as having the responsibility to balance public benefit and private interest and to use properly regulated force when the conditions necessary for the maintenance of public stability and order have descended into a violence and chaos that threaten all civilized life.

For Chamberlain this form of state is the council of fools; for Nietzsche a formation that has been overtaken by events, a servant of the preachers of death; for Grant a haven for bastards, cripples, and the feebleminded (politics flying in the face of scientific reason); for Spencer and Thatcher an ignorance of the realities of self-determining economic life. And, in the pathetic attempt of Huxley and Haddon to reinstate politics when all was about to be lost in the nightmare of Hitler's corporate race hygiene, the appeal was not to the reinstatement of the values of the political state, to a reaffirmation of classical political theory, to resolute political practice, but to a more scientific explanation of how the scientific racists had got it all wrong and how a more scientific politics might get it all right in a better-educated managerial society.

The naive belief that better education, better scientific understanding of the idea of race and racism, better theory, would cure the disease of race-thinking, and end it rationally with a quick fix in a decade or so, pervades the works of those seeking to correct the awful horrors of the concentration camps, the technological charnel houses of the twentieth century—horrors that are already being denied or euphemistically equated with the persecutions of the fifteenth century or attributed to some premodern phenomenon. What I have tried to demonstrate is that the remedies put forward in good faith by the United Nations after the war slavishly followed what Cox sneeringly called "the new orthodoxy of race relations"—an orthodoxy that was picked up willy-nilly in England and thought to be relevant to the problems of postwar immigration. In fact, the Silver Jubilee of statutory "race relations" in Britain has come and gone without celebration. Alas, the dancing in the streets of Notting Hill was not for the impotent Commission for Racial Equality, the pathetic agency left in 1976 to administer as best it could the tattered remnants of the 1960s legislation on equal opportunity and cultural diversity. Neither was there any real attempt to examine intellectually or politically the outcome of "a Myrdal for Britain" to see whether the anniversary was an anniversary of emancipation and restoration in the true sense of jubilee, or nothing more than the anniversary of "a sad botched up job reflecting little credit on anyone who has been involved with it."[26]

I believe that the race relations approach of the social engineers has outlived its purpose and needs to be fundamentally reevaluated in terms of contemporary reality. It has not only failed to prevent the balkanization of the world into a collection of distinctive "ethnic societies,"[27] recognizable from the evidence of the boxes inflicted upon us all, whatever we perceive ourselves to be, but has also accelerated the process by which the natural resentments of narrow tribal units are perceived to be due to ethnicity and to no other factor. In the 1990s nationally and internationally we can now see a new, more correct orthodoxy imposing itself insidiously upon the literature and language of politics, an orthodoxy that seeks to end racial discrimination in all its forms by identifying pernicious race language wherever it appears—in the home, the factory, the school, even the university—and eradicating it from the conversation of mankind.

Above all, my book does not support the thesis that ethnic tension is some inevitable premodern remnant visiting itself upon the modern state like some syphilitic affliction. Neither does it support the view that the self-determining democratic ideologies of the eighteenth and nineteenth centuries will eventually release us from its bondage. On the contrary, it argues that ethnicity is essentially an idea introduced in modern times, and that it has prospered in proportion to the decline in political ideas concerning the disposition of civil affairs. The work of Crick, Watson, Wilkins, and Franklin in the field of genetics has recently provided us with a dramatic account of existence which has been described in *Nature* as "a molecular biology Blitzkrieg that brushes aside cherished ideas, mechanisms, and even personalities in its path" and the realm that it occupies as "a gigantic slaughter house, a molecular Auschwitz in which valuable enzymes, hormones and so on will be extracted instead of gold teeth." The sufferers of genetic diseases are portrayed as "victims of a tragic faustian bargain in which natural selection plays the part of Mephistopheles."[28] And, as Richard Dawkins has since argued, the basic unit of natural selection that leaps from body to body through generations is the gene, and the predominant quality in a successful gene that has survived for millions of years is ruthless selfishness impelled by proficiency. These genes are the survivors; the bodies they inhabit are the survival machines; and individuals mere fleeting presences: "In a few generations the most you can hope for is a large number of descendants, each of whom bears only a tiny portion of you—a few genes—even if a few bear your surname as well." According to Dawkins's analysis all that can be said about human beings is that they are long-lived replicators, some of whom do not survive in the genetic rivalry of the immensely complicated competition for a place in the slot of the chromosomes of future generations. All life is statistical probability on a colossal scale operating cumulatively over aeons by slow and gradual degrees with no purpose in mind: "It does not plan for the future. It has no vision, no foresight, no sight at all. If it can be said to play the role of watchmaker in nature, it is the blind watchmaker."[29] In this blind, unconscious process the races, as we are used to describing them, are little more than gigantic gene pools, ever-shifting chance variables that we have barely begun to understand.

What, then, is there to learn from this genetic chaos? It is that the transformation or transmogrification of individual human beings into groups that have been founded in the past upon prevailing generalizations of racial or ethnic categories may be nothing more than a cruel fiction and a conjurer's delusion—a modern reworking of the arcana of the Cabala, the *Zohar*, Hermes Trismegistus, the astrological "influences" of Jean Bodin, and the Social Darwinism of the nineteenth century? In science there is as yet no Wassermann test that proves the existence or nonexistence of race. All that can be said is that on the basis of genetic evidence and clinal analysis the similarities between human beings, from whatever part of the planet they come, are greater than their dissimilarities. And that is all there is to it.[30]

What science does tell us with force and eloquence is that human existence on this planet has not been for any great length of time, and that the span of years allocated to each one of us, whoever we are, wherever we live, whatever the size of our nose, whatever the color of our skin, whatever the current state of our health, whatever the size of our bank balance, is short and very fragile. Hesiod's didactic poems, with which I began, teach that the real choices in life are between the power of Kronos, and its immensely difficult alternative, the rule of Zeus. I hope that I have shown that the fictitious unities of race and nation whipped up by the philologists, anthropologists, historians, and social scientists of the nineteenth century as alternatives to the antique political state led them to forget a very important past and to invent in its place novel ideological forms of governance that were pursued with vengeance and arrogance and all the cunning skill of the forethinkers. The *nemesis* that followed when the *eunomia* of Zeus was undermined by the power of Kronos we can see in Dachau and Auschwitz, and will see repeated if we are not very careful from the Urals to Shannon, from Gibraltar to Murmansk, and from Breçon to the Balkans as "kinships" shatter into thousands of self-determining fragments.

What, then, are we left with to combat the *hubris* of modernity and mass society? What is it that matters in a political state comprised of many different kinships, many different tribes and clans, many different nations? Is it the color of the skin? Is it the date when people arrived? Is it where they lived, or were assumed to have lived, in some time long since past but not forgotten? Is it the language they speak? Is it the religion they follow? Is it the position they occupy in class or caste? Is it the geographical, chorographical, and topographical milieus of Wapping or St. James, Leeds or Leicester? Is it the innate character, genius, and intelligence of particularly gifted individuals?

It is not that these individual elements and identities are unimportant, but that there is in theory and in practice a more important elected past than the past of kith and kin that needs to be brought out from time to time and dusted down. I have throughout this book tried to show that the arrangements of Greco-Roman political society emphasized citizenship, *nomocracy,* and politics, in avoidance of the worst excesses of tyranny, oligarchy, and democracy. In that notion of political society that prevailed until the great revolutions of the eighteenth century, there was to all intents and purposes a clear understanding of what it meant to be a good citizen (however limited the extent of citizenship) within a general civil association bent on cultivating a civil disposition within and between states comprised of many different kinds of men and opinions. It had something to do with the extremely difficult task of giving priority to smooth and unerring speech, straight talk, interpretation of law, balanced and moderate verdicts, mature judgment, and the bringing of the great disagreements between public and private interest to a skillful settlement through the exercise of political acumen in public places before assembled gatherings of citizens.

It is these aspects of political society and political values that were paralyzed by the racial discourse of the nineteenth century and have led us into the blind alley of bureaucratic multiculturalism and the sterile orthodoxy of an alien race relations rather than into a more mature consideration of those political rules of Zeus that provide a place for all good citizens in an uncertain world where the end is pleasure and death.

I end where I began with a reminder of Primo Levi's warning of what happens when unwittingly we treat "every stranger" as "an enemy" and, on the eve of yet another Sarajevo, add to it the words of a reviewer eminently qualified to speak. In *Shadow and Act* the late Ralph Ellison, accused of filial betrayal, wrote that he had freed himself from the sociological vision by way of the library: "Indeed, I understand a bit more about myself as Negro, because literature has taught me something of my identity as Western man, as political being" (p. 117). Then he described his own slave name, and his given name after the poet Ralph Waldo Emerson as a certain triumph of the human spirit over dismembering pressures: "'Brothers and Sisters,' I once heard a Negro preacher exhort, 'let us make up our faces before the world, and our names shall sound throughout the land with honor! For we ourselves are our *true* names, not their epithets! So let us, I say, Make Up Our Faces and Our Minds!'"

Notes

Classical texts and later works analyzed for their relation to the idea of race are cited in full in the notes where they are first mentioned, including modern editions, if any. Subsequent citations to these works appear in parentheses in the text, usually designating internal divisions only, such as book, section, and line. Italics are mine unless otherwise noted. Secondary sources are cited in the notes.

CHAPTER 1, IN THE BEGINNING

1. Cedric Dover, "Race: The Uses of the Word," *Man* (April 1951):55.
2. José Ortega y Gasset, *Man and People* (London: Allen and Unwin, 1961).
3. See M. Mead, T. Dobzhansky, E. Tobach, Robert E. Light, eds., *The Concept of Race* (New York: Columbia University Press, 1968); Francis Crick, *Life Itself* (London: Macdonald, 1981); Crick, *The Astonishing Hypothesis: The Scientific Search for the Soul* (London: Simon and Schuster, 1994); Ashley Montagu, "The Concept of Race in the Human Species in the Light of Genetics," in *The Concept of Race*, ed. Ashley Montagu (London: Collier Macmillan, 1964); Montagu, *Man's Most Dangerous Myth: The Fallacy of Race*, 4th ed. (New York: World Publishing Co., 1964); Jean Hiernaux, "The Concept of Race and the Taxonomy of Mankind," in *The Concept of Race*, pp. 29–46; Frank Livingstone, "The Nonexistence of Human Races," in *The Concept of Race*, p. 47; S. M. Garn, *Human Races* (Springfield, Ill.: Thomas, 1965); Carleton S. Coon, *The Origin of Races* (New York: Knopf, 1962), including a caustic critique by Ashley Montagu. Biological views of race and a presentation of the "new systematics" are included in C. Loring Brace, "A Non-Racial Approach to the Understanding of Human Diversity," in *The Concept of Race*, pp. 103–52; Paul Erlich and Richard W. Holm, "A Biological View of Race," in *The Concept of Race*, pp. 153–77; and Nigel A. Barnicot, "Taxonomy and Variation in Modern Man," in *The Concept of Race*, pp. 178–216. Carleton S. Coon, with Edward E. Hunt Jr. *The Living Races of Man* (London: Jonathan Cape, 1966) treats race as a zoological concept and does not propose to drop the Linnaean nomenclature.
4. Richard Dawkins, *The Selfish Gene* (New York: Oxford University Press, 1976); Dawkins, *The Blind Watchmaker* (New York: Norton, 1987); Stephen Jay Gould, *The Mismeasure of Man* (New York: Norton, 1981); Gould, *The Flamingo's Smile* (New York: Norton, 1985); Friedrich Vogel and Arno G. Motulsky, *Human Genetics: Problems and Approaches*, 2d ed. (Berlin: Springer, 1986); J. Maynard Smith, "Current Controversies in Evolutionary Biology" in *Dimensions of Darwinism*, ed. M. Grene (New York: Cambridge University Press, 1983), pp. 273–86; R. L. Trivers, *Social Evolution* (Menlo Park, Calif.: Benjamin/Cummings, 1985). There are many provocative articles in *Nature*, including Bryan Sykes, "Genetics Cracks Bone Disease," *Nature*, no. 330 (January 1987): 607–8,

which refers to the discovery of DNA as "a molecular biology Blitzkreig that brushes aside cherished ideas, mechanisms and even personalities in its path." See also J. S. Jones, "How Different Are Human Races," *Nature*, no. 293 (1981): 188–90; R. Dawkins, "Selfish Genes in Race or Politics," *Nature*, no. 289 (1981): 528; Thomas H. Jukes, "Doom and Gloom," *Nature*, no. 330 (January 1987): 514; and Sir David Weatherall, "Molecules and Man," *Nature*, no. 328 (1987): 771–72. Jerome Rotter and Jared Diamond, "What Maintains the Frequencies of Human Genetic Diseases," *Nature*, no. 329 (1987): 289–90, describe sufferers from genetic diseases as "victims of a tragic faustian bargain in which natural selection plays the role of Mephistopheles." See also Rotter and Diamond, "Observing the Founder Effect in Human Evolution," *Nature*, no. 329 (1987): 105–6 for their examination of the founder effect in human evolution in Afrikaner, Cape Colored, and Finnish populations for esoteric diseases as indicators of the evolution of persistent racial characteristics.

5. See John Rex and David Mason, eds., *Theories of Race and Ethnic Relations* (New York: Cambridge University Press, 1986), esp. David Mason, "Introduction: Controversies and Continuities in Race and Ethnic Relations Theory," pp. 1–19; Michael Banton, "Epistemological Assumptions in the Study of Racial Differentiation," pp. 42–63; M. G. Smith, "Pluralism, Race and Ethnicity in Selected African Countries," pp. 187–225. See esp. Stephen Jay Gould's review of Michael Banton, *Racial Theories* (1987), "Why Are 'They' Not Like 'Us'?" *Nature*, no. 332 (1988): 751–52. See also Walter Bodmer and Robin McKie, *The Book of Man: The Quest to Discover Our Genetic Heritage* (London: Little, Brown, 1994).

6. Bernard Crick, *In Defence of Politics* (London: Penguin, 1962), pp. 15–32. See also Bertrand de Jouvenel, *The Pure Theory of Politics* (New Haven: Yale University Press, 1963) as well as Michael Oakeshott, *Rationalism in Politics and Other Essays* (London: Methuen, 1962); Sheldon S. Wolin, *Politics and Vision: Continuity and Innovation in Western Political Thought* (Boston: Little, Brown, 1960); J.G.A. Pocock, *Politics, Language and Time* (New York: Atheneum, 1971); Pocock, *The Machiavellian Moment* (Princeton: Princeton University Press, 1975); Walter Lippmann, *A Preface to Politics* (New York: Mitchell Kennerley, 1913).

7. Martin Bernal, *Black Athena: The Afroasiatic Roots of Classical Civilization*, vol. 1, *The Fabrication of Ancient Greece, 1785–1985* (London: Free Association Books, 1987).

8. Henry Maine, *Ancient Law* (1906; reprint, London: J. M. Dent, 1927).

9. Ludwig Fleck, *Genesis and Development of a Scientific Fact*, trans. Fred Bradley and Thaddeus Trenn, ed. Thaddeus Trenn and Robert K. Merton (Chicago: University of Chicago Press, 1979). Jacques Barzun, *Race: A Study in Superstition* (1937; reprint, New York: AMS Press, 1965), p. xix.

10. Erik Erikson, *Life, History and the Historical Moment* (New York: Norton, 1975), p. 47.

11. Primo Levi, *If There Is a Man*, trans. Stuart Wolf (Harmandworth: Penguin Books, 1979), p. 15.

12. John Dunn, *Modern Revolutions: An Introduction to the Analysis of a Political Phenomenon* (London: Cambridge University Press, 1972).

13. Julian S. Huxley and A. C. Haddon, *We Europeans* (London: Jonathan Cape, 1936). The book was a reaction to Madison Grant, *The Passing of the Great Race; or, The Racial Basis for European History* (New York: Charles Scribner's Sons, 1916). See also Oliver Cromwell Cox, *Caste, Class and Race: A Study in Social Dynamics* (New York: Monthly Review Press, 1948).

CHAPTER 2, THE ANCIENT WORLD

1. J. L. Myres, *The Influence of Anthropology on the Course of Political Science*, Report of the British Association for the Advancement of Science, 1909, London, 1910, in Alfred C. Haddon and A. Hingston Quiggin, *History of Anthropology* (London: Watts & Co., 1910), p. 110.

2. Frank M. Snowden Jr., *Blacks in Antiquity: Ethiopians in the Greco-Roman Experience* (Cambridge, Mass.: Belknap Press of Harvard University Press, 1970), p. 2; Snowden, *Before Color Prejudice: The Ancient View of Blacks* (Cambridge, Mass.: Harvard University Press, 1983), p. 107. See also

Grace Hadley Beardsley, *The Negro in Greek and Roman Civilization: A Study of the Ethiopian Type,* Johns Hopkins Studies in Archaeology (Baltimore, Md.: London, 1929); Lloyd A. Thompson, *Romans and Blacks* (London: Routledge and Oklahoma University Press, 1989); Jean Vercoutter, Jean Le Comte, Frank M. Snowden Jr., and Jehan Desagnes, *The Image of the Black in Western Art* (Cambridge, Mass.: Harvard University Press, for the Menil Foundation, 1976).

3. Michael Oakeshott, *On History, and Other Essays* (Oxford: Basil Blackwood, 1983), p. 46.

4. Homer, *Iliad,* trans. E. V. Rieu (Baltimore, Md.: Penguin Books, 1950), bk. 6, p. 121.

5. Hesiod, *The Poems of Hesiod,* trans. R. M. Frazer (Norman, Okla.: University of Oklahoma Press, 1983). See also the commentary by M. L. West in Hesiod, *Works and Days* (Oxford: Clarendon Press, 1978).

6. See Eric Voegelin, *Order and History,* vol. 2, *The World of the Polis* (Baton Rouge: Louisiana State University Press, 1974), esp. pp. 126–64. Voegelin seems to presume that Hesiod's "ages of the world," which he believes may be a Babylonian myth, are "races of men" (p. 146).

7. Herodotus, *The Histories,* trans. A. D. Godley, Loeb Classical Library (Cambridge, Mass.: Harvard University Press, 1920).

8. Hippocrates, *Airs, Waters, and Places,* trans. W. H. S. Jones, Loeb Classical Library (Cambridge, Mass.: Harvard University Press, 1923). Hippocrates was first translated into English by Peter Low in 1597.

9. John Richard Green, *A Short History of the English People* (1874; reprint, London: J. M. Dent Double Volumes, 1934), pp. 421, 423.

10. Karl R. Popper, *The Open Society and Its Enemies: The Spell of Plato* (London: Routledge and Kegan Paul, 1974), pp. 51–53.

11. Richard Crossman, *Plato Today* (1959; reprint, London: Unwin, 1963), pp. 118, 144–55. See also Bertrand Russell, *The History of Western Philosophy and Its Connection with Political and Social Circumstances from the Earliest Times to the Present Day,* new ed. (London: George Allen and Unwin, 1984). Considering the ethics of Darwinism and race, F. H. Bradley, "Remarks on Punishment," *International Journal of Ethics* 4, no. 3 (April 1894): 269–84, concluded, "And there are views of Plato which, to me at least, every day seem less of an anachronism and more of a prophecy" (p. 284).

12. Plato, *The Republic of Plato,* trans. Francis MacDonald Cornford (1941; reprint, London: Oxford University Press, 1948); Plato, *Timaeus; Critias; Cleitophon; Monexenus; Epistles,* trans. R. G. Bury, Loeb Classical Library 234 (Plato vol. 9) (Cambridge, Mass.: Harvard University Press, 1929).

13. Popper, *Open Society and Its Enemies,* p. 75.

14. Michel Foucault, *The History of Sexuality,* vol. 1, *An Introduction,* trans. Robert Hurely (London: Allen Lane, 1979).

15. Aristotle, *The Works of Aristotle,* ed. William David Ross and John A. Smith (Oxford: Clarendon Press, 1910–37), vol. 6, *Opuscula, De coloribis* and *Physiognomonica,* trans. Thomas Loveday and E. S. Forster; vol. 8, *Metaphysica,* trans. W. D. Ross; Aristotle, *The Politics,* trans. H. Rackham (London: Heinemann, 1932).

16. "*Genus* then is used in all of these ways, (1) in reference to continuous generation of the same kind, (2) in reference to the first mover which is of the same kind as the thing it moves, (3) as matter; for that to which the differentia or quality belongs is the substratum, which we call matter" (28.1024b).

"What then is it that makes man one: why is he one and not many, e.g. animal + biped, especially if there are, as some say, an animal-itself and a bi-ped itself? Why are these Forms themselves the man, so that man would exist by participation not in Man, or in one form, but in two, animal and bi-ped, and in general man would be not one but more than one thing, animal and bi-ped?" (6.1045a.12–19).

For a discussion of genos see D. M. Balme, "Genos and Eidos in Aristotle's *Biology,*" *Classical Quarterly* 12 (1962): 81–98.

Genus and species then differ in epistemological status, and tend to be used not relatively but absolutely. The infima species is abstracted immediately from sense perception, whereas all classes above it are abstracted from abstractions. In Aristotle's theory of substance the form that is actualized in the individual's matter is that of *atoman eidos,* while the successive ranks of genera are successively remote stages of potentiality which can only exist when the infima species is actualized. If the male sperma fails to inform the female matter fully, the offspring may not resemble its parents but only their genus, and this is a step on the way towards the monstrosity: the *teras* (sigh, wonder, marvel) is *zoon ti* (some animal) but no more. (84)

17. Clyde K. M. Kluckhohn, *Anthropology and the Classics,* The Colver Lectures, 1960 (Providence, R.I.: Brown University Press, 1961), pp. 34, 42.

18. Hannah Arendt, *The Origins of Totalitarianism* (New York: Harcourt Brace, 1951). See also Arendt, *The Human Condition: A Study of the Central Dilemma Facing Modern Man* (London: Allen and Unwin, 1967), esp. p. 26.

19. William L. Westermann, *The Slave Systems of Greek and Roman Antiquity* (Philadelphia, Pa.: American Philosophical Society, 1955), argues that it.is totally misleading to see slavery as something the Greeks felt uneasy or unhappy about. Aristotle's theory is grounded on a theory of innate differences both quantitative and qualitative in the moral and intellectual capacities of individuals, and has to be seen alongside a precise definition of citizenship and the quality and character *(arete)* of citizens. "Granting that slave status in general was an unenviable condition, there are many indications that deeper racial and class antipathies, such as those based on skin coloring, were totally lacking in the Greek world" (p. 23). See also *Ethics* 8, 1161a.6–26.

20. H. B. Rackham (London: W. Heinemann, 1926) edition of *Ethica nicomachea* 1149a.9–20 translates *hosper enia gene ton porro barbaron* not as "races" but as "some tribes of remote barbarians" and makes a clear distinction between who are brutish and who are victims of disease, madness, or morbidity.

21. See H. C. Baldry's proposal that the theme of all Greek literature and poetry is that "mankind are united at any rate in feebleness and misery." See also Erwin Schrodinger, *Nature and the Greeks* (Cambridge: Cambridge University Press, 1954); and, for the distinction between Greek and non-Greek and the history of the word *barbarian,* see J. Juthner, *Hellen und Barbaren aus der Geschichte des Nationalbewusstseins* (Leipzig: Dieterich, 1923).

22. See also R. B. Onians, *The Origins of European Thought about the Body, the Mind, the Soul, the World, Time and Fate* (Cambridge: Cambridge University Press, 1988); Moses Hadas, *Humanism: The Greek Ideal and Its Survival* (London: George Allen and Unwin, 1961).

23. Herschel Baker, *The Image of Man* (New York: Harper, 1961), p. 105.

CHAPTER 3, TRANSITIONS FROM GREECE TO ROME

1. Eric Voegelin, "The Growth of the Race Idea," *Review of Politics* (July 1940): 283–317; Hannah Arendt, "Race-Thinking before Racism," *Review of Politics* 6 (January 1944): 36–73.

2. Polybius, *Histories,* 2 vols., trans. Evelyn Schuckburgh (London: 1889), p. 4.40.

3. See also F. W. Walbank, *A Historical Commentary on Polybius* (Oxford: Clarendon Press, 1957), esp. pp. 145, 643–49.

4. Cicero, *De legibus* and *De republica,* Loeb Classical Library (Cambridge, Mass.: Harvard University Press, 1970); Cicero, *Offices, Essays on Friendship and Old Age* and *Selected Letters,* Everyman's Library Series (London: J. M. Dent, 1909).

5. Vergil, *The Aeneid,* trans. H. Rushton Fairclough, Loeb Classical Library (Cambridge, Mass.: Harvard University Press, 1934–35). See also T. J. Haarhoff, *The Stranger at the Gate* (Oxford: Blackwell, 1948), especially on the conclusion of the *Aeneid.*

6. Lucretius, *De rerum natura,* trans. W. H. D. Rouse, rev. ed. by M. F. Smith, Loeb Classical Library (Cambridge, Mass.: Harvard University Press, 1975).

7. Sextus Empiricus, *Outlines of Pyrrhonism (Hypotyposes), Against the Dogmatists, On the Soul and Notes on Medicine,* trans. R. G. Bury (Cambridge, Mass.: Harvard University Press, 1933), gives a full account of the members of his school, and outlines the work of Pyrrho of Elis, who was a natural philosopher maintaining that knowledge of things was impossible and that man must assume an attitude of reserve about everything.

8. Strabo, *The Geographies of Strabo,* trans. H. L. Jones, Loeb Classical Library (Cambridge, Mass.: Harvard University Press, 1917).

9. Vitruvius, *De architectura,* trans. Frank Granger, Loeb Classical Library (Cambridge, Mass.: Harvard University Press, 1956).

10. See also Alfred E. Zimmern, *The Greek Commonwealth: Politics and Economics in Fifth Century Athens* (Oxford: Clarendon Press, 1922), esp. chap. 8.

11. Cornelius Tacitus, *De origine et situ Germanorum,* trans. M. Hutton, revised E. H. Warmington, Loeb Classical Library (Cambridge, Mass.: Harvard University Press, 1970); Tacitus, *Agricola,* trans. M. Hutton, revised R. M. Ogilvie. See E. H. Warmington for distribution of tribes and derivation of names.

12. *Ammianus Marcellinus,* trans. John C. Rolfe, Loeb Classical Library (Cambridge, Mass.: Harvard University Press, 1935).

13. Apuleius, *The Golden Ass, Being the Metamorphosis of Lucius Apuleius,* commentary by S. Gaselee, Loeb Classical Library (Cambridge, Mass.: Heinemann/Harvard University Press, 1915), p. xvii. According to Gaselee the book was translated into English by W. Adlington at University College, Oxford, in 1566, and was reprinted three times during the next thirty years.

14. See Haarhoff, *Stranger at the Gate,* pp. 216–18, for a discussion of Barbarus.

CHAPTER 4, JEWS, CHRISTIANS, MOORS, AND BARBARIANS

1. Flavius Josephus, *Complete Works of Flavius Josephus,* trans. William Whiston (London, 1851).

2. See, generally, Eric Voegelin, *Order and History,* vol. 1, *Israel and Revelation* (Baton Rouge: Louisiana State University Press, 1976), chap. 6, quotations on pp. 165–83.

3. Augustine, *De civitate Dei,* 2 vols. Everyman Series, introd. Sir Ernest Barker (1945).

4. Ancius Manlius Severinus Boethius, *De consolatione philosophiae,* trans. Hush Fraser Stewart, Edward Kennard Rand, and Stanley J. Tester, Loeb Classical Library (Cambridge, Mass.: Harvard University Press, 1973), 3.7.22–31. In *De trinitate,* 1.15–25, Boethius expressed diversity by genus, species, and number, according to Aristotle. In fact the diversity of three or more things lies in the genus or species or number; for often as "same" is said, so often is "diverse" also predicated. Now sameness is predicated in three ways.

By genus, for example, a man is the same as a horse, because they have the same genus, animal. By species, for example, Cato is the same as Cicero, because they have the same species, man. By number, for example, Tully and Cicero, because he is one in number.

5. Frank M. Snowden Jr. has argued that in this discussion, and also in the texts of Origen, Paul, and Saint Jerome, the Ethiopian is the prime motif in the language of conversion, and his color was nothing more than a symbol of his remoteness. See *Blacks in Antiquity.*

6. R. A. Nicholson, *A Literary History of the Arabs,* 2nd ed. (Cambridge: Cambridge University Press, 1977), 169.

7. Leon Roth, *The Legacy of Israel,* ed. Edwyn R. Bevan and Charles Singer (Oxford, 1944).

8. Nicholson, *Literary History,* 248.

9. Lukyn Williams, *Adversus Judaeos* (Cambridge: Cambridge University Press, 1935). See also John Eppstein, *The Catholic Tradition of the Law of Nations* (London: Burns Oates and Washbourne, 1935).

10. Valeriu Marcu, *Expulsion of the Jews from Spain,* trans. Moray Firth (London: Constable, 1935). This beautiful book has no references or footnotes.

11. Americo Castro, *The Spaniards: An Introduction to Their History,* trans. Willard F. King and Selina Margarretten (Berkeley and Los Angeles: University of California Press, 1971), p. 112.

12. Moses Maimonides, *The Guide for the Perplexed,* trans. Michael Friedlander, 2d ed. (London: George Routledge & Sons, 1942).

13. Heinrich Graetz, *History of the Jews from the Earliest Times to the Present Day,* ed. and trans. Bella Lowy (Philadelphia: The Jewish Publication Society of America, 1891), 4:510.

14. Quoted in ibid., 3:516.

15. Quoted in ibid., 3:528.

16. Ibid., 4:114.

17. Marcu, *Expulsion of the Jews from Spain,* p. 25.

18. Valeriu Marcu, *From Conversos to Marranos* (London, Conistable, 1933), p. 43.

19. For the organization and operation of the Inquisition, see Henry Charles Lea, *The Inquisition of the Middle Ages* (London: Eyre and Spotiswoode, 1963), which includes a description of its process: evidence, defense, sentence, confiscation, and stake. See also Lea, *History of the Spanish Inquisition,* 4 vols. (New York: Macmillan, 1906–07), 1:126: "the hatred which of old had been merely a matter of religion had become a matter of race." Lea sees the murder of the inquisitor Pedro Arbues at Saragossa on September 15, 1485, as a significant turning point when popular feeling turned in favor of the Inquisition.

20. Levi, *If This Is a Man,* p. 15.

CHAPTER 5, MONSTERS AND THE OCCULT

1. John Block Friedman, *The Monstrous Races in Medieval Art and Thought* (Cambridge, Mass.: Harvard University Press, 1981), pp. 112–207. These legends are discussed in Margaret Goldsmith, *Mode and Meaning in Beowulf* (London: Athlone Press, 1970); Kenneth Sisam, *Studies in the History of Old English Literature* (Oxford: Clarendon Press, 1962); and Nora Chadwick, "The Monsters and Beowulf," in Peter Clemoes, ed., *The Anglo-saxons* (London: Bowes & Bowes, 1959).

2. *Hermetica,* trans. and ed. Walter Scott (Oxford: Clarendon Press, 1924). Scott's introduction offers helpful interpretations.

3. *The Zohar,* trans. Harry Sperling and Maurice Simon, with an introduction by Joshua Abelson (London: The Soncino Press, 1931).

4. Arthur Edward Waite, *The Doctrine and Literature of the Kabalah* (London: Theosophical Publishing Society, 1902).

5. Joseph Leon Blau, *The Christian Interpretation of the Cabala in the Renaissance* (New York: Columbia University Press, 1944).

6. Ibid., pp. 42–49, 50–59.

7. Henry Cornelius Agrippa, *Three Books of Occult Philosophy or Magic,* ed. Willis F. Whitehead (London: Aquarian Press, 1971).

8. Quoted in Waite, *Doctrine and Literature of the Kabalah,* p. 347.

9. Allen G. Debus, *The Chemical Philosophy: Paracelsian Science and Medicine in the Sixteenth and Seventeenth Centuries* (New York: Science History Publications, 1977).

10. Huxley and Haddon, *We Europeans,* p. 39; John B. de C. M. Saunders and Charles Donald O'Malley, eds., *Andreas Vesalius Bruxellensis: The Bloodletting Letter of 1539* (London: William Heinemann, Medical Books, 1948). See also Karl Sudhoff, *Graphische und typographische Erstlinge der Syphilisliteratur aus den Jahrens 1495 und 1496* (Munich: C. Kuhn, 1912); Sudhoff, *Malfronzo in Italien* (Giessen, 1912); Sudhoff, *Aus der Fruhgeschichte der Syphilis* (Leipzig, 1912), pp. 159 ff. (see *Essays on the History of Medicine,* presented to Karl Sudoff on his seventieth birthday, Charles Singer and Henry Sigerist, eds. [London: Oxford University Press, 1924]); Leo (Johannes) Africanus (Al-Hassan Ibn

Mohammed Al-Wezaz Al Fasi), *The History and Description of Africa,* trans. John Pory, ed. Robert Brown (London: Hakluyt Society, 1896).

CHAPTER 6, NEW METHODS, NEW WORLDS, AND THE SEARCH FOR ORIGINS

1. Castro, *The Spaniards*, pp. 58, 76, 91.

2. Quoted in Lewis Hanke, *Bartolomé Las Casas: An Interpretation of His Life and Writings* (The Hague: Martinus Nijhoff, 1951), p. 82.

3. See Silvio Zavala, *New Viewpoints on the Spanish Colonization of America* (Philadelphia: University of Pennsylvania Press, 1943).

4. See Gilberto Freyre, *The Masters and the Slaves: A Study in the Development of Brazilian Civilization*, trans. Samuel Putnam (London: Weidenfeld and Nicolson, 1963); Stanley Elkins, *Slavery: A Problem in American Institutional and Intellectual Life* (Chicago: University of Chicago Press, 1959).

5. See Enzo Carli, *Sienese Painting* (London: Rainbird, 1958), pp. 44–46, plates 68–81; Quentin Skinner, "Ambrogio Lorenzetti: The Artist as Political Philosopher," *Proceedings of the British Academy* 72 (1986): 1–56.

6. Niccolo Machiavelli, *The Discourses*, ed. and introd. Bernard Crick, trans. Leslie J. Walker (Harmondsworth: Penguin, 1970); Machiavelli, *The Prince and the Discourses*, introd. Max Lerner, Modern Library College Edition (New York: Random House, 1950); Machiavelli, *The Art of War*, introd. Neal Wood, Library of Liberal Arts (Indianapolis: Bobbs-Merrill, 1965). See K. R. Minogue, "Theatricality and Politics: Machiavelli's Concept of Fantasia," in *The Morality of Politics*, ed. Bhikhu Parekh and R. N. Berki (London: Allen and Unwin, 1972). See also Quentin Skinner, *The Foundations of Modern Political Thought* (Cambridge: Cambridge University Press, 1978), 1:88–101, 118–38, for an analysis of political *virtu*, the humanist idea of princely government, and Machiavelli's critique of humanism.

7. Hannah Arendt, *The Human Condition* (Garden City, N.Y.: Doubleday Books, 1968), pp. 9–69: "What remains surprising is that the only postclassical political theorist who, in an extraordinary effort to restore its old dignity to politics, perceived the gulf and understood something of the courage needed to cross it was Machiavelli, who described it in the rise 'of the Condottiere from low condition to high rank,' from privacy to princedom, that is, from circumstances common to all men to the shining glory of great deeds."

8. James Bryce, *Race Sentiment as a Factor in History* (London: Hodder & Stoughton, 1915), p. 15; see also Bryce, *The Relations of the Advanced and the Backward Races of Mankind* (Oxford: Clarendon Press, 1902).

9. Huxley and Haddon, *We Europeans*. John Foxe, *Acts and Monuments of Matters Most Special and Memorable Happening in the Church with an Universal History of the Same* (London: John Day, 1563), p. 18.

10. Jean Bodin, *Methods for the Easy Comprehension of History* (1565), trans. Beatrice Reynolds (New York: Columbia University Press, 1945). Bodin also wrote *Colloquium Heptaplomeres de abditis rerum sublimium arcanis* (1588), first published in 1841 and in complete form in 1857. See Leonard F. Dean, "Bodin's *Methodus* in England before 1625," *Studies in Philology* 39 (April 1942): 160–66.

11. Arendt, "Race-Thinking before Racism," p. 43, n. 12, contests Ernest Seillière's claim, in *La Philosophie de l'Imperialism* (1903–6), that François Hotman was a forerunner of eighteenth-century racial doctrines, as a misconception corrected by Theophile Simar in *Etude Critique sur la Formation de la doctrine des Races au 18e et son expansion au 19e siecle* (1922).

12. François Hotman, *Francogallia*, Latin text by Ralph E. Giesey, trans. J. H. M. Salmon (Cambridge: Cambridge University Press, 1972), p. 137.

13. See Skinner, *Foundations of Modern Political Thought*, preface ix–xv for an overview of his method, and of the new findings reported as resulting from its application; Christopher Morris,

Political Thought in England: Tyndale to Hooker (London: Oxford University Press, 1953), p. 43. Felix Raab, *The English Face of Machiavelli: 1500–1700* (London: Routledge and Kegan Paul, 1964). Louis B. Wright, *Middle-Class Culture in Elizabethan England* (Ithaca, N.Y.: Cornell University Press, 1958), p. 78.

14. See Phillip Mason, *Common Sense about Race* (London: Victor Gollancz, 1961), chap. 2.

15. Fleck, *Genesis and Development of a Scientific Fact.*

16. *Holinshed's Chronicles, England, Scotland, and Ireland,* 6 vols., introd. Vernon F. Snow (New York: AMS Press, 1965). Italics throughout are mine.

17. Annius was a Dominican, Juan Nanni, who had command of many languages. His text, *Commentaria super opera diversorum auctorum de antiquitatibus,* recapitulated works largely declared apocryphal. He was revealed as a forger by Petrus Crinitius in *De honesta disciplina* (1504). A detailed biography of Annius appears in *Enciclopedia Universal Ilustrada Eureopeo-Americana,* vol. 37 (Madrid: Espasa-Calpe S. A., 1942).

18. Richard Hakluyt, *The Principal Navigations, Voyages, Traffiques, and Discoveries of the English Nation* (London: George Bishop and Ralph Newberie, 1589).

19. For contemporaneous accounts of the Creation, see *The Workes of the Right Rev. Father in God Gervase Babington, Bishop of Worcester* (London: George Eld, 1615); *Batman uppon Bartholome, His Book, De Proprietatibus Rerum* (1582), copy in Huntington Library, San Marino, California; Bishop John Aylmer, *An Harborowe for Faithfull and Trewe Subjects against the Late Blown Blast concerning the Government of Women* (1559), copy in British Museum; George Abbot, *A briefe Description of the Whole Worlde* (1599), English Experience, no. 213 (New York: Da Capo Press, 1970); Robert Abbot, *A Mirrour of Popish Subtilties* (1594), copy in British Museum; Guillame de Bartas, *His Devine Weekes and Workes,* trans. Joshua Sylvester (London: Humfrey Lownes, 1611); Thomas Taylor, *Japhet's First Publique Perswasion into Sems Tent* (1612), copy in Huntington Library and Cambridge University; Peter Heylin, *Microcosmos: A Littel Description of the Great World,* 3rd ed. rev. Oxford I. Lichfield, W. Turner, and T. Huggins (1627), copy in Folger Shakespeare Library, Washington, D.C. See also C. H. McIlwain, *The Growth of Political Thought in the West* (New York: Macmillan, 1959), p. 70; Leon Poliakov, *The Aryan Myth: A History of Racist and Nationalist Ideas in Europe,* trans. Edmund Howard (London: Chatto & Windus Heinemann for Sussex University Press, 1974); Kenneth Sisam, "Anglo Saxon Royal Genealogies," *Proceedings of the British Academy* 39 (1953): 287–348.

20. Reginald Scot, *The Discoverie of Witchcraft* (1584; reprint, Wakefield: Ep Publishing Ltd., 1973).

21. Timothy Bright, *A Treatise of Melancholy* (London, 1586), English Experience, no. 212 (New York: Da Capo Press, 1969). See also Bright, *Passion of the Minde* (1601), in which there is a reference to the Latin *races.*

22. Meyrick Heath Carré, *Phases of Thought in England* (Oxford: Oxford University Press, 1949), 178, and Joseph Acosta, *The Natural and Morall Historie of the East and West Indies,* trans. Edward Grimston (London: Val. Sims for Edward Blount and William Apsley, 1604). See also Father Francisco Alvares, *Narrative of the Portuguese Embassy to Abyssinia during the years 1520–27,* trans. Lord Stanley (London: Hakluyt Society, 1881).

23. Samuel Purchas, *Purchas His Pilgrimages; or, Relations of the World and the Religions Observed in All Ages and Places Discovered, from the Creation unto This Present* (London: William Stansby, for Henrie Fetherstone, 1613). The edition I used was from the Exeter Cathedral Library, and until I read it in 1970 the pages had not been cut. There were other editions in 1614, 1617, 1619, and 1625.

24. John Florio, *His First Fruites* (London, 1578), English Experience, no. 95 (New York: Da Capo Press, 1969); Florio, *Queen Anna's New World of Words* (1611; reprint, Menston [Yorks]: Scolar Press, 1968). See also Frances A. Yates, *John Florio: The Life of an Italian in Shakespeare's England* (Cambridge: Cambridge University Press, 1934), p. 239. Yates not only regards Florio's work as an important landmark in the history of Italian scholarship in England and immensely influential

but cites T. S. Eliot's regard for his translation of Montaigne as second only to the Authorized Version of the Bible.

25. Pierre Charron, *Of Wisdom: Three Bookes Written in French by Pierre Charron, Doctor of Laws*, trans. Samson Lennard (London: Eliot's Court Press, 1612).

26. Thomas Blundeville, *Description of Mappes and Cardes* (London, 1589), English Experience, no. 438 (New York: Da Capo Press, 1972). See also Blundeville, *His Exercises Containing Sixe Treatises* (1594), English Experience, no. 361 (New York: Da Capo Press, 1971); Blundeville, *The Art of Logike* (1599; reprint, Menston [Yorks]: Scolar Press, 1967).

27. Francis Bacon, *The Twoo Bookes of the Proficience and Advancement of Learning* (London, 1605), English Experience, no. 218 (New York: Da Capo Press, 1970).

28. Richard Verstegan, *A Restitution of Decayed Intelligence in Antiquities concerning the Most Noble and Renowned Engish Nation* (Antwerp: R. Brunley, 1605).

CHAPTER 7, THE FIRST STAGE IN THE DEVELOPMENT OF AN IDEA OF RACE, 1684–1815

1. Arendt, *Origins of Totalitarianism*.

2. Thomas Hobbes, *The Leviathan* (1651), ed. C. B. Macpherson (Harmondsworth: Pelican Classics, 1968).

3. See Stanley Elkins, *Slavery: A Problem in American Institutional and Intellectual Life* (Chicago: University of Chicago Press, 1959), for an analysis of the development in a vacuum of a peculiar institution that had no place in English traditions. See also Arnold Sio, "Interpretations of Slavery: The Slave Status in the Americas," *Comparative Studies in Society and History* 7 (April 1965): 289–308; and David Brion Davis, *The Problem of Slavery in Western Culture* (Ithaca, N.Y.: Cornell University Press, 1966), pp. 224–25.

4. Thomas Hobbes, *The Elements of Law; Natural and Politic* (1650), ed. Ferdinand Tonnies, introd. M. M. Goldsmith (London: Frank Cass & Co., 1984), p. 21.

5. John Locke, *An Essay Concerning Human Understanding* (1690), ed. Peter H. Nidditch (Oxford: Clarendon Press, 1975).

6. Jacques Barzun, *The French Race: Theories of Its Origins and Their Social and Political Implications prior to the Revolution*, Columbia University Studies in History (New York: Columbia University Press, 1932), pp. 375–76; see also pp. 167–83.

7. Dubos is the basis for the argument of Theophile Simar, *Etude critique sur la formation de las doctrine des races au XVIIIe siècle et son expansion au XIXe siècle*, Royal Academy of Belgium Memoires, 2d ser., Bk. 16, ed. Maurice Lamertin, Brussels, 1922.

8. Charles de Secondat, baron de Montesquieu, *The Spirit of the Laws* (1748), trans. Thomas Nugent, rev. J. V. Prichard (Chicago: University of Chicago Press, 1952).

9. Quoted from Linnaeus, *Systema Natura*, in Johann Friedrich Blumenbach, *De Generis Humani*, 3rd ed. (1795), 1.18.183.

10. Johann Friedrich Blumenbach, *The Anthropological Treatises of Johann Friedrich Blumenbach*, trans. Thomas Bendyshe (London: Anthropological Society, 1865). The versions considered in the following discussions are the first and third (or last) editions of *On the Natural Variety of Mankind*, published in 1775 and 1795 respectively. The London translation includes the memoirs of Blumenbach's colleague, Karl Marx, who had published them previously in the *Edinburgh New Philosophical Magazine*, and an appreciation by M. J. P. Flourens (1794–1867), the editor of the complete works of Buffon.

11. Voegelin, "Growth of the Race Idea," pp. 283–317.

12. See Poliakov, *Aryan Myth*, p. 163; Poliakov, *History of Anti-Semitism* (London: Routledge & Kegan Paul, 1974–85), 4 vols, 3:157.

13. Arthur O. Lovejoy, *The Great Chain of Being: A Study of the History of an Idea* (New York: Harper & Row, 1965), especially chapter 6.

14. J. F. Blumenbach, "On the Capacity and the Manners of the Savages," *Göttingen Magazine* 2, no. 6 (1781): 409–25.

15. Simar argues that "L'heure du 'polygenisme radical' n'avait pas encore sonné" (1.10). Neither Buffon nor Lamarck had made race an entity overarching the idea of the unity of species, and developing a law unto itself in natural selection. The origins of the theory of race lie in modern civilization and the self-determining psychological principles of diversity concocted in the nineteenth century.

16. David Hume, "Of National Characters," (1748), in *The Philosophical Works,* ed. Thomas Hill Green and Thomas Hodge Grose (London, 1882; reprint Aalen: Scientia Verlag, 1964) 3.

17. Gotthold Ephraim Lessing, *Briefe, die neueste Literatur betreffend* (mm); Lessing, *Laocoön* (mm, 1766); Lessing, *mmm* (mm); Lessing, *Nathan der Weise* (mm, 1779); Lessing, *Minna von Barnhelm* (1763), trans. W. A. Steel, Everyman's Library (London: 1959); Lessing, *Wolfenbutteler Fragmente* (mm 1774–78); Lessing, *Die Juden* (mm, 1745).

18. Immanuel Kant, *Anthropology from a Pragmatic Point of View*, trans. Mary J. Gregor (The Hague: Nijhoff, 1974).

19. On Schiller, see J. Holland Rose, *Nationality as a Factor in History* (London: Rivingtons, 1916).

20. Johann Gottlieb Fichte, *Beitrage* zur Berichtigung der Urteile des Publikums über die französische Revolution (Contribution to the Formation of a Correct Judgment on the French Revolution).

21. Rose, *Nationality as a Factor in History*, lecture 3 of a series delivered at Christ's, Cambridge, Michaelmas term, 1915.

22. See John Rex and David Mason, eds., *Theories of Race and Ethnic Relations* (New York: Cambridge University Press, 1986), especially Michael Banton's essay, "Epistemological Assumptions in the Study of Racial Differentiation," 2:42–63, on "Hegel-inspired" and "Kant-inspired" theories.

23. Hannah Arendt, "Race thinking before racism," *Review of Politics* 6, no. 1 (January 1944): 60–73.

24. Edmund Burke, *Two Speeches on Conciliation with America, Two Letters on Irish Questions* (1778, 1792) (London: Routledge and Sons, 1889), *Reflections on the Revolution in France,* 5th ed. (London: J. Dodsley, 1790).

25. R. G. Collingwood, *The Idea of History* (Oxford: Oxford University Press, 1970), pp. 90–91, 92.

26. Johann Gottfried von Herder, *Reflections on the Philosophy of the History of Mankind* (1784–91), abridged with an introduction by Frank E. Manuel (Chicago: University of Chicago Press, 1968).

CHAPTER 8, THE SEARCH FOR HISTORICAL
AND BIOLOGICAL ORIGINS

1. Arthur, comte de Gobineau, *The Inequality of the Races*, trans. Adrian Collins, introd. Oscar Levy (New York: G. P. Putnum's Sons, 1915), p. xii.

2. Barthold G. Niebuhr, *The History of Rome,* vols. 1–2 trans. Julius Charles Hare and Connop Thirlwall (Cambridge and London: Longmans, 1835) vol. 3 trans. William Smith and Leonhard Schmitz; Niebuhr, *Lectures on Ancient Ethnography and Geography,* trans. Leonhard Schmitz (London: Walton and Maberly, 1853); Niebuhr, *A Dissertation on the Geography of Herodotus: Researches into the History of the Scythians, Getae and Sarmatians* (1828) (Oxford: D. A. Tallboys, 1830).

3. Augustin Thierry's works include *Histoire de la conquête de l'Angleterre par les Normands* (1821–25), *Lettres sur l'histoire de France* (1828), *Essai sur l'histoire de la formation et des progrè du Tiers État*

(1844); and *Dix ans d'etudes historiques* (1842), the preface of which refers to the discovery of the theory of conquest. On Thierry, see M. Seliger, "Augustin Thierry: Race Thinking during the Restoration," *Journal of the History of Ideas* 19 (1958): 273–82; Kieran Joseph Carroll, *Some Aspects of the Historical Thought of Augustin Thierry (1795–1856)* (Washington: Catholic University of America Press, 1951); Rulon Nephi Smithson, *Augustin Thierry: Social and Political Consciousness in the Evolution of Historical Method* (Geneva: Librarie Droz, 1973), pp. 283–303.

4. See G. P. Gooch, *Studies in German History* (London: Longmans, 1948).

5. Leon Poliakov, *The Ryan Myth: A History of Racist and Nationalist Ideas in Europe* (London: Hatto, Heinemann, for Sussex University Press, 1974).

6. Butterfield, *Man on His Past,* pp. 39–61.

7. Thomas Carlyle's works include *Critical and Miscellaneous Essays* (London: Chapman and Hall, 1847). See also Carlyle, "Occasional Discourse on the Negro Question," *Frazer's Magazine* 40 (December 1849): 670–79.

8. John Mitchell Kemble, *The Saxons in England: A History of the English Commonwealth to the Period of the Norman Conquest,* 2 vols. (London: Longman, Brown, Green and Longmans, 1849).

9. Charles Kingsley, *The Roman and the Teuton* (London: Macmillan and Co., 1884), p. 49.

10. On Hippolyte Taine, see Leo Weinstein, *Hippolyte Taine* (New York: Twayne Publishers, 1972), esp. chap 4; John S. White, "Taine on Race and Genius," *Social Research* 10 (February 1943); Arendt, "Race Thinking before Racism," p. 59; and Maurice Baring's article on Taine in vol. 26 of the 11th ed. (1911) of the *Encyclopaedia Britannica*.

11. Joseph Ernest Renan, *The Poetry of the Celtic Races, and Other Studies* (1857), trans. William G. Hutchinson (London: W. Scott, 1896; reprint, Port Washington, N.Y.: Kennikat Press, 1970). On Renan, see H. W. Wardman, *Ernest Renan: A Critical Biography* (London: Athlone Press, 1964).

12. Joseph Ernest Renan, "Réflexions sur l'état des esprits," *La Liberté de penser* (1849), from H. Wardman, *Ernest Renan: A Critical Biography* (London: Athlone Press, 1964) p. 40.

13. Arendt, "Race Thinking before Racism," p. 59.

14. Joseph Ernest Renan, *Intolerance of Skepticism,* p. 135.

15. Jules Michelet, *The People,* trans. John P. McKay (Urbana: University of Illinois Press, 1973). On Michelet, see Anne R. Pugh, *Michelet and his Ideas on Social Reform* (New York: Columbia University Press, 1923).

16. Poliakov, *Aryan Myth,* esp. pp. 131–54, 175–178.

17. Simar, *Etude critique sur la formation de la doctrine des races.*

18. Alexander von Humboldt, *Cosmos: Sketch of a Physical Description of the Universe,* trans. Edward Sabine, 7th ed. (London: Longman, Brown, Green and Longmans, 1849).

19. Arthur, comte de Gobineau, *The Inequality of the Human Races,* trans. Adrian Collins, introd. Oscar Levy (New York: G. P. Putnam's Sons, 1915), pp. xi–xii.

20. Jacques Barzun, *Race: A Study in Superstition* (New York and London: Harper and Row, 1965), p. 155.

21. Houston Stewart Chamberlain, *The Origins of the Nineteenth,* trans. John Lees (London: John Lane, The Bodley Head, 1912).

22. Dawkins, *Blind Watchmaker* and *Selfish Gene.*

23. This quote first appeared in the *Contemporary Review* 45 (April 1984) and was reprinted in "Man versus the State" in *Great Political Thinkers,* 4th edition, ed. William Ebenstein (New York: Holt, Rhinehart, and Winston, 1969), pp. 669–70.

24. Quoted in William Ebenstein, *Great Political Thinkers: Plato to the Present,* 4th ed. (New York: Holt, Rinehart and Winston, 1969), pp. 669–70, where the full extract of "The Coming Slavery," from *Man Versus the State* (1884) appears (pp. 654–670), together with an extract from *Social Statics* (1851) on the survival of the fittest (pp. 650–54). See also Robert L. Trivers, foreword to Dawkins, *Selfish Gene,* pp. viii–ix and David Concar, "Challenging Darwin's Sacred Theory of Life," *Times* (London), August 30, 1980.

CHAPTER 9, THE RISE OF THE RACE-STATE AND THE INVENTION
OF ANTISEMITISM, 1870–1900

1. An abstract of Hunt's "On the Negro's Place in Nature" appears in *Memoirs Read Before
the Anthropological Society of London,* 1 (1863–64), pp. 1–60. For an understanding of how far anthropology had strayed from Blumenbach's original intent to establish a disinterested science observing three cardinal rules, see Alfred C. Haddon and A. Hingston Quiggin, *History of Anthropology*
(London: Rationalist Press, Watts & Co., 1910).

2. Charles Wentworth Dilke, *Greater Britain: A record of Travel in English Speaking Countries, 1866
and 1867* (London: Macmillan and Co., 1869), pp. 192, 223. See also Israel Zangwill, *The Melting
Pot* (New York: Macmillan, 1909), a play that opened in New York in 1908.

3. E. H. Dance, *The Victorian Illusion* (London: William Heinemann, 1928), p. 8.

4. Matthew Arnold, *Culture and Anarchy* and *Friendship's Garland* published in serial form from
Feb. 1866–Nov. 1870. On Arnold, see James Simpson, "Arnold and Goethe," in *Writers and Their
Backgrounds: Matthew Arnold,* ed. Kenneth Allot (London: G. Bell and Sons, 1975), pp. 286–318.
Quotes from *Culture and Anarchy.*

5. P. J. Keating, "Arnold's Social and Political Thought," in *Writers and Their Backgrounds:
Matthew Arnold,* ed. Allot, pp. 307–35.

6. Walter Bagehot, *Physics and Politics; or, Thoughts on the Application of the Principles of "Natural
Selection" and "Inheritance" to Political Society* (London: Henry S. King, 1872; reprint, Gregg International Publishers, 1971).

7. J. R. Green, *A Short History of the English People* (1874; reprint, London: J. M. Dent and
Sons, 1934), pp. 14, xi. William Stubbs, *The Constitutional History of England: Its Origin and Development,*
3 vols. (Oxford: Clarendon Press, 1874–78), 1:2.

8. J. R. Seeley, *The Expansion of England* (1883; 2d ed., London: Macmillan and Co., 1891),
p. 8.

9. Jean-Louis Armand de Quatrefages, *The Prussian Race: Ethnologically Considered,* trans. Isabella Innes (London: Virtue & Co., 1872), p. 3.

10. Ernst Haeckel, *Anthropogonie oder Entwickelungsgeschichte des Menschens* (Leipzig: N. Engel-
mann, 1903), p. 354. See also Daniel Gasman, *The Scientific Origins of National Socialism: Social Darwinism in Ernst Haeckel and the German Monist League* (London: Macdonald & Co., 1971).

11. See G. R. Searle, *Eugenics and Politics in Britain, 1900–1914,* Science in History Series
(Leiden: Noordhoff International Publishers, 1976), p. 1.

12. Simar, *Étude critique sur la formation de la doctrine des races,* p. 191.

13. G. Vacher de Lapouge, *Les Selections Sociales,* 3 vols. (Paris: 1896).

14. On Bismarck, see J.C.G. Rohl, *From Bismarck to Hitler: The Problem of Continuity in German
History* (London: Longman, 1970), esp. pp. 13–16, 35–36, 41–42. On the influence of Droysen,
Sybel, and Treitschke, see Gooch, *History and Historians in the Nineteenth Century,* pp. 134–40.

15. Friedrich Wilhelm Nietzsche, *The Birth of Tragedy (Out of the Spirit of Music),* trans. and
ed. Walter Kaufman (New York: Modern Library, 1968).

16. Ludwig Gumplowicz, *Rasse und Staat* (1875)

17. Ludwig Gumplowicz, *Der Rassenkampf: Soziologische Untersuchungen* (Innsbruck, 1883)

18. Ernest Renan, "Qu'est ce qui un nation?" in his *The Poetry of the Celtic Races, and Other
Studies,* trans. William G. Hutchinson (New York: Kennikat Press, 1970).

19. F. Max Müller, *Biographies of Words: The Home of the Aryas* (London: Longmans, Green &
Co., 1888).

20. Heinrich von Treitschke, *History of Germany in the Nineteenth Century,* trans. Eden and Cedar
Paul, ed. William Harbutt Dawson, 7 vols. (New York: McBride, Nast & Company 1915–19).

21. Friedrich Wilhelm Nietzsche, *Basic Writings of Nietzsche,* trans. and ed. Walter Kaufmann
(New York: Modern Library, 1968), p. 386.

22. Friedrich Wilhelm Nietzsche, *Thus Spake Zarathustra,* trans. R. J. Hollingdale (London:
Penguin, 1974).

23. Friedrich Wilhelm Nietzsche, "Beyond Good and Evil," *Basic Writings of Nietzsche*. For the concept of "blood," see Walter Kaufmann, *Nietzsche: Philosopher, Psychologist, Antichrist*, 4th ed. (Princeton, N.J.: Princeton University Press, 1974), chap. 10. Kaufmann argues that Nietzsche believed that Lamarck's concept of inherited characteristics applied to spiritual nobility.

24. Arendt, "Race Thinking before Racism"; Ernest Barker, *National Character and the Factors in Its Formation* (1927), 4th ed. (London: Methuen, 1948); Kaufmann, *Nietzsche: Philosopher, Psychologist, Antichrist*, chap. 10, [and the footnote to the First Essay of *The Genealogy of Morals*, Section 11.]; R. Hinton Thomas, *Nietzsche in German Politics and Society 1890–1918* (Manchester: Manchester University Press, 1983); Barker, *Nietzsche and Treitschke: The Worship of Power in Modern Germany* (London: Oxford University Press, 1914).

25. In addition to Arendt, *Origins of Totalitarianism*, see Simar, *Étude critique sur la formation de la doctrine des races*; G. L. Mosse, "The Mystical Origins of National Socialism," *Journal of the History of Ideas* 22 (1961): 81–96; G. L. Mosse, *Toward the Final Solution: A History of European Racism* (Madison, Wisconsin: University of Wisconsin Press, 1985); Leon Poliakov, *Histoire de l'antisémitisen*, 4 vols. (London: Routledge & Kegan Paul, 1974–85); Norman Cohn, *Warrant for Genocide* (Harmondsworth: Penguin, 1970); Louis L. Snyder, *The Idea of Racialism*, vol. 8 (Princeton, N.J.: Van Nostrand, 1962), pp. 76–81.

26. Poliakov, *Aryan Myth*, pp. 294, 300; Simar, *Étude critique sur la formation de la doctrine des races*, chap. 10; Mosse, "Mystical Origins of National Socialism"; and Mosse, *Toward the Final Solution*, pp. 65 et seq.

27. Edouard Drumont, *La France Juive*, 2 vols. (1886). See also J. S. McClelland, ed., *The French Right (from de Maistre to Maurras)*, esp. pp. 85–116; see also Robert F. Byrnes, *Anti-Semitism in Modern France* (New York: Howard Fertig, 1969).

28. Arendt, *Origins of Totalitarianism*, pp. 94–95.

29. Arendt, *Origins of Totalitarianism*, p. 103.

30. Arendt, *Human Condition*, pp. 28–29.

CHAPTER 10, RACE IS ALL, 1890–1939

1. Nicholas Goodrick-Clarke, *The Occult Roots of Nazism: Secret Aryan Cults and Their Influence on Nazi Biology—The Ariosophists of Austria and Germany, 1890–1935* (London and New York: I. B. Tauris, 1992).

2. William Z. Ripley, *The Races of Europe* (New York: D. Appleton and Co., 1899), p. 546.

3. Francis Galton, "Eugenics: Its Definition, Scope and Aims," *Nature* 70 (1904): 82. See also *Papers of the Sociological Society of London* (1905), translated in *Archiv für Rass und Gesellschafisbiologie* (1905), pp. 5–6 & 812.

4. For an insight into intellectual attitudes toward the new industrial civilization, see Karl Pearson, *National Life from the Standpoint of Science*, Eugenics Lecture Series 11, University of London (London: A. and C. Black, 1901). First delivered in 1900 to the Literary and Philosophical Society to focus attention on national deterioration and the national value of science, it was so popular it was reprinted in 1905.

5. George L. Mosse, *Toward the Final Solution: A History of European Racism* (London: J. M. Dent, 1978), esp. pp. 81, 191–214; Daniel Kevles, *In the Name of Eugenics: Genetics and the Uses of Human Heredity* (Cambridge: Harvard University Press, 1985). See also Searle, *Eugenics and Politics in Britain 1900–1914*.

6. For a discussion of the *Protocols*, see Cohn, *Warrant for Genocide*.

7. For an account of Social Darwinism and social evolutionism in the United States, see Richard Hofstadter, *Social Darwinism in American Thought*, rev. ed. (Boston: Beacon Press, 1955) and A. J. Beitzinger, *A History of American Political Thought* (New York: Dodd, Mead & Co., 1972).

8. William Graham Sumner, *What the Social Classes Owe to Each Other* (New York: Harper Bros., 1883), pp. 113, 167–8.

9. Charles H. Pearson, *National Life and Character: A Forecast* (London: Macmillan, 1893), p. 17.

10. William I. Thomas, "The Psychology of Race Prejudice," *American Journal of Sociology* 9, no. 5 (March 1904): 593–611, quotations on pp. 607, 609, reprinted in *Source Book for Social Origins*, 6th ed. (Boston: The Gorham Press, 1909). On Thomas, see Franz Samuelson, "From Race Psychology to Studies in Prejudice," *Journal of the History of the Behavioral Sciences* 14 (1978): 265–78; Donald Fleming, "Attitude: The History of a Concept," *Perspectives in American History*, ed. Bernard Bailyn (Cambridge: Cambridge University Press, 1967), 1:287–365.

11. John Emerich Edward Dalberg Acton, *Essays on Freedom and Power* (London: Thames and Hudson, 1956), chap. 5, on nationality.

12. James Bryce, *The Holy Roman Empire*, 4th ed. (Macmillan, 1897), p. 444.

13. Woodrow Wilson, *The State* (1899; reprint, Boston: D. C. Heath and Co., 1904), pp. 2, 23.

14. Henry Fairfield Osborn, *From the Greeks to Darwin* (New York: Macmillan, 1894), pp. 5, 7.

15. William McDougall, *Is America Safe for Democracy?* (New York: Charles Scribner's Sons, 1921), p. 12.

16. Graham Wallas, *Human Nature in Politics* (London: Constable, 1910), p. 294.

17. Walter Lippmann, *A Preface to Politics* (New York: Mitchell Kennerley, 1913), p. 156.

18. Houston Stewart Chamberlain, *The Foundations of the Nineteenth Century* (1899), trans. John Lees, introd. Lord Redesdale (London: John Lane, 1912). On Chamberlain, see Rohl, *From Bismarck to Hitler*, esp. pp. 43–45, 52–53.

19. Henry Fairfield Osborn, preface to Grant, *Passing of the Great Race*, p. vii.

20. Theodore Lothrop Stoddard, *The Revolt against Civilization: The Menace of the Under Man* (New York: Charles Scribner's Sons, 1922), p. 36.

21. Hans Gunther, *The Racial Elements of European History*, trans. G. C. Wheeler (London: Methuen, 1927), p. 246.

22. H. G. Wells, *The Complete Short Stories of H. G. Wells* (1927; reprinted London: E. Benn, 1974), p. 284.

23. On race in fiction, Gina M. Mitchell, "John Buchan's Popular Fiction: A Hierarchy of Race," *Patterns of Prejudice* 7 (November/December 1975): 24–30, is of interest. See also E. M. Forster, *Two Cheers for Democracy* (London: Edward Arnold & Co., 1951), pp. 24–26, 29–32.

24. Adolf Hitler, *Mein Kampf*, ed. D. C. Watt, trans. Ralph Mannheim (London: Hutchinson, 1969). See also Rohl, *From Bismarck to Hitler*.

25. Michael Oakeshott, *The Social and Political Doctrines of Contemporary Europe*, 2d. ed. (Cambridge: The University Press, 1941).

26. Cesare Santoro, *Hitler's Germany As Seen by a Foreigner*, 3rd. ed. (Berlin: Internationaler Verlag, 1938), p. 130.

27. Ibid., pp. 121–32.

28. Ibid., p. 36.

29. Ibid., p. 126.

30. Ibid., p. 121.

CHAPTER 11, REACTIONS, RETRACTIONS, AND NEW ORTHODOXIES, 1920 TO THE PRESENT

1. Barker, *National Character*, introd. to the 4th ed., p. 17. See also Barker, *Nietzsche and Treitschke*.

2. Hilaire Belloc, *The Crisis of Our Civilization* (London: Cassell & Co., 1937), p. 122.

3. G. K. Chesterton, *Eugenics and Other Evils* (London: Cassell & Co., 1922), p. 32.

4. Franz Boas, *Anthropology and Modern Life* (New York: Norton, 1928), p. 35.

5. Huxley and Haddon, *We Europeans,* p. 61.

6. Fleck, *Genesis and Development of a Scientific Fact.* See also Gould, *Mismeasure of Man.*

7. Ralph J. Bunche, *A World View of Race* (1936; reprint, Port Washington, N.Y.: Kennikat Press, 1968), pp. 67, 96.

8. Barzun, *Race.* See also Barzun, *Race: Theories of Its Origins and Their Social and Political Implications Prior to the Revolution,* Columbia Studies in History, 375–76 (New York: Columbia University Press, 1932).

9. Erikson, *Life, History and the Historical Moment,* (pp. 47, 178). For a new and troubling dimension, see Peter Skerry, "E Pluribus Hispanic," *Wilson Quarterly* 16, no. 3 (Summer 1992): 62–73.

10. Donald L. Horowitz, *Ethnic Groups in Conflict* (Berkeley: University of California Press, 1985), pp. 58–9, 74–5; Levi, *If This Is a Man,* p. 15. See also Anthony D. Smith, *The Ethnic Revival* (Cambridge: Cambridge University Press, 1981); and Michael Novak, "The New Ethnicity," *Center Magazine* 7, no. 4 (July/August 1974): 18–25.

11. Robert Ezra Park, *The Collected Papers of Robert Ezra Park,* intro. by Everett Cherrington Hughes (Glencoe, Ill.: Free Press, 1950). See also Park and Ernest Watson Burgess, *Introduction to the Science of Sociology,* (Chicago: University of Chicago Press, 1924) and Edgar T. Thompson, ed., *Race Relations and the Race Problem: A Definition and an Analysis* (Durham: Duke University Press, 1939). For a bibliography of Park, see Edna Cooper, *Phylon* 6, no. 4 (Winter 1945): 372–83. See also Werner J. Cahnman, "Robert E. Park at Fisk," *Journal of the History of the Behavioral Sciences* 14, no. 4 (October 1978): 328–36.

12. Peter I. Rose, *The Subject is Race: Traditional Ideologies and the Teaching of Race Relations,* foreword by Everett C. Hughes (New York: Oxford University Press, 1968).

13. Gunnar Myrdal, *An American Dilemma: The Negro Problem and Modern Democracy* (1944; 2d ed., New York: Harper & Row, 1962). Most of the material for Myrdal's study was deposited in the Schomberg Collection at the New York Public Library. See also Gunnar Myrdal, "The Case against Romantic Ethnicity," *Center Magazine* 7, no. 4 (July/August 1974): 26–30; Walter A. Jackson, *Gunnar Myrdal and America's Conscience: Social Engineering and Racial Liberalism, 1938–1987* (Chapel Hill: University of North Carolina Press, 1990); Louis Wirth, "Problems and Orientations of Research in Race Relations in the United States," *British Journal of Sociology* 1 (1950): 117–25; Wirth, "The Unfinished Business of American Democracy," *Annals of the American Academy of Political and Social Science* 244 (March 1946); Helen V. McLean, "Psychodynamic Factors in Racial Relations," *Annals of the American Academy of Political and Social Science* 244 (March 1946): 159–66.

14. Cox, *Caste, Class and Race,* p. 474. See also Cox, "An American Dilemma: A Mystical Approach to the Study of Race Relations," *Journal of Negro Education* 14 (Spring 1945): 132–48. For the Herbert Aptheker–Myrdal controversy, see Ernest Kaiser, "Racial Dialectics," *Phylon* 9, no. 4 (1948): 295–302.

15. For the "caste hypothesis," see W. Lloyd Warner, "American Caste and Class," *American Journal of Sociology* 42 (September 1936): 234–37; Charles Sumner, *The Question of Caste* (Boston: Wright & Potter, 1869); Herbert Risley, *The People of India* (London: W. Thacker & Co., 1908) and *Census of India,* 1901; Thomas, "Psychology of Race Prejudice."

16. Cox critiqued the following: Edvard Westermarck, *History of Human Marriage* (New York: Allerton Book Company, 1922); Risley, *The People of India*; Nripendra Kumar Dutt, *Origin and Growth of Caste in India* (London: K. Paul, Trench, Trubner & Co., 1931); Shridhar V. Ketkar, *The History of Caste in India* (New York and London: Luzac & Co., 1909–11); James Bryce, *The Relations of the Advanced and Backward Races of Mankind,* 2d ed. (Oxford: The Clarendon Press, 1902); H. J. Fleure, *The Dravidian Element in Indian Culture* (London: E. Benn, 1924); and J. N. Farquhar, *The Religious Quest of India: An Outline of the Religious Literature of India* (London: Humphrey Milford, 1920). Cox also carefully analyzed the literature of the Mahabharata, reading John Muir, *Original Sanskrit Texts on the Origin and History of the People of India* (London: 1872–74).

17. Ralph Ellison, *Shadow and Act* (New York: Random House, 1964), p. 316.

18. For the UNESCO Statement on Race, July 18, 1950, and June 8, 1951, see Snyder, *Idea of Racialism* (pp. 92–183).

19. Louis L. Snyder, *The Ideas of Racialism* (Princeton, NJ: Van Nostrand, 1962), pp. 97–8.

20. The essays by Claude Levi-Strauss, Kenneth Little, Michael Leiris, G. M. Morant, Otto Kleineberg, and Arnold Rose are in *The Race Question in Modern Science* (New York: Whiteside and Morrow, for UNESCO, 1956). See also the essays by Juan Comas and L. C. Dunn.

21. Ruth Benedict and Gene Weltfish, *Race: Science and Politics,* foreword by Margaret Mead (New York: Viking Press, 1958), p. 38.

22. Ashley Montagu, *Race, Science and Humanity* (Princeton, NJ: Van Nostrand, 1963), p. 6. See also Montagu, *Man's Most Dangerous Myth* and M. Mead, T. Dobzhansky, E. Toback, and Robert E. Light, eds., *Science and the Concept of Race* (New York: Columbia University Press, 1968).

23. Montagu, ed., *Concept of Race,* p. 5. This collection includes not only lectures and essays by Montagu but also contributions by Jean Hiernaux, Frank Livingstone, Thomas Dobzhansky, S. M. Garn, Carleton S. Coon, Robert T. Anderson, Lancelot Hogben, C. Loring Brace, Paul Ehrlich, Richard W. Holm, and Nigel Barnicot.

24. P. L. Van den Berghe, *Race and Racism* (New York: John Wiley & Sons, 1967), p. 6. Also see also Thomas F. Gossett, *Race; The History of an Idea in America* (Dallas: Southern Methodist University Press, 1963).

25. Rex and Mason, ed., *Theories of Race and Ethnic Relations,* esp. Rex's preface (pp. ix–xii), Mason's introduction (pp. 1–9), and Banton, "Epistemological Assumptions in the Study of Racial Differentiation" (pp. 42–63). On approaches to race relations in Britain see Frank Palmer, ed., *Anti-Racism: An Assault on Education and Value* (London: Sherwood Press, 1986); Kenneth L. Little, *Negroes in Britain* (London: Keegan Paul, 1948); M. P. Banton, "Changing Position of the Negro in Britain," *Phylon* 14, no. 1 (1953): 74–83; Banton, *Race Relations* (London: Tavistock Publications, 1967); Banton, *Racial Theories* (Cambridge: Cambridge University Press, 1987); Banton, *Racial Consciousness* (London: Longman, 1988); Charles Husband, ed., *"Race" in Britain: Continuity and Change* (London: Hutchinson, 1982), E. J. B. Rose, *Colour and Citizenship: A Report on British Race Relations* (London: Oxford University Press, 1969); Sally Herbert Frankel, *The Economic Impact on Underdeveloped Society* (Oxford: Blackwell, 1953); Eric Williams, *Capitalism and Slavery* (Chapel Hill: University of North Carolina Press, 1944); Anthony H. Richmond, *The Colour Problem* (Baltimore: Pelican Books, 1961); John Solomos, *Race and Racism in Contemporary Britain* (London: Macmillan, 1989); and John Rex, *Race and Ethnicity* (Milton Keynes, England: Open University Press, 1986).

26. Cedric Thornberry, *The Stranger at the Gate: A Study of the Law on Aliens and Commonwealth Citizens* (London: Fabian Society, 1964), and "Commitment or Withdrawal," *Race: The Journal of the Institute of Race Relations* 1 (July 1965): 73. For additional insight into the course of race relations in Britain, see the following articles in *Race: The Journal of the Institute of Race Relations* 1 (November 1959): Michael Banton, "Sociology and Race Relations," pp. 3–14; H. S. Deighton, "History and the Study of Race Relations," pp. 15–24; and Philip Mason, "An Approach to Race Relations," pp. 41–52. See also J. H. Newsom, *Half Our Future: A Report on the Central Advisory Council for Education (England)* (London: HMSO, 1963); *Children and Their Primary Schools: A Report of the Central Advisory Council for Education (England)* (London: HMSO, January 1967). Lord Scarmen, *The Brixton Disorders,* CMND 8427 (London: HMSO, 1981).

27. See also *Research on Racial Relations* (Paris: UNESCO, 1966)—articles reprinted from *International Social Science Journal* 13, no. 2 (1961) and *International Social Science Bulletin* 10, no. 3 (1958).

28. Sykes, "Genetics Cracks Bone Disease."

29. Dawkins, *The Selfish Gene,* p. 37; Dawkins, *The Blind Watchmaker,* p. 5.

30. See Jean Hiernaux, "The Concept of Race and the Taxonomy of Mankind" and Frank B. Livingstone, "The Non-Existence of Human Races," in Montagu, ed., *Concept of Race,* pp. 38, 47.

Index

A

Abd Al Mumin, 102

Abdar-Rahman, 102

Abel (biblical figure), 89, 90, 132, 133. *See also* Cain (biblical figure)

Abraham (biblical figure), 109

Abu-Abdullah Mahomet Alnasir, 115

Abu-Yussuff Almansur, 114–15

Acosta, Joseph, 168–69, 171, 181, 183

Action Française, 319

Acton, John Emerich Acton, Lord, 10, 51, 341–44, 356, 369, 387, 396

Acts and Monuments (Foxe), 155

Adam (biblical figure), 97; archetype of, 136–37; descent from, 93, 94, 107, 123, 164, 269, 279, 289, 358; and the Fall, 89–90, 135, 272

Aeneid (Vergil), 62, 68–72, 84, 311

Aeschylus, 77

Africans, 158; color of, 171; as descendants of Ham, 94–95, 135; encounters of, with Europeans, 19–20, 143, 149; enslavement of, 384; portrayals of, 167. *See also* Ethiopians; Negroes; slavery

Against the Dogmatists (Sextus Empiricus), 73

agenealogetos, 22

Ages of Man myth, 24–25

"agnostic," 261, 278

agora, 10, 22

Agricola (Tacitus), 62, 80, 81

Agricola, Gnaeus Julius, 81

Agrippa, Henry Cornelius, 36, 138, 139–43, 146, 167, 221, 326

Airs, Waters, and Places (Hippocrates), 20, 28–30, 210

Albertus Magnus, 141, 180

Albigensian heresy, 113–14, 125

Albion (giant), 164, 181

alchemy, 131, 144, 145

Alcmaeon of Croton, 72, 77

Aleric, 89

Alexander VI (pope), 122, 124, 384

Alfonso the Noble (king of Castile), 113, 114

Alfonso X (king of Léon and Castile), 104

Algeria, 338, 339

Ali (descendent of Muhammad), 101

aljamas (Moorish ghettos), 104–6, 120, 122

Allah, 97–99, 103

Allen, Grant A., 344

Allgemeine Kultur: Geschichte der Menschheit (Klemm), 259

Almoravid dynasty, 102

alphabet (letters), 132–34, 136, 138, 143

"Alpine man," 292–93, 329, 360, 374

Also Sprach Zarathustra (Nietzsche), 311, 312

'am (Hebrew word), 88

An American Dilemma (Myrdal), 378, 385

American Revolution, 6, 284, 286, 302

Ammianus Marcellinus, 62, 80–83, 199

Ammon, Otto, 326–31, 333, 389

anatomy. *See* biology; body; physical anthropology

Anaxagoras of Clazomenae, 45

Anaximander, 18

Anaximenes, 45